Rabindranath Tagore's
Gorā

Translated by
Mohit K. Ray
Rama Kundu

Published by

ATLANTIC

PUBLISHERS & DISTRIBUTORS (P) LTD

7/22, Ansari Road, Darya Ganj,
New Delhi-110002
Phones : +91-11-40775252, 23273880, 23275880, 23280451
Fax : +91-11-23285873
Web : www.atlanticbooks.com
E-mail : orders@atlanticbooks.com

Branch Office
5, Nallathambi Street, Wallajah Road,
Chennai-600002
Phones : +91-44-64611085, 32413319
E-mail : chennai@atlanticbooks.com

Printed in India at Glorious Printers, A-13, D.S.I.D.C., Jhilmil Industrial Area, Delhi-110095

Translators' Note

Tagore once said, "I enter into my real self when I write poetry", and Tagore is essentially a poet. As his criticism is more creative than critical, his creative writings in prose are also highly poetical in the sense that there is an abundance of the use of images, symbols and metaphors, and not infrequently, a rhythm which makes it eminently amenable to a breaking up into free verse by imaginative lineation. This is, of course, most true, as Sibabrata Chattopadhyay has shown in his extremely well-researched book, *Nātya Aitihya O Laghu Nāṭak* (*Theatrical Tradition and Light Drama*, Burdwan University, 2005) in the case of drama; prose lines of a drama are broken up into several lines of a free verse. Then there is the problem of culture. It is much easier to translate from Bengali into Hindi or Gujarati, for example, than to translate into English or French, because of the cultural differences, i.e. in customs, rituals, forms of greeting and other subtle aspects of Indian sensibility and world view. The idea of *praṇām* (literally, bending down), touching the feet of a respectable elderly person is simply absent in the Western culture. In India whenever somebody meets a respectable person he/she touches that person's feet as a mark of respect. The idea of *ěto* or contamination of food is difficult for a Westerner to comprehend. And, mind you, there are different degrees of *ěto;* an item like rice or fish may be *ěto* in itself, or the leftover, something lying on the plate of a person who has finished eating, or in its worst form something that has been put into the mouth and then taken out without eating, etc.

Then there is the problem of world view, which is invariably reflected in the structure of a language. In Bengali—in fact in most Indian languages—there is an abundant use of passive construction. Literally translated, a Bengali will say: "My pencil is lost", while in the same situation an Englishman would say: "I have lost my pencil" or a Frenchman would say: "*J'ai perdu mon crayon*". The passive structure reflects the Indian philosophy of life that believes in the doctrine of predestination.

What would a translator do then? If he has to preserve the Indian sensibility he has to retain the passive construction, but if he wants to conform to the genius of the English language he has to strike a balance between fidelity and freedom. The recent tendency in the creative writings in the postcolonial literature is to include many indigenous words and use them as such without translating them into English and without even giving a gloss at times. It is presumed that the context—for after all words are used not in vacuum but in a particular situation—will give an idea of the meaning, and repeated use of the word in the same novel will make its denotations and connotations clear to the native speaker of the English language. When Amos Tutuola's *The Palm-Wine Drinkard* was published in 1952 the purists were shocked by Tutuola's irreverent use of the English language—"irreverent", because of his use of Yoruba folk materials. Dylan Thomas described it as "young English by a West African" while Anthony West remarked: "One catches a glimpse of the very beginning of literature, that moment when writing at last seizes and pins down the myths and legends in an alphabetic culture." Lee Rogow referred to it as a "fantastic primitive...written in English, but...an English with inflections and phrasings which make it seem like a new-born language...." The problem that Chinua Achebe raises in this connection is equally applicable to the Indian language as well. Achebe writes in "The Role of a Writer in a New Nation" (1964):

> For an African, writing in English is not without its serious setbacks. He often finds himself describing situations and modes of thought which have no direct equivalent in the English way of life. Caught in that situation he can do one of the two things. He can try and contain what he wants to say within the limits of conventional English or he can push back those limits to accommodate his idea.
>
> The first method produces competent, uninspired and rather flat work. The second method produces something new and valuable to the English language as well as to the material he is trying to put over. *But* it can also get out of hand. It can lead simply to *bad* English being accepted and defended as African or Nigerian. I submit that those who can do the work of extending the frontiers of English so as to accommodate African thought-patterns must do it through their mastery of English and not out of innocence.

A real word of caution indeed, because the most important point is intelligibility. If the language becomes too literal or appears distorted beyond recognition by the native speaker of English then the very purpose of the original creative writing or its translation fails to achieve communication. So, while it is true, to quote Achebe again, that the "price a world language (English) must be prepared to pay is submission to many different kinds in use" ("English and the African Writer", 1965), it is also necessary for the translator to reconcile freedom and fidelity while translating a literary text. Matthew Arnold referred to Newman's dictum that the translator's first duty is to be faithful, and said, "but the question at issue...is, in what faithfulness consists" ("On Translating Homer"). The entire history of translation theory, in fact, is the history of the debate between two opposing views about translation: fidelity versus freedom. Should translation be rigorously faithful to the original by being meticulously literal, or should it exercise freedom in its attempt to convey the spirit of the original and not the letter? It may sometimes be necessary to be a traitor to the letter in order to be faithful to the spirit of the text, because the soul is more important than the body.

While translating *Gorā* we have constantly faced this problem. On the one hand lies the highly poetic language of Tagore, an artist of the first order, and the differences between Western culture and the Indian; on the other we have tried to remain as loyal to Tagore as possible without taking too much liberty with the genius of the English language, because we believe that this translation is primarily meant for those who do not know Bengali or who do not have enough proficiency in Bengali to understand and enjoy a Bengali novel written by no less a mighty literary figure than Rabindranath Tagore.

This translation is a modest homage to Tagore whom we hold close to our heart in love and reverence.

Mohit K. Ray
Rama Kundu

Gorā: A Critical Introduction

It is at once a privilege and a challenge to introduce a work of Rabindranath Tagore to the vast non-Bengali readership of India and abroad.

Whereas the extraordinary and multifaceted genius of Rabindranath Tagore (1861-1941), his immensely rich creative harvest, which included an overwhelming diversity of literary forms—from poetry, song, play, dance drama to fiction, short story, essay, literary criticism, fine polemics, travelogue, memoir, sketch, letter, journal, children's literature, original textbook for children on language and other disciplines—in addition to painting, music, ballet, performing arts, has substantially conditioned the cultural life of the two Bengals (West Bengal and Bangladesh), Tagore study has been consistently on the rise beyond Bengal, and across India and abroad. And even more than seven decades after his death the continuing relevance and appeal of Tagore are apparent.

As Rabindranath continually evolved in perception and technique through reflection, innovation and experimentation, and achieved spectacular success in all the literary genres/forms and art forms he tried his hand at, he has left a monumental heritage behind. Tagore's contribution to the development of the Bengali literature and language is immeasurable; it was in his hands that it achieved its final leap into modernity.

Among Rabindranath's major fictional works *Gorā* (1910) is the sixth in the chronological order, and bears evidence of the maturity of the writer in its superb handling of certain topical social-religious-political controversies while reflecting, at the same time, some of Tagore's major preoccupations and convictions like the value of truth, freedom, dignity of the individual, which remained with him all along as a driving force behind his personal life as well as his great creative and critical oeuvre.

One can trace four definable clusters forming distinct stages in Rabindranath Tagore's novelistic oeuvre. The first stage which can be called the phase of apprenticeship, and was over by the end of the nineteenth century, included two novels: *Bauthākurāṇīr Hāt* (1883) and *Rājarṣi* (1887). These were based on two historical situations of Bengal and Tripura respectively, and depicted the stories of royal families; nevertheless even at this early stage the narrative focus is constituted by the conflict between familial and religious loyalties on the one hand, and the values of truth, humanism and individual dissent on the other. These were the values that remained of supreme concern for the writer and continued to resurface in his subsequent novels (as well as other writings), including *Gorā*. This was followed by a cluster of three novels forming the second stage—*Cokher Bāli* (1903), *Prajāpatir Nirbandha* (1904), and *Naukādubi* (1906)—probing the intricacies and nuances of individual human relationship, along with its stresses and subtleties—a subject that reappeared in *Caturanga* (1916).

Following a pause after *Naukādubi*, *Gorā* (1910) ushered in a new direction in Tagore's fiction which subsequently came to the fore in the next novel *Ghare Bāire* (1916), and years later in his last novel *Cār Adhyāya* (1934). These three novels, generally considered his best, should be studied together, as in each of these Tagore explored individual characters and nuances of human relationships in relation to the immediate social-cultural-political backdrop, while probing the issues of cultural nationalism, extremism, terrorism in his contemporary context; and, as a result, the private lives of individuals get interwoven with the contemporary political/religious turbulence/controversies that characterized Bengal and much of India at the time.

Besides these Tagore had written *Śeṣer Kabitā* (1929), *Yogāyog* (1929), *Dui Bon* (1933), *Mālaṇca* (1934)—novels which made daring and sharp projection of psychological subtleties of characters and complex human relationships against the backdrop of Tagore's contemporary elite society of urban Bengal.

Gorā is generally considered the best novel of Tagore's middle phase, and according to many a critic, *Gorā* can be judged as the best novel of Tagore, in terms of the maturity of vision and excellence of artifice, as it combines all the characteristic features of Tagore's thoughts on the country and the world, his observation of the times and people, and weaves them into a fine narrative structure punctuated by superb lyrical passages, brilliant intellectual dialogues, and delightfully witty touches.

One of course feels rather diffident to make a summary of a text by Tagore, as much is bound to disappear in course of the summation. Anyway, briefly outlined, it is the story of an orphan, born of Irish parents during the turbulent days of the Sepoy mutiny of 1857, and brought up in the home of a childless Bengali Brahmin couple as their own son. Even as a small boy Gora stood out from his schoolmates and playfellows both by appearance and temperament, while his closest friend Binoy was just his opposite—a soft-spoken, mild natured, sensitive, tender boy. In his early youth Gora becomes a staunch proponent of *swadeś* and Hinduism and is ready to challenge any one on the issue. In the meantime Gora's foster parents drift with time in opposite directions: whereas Krishnadayal, his foster-father has made a *volte face* to his youthful adventurism and turned an extreme obscurantist, his wife Anandamoyee has given up all rituals, customs, mores of the orthodox Hindu ways, has withdrawn from relatives and friends, and has emerged as a fully blossomed, mellowed, yet fearless self-confident personality. Eventually Binoy and Gora come in touch with Pareshbabu and his family who belong to the Brahmo community, get involved with Lalita and Sucharita, Pareshbabu's daughter and his friend's daughter respectively. A phase follows when their friendship is put under severe strain, when Binoy and Lalita get married with the blessings of Pareshbabu and Anandamoyee. Throughout this period Gora also remains restless and unsettled, caught up as he is in an intense search for the 'real' India, and for the 'real' mission of his own life. Though Gora is strongly drawn towards Sucharita, he is on the point of sacrificing the prospect of happiness for both himself and Sucharita for the good of the 'cause' of *Swadeś* and Hinduism. Ultimately tragedy is averted by the disclosure of Krishnadayal; prompted by a sudden illness, he tells Gora about his Irish descent. Gora comes to Pareshbabu to seek his blessing on this occasion of his 're-birth' and to claim Sucharita as his partner in this new life. At the end of the long day we see him returning to Anandamoyee with the ecstatic exclamation of his epiphanic vision, 'You are my Bharatbarsha.'

True, the novel appears to have been woven around the subtleties and intricacies of human relationships. The external events of the social-political context help to bring out the dormant psychological potentialities of the characters to the fore. However, in the story, which is, in a way, broadly speaking, about two pairs of young lovers from two different kinds of social-religious orientation, the inner circle of individual characters and their personal relationships is vitally related to the outer circle of a society which had been undergoing a state of transition after centuries of stagnation. The six individuals—four young people and two elderly parental figures—who make the inner circle, are embedded within the space of the outer circle, the chronotope of contemporary time and milieu.

Apparently *Gorā* is not just another story of personal relationships, though at the centre of the narrative the two love stories coalesce—one between Gora and Sucharita, the other between Binoy and Lalita. Then how to categorise the novel? Is it a political novel, or a sociological discourse, or a psychological story? Like *Ghare-Bāire* there is, or rather there are, two love stories at the centre, but these are used to foreground a far wider spectrum. The novel is set against the atmosphere of political excitement and religious debates that characterized the first decades of the twentieth century in Bengal and India. In the words of Asit Bandyopadhyaya: "*Gorā* is not only an epoch-making novel of modern Indian literature; it is certainly comparable with any epic novel of Europe in shape and size, in treatment and in execution. *Gorā* has an epic dimension, it contains, in essence, the crisis of the whole nation." In a similar vein Niharranjan Roy, the eminent historian, eulogized *Gorā* for having "the amplitude of ancient epics", Sukumar Sen, the renowned scholar, hailed the novel as "a *Mahabharata* of modern India", while Tagore's biographer Krishna Kripalani praised the novel as "the epic of India in 'transition'", and compared it to Tolstoy's *War and Peace.* Indeed, it is a novel that encapsulates the 'race', the 'milieu', and the 'moment' within its epic ambience.

Tagore's consistent, profound and lifelong exploration of the two issues—i.e. religion and nationalism—which necessarily got intersected during those days of newly awakened cultural nationalism, found reflection in the novel. He posited his own ideas against the backdrop of contemporary controversies surrounding these two vital issues which were of central importance to him. His own idealism and ideals about India, his thoughts, activities, his anguish, his dreams and disillusionment, all are woven into the texture of *Gorā.*

Significantly, in spite of all this *Gorā* does not end up as a social-political treatise or discourse; neither does this relegate the importance of the characters of the protagonists; rather, in the context of the epic spectrum the protagonists assume a very special vivacity and significance.

The time frame of the novel is just a few years behind the immediate 'moment' of its composition. Gora, as we can guess, was born in 1857, and thus, considered chronologically, Gora seems to be almost the same age as his author (born 1861). Both grew up from childhood to adolescence and into youth in the same chronotope of Calcutta in the last decades of the nineteenth century; it is the same city along with its horse-driven carriages and palanquins, its road-map, skyline and demographic formation—extending to the outskirts which included miles of fallow land spotted by sprawling gardens with some occasional villas inside, along the banks of Ganga—amidst which Tagore himself grew up, and about which he wrote so nostalgically in his poetic autobiography *Jīvansmṛti.*

The novel derived directly from the author's own first-hand experience of the times too. In order to understand and appreciate Tagore's depiction of his times in the novel, one may take into account, however briefly, Tagore's own views on *swadeś* and nationalism. Like many an elite of the late nineteenth and early twentieth century India, Tagore had also been carried away along the crest of the first wave of the Swadeshi movement. Apart from taking part in the many spontaneous and enthusiastic nationalistic activities of the extended Tagore family, Rabindranath inaugurated the 1896 Indian National Congress session of Calcutta by singing Bankimchandra's '*Vande Mataram*'; stirred by Bal Gangadhar Tilak's Shivaji festival, wrote his famous poem '*Shivaji-utsav*'; sent aids to Tilak from Bengal during his trial by the British court; sang the national song in the Provincial Congress of Dacca in 1305 B.S.; wrote inspiring patriotic essays in the columns of *Sādhanā, Baṅgadarśan,* and *Bhāratī*; composed excellent songs and poems on Swadesh which provided inspiration to many a freedom fighter. Tagore had actively participated in the protest movement against the proposed partition of Bengal in 1905. One may also recall his spirited protest of the Jalianwalla Bagh massacre.

Though *Gorā* came out only in 1910, understandably Tagore had started writing it quite a few years ago; and in order to understand *Gorā* as novel and Gora as character one has to look back to 1905, that turbulent year in our national history. Lord Curzon's proposal for partitioning Bengal had provoked a tremendous protest and as a result unleashed a high tide of patriotism. Riding on the crest of this strong wave of nationalism Tagore emerged as one of the leaders of the anti-partition movement during the initial phase of this surge. This was perhaps the period in Tagore's life when he enjoyed the highest ever popularity, and the only period when he was not target of petty maligning. However, it did not take long for the young poet to become disillusioned and immediately he extricated himself from the potentially enmeshing popularity and stood up defiantly against the current. But why?

In order to find the answer we have to remember some of Tagore's lifelong convictions regarding *swadeś* (literally, one's own land) or motherland:

[1] '*Deś*' or Bharatbarsha manifested to him an age-old and continuing tendency towards reconciliation, absorption and harmony.

> "Here came the Aryans, the non-Aryans, here came the Dravidians, the Chinese—
>
> The Saks, the Huns, the Pathans, the Mughals—and all got merged into one body...
>
> Those who came once as the fierce enemy marching in with triumphant frenzy
>
> Traversing desert tracts, defeating mountain ridges
>
> All of them dwell within me, no one is turned away, no one
>
> My blood resonates with the rich tune of this great orchestra...."

Even the West is not to be left out from this great harmonizing principle:

> The West opens out its doors today, to offer gifts and receive, and won't be turned away from this great ocean of humanity.

This is the idea Tagore articulated in poems like '*Bhārat-tīrtha*' as well as essays like '*Bhāratbarṣer Itihās*', where he underscored the uniqueness of Indian history in unequivocal terms: "I perceive that all along India has pursued the single goal of accommodating diversities within one broad unity, of converging various ways and channelizing them along the same direction, of envisioning the one within the heart of the many—foregrounding the deeper affinity of things without destroying their distinctive marks." This is the idea Tagore goes on consistently reiterating in various ways.

[2] The other facet of Tagore's thoughts on *swadeś* was the conviction that true patriotism constituted in serving the poorest of the country by means of working patiently toward their economic upliftment and restoration of individual dignity. The Tagore family at Jorasanko had evolved a distinct sense of patriotism long before 1905; they had tried to cultivate and propagate nationalistic awareness by organizing programmes like Hindu Mela, and by launching projects of indigenous

economic productions (all of which failed though) with the aim to promote indigenous commerce and industry. In *Jīvansmṛti* one comes across Tagore's fond nostalgic reminiscences of those innocent impractical activities, including his own brother Jyotirindranath's idealistic enterprises. Tagore himself, during his visits to Silaidaha, had initiated cooperative ventures, and much later set up the vocational institution of Sriniketan on the fringe of his Santiniketan. Serving one's country, for Tagore, thus often involved going against the current.

Tagore's various essays—like '*Ātmaśakti*' or '*Kartār Ichhāy Karma*', for instance—written from time to time on the subjects of *swadeś* and *samāj* emphasize this idea; so do his other novels like *Ghare-Bāire*, *Cār Adhyāy*, etc. Tagore was less interested in the exciting programmes of political agitation, and more concerned with the long-term tough work towards self-reliance which required greater patience, tenacity, and wisdom. In his famous essay, '*Swadeśi Samāj*', Tagore had chalked out an elaborate programme for self-reliance of the mass by means of planned organization of villages, education of the common people, social self-administration, cooperative movements, etc. He had tried to apply some of these ideas in his own estate in Silaidaha (now in Bangladesh), and later in Santiniketan-Sriniketan. Tagore had wanted his countrymen to be aware of their own individual strength, and to exert the same in order to break not only the external shackles, but also the internal ones. He did not believe in the shallow excitement of destructive activism or exclusivist sectarianism (whether it appeared in its ancient form or behind a mask of 'modernism'); instead he unequivocally expressed his preference for sustained constructive work for the country which would really benefit the helpless poor common man. No wonder, that he should have been so often misunderstood and abused during his own time. A look at this personal background helps the reader to follow the clash of the contrary viewpoints in *Gorā* on the subject of *swadeś*, *swadeśi*, and patriotism/nationalism.

Another important dimension of Tagore's patriotism, which becomes particularly relevant in the context of *Gorā*, is constituted by his approach of transcendental universalism and humanism. Tagore had indeed lent an extraordinary imaginative richness to the concept of *swadeś*; in his poems and songs he had again and again projected a sublime vision of *swadeś* and paid wonderful tributes to the empirical beauty and spiritual heritage of the country which he had envisaged as '*Bhuban-mana-mohinī*' and '*Bhārat-tīrtha*'. At the same time, he carefully kept himself above all narrow parochialism and chauvinism. Indeed, Tagore's unique nationalism can be traced back to the influence of Raja Rammohun Roy's broad human perceptions. His basic values were truth, humanity, justice, and his patriotism too was founded on these basic values. He was incapable of accepting anything demeaning, disgraceful, or dishonourable in the name of the country or the people. Whatever was false or wrong had to be rejected, even if it was of one's country. His love for the country, *swadeś*, was governed by another transcendental philosophy or wisdom. As he was not prepared to accept injustice of any sort, he protested against the injustice that had been perpetrated on his country by the foreign rule. As he was against exploitation he rejected the British exploitation of India. But as he felt for his own country and the countrymen, so he felt for the world and its citizens. His patriotism had risen above all sorts of sectarianism. Many of Tagore's contemporaries, in their excited involvement in the moment, failed to understand the broad nature of his nationalism which embraced the values of internationalism and basic humanism. He believed that if the good of man was sacrificed in the name of nationalism, then nationalism would also be surrendered for the sake of personal benefits. Hence his unhesitant rejection of those who would destroy good and enhance evil, whose misdirected minds would promote injustice and divisiveness in the name of either 'nationalism' or 'progress'. He powerfully portrayed in his novel the unscrupulousness of dishonest politicians and sectarian religious leaders side by side with the picture of genuine devotion of an honest sincere individual to his country and people. By the time Tagore came to write *Gorā* he had already formulated his ideas regarding the issues of nationalism, patriotism, commitment to one's motherland, and the vision of India as a wonderful poetic image as well as a vast mass of overwhelmingly suffering humanity. These are some of the basic issues that surface in *Gorā*.

Gora is shown to launch on extensive tours on foot through the length of rural India. This project of Gora reflects the author's own rejection of fashionable, insensitized arm-chair politics, and his preference for a genuine knowledge and feeling for the real India, its real condition, and willingness to pay for this knowledge in terms of pain—pain at the condition of the land and people. Gora's experience of working at the grass-roots level forces him to face another Bharat, the Bharat of countless poor disempowered people, who have been leading a death-in-life existence in the obscure backwaters of the country. During his extensive tour through the land

> ...for the first time Gora saw what the country was like beyond the pale of the genteel elite circle of the Calcutta society. This remote, vast, rural India—how fragmented it was, how narrow, how weak, how completely unaware of its own strength, ignorant and indifferent to betterment—how different it was at the interval of every ten to fourteen miles, how debarred from the big world by its own self-imposed imaginary obstacles, how obsessed with trivialities and rigidly resistant to any change or reform; what stagnation of mind, paucity of life, feebleness of effort!

In 1893 Tagore had already written his extraordinary poem '*Ebār Phirāo More*' (Bring me back), anthologized in *Citrā*. There he foregrounds the image of an orphaned girl in chains, thrown into some deep dark dungeon, and seeking succour while demonic insolence sucks the life-blood of the powerless with its million mouths, arrogant injustice mocks the pain of the victim, and the scared slave cowers.

> There they are, with bent head
> Speechless, carrying the story of millennia's suffering scribed
> On the lines of joyless face; the back weighed down with growing load
> They trudge on till the end—

then pass it on to the children—generation after generation—

do not blame fortune, do not accuse god or man, do not know resentment,

Only manage bare survival by pecking a few grains.

When even this small bowl is snatched away, even this gaunt body is crushed under the cruel wheels of proud power they do not know where to seek justice and silently die with a sigh.... [Translation ours]

The poet defines his own duty, and that of the youth of the country—to stir hope for some better future.

...to restore voice to these dumb dry benumbed lips; to resonate with hope these tired, withered broken hearts....

You poet, arise....

Such great misery, so much pain—life of such immense suffering around—

So poor, empty, so narrow, imprisoning, dark!

Clamour for food, for life, for light, for open air

For strength, for health, for joyous bright vivacity, for challenge, for courage.

Oh Poet, amidst this deep misery

Please hold up once again the divine vision of hope. [Translation ours]

This poem deserves mention in the present context because there is unmistakable correspondence between the poem and the novel; all these ideas are reiterated, almost verbatim, in the novel through Gora's anguish for the endless suffering of his countrymen, and his painful search for his own mission in this context. All these crowd in to form the background of *Gorā*, to provide the ideational frame of the novel. It is the same image of the country drawn up on a huge canvas.

Apart from the issue of nationalism Tagore also captures another facet of his times in *Gorā*; it is the religious debate that raged through Calcutta during those days. Tagore captures this atmosphere down to its vivid details. Again, in order to gain a right perspective on this aspect the reader should take into account Tagore's own deep sense of religion, his own personal search for a personal God, and a personal religious philosophy, his own interrogations of so-called religion, his pained perception of the dehumanizing impact of orthodoxy upon society and individual. As he said in a speech:

> "Generally speaking, in the name of religion, our minds are moulded according to the one uniform sectarian standard prevalent in our own community. Therefore, with the exception of those who have rare spiritual gifts, the generality of men, without their knowing it, are godless. They are pious, but not religious; they have not the courage of faith, but the habit of conformity....
>
> Religion is the expression of human aspiration seeking the fundamental unity of truth in the divine person of God. Whereas sectarianism uses religion itself to create disunion among men, sharpening its sword for the killing of brothers as a part of the ritual of the Father's worship. Sectarianism is the dangerous form of worldliness that claims exclusive right to spiritual illumination within its own narrow enclosure, and in the name of God refuses recognition to God himself where He is for all...."
>
> ['Parliament of Religions' (1929), *Boundless Sky*, 263-64]

Nikhilesh, the alienated hero in Tagore's *Ghare-Bāire*, arrives at the conviction through his ordeal of pain: "If we should perish in the attempt to save the country from the thousand-and-one snares—of religion, custom and selfishness... we shall at least die happy."

The vast spectrum of conflicting and corresponding ideas, notions, issues regarding religion which we encounter in *Gorā* was in the air; these were part of the 'moment', and were as operative behind Tagore's imagination during the time of writing *Gorā* as were the various currents and cross-currents of political-social ideas regarding nation, nationality, motherland, patriotism, etc., as they clashed and cohered through that entire phase of nascent freedom movement. However, religion in this novel is not just to provide an atmospheric element; it is also shown, in its profoundest form, as a deeply felt personal experience towards truth and humanism.

In this wonderful love story, woven as it is into the vast canvas of nationalism and religion, Tagore's thoughts, imagination, and vision of 'Bharatbarṣa' finally crystallize into one beautiful image; it is Anandamoyee, the all-forgiving, all-embracing, superb mother figure, who comes to manifest this vision. For Anandamoyee affection is the only guideline; she does not require anything else in deciding her course of action. Anandamoyee seems to be Tagore's vision of India incarnate in the form of a mother whose affection knows no barrier of cult or race. As Tagore wrote in his landmark poem, '*Bhārat-tīrtha*':

> Come Ye Aryan, come you non-Aryan, Hindu, and Muslim,
> come ye English, come ye Christians, welcome to all of you
> come Brahmin, cleanse your mind and clasp the hand of all,
> come ye outcaste, to take off the load of all ignominy!
> Come one and all, to the Mother's Crowning, the sacred
> jar is yet to fill, and
> all must join so that the water be consecrated
> by this vast sea of humanity that is India.

Anandamoyee is the microcosmic representation of that macrocosmic India of Tagore's vision, at whose feet the 'great ocean of humanity' can gather, because she can reach out to, and embrace all religions and nationalities through her all-absorbing love. It was in order to underscore the uniqueness of this all-embracing love that Gora had to be made a child of Irish descent.

Tagore's vision of religion and India get merged in the one beautiful composite figure of Anandamoyee. At the end of the novel, and at the end of his long day following the crucial disclosure of the secret of his birth Gora comes home to greet Anandamoyee with the joy of his wonderful discovery: "Gora said, 'Ma, it is you and you alone who is my mother! I had been looking for the *mother* outside while all the time she was here in my own house. You have no consideration of race, no discrimination, no hatred—you are the image of benediction! It is you who are my Bharatbarsha....'"

Years later, in *The Religion of Man* (1931) Tagore emphasized the same all-embracing love as the highest truth of all religion:

> We are made conscious of this truth of relationship immediately within us in our love, in our joy; and from the experience of ours we have the right to say that the Supreme One who relates all things, comprehends the universe, is all love—the love that is the highest truth being the most perfect relationship.

The same humanism which constituted the ground of Tagore's vision of *swadeś*, also worked as the keystone in evolving his religious philosophy. As Tagore explains the 'religion of man' in *Ātmaparicaya*:

> What is his religion? It is the religion that lies concealed in his mind to create himself. It is the inherent life-force that creates the living beings of the animal kingdom. The animals need not know anything about this life-force. But man has another entity, which is bigger that his sentient being—his humanism. This creative force within his life is his religion.

Besides Tagore's thoughts about *swadeśi* and religion, some other recurrent themes of Tagore's works reappear in this novel. One such theme is the predicament of the thinking, conscientious and necessarily lonely individual who gets alienated from, and is persecuted by, the thoughtless fanatic collective.

The attainment of fulfillment by realizing the truth through great suffering is another major theme of Tagore which finds articulation here in Anandamoyee's superb poise, and Gora's eventual self-discovery at the end of prolonged turbulence.

Again, the novel repeats in a way one continuous and consistent theme of Tagore's works—the relation between the small and the vast, the finite and the infinite; in an encounter between the two the finite may be traumatized, or even crushed for a time but then it absorbs the sustaining strength of the infinite, and emerges stronger than before.

Gora is the focus of the novel, and it is in his story that all these themes meet, intersect and flash into illuminating radiance of meanings. Gora also serves as the narrative centre unifying the rich and varied material. In the words of K.R. Srinivasa Iyengar, "Notwithstanding the wide canvas and the multiplicity of character, incident and dialogue, the novel is a unity—and this comes from Gora himself, who is both centre and circumference."

Gora is restless from the start. This cannot be attributed to the secret of his birth as Gora does not come to know about his Irish descent till the penultimate chapter. Actually the cause of this mental restiveness lies much deeper. It is a turmoil which Tagore himself might have shared with his protagonist. Through Gora Tagore seems to have projected the angst experienced by the serious, sincere and sensitive youth of his time who could be caught up in a similar disquieting search for the real mission, for the 'real' Bharat. Gora represents the author's dream vision of the new age youth of India as an irresistible, indomitable liberating force committed to the upliftment of the land and its people. Gora represents the youth of his times, torn as it was between the opposite pulls of orthodoxy and liberalism, revivalism and reform, tradition and modernity, proponents of orthodox Hinduism on the one hand, and initially dynamic but eventually stultified Brahmo-ism on the other. Parallel to this surged the newly emerging wave of nationalism. Initially Gora, being stirred by the new spirit of cultural nationalism, proudly embraces even the obscurantist form of Hinduism without question; but eventually as he comes in direct contact with the people he has his hunches about the validity of the orthodox ways; for example, while refusing the offer of hospitality from the Brahmin collector of the indigo-plant, Gora wonders: "We have made purity an external thing, and what an aberration this is from religion. My caste is saved by eating with one who is playing host to criminals for torturing Musalmans. And I shall ruin my caste status by eating with the man who protects a Musalman child in the face of threats and is ready to run the risk of social censure!"

Yet the persistent assaults from the British and their henchmen, the so-called liberals—only make him more desperate and push him further into the fold until he is redeemed by the sudden tremendous blow of the disclosure. Gora's obscurantism is thus generated by a proud spirit of protest against the colonial snobbery, which marked his times and was to continue for decades to follow.

It may also be interesting to remember in this context Krishna Kripalani's observation regarding the genesis of *Gorā* during a meeting between the author and Sister Nivedita:

> It is said that the main character in the novel, Gora... was suggested to him by the personality of Sister Nivedita, the Irish lady who became a disciple of Swami Vivekananda, the eloquent apostle of neo-Hinduism. Those who have read her books know what a passionate advocate she was of everything Hindu. Tagore, who liked her for her sincerity and courage, must often have smiled when she preached orthodoxy to him—more Hindu than the Hindu. Once when she was staying as his guest at his Silaidah estate, she would insist, when they sat out on the deck of the house-boat in the evening, that he tell her a story. So he began telling her the story of Gora and later wrote it down. (*Tagore: A Biography*, 214)

There may also be a shadow of Brahmabandhab Upadhyaya behind Gora, a freedom fighter who had attracted Tagore once by his sharp mind and dedication but eventually got involved in aggressive nationalism and terrorist activities; Tagore's brief poignant recollection of their last meeting is to be found in his foreword to *Cār Adhyāy*, his last novel.

Anyway, Gora, who can indeed remind one of Upadhyaya by virtue of his spiritedness and commitment, yet virtually journeys in the opposite direction; and Gora's progress from aggressive religious obscurantism to liberating universal humanism does not seem odd or anachronistic; because all along he has been a sincere honest searcher, and followed the dictate of none other than his own idealism. Whatever he did, it was done with a total commitment. So at the end when he is suddenly granted the illumination he can accept the truth with courage and confidence. At this moment Gora can think of only one person to whom he can rush with his newly gained freedom. Gora says to Pareshbabu, "You alone know the mantra of this freedom. That is why you have no place today in any society. You make me your disciple. You teach me the mantra of that God, who is the god of all—be they Hindu, Musalman, Christian, Brahmo, and whatever else—whose temple doors do not shut out any race, any caste, any individual, who is not just the God of the Hindus, but the God of Bharatbarsha!" As Gora's anguished search all these years now meets its end he can recognize in Pareshbabu the emissary of a religion of universal humanism, and in Anandamoyee the living incarnation of *Swadeś*.

Binoy represents another face of this new youth; Binoy represents the youth who has accepted the challenge of his times, but in a quieter and more pragmatic way. Binoy is the evidence that the author had no dislike or reservation for this model of the educated gentleman Bengali youth. That Tagore held the youth of contemporary Bengal in affection and trust can be felt in a number of his short stories as well; Apurba in '*Samāpti*', for example. In both of the two waves of stories—*Galpaguchha*, first series, preceding *Gorā*, and *Galpaguchha*, second series, following *Gorā* we come across many such educated youths who are idealistic, high-minded, and yet tender, sensitive, compassionate.

The two characters who have been done by the author with great admiration and command the same from the reader are Pareshbabu and Anandamoyee. While Pareshbabu with his tolerance, humility, spirituality and ambience represents the best face of modern liberalism, Anandamoyee is such an exceptional person as to evade all definitive or reductive categorization; she has no hesitation to discard many an inhibition and ignore the society out of her sheer love for Gora, yet she can refuse to be carried away by Gora's obscurantist impositions, be it regarding Lachmya's glass of water, or Binoy's marriage with Lalita; in the latter case she alone can take a stand against two opposed brands of sectarianism, and have her way.

Tagore's central characters, especially his women protagonists, seem to carry all along a wonderful fine fragrance of an ethereal essence, as it were. His women, exceptional by any standard, get transferred from the domain of mundane realism to another elevated finer realm of poetic truth. Thus Sucharita with her quiet grace and superb dignity, and Lalita with her dazzling splendour of spiritedness and self-respect can be placed in a long line of Tagorean women—from Kumudini (*Yogāyog*), to Labanya (*Śeṡer Kabitā*), Nandini (*Red Oleander*) to Ela (*Cār Adhyāya*).

Indeed the focal characters—both male and female—of Tagore's novels and plays seem to belong to another mental world, a world marked by a subtler, finer, sublime imagination, aesthetic sense and personal ethics. They mentally live on an elevated plane than the average bystanders. Even their articulation is different. Generally in Tagore's verse drama too, the crowd speak in prose (*Bisarjan*, *Rājā O Rāṇī*) whereas the protagonists speak fine poetry; the central characters are distinctly identified by name, the crowd is mentioned as numbers—1,2, etc. However, this does not mean that Tagore could not perceive or portray commoners. The novels bear ample evidence to Tagore's power of observation—sometimes amused, sometimes compassionate—which is often brought out by means of sharp flashes, and minute cute touches of a casual stroke of brush. Hence the long pageant of ordinary people in *Gorā*—from Baradasundari to Harimohini, from Kailash to Mahim, from Krishnadayal to Haranbabu, from Mahim's wife to Labanya, and from the reptilian Madhab Chatterjee to the vulturish police inspector, the arrogant magistrate Brownlow, the brute policemen—amusingly/revoltingly small and mean, is no less vivacious and entertaining. These flashes adequately show that Tagore could be as realistic as any of the valorized realistic writers (Saratchandra, for instance); like Gulliver holding the Liliputians on his palm, Tagore could at ease pick these small people up for instantaneous playful observation and then leave them indifferently on the roadside to go ahead with his main characters. These mundane people of mundane outlook, mindset and ways are not his protagonists; they are bystanders—

the insignificant but vivid people strewn on the roadside. Similarly, just with a few brush strokes he can also bring out the poignancy of the tragic death of Harimohini's daughter Manorama for dowry, or the pitiful death of Nanda, the young carpenter due to the community's superstition, the brute oppression of the hapless farmers under the British indigo planters and magistrate, and also the quiet courage of the lone Hindu barber protecting the Muslim child.

But Tagore's central characters, high-minded, cultured, devoid of narrowness as they are, attain an altogether different level—a philosophical-imaginative-mental level of higher altitude. In course of undergoing the creative process of imaginative transcendence the concrete assumes an impalpable dimension, while the sensuous image (*Rūp*) becomes transformed into essence or idea (*Bhāb*).

The secret of Gora's birth, about which Gora is kept in the dark till the penultimate chapter, but the reader has been taken into confidence, contributes to an element of irony which persists through the narration enriching its suggestion and effect.

To conclude with Krishna Kripalani's succinct commentary which offers one of the best insights into *Gorā*:

> *Gorā* is more than a mere novel; it is the epic of India in transition at the most crucially intellectual period of its modern history. Though not so vast in its scope and sweep of events nor so rich and so varied in its gallery of portraits, it is to Bengali fiction what Tolstoy's *War and Peace* is to the Russian. No other book can claim so masterly an analysis of the Bengali intelligentsia of the period, with their divided loyalties, their aspirations and inhibitions, or of the character of Indian nationalism which draws its roots from renascent Hinduism and stretches out its arms towards universal humanism. Nor is it any the less interesting as a novel. The characters are well drawn, not as individual freaks but as types, clearly recognizable, and their conflicts, both as between themselves and within themselves as living and growing

> characters, are delineated with great insight and sympathy. Despite the abundance of polemics in the book, inevitable in view of its theme, the author does not lose the thread of the main narrative, whose interest is sustained to the end. (*Rabindranath Tagore: A Biography,* 213)

Finally, as a major work of Tagore's middle phase, *Gorā* connects back and forth to the previous and succeeding works of Tagore, sending back its tentacles of ideas, and radiating forth its beautiful significances through Tagore's wonderful oeuvre.

Mohit K. Ray
Rama Kundu

Gorā

1

Although it was the month of *Śrāvaṇ*, the high tide of monsoon, the sky had cleared in the morning and shimmering sunlight had filled the air of Kolkata. The roads were busy as usual with continuous flow of traffic. The vendors were ceaselessly hawking their wares. Vendors carrying baskets of fish and vegetable had already done their brisk business at the doorstep of those who were set for office, college or court. Smoke was curling up from kitchens. Still, all the myriads of streets, lanes and by-lanes of Kolkata—this huge busy and concretized city—seemed to have been flooded this morning by a stream of golden light which was, as it were, an epitome of the exquisite flow of youth.

On such a morning, Binoybhushan, standing alone on the first-floor balcony of his apartment, was looking in a leisurely mood at the moving crowd in the street. He had finished his college education quite sometime ago, and yet has not started leading family life. This is the present situation of Binoy. He has engaged himself to the mission of conducting meetings and seminars, and writing for newspapers. But that has not given full satisfaction to his entire mind. At least this morning he was feeling restive as he could not decide how to preoccupy himself right at the moment. From the neighbouring roof-top some three crows were loudly exchanging notes, while at one corner of his own balcony a sparrow couple were encouraging each other in soft twittering regarding their nest-building project. All this lisping melody had been stirring up some vague emotions in Binoy.

A *bāul* in flowing robe stopped in front of the shop nearby and started singing—

How does the strange bird fly in and out of the cage,
If I could, I would have fettered her within my mind.

Binoy wished he could take down this song about the strange bird by calling the *bāul.* But just as one feels slightly chilly towards dawn, and yet does not feel like pulling on the blanket, Binoy too felt pleasantly lazy so that the singer was not called, neither was the song taken down; only the melody continued to resonate within his mind, when suddenly just in front of his house a huge carriage came down headlong upon a small cab, smashed one of its wheels and dashed off in high speed without looking back. The cab, instead of being overturned, slumped on one side.

Binoy rushed out on the streets and saw that a girl of seventeen to eighteen had already come out from the cab and an elderly gentleman was trying to get down.

Binoy helped him out and on seeing his pale face asked, 'I hope you aren't hurt!' He tried to force a smile saying, 'Oh, no—not at all'; but before he could finish the smile faded and he was on the point of fainting. Binoy at once caught him and told the anxious girl, 'My house is just in front. Please come in.'

When the elderly man was laid on the bed, the girl looked around and spotted an earthen pitcher. At once she poured some water from the pitcher into a glass and started sprinkling it on the old man's face while fanning him at the same time, and suggested to Binoy, "Shouldn't we call in a doctor?"

A doctor lived nearby. Binoy sent his servant to call him in.

On a table at one corner of the room there were a mirror, a bottle of hair oil, a comb, etc. While standing behind the girl Binoy looked into the mirror and became spellbound.

Since childhood Binoy had been at Calcutta in rented houses in connection with his studies. Whatever knowledge he had gathered about life and the world was entirely through books. He had never come in contact with any woman other than his relatives.

He stared at the mirrored image—what a beautiful image it was! He was not experienced enough to see and judge the features and lineaments separately. It was only the soft luminosity of that young face, bending in anxious affection that struck Binoy as a freshly revealed unique wonder of creation.

Soon the old man slowly opened his eyes and sighed saying '*Ma*'. The girl tearfully bent her face close to the old man's face and asked anxiously, 'Baba, where does it hurt?'

'What is this place? Why am I here?',—the old man tried to get up. Instantly Binoy stepped forward and intervened, 'Please don't move. Take a little rest. The doctor is coming.'

Then he remembered everything and said, 'A slight pain is here at this spot on the head but it is nothing serious.' At the very same moment the doctor arrived raising smart sound with his squeaking shoes; he too assured, 'nothing serious'. As soon as the doctor left after advising a little dose of brandy in a little milk, the old gentleman appeared extremely embarrassed and restless. Understanding his feelings the daughter said, 'Baba, why are you getting fidgety? After we go home we shall send the doctor's visit and the medicinal cost.' Saying this she turned her eyes towards Binoy.

What strange eyes those were! Whether they were big or small, black or blonde—these small details did not simply occur to the viewer. What one at once felt after one first glimpse of them was that these eyes had an irrefutable impact. There was no hesitation in their gaze, no embarrassment; it denoted an inner strength and certitude.

Binoy tried to say, 'The fee for the doctor's visit is nominal, it is not...you needn't...I will...', but as the girl continued to stare at him he could not even properly finish his say. Only he was not left with the least doubt that he must accept the reimbursement of the doctor's fees.

The old gentleman said, 'Look here, I don't need brandy—'

The daughter intercepted, 'Why *baba*? It was the doctor who advised so.'

The old man said, 'It is like the doctors; it is their superstition. Just a little warm milk will be enough to get over the slight weakness that I feel at the moment.'

After the milk the old man felt stronger and said to Binoy, 'Now allow us to take leave. Sorry for causing you lot of trouble.'

The girl turned to Binoy, 'A carriage—'

The old man shyly said, 'Why bother him again? We live close by. Let us walk down.'

The girl remonstrated, 'Oh no *baba*, that cannot be.'

The old man did not contest and Binoy himself fetched in a coach. Before boarding the coach, the old man asked, 'May I know your name please?'

'My name is Binoybhushan Chattopadhyaya.'

The old man said, 'I am Pareshchandra Bhattacharya. I live in number 78 in the next lane. If you find some time to visit us we shall be very pleased.'

The girl silently raised her eyes to Binoy and indicated her silent approval of the invitation. Binoy was ready to instantly board the very same coach and pay the requested visit; but as he was not sure whether that should be appropriate or socially right manners, he just stood there. On the eve of leaving the girl made a small *namaskār* with folded hands. Binoy was not at all ready for this. So, being taken completely by surprise he got confused and failed to reciprocate the beautiful gesture. On returning home he reproached himself again and again. He turned the entire encounter from the first to the last over in his mind, reviewed his own performance—and concluded that his behaviour all along had been uncivil in every respect. He continued to feel disturbed over questions like what he should have really said or done at which particular moment. Coming back to his room Binoy saw a handkerchief left on his bed. It was the handkerchief the girl had used to wipe her father's face. He quickly picked it up. The *bāul*'s song continued to resonate within his mind—

'How does the strange bird fly in and out of the cage!'

The day rolled on, the monsoon sun became hot, the endless stream of vehicles rushed by. Binoy could not concentrate on any of his regular daily work. He had never experienced such deep sadness juxtaposed with such exquisite delight. His small apartment and the ugly Kolkata around it became transformed into some charmed land—a land where impossible things can happen, the unachievable is achieved, and the indescribable takes the form of manifest beauty. Binoy felt as if he were moving around in one such absurd land. The luminous beauty of this monsoon morning seeped into his brain, pulsated in his veins, and came down before his consciousness like some radiant curtain that completely covered up all the mundane trivialities of daily life. Binoy longed to express in some wonderful way this feeling of self-fulfillment, but finding no chance to do it, only felt distressed. The image in which he could envision himself showed just a very ordinary person—the apartment was most ordinary, the articles were in disarray and the bed was most untidy. On some days he happens to keep a bouquet of flowers in his room, but today as ill luck would have it, there was not a single petal. People used to say—the way Binoybabu can deliver fine extempore speeches in public meeting, he will eventually emerge as a great orator. But today he had not uttered a single word which might prove his intelligence. He repeatedly rehearsed the scene in his mind—'Suppose it so happened that just at the moment the big carriage was on the point of colliding with their cab, I rushed out in a flash to the spot and reined back the wild horses with visible ease!' As the image of his own heroism became vivid to him he could not rest without having a look at his reflection in the mirror.

At this time he saw a boy of seven or eight in the street, where he stood trying to decipher the number of the house. Binoy said from above, 'Here, yes, this is the house.'

He did not have the least doubt that the boy was looking for his house. He quickly scrambled down with the slipper flapping on the steps. He warmly received the boy and taking him indoors looked askance at his face. The boy said, 'Didi has sent me.' Saying this he handed in an envelope to Binoy.

Taking the letter Binoy looked on the envelope to find his own name superscribed in English in clear feminine hand. Inside there was no letter or message, but only some money.

The boy was about to leave, but Binoy would not let him go by any means. He put his arm round the boy's shoulder and took him upstairs to his first-floor room. The boy was darker than his elder sister, but Binoy thought there was a family resemblance in the features. Looking at the boy Binoy felt a stirring of affection and joy within.

The boy was quite smart. Immediately on entering the room he spotted a photograph on the wall and asked, 'Who is he?'

Binoy said, 'He is a friend of mine.'

The boy asked again, 'A friend's picture? Who is your friend?'

Binoy smiled, 'You won't know him. My friend is Gaurmohan. I call him Gora. We have been pals since our schooldays.'

'Are you a student still?'

'No, I don't have to study any more.'

'So you have finished reading e—verything?'

Binoy could not restrain the desire to show off to this little fellow, and said, 'yes, *everything*'.

The boy was surprised and sighed a little. Perhaps he thought how long will it take him to read as much.

Binoy. 'What is your name?'

'My name is Sri Satishchandra Mukhopadhyay.'

Now it was the turn of Binoy to be surprised, 'Mukhopadhyay'?

Then bit by bit he gathered the information—that Pareshbabu was not his father—that he had brought up the brother and the sister since their childhood. Previously the name of his elder sister was Radharani; subsequently Pareshbabu's wife has replaced it with 'Sucharita'.

Before long Satish and Binoy became quite friendly. When Satish was about to start for home, Binoy said, 'Will you be able to go alone?'

Satish proudly replied, 'I always go alone.'

Binoy said, 'Let me accompany you.'

Satish resented what seemed to be a lack of confidence in his ability, and remonstrated, 'Why must you come? I can go alone.' He continued to cite a number of amazing instances in support of his claim regarding his ability to move about by himself. And the poor child could not understand why even after this Binoy went along with him till he reached home.

Satish aked, 'Won't you come in?'

Binoy said, suppressing his strong inclinations, 'Another day.'

Coming back home Binoy took out the envelope from his pocket and took a long look at the handwritten address—the curves and patterns of every letter became almost inscribed in his memory; then he put back the envelope along with the money carefully inside the suitcase. There remained no chance that he would spend this money on any emergency.

2

The moist darkness of the sky seemed to hang heavily over the monsoon evening. Under the oppressive silence of unvariegated grey clouds the city of Kolkata was lying motionless like some huge cheerless dog curled up and resting its head on its tail. Since last evening it has been drizzling incessantly. The drizzle had turned the dust of the road into mud, but did not have the power to wash the mud away. Since four o'clock in the afternoon today the rain has stopped, but the cloud still looks ominous. On such an evening threatened by imminent rain when being alone indoors you feel restive, and yet do not find any comfort outside, two people are seen sitting on two light cane stools on the damp roof top of a three-storeyed house.

When these two friends were kids how often after school they would play and run around on this roof top. Again, on exam eves they would endlessly walk from end to end of this space with excited brisk steps while loudly memorizing the lessons. How often during summer afternoons they would come back from college to take their dinner on this very roof top, and then would debate or talk on till the small hours to wake up only when the morning sun struck them and realize that they had dropped into sleep on the *madur*. When all the college exams were over one by one, then this same roof space had been the venue of the monthly meetings of the 'Friends of Hindu' organization, of which one of these two comrades were the President while the other was the Secretary.

The President's name was Gaurmohan; friends and relatives called him 'Gora'. He seemed to have absurdly outgrown all who had surrounded him. The *Pundit* of their college used to address him as 'the rajatgiri' or silver hill. His complexion was rather too white, without any touch of the yellowish to offset it. Nearly six feet tall, Gora was big-boned, and with palms as big as a tiger's paws. His voice was so thick and deep that it could startle one to exclaim, 'Ah! who's it!' The face too was unnecessarily big and excessively strong-looking, with jaw bones and chins firm like the bars of the fortress door. The eyebrow was next to none and the brow stretched wide towards the ears; the lips were thin and tightly pressed, with the nose hanging on them like a *khāndā*. The eyes were small but sharp. Their look seemed to be like the tip of an arrow about to shoot a distant object and would yet turn back in an instant like lightning to strike the nearest object. Gaur could not be called exactly goodlooking, but he could never pass unnoticed; he was bound to attract attention amidst a crowd.

On the other hand, Binoy was like an average educated Bengali gentleman,—modest yet bright; delicate temperament and sharp intelligence had joined to lend a special charm to his features. At college he had all along secured high marks and scholarship. Gora could not keep up with him by any means. Indeed, Gora had little interest in prescribed studies in the syllabi. Nor could he follow or remember the lessons as promptly as Binoy. It was Binoy who had acted as his main support through the college exams and carried him along.

Gora had been saying, "Look here. That Abinash had been disparaging the 'Brahmos' only proves that the man is normal and in right state of mind. Why did you suddenly get so excited over this?"

Binoy. 'How strange! I could not even imagine that this would be an issue!'

Gora. Then you must have developed a wrong mindset. A group of people would defy all rules of the society and act aberrantly in every matter, and the society would remain calm and treat them with every fairness—that is not the law of nature. Society is bound to misunderstand them; whatever they do as the right thing would surely appear distorted to the perception of others—and this is as it should be. This is one of the various retributions that await the wilful non-conformists.

Binoy. I cannot agree to the proposition that whatever is natural is also good or desirable.

Gora warmed up a bit and said, 'I do not need the "good". If the world must have a few goodies let her have it, but let the rest be normal. Otherwise it remains neither workable, nor livable. Those who want to boast of their 'brahmo' status, must also accept this little trouble of being misunderstood and vilified by the non-Brahmos for their every activity. They will swagger about, and their antagonists will follow them applauding,—this is something that does not happen in this world, and even if it did happen it would not have come to much avail.'

Binoy. I do not mean criticizing the group. But personal attack—.

Gora. Attacking the group—do you call it an attack! That is just discussion of opinions. What we need is personal attack. Well, my dear Mr Saintly, didn't you indulge in the same practice till the other day?

Binoy. Yes. I did. I did a lot. But I feel really ashamed of that.

Gora clenched his right fist and said, 'No, Binoy, this cannot be, by no means....'

Binoy fell silent for a few seconds, then said, 'Why? What has happened? What scares you?'

Gora. 'I can clearly see that you are getting weak.'

Binoy got slightly excited: 'Weak! You know, if I want I can visit their place any moment—they invited me too—but I did not go.'

Gora. But neither can you get over the fact that you did not go. Day and night you have been only thinking, 'Oh, I have not gone, have not gone, Oh I have not gone to them'—It would have been better if you really clinched the thing.

Binoy. Then do you advise me to go?

Gora slapped his own knees and shouted, "No, I don't. But I can give you in black and white, that the day you go there you will go the whole hog. From the next morning you will start taking their food and before long you will formally join the *Brahmo* samaj to become a celebrated preacher.

Binoy. Indeed! What next?

Gora. There is no next. What can be worse than death? A Brahmin by birth, you will end up in the slaughter yard for the cattle, with all your rites and rituals thrown away, with your sense of direction lost like some captain with broken compass in the far seas. Then you will think that steering the ship to the port is superstition, narrowness, and just drifting about is real navigation. But such argument taxes my patience. I tell you, 'Go'. Why do you keep us too in suspense by standing on the brink of damnation, your feet already making it towards the abyss?

Binoy laughed aloud and said, 'It is not that the patient should necessarily die the moment the doctor gives up hopes. At least I don't see any symptom of an imminent catastrophe.'

Gora. Don't you?

Binoy. No.

Gora. Don't you feel the pulse sinking?

Binoy. No. It's going fine and strong.

Gora. Aren't you dreaming that, served by some graceful hand, the heathen's food could be as good as divine delicacies?

Binoy shrank at this; he said, 'Gora please! Stop here.'

Gora. Why? Privacy cannot be an issue here. The 'graceful hand' is not in purdah. It can shake male hands; and yet you cannot stand even the mention of this sacred soft palm, it proves you are already mulled. *Tadā nāśangse maraṇāya Sanjaya*! So, you are lost.

Binoy. Look here, Gora. I respect the womenfolk—our scriptures too—.

Gora. Don't cite the scripture to justify your way of showing respect to womenfolk. It is not respect. If I tell you what it is you will thrash me.

Binoy. That is *argumentum ad baculum.*

Gora. The scriptures mention that women should be worshipped, because they impart radiance to home. They are to be worshipped because they make the *house* radiant, not the *male heart* for which they may be valued in the West—that is better not called worship.

Binoy. Should you thus mock a noble emotion just because of its occasional aberrations?

Gora lost his patience: 'Binu, now that you have lost the capacity of reasoning, please accept my observation—I say, the driving force behind all the exaggerations in the Western culture regarding women is simply lust. The proper place to worship women is in her position as mother, as the chaste modest housewife. The reason why your mind is revolving round the house of Pareshbabu like the moth around flame is called "love" in English. I can only wish that you are not carried away by such foolhardiness of aping the British as to worship that "love" as the supreme goal of life.'

Binoy sprang up like a strong horse under lash and cried, 'Oh Gora. Please stop it! Enough of it!'

Gora. Enough! It has been nothing. It has been so because we have not learnt to properly place man and woman in their own distinct positions that we have been poeticizing reality.

Binoy said, 'Well. I accept that driven by instinctual motivation we tend to forget the right and appropriate relation between man and woman. But is it exclusively a lapse of the West? If the poeticism of the English regarding this is a mistake then what about our overdoing of the so-called abdication of "*kāminī-kancan*"? Is it not wrong? There are things which can easily make man forget himself; some try to lend glory to the beautiful aspect of love which can cover up its seamy side; some others issue the dictum of foregoing woman and wealth. These are just two different ways devised by people of two different temperaments. If you criticize one you should not overlook the other.'

Gora. Oh no. I had misunderstood you. Now I find you are not lost altogether as yet. Since you can still philosophize, you may safely make your love, but do cry halt in time—that is the earnest appeal of your well-wishing friends.

Binoy at once protested: 'Ah! Have you gone mad! "Love" for me? Anyway, I must admit this much, that so far as I have come to know about Pareshbabu and his family, I have felt real regard for them. Perhaps that is why I felt interested to know about their life and ways from inside.'

Gora. Very good, it is this interest that you have to keep under control. Why not leave the zoology chapter regarding them undiscovered? Specially since they are the predatory type, it is possible that your search for knowledge about them may entice you so far in as to make you disappear altogether.

Binoy. Listen Gora, you have one serious fault. You assume that God has given all the strength to you alone, and the rest of us are all weaklings.

The observation instantly struck Gora's imagination. Happily he slapped Binoy on the back and agreed, 'Yes—you are perfectly right—precisely that is my fault—a big fault.'

Binoy exclaimed in pain: 'Oh! you have an even bigger fault: you have no idea regarding the capacity of a person's backbone towards absorbing hurt.'

At this point Gora's elder stepbrother Mahim came up gasping under the weight of his heavy body, and called, 'Gora!'

Gora instantly stood up from the stool and respectfully replied, 'Yes, *dādā*!'

Mahim. I came to see if the heavy cloud of the monsoon has come to land right on our own roof top. What's the matter today? Have you seen off the English halfway across the Indian ocean? In any case I do not see the English suffering much loss, but your sister-in-law downstairs, floored by her headache, has to take the brunt of this lion-roar.

Saying this Mahim left them.

Gora stood embarrassed—also a little angry; one cannot be sure if this anger was directed against himself or somebody else. After some time he said slowly, as if to himself, 'In everything, I tend to apply much more pressure than what is needed; I do not remember how unbearable that can be to another.'

Binoy came up to Gora and affectionately held his hand.

3

Gora and Binoy were about to leave the roof top when Gora's mother came up. Binoy greeted her by touching her feet.

Seeing Anandamoyee one would hardly guess her to be Gora's mother. She was slim, tightly built; if a few wisps of hair had been graying those were not readily visible; a casual look would lead one to assume she was on this side of forty. The face was very delicately curved; the nose, the lips, the chin, the forehead were as it were sculpted with great care. The body was devoid of any extra fat—the face always expressed a clear and lively intelligence. Her complexion was darkish, and not at all comparable to Gora's dazzling fair skin. The obvious thing that struck one about her appearance was that she used to wear chemise under her *sārī*. The time about which we are talking had already seen the introduction of blouse or chemise in the outfit of young Bengali girls; but still the elderly housewives generally disapproved it as smacking of Christian culture. Anandamoyee's husband Krishnadayalbabu had once worked with the 'Commisseriat'; since her girlhood Anandamoyee had to live with him in the Western parts of India. So, it had never occurred to her that properly covering one's body could be a cause for shame. Even after scrubbing and cleaning the house, doing the washing, cooking and serving food, sewing, keeping the accounts, sunning and ordering the various domestic articles, keeping contact with relatives-friends-neighbours, she seemed to have more time on her hands. She would never care even when she was sick; and would say instead, 'Sickness can't do anything to me, but how can I live without work?'

Gora's mother came up saying, 'As soon as I hear Gora's voice downstairs I know Binu must be there. For the last few days the house was dead silent. What happened sonny? Tell me. Why didn't you come? I hope you didn't fall ill.'

Binoy shyly said, 'No *mā*—it was just this weather—so inclement!'

Gora retorted, 'Indeed! After this when the rains are over Binoy will say, "Oh, so hot it is!" When you put it on the gods they do not answer back—but the real cause is known only to the all-knowing God.'

Binoy said, 'Gora, what nonsense are you babbling!'

Anandamoyee rejoined, 'Truly son, you should not speak like that. It is the question of mood or mental condition; sometimes it is fine, sometimes it may not be; you can never have it uniform. If you start arguing about it, that amounts to a kind of disturbance. Well, Binu, come along to my room. I have readied dinner for thee.'

Gora vehemently protested, 'No, *mā*, that cannot be. I won't allow Binu to have his dinner in your room.'

Anandamoyee. 'Oh! indeed! Why son? Do I ever call you to dine in my room? Your father too has grown terribly fastidious and ritualistic these days; he won't take anything unless it is cooked by himself. Binu is my darling son, he is not orthodox like you; it is you who try to hold him back by force.'

Gora. 'Yes. You are right. I will hold him back by force. Until you dismiss that Christian maid of yours—Lachmya, we won't take food in your room.'

Anandamoyee. 'Gora dear, you please don't utter such a thing. All along she has fed you, she has reared you since childhood. Till the other day a meal seemed tasteless to you without the sauce prepared by her. When you had an attack of small pox in your infancy, it was Lachmya who had saved you, nursed you back to health; how can I ever forget that?'

Gora. You provide her with pension, buy a plot of land, build a cottage, do whatever you like, but she must not be allowed to stay on in this house.

Anandamoyee. Gora, it seems you think all debts can be paid back by money! She does not want land or house; but she will die if she cannot see you.

Gora. O.K. Then have her if you like. But I cannot let Binu eat in your room. What is rule is rule; rules must be obeyed by any means. *Mā*, in spite of being the daughter of such a renowned family of professors, you do not observe the rituals or regulations, it is—.

Anandamoyee. My dear, there was a time when your mother used to observe each and every rule; had to shed such tears over them indeed! Where were you then? Every day as I moulded my own small earthen 'Shiva' and sat down for worship, your dad would rush in to throw it away. Those days I felt nauseated to eat rice cooked even by a '*bāmun*' who was not known to us. The railroads did not cover much of the land then—so many days I had just fasted while journeying by bullock carts, horse-driven carriage, palanquin or riding camel. Was it easy for your father to break down my old ways? Again, was it for nothing that he did this? It was precisely because he used to take his wife with him everywhere he went that his English bosses plauded him, his emoluments soared—he could stay on at one place for long terms, was indeed rarely transferred. Now, arrived at old age, he has resigned his job after securing a lump sum and has suddenly done a somersault towards orthodoxy. But I cannot do it. My habits and beliefs, acquired through the accumulated practice of seven generations have been wrenched up and destroyed one by one—now they cannot be restored for a song.

Gora. O.K. Forget your ancestors. They at least won't come back to raise objection. But for our sake you must accept certain things. Well, you may not do it for the sake of the scripture; but won't you do it for the sake of affection?

Anandamoyee. 'Oho! Do you need all these arguments in order to convince me? I alone know what is going on within my mind. What happiness remains for me if my husband, my son have to clash with me at every step? But do you know that I have thrown orthodox rituals overboard the very day I picked you up into my bosom? The moment one holds an infant in one's bosom, one realizes nobody in this world is born with a racial identity. The day I came to learn this, I also got the conviction that if I hate one for being Christian or low class, God will snatch you away from me. May God keep you to fill my house, my life with light and joy; I will take my food and drink from members of all races of the world.

Today, while listening to Anandamoyee, a sudden cloud of vague uncertainty floated across Binoy's mind. He looked from Anandamoyee's face to Gora's, but instantly dismissed his hunches.

Gora said, 'Ma, I don't quite get your logic. Those who strictly follow the scriptures have also children and they survive too; yet why should God apply his special law only in your case! Who gave you such ideas?'

Anandamoyee. He, who has given you, has also given the ideas. So, tell me what can I do, I have no control over this. But o my crazy son, I don't know if I should laugh or weep at your madness. Anyway, let us stop this. Then Binoy, won't you have your dinner at my room?

Gora. Left to himself, he will at once rush to your room, the glutton that he is. But *Mā*, I won't let him. He is the son of a Brahmin, and he should not be allowed to forget the fact just for the sake of a pair of sweet cakes. He must sacrifice a lot, restrain his instincts. Only then would he be able to live up to the mark as designated by his birth. *Mā*, please don't be angry. I am touching your feet.

Anandamoyee. Me angry! What do you say! I just want to say you this much that whatever you are doing, it is done in ignorance. This is my pain that although I brought you up...—anyway, I cannot accept what you call 'dharma'. For that you may not eat the food I cook or serve—well, don't—but still I can see you twice a day. That is enough for me. Binoy, my dear, please don't look so cast down. You are soft-hearted; you are thinking perhaps you have made me unhappy. Not at all, my son. I shall invite you another day and arrange for a very authentic *bāmun* to cook and serve—don't worry. For myself, however, my sons, I am leaving with this clear declaration that I shall have my food and drink served by Lachmya.

Gora's mother went downstairs. Binoy stood silent for some time; then slowly said, 'Gora, this seems a bit overdoing.'

Gora. 'Whose overdoing?'

Binoy. Your....

Gora. Not a bit. I just want to maintain the limits. Once you concede to forego the smallest ground you end up losing everything.

Binoy. But it is *Mā*!

Gora. I know what is *Mā*. Must you remind me? How many have mothers like my *Mā*? But if I stop respecting the laws a day may come when I will not even respect *Mā*. Look here Binoy, let me tell you, please remember, emotion is a fine thing, but it is not the finest of all.

After a little hesitation Binoy said, 'Listen Gora, today I feel a strange disturbance in my mind after listening to *Mā*. I feel, *Mā* has something to say, but she cannot convey that to us and has been suffering thereby.'

Gora impatiently cried out: 'Oho Binoy, please don't imagine too much—that only eats away your time, and is of no avail.

Binoy. You do not look closely at the world around. Or whatever evades your sight is dismissed by you as imaginary. But I am telling you I have felt it many a time that *Mā* has some thought or idea which she has not been able to give up or get reconciled to—that's why she always carries a sadness hidden under her busy schedule. Gora, please lend your ears patiently to what she says.

Gora. I always hear what can be heard by lending one's ears—If I try to hear more there's the risk of making mistakes. O, I don't try that way at all.

4

You can calmly consider a proposition so long as it is an abstract idea, but when you come to apply the same to a real human being you cannot retain that detached attitude—at least Binoy could not do it. Binoy was a man of strong emotions. So, during a debate he would speak vehemently in support of some opinion, but when it came to practical application he could never cling to the idea and place the idea above the real man. In fact, regarding his acceptance of Gora's preachings, it is difficult to say how far he did it for the sake of the opinion itself, and how far it was conditioned by his genuine love for Gora.

As Binoy was walking back from Gora's house to his own apartment, cautiously stepping over the muddy spots on the road, mentally he was engaged in a conflict between abstract idea and the concrete human.

Binoy had no problem in accepting from Gora the view that if the society had to protect itself from implicit and explicit assaults of the day, it had to be extra careful regarding all sorts of taboos in matters of eating, touching, etc. He had also sharply argued with people on the issue; he has said, when the enemy surrounds the fort from all sides, sealing all the holes and passages into the fort for self-protection is a necessity and not lack of generosity.

But that Gora had imposed embargo today against his eating in Anandamoyee's kitchen, continued to haunt him as a nagging pain.

Binoy did not remember his father. He had also lost his mother at a tender age. There was an uncle in the ancestral house in a remote village, and since boyhood he had grown up alone in apartments of Calcutta through his student life. Since the day he came to know Anandamoyee through his friendship with Gora, he has looked up to her as his own mother. So many times he has stormed into her room and enjoyed the food with gay abandon. So many times he has feigned jealousy at Anandamoyee's supposed partiality for Gora regarding the distribution of food. Binoy knew very well how Anandamoyee got anxious if Binoy failed to turn up for a few days, how she waited eagerly for their meetings to end so that she could lovingly treat Binoy to her delicacies in the privacy of her room. If Binoy stopped all this today just for the sake of social disapproval, could she bear it, or could Binoy himself bear it either?

'From now on *Mā* will offer me food through authentic "*bāmun*". *Mā* said this smilingly, but is it not a terrible decision!' Binoy repeated this again and again in his mind as he trudged on towards his apartment.

The empty room was plunged in darkness. Books and papers were scattered all around. Striking a match stick Binoy lighted an oil lamp—the glass lamp bore the many finger prints of the attendant. The white cloth cover on the writing table was spotted with marks of ink and oil. He felt claustrophobic in this room. The lack of human company and affection seemed to weigh down heavily on his heart. To restore the country, to protect the society—this sort of duties seemed to be too vague and untrue. In comparison that strange bird seemed to be much more authentic,—the bird that had come close to the cage one luminous beautiful *śrāvaṇ* morning and then had again flown far away. But no. He must not pay any heed to that strange bird,—no, never by any means. In order to stick to his resolve Binoy tried to distract himself by mentally redrawing the picture of Anandamoyee's room, the room from which Gora had forced him back.

The *pankh*-decorated, polished bright clean floor was gleaming; at one corner a bed—soft and clean like the wings of a white swan—was spread on a wooden plank; right by the bed on the small stool the oil lamp had been lit by now; *Mā* was certainly bending over embroidery work with colored threads on a coverlet near that light, while sitting on the floor Lachmya was talking ceaselessly in her broken Bengali, with *Mā* registering little or none of her ramblings. Whenever *Mā* is hurt she preoccupies herself with some artistic work. Binoy envisioned that silent absorbed face, and concentrating his imagination on it, prayed silently, 'the love and affection behind this face may protect me from all sorts of aberrations. Let this face be for me the epitome of my motherland, let it motivate me to duties and keep me firm in them.' Binoy silently addressed her once as '*Mā*', and said, 'No scriptural code can ever convince me that your food is not my nectar.'

In the big silent room the clock ticked on. Binoy could not bear it any more. A lizard was pursuing some insect on the wall near the light. Binoy watched it for a while; then suddenly sprang up and picking up the umbrella set out.

He was not very clear about what he would do. Perhaps his intention was to go back to Anandamoyee. But then it occurred to him, 'It is Sunday. Let me go to listen to Keshabbabu's address at the Brahmo-sabha.' As soon as he thought this he started walking briskly. Although he was aware that there might not be enough time to reach before the address, still he was not deterred.

On reaching his destination Binoy found that the devotees were coming out. Opening the umbrella he stood on one side of the road. Just at that moment Pareshbabu, looking calm and benign, came out from the temple. He was accompanied by four or five members of his family. Binoy spotted out among them only a single young face for only a single fraction of a moment in the gas light of the street. Then he heard the wheels rolling; the vision was lost like a bubble in the ocean of darkness.

Binoy had read lots of English novels; but how could he get over the inhibitions of the typical middleclass Bengali gentleman? He could not persuade himself by any logic that there was nothing wrong—either towards the woman or for himself—in so eagerly waiting by the roadside to steal a glance at some particular woman. So Binoy simultaneously felt a strange joy and a deep shame. He thought, 'Perhaps I am having a sort of degeneration.' Although he has all along argued with Gora about this, still thus looking at a woman with love—especially where there was no social sanction—seemed to clash with his lifelong inhibitions.

Going back to Gora's house remained an unaccomplished fact. Binoy walked back home with his mind in a state of turmoil.

When he at last reached Gora's place the following day after setting out from the apartment and much aimless roaming hither and thither, the long day of the rainy season was already over and the darkness of the evening had been thickening. Gora had lighted the lamp and sat at the writing desk.

Without raising his face from the paper Gora asked, 'Well, my dear Binoy, in which direction is the wind blowing today?'

Binoy took no account of this and said, 'Gora, I want to know something. What is India in your vision? Is it very true? Very clear? I know you think about her day and night. But how do you imagine her? In what form?'

Gora stopped writing and looked sharply at Binoy for a while. Then he put down his pen and reclining against the backrest said, 'As the captain of a ship on a voyage out remembers the port beyond the sea in all his work and leisure, duty and pleasure, so I bear my India in my mind.'

Binoy. Where is that India of yours?

Gora placed his hand on his chest and said, 'It is where the compass within me is constantly pointing at; it is not in your Marshman Sahib's *History of India*.'

Binoy. Is there really anything to be found by following the direction of your compass?

Gora excitedly cried out, 'Of course! I may lose the way. I may sink. But that prosperous port of my dream is there. That is my vision of India in its fullness—it is full of wealth, wisdom, faith—that India does not exist in reality! Real is only this sordid illusion around us! This your Calcutta city, this office, this court, this bubble of assembled brick and mortar! Pooh!'

Saying this Gora stared at Binoy for some time. Binoy pondered in silence. Gora said, 'This our pursuit of educational degrees, our search for jobs, our day-long purposeless endless labour,—we have decided that this false bewitched India is the truth. That is why a mass of twenty-five millions are madly running day and night after false prestige, false work, in a state of complete confusion—shall we ever come out of this spell, this pursuit of mirage! So we are withering up, dying every day. But there is a true India—a full India. Unless we get our mind anchored in the vision of this India we shall never be able to get at the source of life-energy, be it in intellect or be it in emotion. So, I say, let us forget everything else—all the bookish knowledge, the lure of titles, the temptation of small profits—let us throw all overboard and sail ahead towards that port—Let us sink if we have to; let us die if we have to. Is it for nothing that I can never forget this true vision, this complete image of India!'

Binoy. Are you sure that this is not just excited fantasy? Are you sure this is true?

Gora thundered, 'Yes, it is true indeed.'

Binoy. What about those who cannot envision like you?

Gora clenched his fist and said, 'They have to be shown. This is precisely what should be our mission. If people cannot clearly see the image of truth, to what mirage would they surrender? Hold up the complete vision of India before all—people will be overwhelmed. Then you won't have to appeal from door to door for small subscriptions. There will be competition for self-sacrifice.'

Binoy. Either you let me drift away like the average man, or show me that image.

Gora. Practise perseverance. If you have faith the very act of committed perseverance will make you happy. Our amateur patriots have no real faith, that's why they cannot emphatically demand anything either from themselves or from others. If Kuber himself appeared in person before them and offered gift, they would not dare to demand more than the gilded epaulette of the governor's attendant. They do not have faith; therefore they do not have hope.

Binoy. Gora, everybody is not born with the same temperament. You have discovered your faith within your own soul, you can sustain that faith by means of your own strength. But you cannot exactly understand the position of others. I say, you engage me in some work, slave me day and night—otherwise so long as I am with you it is all right; but once I am away from you I don't find anything that I can cling to.

Gora. Since you speak of work, now our only work should be evolving a complete unquestioning uninhibited regard for everything of the motherland and transmitting the same feeling in the minds of fellow countrymen. Our inferiority complex regarding our own country has enfeebled us by instilling the poison of slavish mentality; only after each of us sets an example it can be cured, and it is only then that we shall find the scope to do our own work. Now whatever we attempt becomes a mimicry of others' work following the line of prescribed school texts of history. Can we ever dedicate ourselves heart and soul to the pursuit of such phoney work? That would only help us to sink even lower.

At this point Mahim sailed into the room in his relaxed leisurely gait, hookah in hand. For Mahim this is the time of the day when he, after returning from office, and having good refreshment, pushes a betel leaf into his mouth, puts another six in the betel-box, and squatting on the roadside balcony enjoys puffs from the hookah. Before long friends from neighbourhood would start dropping in one by one; then game of cards will begin in the room by the front door.

As Mahim entered Gora at once stood up from his chair. Mahim took another puff at the hookah and said, 'Busy as you are in saving India, can you do something to save your brother for the time being?'

Gora stared at Mahim. Mahim said, 'It is about the new boss in our office. He looks like a bulldog—a very nasty fellow. He calls the "babus" baboon; refuses to sanction leave to the employees even on the occasion of one's mother's death; no Bengali officer gets the chance to carry home the pay packet intact. With fines upon fines he would burn holes into our purse. There was an open letter against him in the newspaper. The scoundrel has guessed that it is my handiwork; can't say he is altogether wrong in guessing. Now, therefore, for the sake of survival, I have to write a strong protest against the same and in my own name this time. Here you are, the two gems that have been churned up from the ocean, that is, the university; you please draft this letter in polished language. Also garnish it with

such choice phrases as "even-handed justice", "never-failing generosity", "kind courteousness", etc., etc.'

Gora kept silent. Binoy laughed and said, 'Dada, so many false epithets in the same breath…?'

Mahim. Tit for tat. Or pay them back in their own coin. I have been in their proximity for a long time, and I know them well. The way they can build up lies is simply admirable. If the occasion demands they can stoop to any level. If one of them just starts off a lie, all the others will sing in the same tune like a pack of foxes. They do not have the habit of sneaking into favour by betraying a colleague. Take this from me that there is no sin in cheating them, of course on condition that you are not caught.

Saying this Mahim laughed out loud and long. Binoy could not refrain from joining.

Mahim said, 'You want to put them in embarrassment by flaunting the truth in their face. It is no wonder that the country should be in such a shape. Don't you understand that one who has the power does not necessarily hang his head in shame at being caught red-handed. Rather he would flaunt his *sīdhkāṭi* and hit back with the same while assuming the posture of Mr Clean. Tell me if I am right or not.'

Binoy. Right indeed.

Mahim. It is better to squeeze out a few drops of cost-free oil from the mill of falsehood and massage the Saheb's feet with it while pleading, 'Oh Mr Clean Sir, oh thou great saintly being, be kind enough to shake your purse a little. Even particles of dust from that bag would go a long way to save me.' In that case at least a portion of your own dues can be restored to you, and at the same time there is no risk of any trouble. If you can understand rightly this is what is called patriotism. Anyway, my brother is getting angry. Of course, since he has turned the staunch 'Hindu' he has been behaving quite respectfully toward his elder brother. But what can I do brother! I must also say the truth about falsehood. Binoy, I must have the draft. Just wait a bit, I have jotted some notes; have a look at them.

Saying this Mahim went out while taking puffs from the hookah. Gora told Binoy, 'Binu. Please go to Dada's room and stop him. Let me finish this article in the meantime.'

5

'Do you hear me? Don't worry, I am not entering your *pūjā* room. After you finish your prayer please come to my room. I have something to discuss with you. Since two new mendicants have arrived I know you will be inaccessible for the next few days. Hence this call. Don't forget. Please drop in once.'

Saying this Anandamoyee went back to her domestic chores.

Krishnadayalbabu is a squarely built man, not very tall; the most prominent thing about his face is the pair of large eyes, the rest being almost totally covered by grey-black beard and moustache. He is always in saffron-coloured raw silk, with a brass *kamandalu* near his hand, and feet in wooden clogs. The front part of the head has started balding; the rest of the hair which had been left to grow long, are tied up into a knot at the top of the head.

There was a time when, during his years in the Western India in connection with his service under the British militia, he had freely indulged in all sorts of earthly pleasures including meat and alcohol. In those days he used to consider it an act of bravado to offend—without any provocation—the priestly or the mendicant class among his countrymen. Nowadays there is nothing that he does not pay his obeisance to. Whenever he encounters a new mendicant he would sit at his feet to learn some new method of prayer or worship. His greed for access to occult methods for *mukti* and occult ways of *Yoga* is boundless. Recently he had been taking lessons for practising the *Tāntrik* method, when he got news of some Buddhist priest and became restive at once.

When his first wife died after delivering a male baby, Krishnadayal was just twenty-three. Holding the baby responsible for the mother's death, Krishnadayal resentfully left it in his in-laws' house and in his wild grief and disdain of life headed straight for the far West of the country, and within six months married Anandamoyee, the orphaned granddaughter of a renowned scholar who had settled in Varanasi.

Krishnadayal had secured a job in the West and had struck good rapport with his employers by various means. In the meantime Anandamoyee's grandfather died. In the absence of any other guardian he had to bring along his wife and keep her with him.

Eventually, as the Sepoy Mutiny broke out, he tactfully saved the live/s of one or two highly-placed Englishmen, and thus managed to earn both reputation and landed property. Soon after the Mutiny he resigned his job, and spent some years in Varanasi with Gora, an infant at the time. When Gora grew up to a boy of five Krishnadayal came to Calcutta, brought his eldest son Mahim back from the house of his maternal uncle, and brought him up. Now Mahim, thanks to the favour of his father's patrons, is working with gusto at the local settlement office of the British government.

Since childhood Gora had been the natural leader of children in the locality and at school. His main engagement and entertainment was teasing the stern teachers. When he was just a little grown up, he began to cite *'Swādhīnatāhīnatāy ke bācite cāy re...'* (Who wants to live without freedom?), and 'We are twenty millions...' etc. and deliver speeches in English at the students' club, which soon made him a leader of the small rebels. When at last he burst out of the eggshell of the Students' Club and started cackling at the adults' meet, Krishnadayalbabu took it as great fun.

In the world outside home Gora's popularity swelled quickly. But the family members did not take him seriously. Mahim had already joined service. He tried to discourage Gora in various ways,—sometimes by calling him 'Patriot Uncle', sometimes 'Harish Mukhujjee the Second', etc. In those days the two brothers often came nearly to the point of fighting. Anandamoyee felt extremely disturbed at Gora's hostility towards the British; she tried to contain him in various ways, but with no result. Gora would consider it an occasion of supreme happiness if he could get any chance of forcing a showdown upon some Englishman in the street and giving him a good thrashing.

Around this time Gora became charmed by the speech of Keshabbabu, as a result of which he felt a strong attraction towards the *Brāhmosamāj*. Again, it was about the same time that Krishnadayal too turned extremely orthodox and ritualistic; so much so that even if Gora himself chanced to happen to step into his room he was annoyed. He marked out a few rooms for his own separate suite and pompously hung up a wooden plate at the entrance to his suite, with the word '*Sādhanāshram*' painted on it.

Gora felt rebellious at such activities of his father. He announced: 'I cannot stand this stupidity—this is an eyesore for me.' Gora was about to sever all relations with his father on this issue and leave home altogether; it was Anandamoyee who had stopped him at great effort.

Whenever he got the chance Gora started debating with the Brahmins and scholars who began to visit his father. It is better described as blows rather than arguments. Many of them had little scholarship and great greed for money. They were no match for Gora, and were scared of him like anything. Among the whole lot it was only Harachandra Bidyabagish who stirred respect in Gora.

Krishnadayal had engaged Bidyabagish for helping him to study the *Vedānta*. As usual Gora threw his gauntlet at him too with the habitual haughtiness, but then realized to his surprise that here was someone with whom you could not fight. Not only was he a genuine scholar; but also had a wonderful openness of mind. Gora could never imagine that just by reading Sanskrit one could come to acquire such sharp yet embracing intelligence. Bidyabagish commanded such an unruffled patience and profundity, his nature so brimming with love and benevolence, that it was altogether impossible for Gora not to restrain his arrogance before such a man. Gora started studying the *Vedānta* with Harachandra. Gora could not leave anything done halfway. Therefore, he plunged headlong down into the study of philosophy.

Incidentally, around this time an English missionary threw a challenge through some newspaper at the people of India by inviting them to contest his aggressive remarks on the Hindu scripture and society. Gora flew into a rage. Although he used to criticize the scripture and conventions at every chance and thereby hurt their supporters to any extent, yet a foreigner's explicit contempt for the Hindu society seemed to provoke him like a wounded elephant hurt by the needled club.

Gora picked up the gauntlet and the duel (in the newspaper) started. Gora on his part did not admit a single accusation against the Hindu society. After many attack and counterattack from both sides the editor at last put his foot down and declared, 'We won't publish any further rejoinders on the issue.'

But by then Gora had become adamant. He started writing a book in English on 'Hinduism'. There he tried to marshal to his best ability all possible proofs, arguments and evidences in support of the unquestionable superiority of the Hindu society.

In course of this prolonged debate with the missionary opponent Gora at last realized the lacunae of this process. He perceived, 'We should not allow ourselves to be dragged into such debates where my own country is put in the position of the accused, and the argument or judgment is done according to the rules laid down by a foreign court and decided by their foreign standards. We should refuse to be ashamed if it does not fit into the foreign frame, nor need we feel elated if it does. We won't cringe for the rites, faith, heritage or society of the land in which we have been born. We shall hold up with pride and strength whatever our land has to offer, and thus we shall resist humiliation of ourselves and our motherland.'

On arriving at this conviction Gora started to take holy dip in Ganga, to pray twice a day, to keep *tiki*, and became selective and exclusivist regarding food and touch. From now on he began to touch the feet of his parents every morning. Earlier he would take every chance to mention Mahim as 'cad', 'snob', etc.; now he stands up to greet the same man, and touches his feet too. Mahim says whatever he feels like regarding this sudden reverence, but Gora does not hit back.

Gora's new opinions and activities had a special appeal to a section of countrymen. They seemed to be waking up. They were apparently released from a tension, and happily exclaimed, 'We do not seek to justify ourselves—we do not care whether we are good or bad, civilized or uncivilized—we only want to feel exactly our distinct uniqueness, that we are just what we are.'

But, it did not seem that Krishnadayal was happy at this new turn of Gora. In fact, he even called Gora one day and said, 'Look here my son, Hindu theology is a very profound thing. The religion that the sages had established is too deep for an average man. So far as I understand, it is better not to get involved in it without adequate initiation. You are young; all along you have received Western education. That you had become inclined earlier towards the *Brāhmosamāj* was the right thing to do for you. I did not resent it in the least. On the contrary I was glad. But now the way you are going does not seem good. It is not your path at all.'

Gora was surprised, 'What are you saying, Dad! I am a Hindu. If I cannot plumb the depths of its mystery today I shall do it tomorrow. Even if I never penetrate it still this is my only way. It is precisely because I could not overcome my involvement with the Hindu society in my last incarnation that I have again been born in this incarnation in a Brahmin home. It is along the route of such successive incarnations in Hindu homes and Hindu religions that ultimately I shall reach the acme, the last destination. If I get slightly inclined to some other road by mistake, I will have to come back to it with redoubled energy.'

Krishnadayal continued to nod his head in disagreement, 'But my son, you cannot be a Hindu just by staking the claim. Being Muslim is easier; anybody can be a Christian. But being a Hindu!—Oh my God! It is very difficult.'

Gora. That's true. But, since I am born into Hinduism I have already crossed the crucial gateway of the palace. Now if I can properly go on with my pursuit, that should be enough to help me progress gradually.

Krishnadayal. Son, I cannot exactly clarify by arguing what I want to say. Anyway, what you are saying is also true. The pre-destined consequence of one's action, one's pre-destined religion are things to which one must come back some day—none can prevent it. Everything is willed by God. What can we do? We are just instruments.

Be it the consequence of one's action or God's will, divinity of man, or the cult of devotion, all such contrary concepts and theories were equally accepted by Krishnadayal; he did not feel the least need of reconciling or harmonizing them in any way.

6

Today after finishing his meditation, bath and lunch, Krishnadayal entered Anandamoyee's room after many days. Spreading his personal and exclusive rug on the floor he sat up straight as if he was cautiously holding himself aloof from the contact of everything around.

Anandamoyee said, 'You are absorbed in your meditations; you have no time to think of home. But I am terribly worried about Gora. I am so scared indeed!'

Krishnadayal. Why? What's the scare about?

Anandamoyee. That I cannot exactly define. But these days I have been having a hunch that the obsessive Hinduism that Gora has started practicing recently will never suit him in the long run. If he goes on this way perhaps eventually it will explode into some catastrophe or crisis. Didn't I tell you not to give him the sacred thread? But those days you used to care for nothing; you said, 'Let it be. Hanging a piece of thread round one's neck does not affect anyone. But now, how to control him!'

Krishnadayal. Well. But is it entirely my doing! The initial blunder was yours. You did not agree to give him up by any means. I was also a sort of dare-devil then, and had no idea of religion or rites. Could I act like that today!

Anandamoyee. But whatever you may say, I shall never accept that I have done anything wrong or against God. I hope you remember how desperate I had become for a baby—had tried every device prescribed by everybody—you know best how many *madulis* and *mantras* I had collected. Then one night I dreamt, as if I was sitting to worship my god with a basket full of white Tagar petals—when suddenly I found the flowers had disappeared. In their place there was a baby, white and beautiful like the flowers. Ah! So beautiful it was,—how can I describe! Tears filled my eyes; as I rushed to pick it up the dream was over. Within ten days after this I got Gora—he is my God's gift—is he anybody else's that I can return him? Perhaps in the last incarnation I had suffered greatly by carrying him in my womb. That is why he has come back in this life to call me, '*Mā*'. How did he reach us, wherefrom did he come? Just think of it. When all around it was violence, massacre, chaos, we ourselves nearly dead in fear, how the '*memsāheb*' came to hide in our house in that dark midnight. You were afraid to shelter her—I secretly hid her in the cowshed. She passed away that very night just after delivering the baby. If I had not saved that orphaned baby could he survive? What did you care? You had even wanted to hand him over to the Church? Why? Why should I hand him over to the Father? Was the Father his mom or dad? Did the father save his life? The baby I received in such circumstances—is it in any way less than receiving it in my womb? You may say anything. But—unless the giver himself takes him back—I won't allow anybody to snatch him away.

Krishnadayal. I know that very well. You live with your Gora. Did I ever raise any objection to that? But, if you passed him on as your own son, and yet did not give him the sacred thread, then the society would not have accepted that. So we had to do it. Now I think the real issues are only two: legally, all my property should go to Mahim—therefore—

Anandamoyee. Who wants a share in your property? Give all the money you have to Mahim. Gora will not take a penny of it. He is a man, has received education; he will work hard for his living. Why should he go to grab somebody else's wealth? May he survive healthy and happy, that is enough for me. I need no other treasure.

Krishnadayal. No, I won't deprive him altogether. In fact, I will give away the plot of land I had received as *jāgīr* to him; in course of time the annual profit from the plot may come to a thousand rupees. Now the main problem is his marriage. What I have done in the past is a separate story. But now I cannot arrange his marriage in some Hindu Brahmin family according to Hindu customs. If you get angry at this I have nothing to do.

Anandamoyee. Alas, indeed! Do you think that just because you are sprinkling Ganga-water and cowdung everywhere, no one else has any sense of right and wrong? Why should I marry him into a Brahmin home, or why should I be angry either on this issue?

Krishnadayal was astonished, 'Indeed! But you yourself hail from a Brahmin family!'

Anandamoyee. I don't contest that. But you know how I have given up the Brahministic ways. Don't you remember the fuss some of the relatives made about this on the occasion of Mahim's marriage? I had deliberately kept aloof, without a word of protest. The whole world calls me Christian, says so many more abusive things—I accept all and say, 'So what? Isn't a Christian a human? If you are really so superior a race, such a special favorite of God as you claim, then why does God so humiliate you again and again—now at the feet of the Pathan, next at the Moghul's, then at the Christian's?'

Krishnadayal. That is a complicated issue. You, a mere woman, won't understand all this. But, you should understand at least this much that there is a thing called society, and that it is desirable that you observe its norms.

Anandamoyee. I don't have any need to understand. What I understand is this—since I have brought up Gora as my own child, any hypocrisy on my part regarding social rituals would go against my own true religion. It is out of my respect for this religion that I never seek to hide anything—I let everybody know that I do not conform to the social regulations and though as a result I invite hatred from all and sundry I keep mum. I have concealed only one thing, and it is because of this that I suffer such anxiety day and night. All the time I am haunted by one tension,—what may happen and when. Listen, I have the feeling that I should tell Gora everything; after that what is pre-destined will happen.

Krishnadayal was instantly nervous. 'Oh no! No! As long as I live this must not be. Don't you know Gora's nature? You can never tell how he will react when he learns the truth. There will also be a hue and cry in the society. Not only that. You cannot be sure about the Government's reaction either. Although Gora's father was killed in the war, his mother too died, but still they may say, "You should have informed the administration after the mutiny was over." If some trouble is brewed up now over the issue then all my worship and meditation will be thrown out of gear and you can never tell what other troubles may follow.'

Anandamoyee did not say a word. After some time Krishnadayal said, 'I have thought about a plan regarding Gora's marriage. I had a school pal named Paresh Bhatchaj. Recently he has retired from his job of school-inspector and has settled in Calcutta. He is a keen Brahma. I have gathered that he has quite a few daughters as well. If Gora could be somehow introduced to them, then in course of social visits he might take a fancy for any of Paresh's daughters. Finally, of course, all is God's will.'

Anandamoyee. What do you say! Would Gora ever visit a Brahmo family! Gone are those days....

Before she could finish Gora's bass voice calling '*Mā*' was heard and Gora strode into the room. Seeing Krishnadayal here he was a little surprised. Anandamoyee at once stood up and reached out to Gora, her eyes radiant with affection, 'Come in son. Do you need anything?'

'No, nothing important, don't bother',—mumbling this he was about to go back when Krishnadayal said, 'Please wait a bit. Be seated here, I wanted to tell you something. A Brahmo friend of mine has recently arrived at Calcutta. He is at present staying at Hedo.'

Gora. Do you mean Pareshbabu?

Krishnadayal. How did you know him?

Gora. Binoy lives in the neighbourhood. I have heard Binoy talking about them.

Krishnadayal. I wish you pay them a visit and find out how things are going with them.

Gora pondered a while, and then suddenly blurted out, 'Okay. I shall go by tomorrow itself.'

Anandamoyee was surprised a bit.

Again Gora seemed to remember something and said, 'No. I can't go tomorrow.'

Krishnadayal. Why?

Gora. Tomorrow I am going to Triveni.

Krishnadayal was genuinely puzzled. 'Triveni!'

Gora. For taking a dip on the occasion of the solar eclipse which will fall tomorrow....

Anandamoyee. You amaze us, Gora! If you wanted to take a dip don't we have Ganga flowing by Calcutta? But you must have your dip either at Triveni or nowhere—It seems you have surpassed all the countrymen.

Gora left without an answer.

The reason that motivated Gora for the Triveni dip was that many pilgrims would be gathering there on the occasion. Gora wanted to get merged into that mass and thereby surrender himself to the great flowing life of the country, and feel the pulsation of the great national life within his own heartbeats.

7

Getting up in the morning Binoy saw the sky had cleared during the previous night. The morning light had come out clean and beautiful like an infant's smile. One or two light white cloudlets were aimlessly drifting about in the sky.

Standing in his balcony Binoy was getting into an ecstasy by recalling another such morning when Pareshbabu appeared at the end of the road. He had a stick in one hand and holding Satish's hand with the other while slowly walking along the road. As soon as Satish could spot Binoy on the balcony he clapped and shouted, 'Binoybabu!' Paresh also looked up and saw Binoy. Binoy hurried down, and at the same moment Paresh also entered his house followed by Satish.

Satish held Binoy's hand, and said, 'Binoybabu, that day you promised to visit our place. What about your promise?'

Binoy affectionately patted Satish on the back and continued smiling. Paresh carefully placed his stick against the table and taking his seat on the couch said, 'We would have been in great trouble without you that morning. You helped us so much!'

Binoy fidgeted, 'Don't mention it, please, it's nothing as such....'

Satish suddenly interrupted, 'One thing, Binoybabu, don't you have a dog?'

Binoy smiled, 'Dog? No, I don't have a dog.'

Satish. Why? Why don't you keep a dog?

Binoy. Actually it has never occurred to me.

Paresh intervened, 'I learnt that Satish came to you the other day. I am afraid he has disturbed you a lot. He is so talkative indeed, that his sisters have rechristened him as Bakhtiyār Khilji.'

Binoy assured, 'I also talk a lot. That is why we have become very good friends. Haven't we, Mr Satish?'

Satish did not answer. But he grew nervous lest his prestige with Binoy suffers on account of his new name and hurriedly went on, 'Alright. What's wrong about Bakhtiyār Khilji? Wasn't he a real fighter? Didn't he win Bangladesh?'

Binoy laughed, 'Yes, he used to fight in the past, but nowadays fighting has become redundant; these days he only delivers speeches, and even conquers Bangladesh that way.

Thus the conversation went on for quite a time. Paresh talked least. Sitting peaceful and serene there, he joined them only with his benign smile and occasional brief participation. While taking leave Pareshbabu said, 'Our house is No. 78,—go straight from here and take the right turn and—

Satish intercepted, 'He knows our house. The other day he had seen me off right to our front door.'

This was no cause for embarrassment; still Binoy felt embarrassed; as if some secret got exposed.

The old man said, 'So you know our house. Then, in case if you—'

Binoy. Of course, of course—whenever—

Paresh. We live in the same locality. Had it not been Calcutta we should have met earlier.

Binoy came with Paresh to the road. He stood at the door for some time as Paresh, holding the stick, went off slowly and Satish followed him along with his non-stop babbling.

Binoy told himself, 'I have never seen another such elderly gentleman. I feel like touching his feet. And, Satish—what a nice boy he is! In course of time he is bound to shine—so intelligent as he is, and so simple too!'

Howsoever nice the old man and the boy might be, it was a bit unlikely that such a brief encounter should affect one to be so carried away with reverence and affection. But the state of Binoy's mind was such that he did not need to wait for more impressions.

The thought that followed next was, 'I must pay them a visit. Sheer politeness demands it.'

But through the voice of Gora the 'Bharatbársha' of their party continued to warn him, 'No. It is forbidden for you. Remember.'

Binoy had obeyed many of such bans of this 'Bharatbarsha' of their party; sometimes he had hesitations; still he did not disobey. Today he felt rebellious. He felt this Bharatbarsha was constituted of just so many bans.

The servant came to call for lunch,—but Binoy had not yet taken his bath even. It was already twelve. After a time Binoy shook his head with sudden vehemence, called out to the servants, 'I won't lunch today. You can go home', and picking up the umbrella set out on the road. He did not even care to take a *cādar* on the shoulders.

Binoy made a beeline for Gora's residence. He knew that the '*Hinduhitaiṣī*'(Well-wishers of the Hindu) had recently opened an office at a rented room at Amherst Street, and everyday Gora went there around midday to write and send letters to all the friends of the organization in all corners of the state, thereby keeping them alert about their duties. It was here that his admirers used to come to listen to his instructions and to feel elated by assisting in his work.

Today too, Gora had gone to his office as usual. Binoy almost flew into the inner house and landed straight into Anandamoyee's room. Anandamoyee had just started her lunch, and Lachmya, squatting near her, was waving the palm-leaf fan.

Binoy slumped down in front of her and said, '*Mā*, I am very hungry, please give me something to eat at once.'

Anandamoyee looked confused, 'Ah what a mess it is! The *bāmun* cook has left—and you can't—'

Binoy remonstrated, 'Have I come for the food cooked by the *bāmun*! Then what was wrong with my own cook? I came to have *prasād* from your plate. Lachmya, bring me a glass of water. Quick!'

As soon as Lachmya brought the glass Binoy gulped it down. Then Anandamoyee asked for another plate, and passed on in small measures, and with great care and love, the rice and curry of her own plate to the plate of Binoy; and Binoy ate it eagerly like someone who had been starving for days on end.

A weight of pain was lifted from her mind today. Looking at the serene happiness of her face Binoy too felt relieved and happy. Anandamoyee sat down to sew up pillow-covers. The fragrance of Keya flowers—collected for making betel-spice and stored in the adjoining room—came floating in; Binoy lay half-reclining at her feet, resting his head on one raised hand; he forgot all his troubles, and babbled on happily just like the good old days.

8

As he got over the first barrier the fresh flood within Binoy's heart swelled up beyond control. After emerging from Anandamoyee's room he seemed to be almost on wings; his feet did not seem to touch the ground as it were. He longed to proudly declare to the world his intimate secret which had been oppressing his mind with hesitation and diffidence for the last few days.

Binoy reached the door of No. 78 exactly at the same moment when Paresh also arrived there from the opposite direction.

'Come in, come in, Binoybabu, I am so glad', saying this Paresh took Binoy to his sitting room facing the road and helped him to the couch. There was a small table; on one side of it was a bench with backrest, on the other side stood a wooden chair and a cane couch. On one wall hung a coloured picture of Jesus Christ, on another a photograph of Keshabbabu. A few recent newspapers neatly folded under a lead paper weight were lying on the table. In one corner stood a small cupboard, the upper stack of which displayed a row of works by Theodore Parker. A cloth-covered globe stood on top.

Binoy sat down. But his heart throbbed; he waited for someone to enter the room through the open door behind him.

Paresh said, 'On Mondays Sucharita goes to coach my friend's daughter. As they have a boy of Satish's age, he also has gone with her. I am just coming after having dropped them there. I would have missed you in case I was delayed even a bit more.'

On hearing this Binoy simultaneously felt a pang of disappointment as well as a strange comfort. Soon he was perfectly at ease with Paresh.

In course of the evening Paresh came to learn bit by bit all about Binoy. Binoy had lost his parents. An uncle lived in the ancestral countryhouse with his wife and looked after the family property. His two cousins lived in a rented house in Calcutta for their studies; the elder one has become an advocate and is now practicing at their district court while the younger one died of cholera during his stay in Calcutta. Uncle wished that Binoy should try for the job of deputy magistrate, but Binoy has made no effort in that direction, and instead is engaged in useless activities.

Thus one full hour slipped by. Staying on too long without any apparent reason looks odd. So Binoy had to get up. He said,

'I am sorry that I could not meet my friend Satish. Please tell him I came.'

Pareshbabu suggested, 'If you could wait a little more you might meet them. They must be returning soon.'

Binoy, however, felt shy to take advantage of this polite gesture and sit down again. Perhaps a little more insistence would have helped him. But Pareshbabu was not one to insist or talk much. Therefore, he had to take leave. Paresh said, 'I shall be happy if you cán drop in occasionally.'

Coming out on the road Binoy felt no inclination for going home. He had no business there. Binoy used to write for the newspapers. Readers generally appreciated his command of English. But since the last few days writing eluded him. Indeed it seems impossible to sit at the writing desk for some stretch. The mind becomes restless. Binoy, therefore, set off for the opposite direction today though without any apparent reason.

Before long he heard a boyish voice shouting, 'Binoybabu, Binoybabu!'

He looked up to see Satish calling out at him from the door of a hired cabbie. The portion of a sari, and the fraction of the white sleeve that were visible inside left no doubt about the identity of the passenger within.

It was impolite for Binoy, according to the rules of Bengali decorum, to stare at the interior of the cabbie. In the meantime Satish had already come down and holding his hand, implored: 'Come along to our house.'

Binoy said, 'It is from there that I am coming now.'

Satish remonstrated: 'But we were not there; please come with us again.'

Binoy could not ignore this appeal. Satish marched into the house with his prisoner, and announced in high pitch: '*Bābā*, see whom I have brought.'

Paresh came out and smiled, 'You have been at the hands of a tough jailor. I don't think there is hope for an early reprieve. Satish, go and send your *Didi*.'

Binoy entered the room again and sat down. His heartbeat increased. Paresh said soothingly, 'Seems you are exhausted! Satish is really very exasperating.'

When Satish came back with his *Didi* Binoy dimly felt the sensation of a mild fragrance. Then he heard Pareshbabu saying, 'Radhe, here is Binoybabu. You know him, don't you?'

Binoy looked up for the fraction of a second to see that Sucharita had greeted him with a *namaskār* before taking her seat on the couch. This time Binoy did not miss on the counter *namaskār*.

Sucharita said, 'He was walking in the street. The moment Satish spotted him he could not be stopped. He just left the cab and dragged him back. Perhaps you had some other work. I hope we are not causing you any inconvenience?'

Binoy had indeed never expected that Sucharita would directly address Binoy. He became very embarrassed and hurriedly said, 'No, No, I had no work as such. No problem at all.'

Satish pulled at the end of Sucharita's *sārī*, 'Didi, give me the key please! I shall show our organ to Binoybabu.'

Sucharita smiled, 'So it starts again! Whoever becomes a friend to our Bakhtiyār has no respite—he must listen to the organ—and is destined for many other ordeals. Binoybabu, this friend of yours is small in size, but his demands are high. I hope you can bear with him.'

Binoy did not know how to respond with ease to such free manners and talk. In spite of his resolve against feeling shy Binoy could just manage to make out a semblance of answer: 'No, no, not at all. He—I—I quite like this—'

Satish managed the keys from his *Didi* and brought down the organ. It was just a toy ship on blue cloth in imitation of wavy sea, and placed inside a square glass case. As Satish winded the spring with the key, the ship swayed in tune with an organ note. As Satish looked alternately at the ship and at Binoy's face he could hardly restrain his excitement.

Thus with Satish between them Binoy got over his shyness by degrees, and eventually it was not even impossible for him to look straight into Sucharita's face while talking with her.

Suddenly without any reference to a context Satish asked, 'Won't you bring your friend here someday?'

This diverted the talk to Binoy's friend. Pareshbabu and his family were newcomers to Calcutta. They knew nothing about Gora. While speaking about his friend Binoy slowly warmed up. He could not, as it were, speak enough about Gora's extraordinary talent, his expansive heart, his firmness and strength. He stressed that he did not have the least doubt that in future Gora will emerge as the radiant meridian sun shining over entire India.

As he had been saying this a lustre illumined his face, all his hesitations disappeared. He even had some small differences with Pareshbabu regarding Gora's religious opinions. Binoy stressed, 'That Gora can unquestioningly accept everything of the Hindu society is because he envisions his India from a very broad perspective. In his vision all great and small things of India are harmonized into the unity of a sublime music. It is because the average countryman cannot attain that vision that we think of India in terms of fragmentary images in terms of European ideologies, and thereby perpetrate grave and continuous injustice on her.'

Sucharita asked, 'Do you accept the caste-system?'

She put the question in such a way as if there cannot be any controversy on the issue.

Binoy said, 'the caste system is neither good, nor bad in itself. That is, it depends on the context. If you ask, is the hand a good thing', I should answer, 'see it in relation to the entire body. If you ask whether the hand is good for flying I must say, "no". Similarly, wings are not good for holding things.'

Sucharita became excited, 'I don't follow your logic. Tell me clearly. Do you accept the caste system or do you not?'

Had it been an argument with some other person, Binoy would have said emphatically, 'Yes, I do accept.' But today something held him back. Was it his cowardice, or is it possible that today he did not feel like going to that extent mentally—the extent that would be implied by an assertion: 'I accept the caste system.' Who can tell? Lest the debate went too far—Paresh stopped it at this point by saying, 'Radhe, call your *Mā* and the others inside—let him be introduced to all of us.'

Sucharita went out and Satish at once followed her with bouncing steps.

After some time Sucharita re-entered and said, 'Baba, *Mā* asks you to come to the upstairs balcony'.

9

On the upstairs balcony, which hung above the garage, there was a table covered with white cloth and chairs all around it. Alongside the rails there were seasonal flowers and greeneries in small earthen pots. From the balcony one could see the glistening twigs of the rain-washed *sirish* and *jacaranda* trees on the wayside.

The sun had not yet gone down; the mellowed light from the western sky was falling straight on a side of the balcony.

No one was yet there. Soon Satish entered with a small puppy in mixed black-and-white. Its name was *khude*. Satish made the puppy demonstrate all the skills it had been taught. It saluted by lifting one leg, bowed by touching head on the floor; on being shown a piece of biscuit at once sat down with folded legs and begged for it. The credit of Khude's performance was completely appropriated by Satish, about which the dog showed no interest; apparently the piece of biscuit was more important to him than admiration.

From some adjacent room feminine voices were audible—sudden bursts of laughter and fun—along with a male voice. This uninhibited mirth stirred in Binoy a sensation of exquisite sweetness tinged with the pain of a faint jealousy. Since attaining adulthood he had never listened like this to the merry note of female voices inside a room. This sweet joy was springing up so close to him, yet so far he was from all this!

Satish was continuously buzzing into his ear, but he could hardly pay any attention.

Pareshbabu came up to the roof top balcony followed by his wife and three daughters. Another youth also accompanied them. He was a distant relative.

The name of Pareshbabu's wife was Baradasundari. She was not quite young, but it was obvious that she dressed up with particular care. After living like a rural woman well into advanced age, suddenly she had become keen to catch up with the pace of the modern times. Perhaps that's the reason why her silk *sārī* rustles a bit too audibly, and her high heels clatter a bit louder than others'. She is always very alert in maintaining the distinction between what is Brahmo and what is non-Brahmo. It is precisely because of this that she has re-christened Radharani as Sucharita. Some cousin of her father, on his return home after long years, had sent them *tattwa* on the occasion of *Jāmāiśaṣthī*; at that time Pareshbabu was out of station in connection with some official work. Baradasundari had sent back all the gifts, since such things were considered by her as epitome of superstition and idolatry. She was so serious about using socks and hats for women when outdoors as if these too were part of the Brahmo religious ideology. Once seeing some Brahmo family taking their meal by sitting on floor she had expressed the anxiety that these days Brahma society was regressing towards heathenism.

Her elder daughter's name was Labanya. She was a buxom, jolly girl, and loved company and gossip. She had a round face, large eyes, and shady but clear complexion. Left to herself she would not care much about dress-up, but she had to obey her mother's strictures about such matters. She did not feel quite comfortable in high heels, but had no choice. During afternoon dress-up her mother used to rub powder and rouge with her own hand on both the cheeks of the poor girl. As she was a bit fatty, Baradasundari tailored her dress so tight-fitting that when she came out after dressing for outdoors she looked like a sack of jute bags that had been packed tight under hydraulic press.

The second daughter was called Lalita. She appeared a contrast to Labanya; taller than her *didi*, slim, darker, a person of few words, Lalita followed her own ways, and could give a piece of her mind to people if she so desired. Baradasundari was a bit scared of her, and usually did not dare to provoke her.

The youngest, Leela, was around ten. She was the tomboy type, expert in sports and various mischiefs. Leela and Satish would always be fighting on one or another issue. Especially, regarding the proprietorship over Khude, they had not been able as yet to come to any amicable settlement. If the poor dog's own opinion were sought perhaps it would not have accepted either of them as its boss. Still it seemed among the two it was slightly better inclined towards Satish; because it was not easy for this small creature to bear the brunt of Leela's excessive affection. The poor creature preferred the boy's oppression to the girl's affection.

As soon as Baradasundari entered, Binoy stood up, and bending down touched her feet. Pareshbabu said, 'It was in his house the other morning that we....'

Barada said, 'Oh! You have been very kind. We are grateful to you.'

At this Binoy was so embarrassed that he did not know what to say in reply.

The young man who entered along with the girls was also introduced. His name was Sudhir. He was studying in college for graduation. He was good looking, bespectacled, with a fair complexion, and a faint line of moustache. He looked very restive and lively, always eager to do something, never showing a sign of sitting down for a quiet moment. He had been continuously teasing the girls, cutting jokes, and thus keeping them on edge. The girls too were always scolding him, yet Sudhir was indispensable to them. Be it going to the circus, or visiting the zoo, or purchasing some delicacies, Sudhir was ever there ready to help. Sudhir's free exchange and friendship with the girls was something new and amazing to Binoy. At the start he thought this improper, but a shade of envy also seemed to sneak into his disapproval.

Baradasundari said, 'I think I have seen you some time in the Samaj.'

Binoy felt as if he has been caught in the midst of some misdeed. He was unnecessarily apologetic in replying, 'Yes, sometimes I go there to hear Keshabbabu speaking.'

Baradasundari asked, 'Are you a college student?'

Binoy replied, 'No, I do not go to the college any more.'

Barada again inquired, 'How far have you studied?'

Binoy said, 'I have passed the M.A.'

At this Baradasundari felt respectful towards this boyish-looking youth.

She sighed and turned to Paresh, 'If my Manu were alive he too would have completed his M.A. by now.'

Barada's first issue, Manoranjan, had died at the age of nine. Whenever Barada heard of any youth getting a good degree, or high post, or authoring some good book, or attaining some notable achievement, she immediately came to conclude that if Manu had survived he would have done exactly these very things. Anyway, since he was no more, her special mission at present was to give good publicity in the society around of the various accomplishments of her three daughters. Barada took care to inform Binoy that her daughters were highly educated. Binoy also came to learn about the Mem's appreciatory comments regarding her daughters' intelligence and accomplishments. Binoy was also informed that when the lieutenant-governor and his wife came to the girls' school on the occasion of the annual prize distribution ceremony, it was Labanya who was selected among all the students for presenting the bouquet to them; and the sweet word of encouragement that the governor's wife had to spare for Labanya was repeated for the consumption of Binoy.

Eventually Barada told Labanya, 'Bring that piece of embroidery dear,—the one for which you got the prize.'

A parrot's replica sewn with woolen threads had become famous among friends and relatives of the family. Labanya had produced this with the help of '*Mem*' years ago; not that she could claim much credit for it either. But it was taken for granted that every newcomer in the house must be shown it.

Earlier Paresh tried to protest, but knowing that it was completely futile he had eventually given in. When Binoy was wide-eyed with wonder at the artistic skill behind the woolen parrot a servant came up to hand in a letter to Paresh.

On reading the message Paresh looked delighted, and said, 'Bring him here.'

Barada asked, 'Who is he?'

Paresh said, 'My old pal Krishnadayal has sent his son to get introduced to us.'

Suddenly Binoy felt his heart leap up, he turned pale. Next moment he clenched his fist and sat up, as if he was gathering strength to fight some aggressive opponent. The apprehension that Gora would view this family with disrespect, and judge them accordingly, seemed to make Binoy a bit excited in advance.

10

As Sucharita came in after arranging tea and snacks on the lace-covered tray, which was carried in by the servant, Gora too, ushered in by the gateman, entered the room. All were instantly struck by the extraordinary appearance and dress of the tall fair youth.

His forehead was smeared with sediments from Ganga bank; he wore a coarse *dhoti*, a shirt tied with strings, a coarse cloak on top of it, and had the traditional heavy *Katki* slipper for footwear. He appeared like the embodiment of revolt against the modern times. Even Binoy had never seen him earlier dressed like this.

Today a fire of challenge was already aflame in Gora's mind. There were reasons too.

On the occasion of the solar eclipse a steamer company had started early in the morning with its passengers. On the way many women passengers, escorted by one or two men, were boarding the steamer at various stops. There was a lot of jostling and rush for getting a foothold on the board. As some had been coming with muddy feet the plank connecting the ground with deck had become slippery and some were slipping into the water, their dress in a shambles, exposing parts of the body to the public eye; some were being pushed off by the crew; some was nervy at finding that though she herself had somehow managed to get on board her companion was left behind; occasional showers left them drenched; the seats had been splattered with mud. Their faces bore an anxious pitiful appealing expression. They had absolutely no power, and they knew fully well they were so insignificant that no one—from the crew to the captain—of the ship would respond to their appeal. This painful certitude was evident in their nervous movements. In such a situation Gora had been trying his best to assist the passengers. On the first-class deck upstairs there stood an Englishman and a Bengali *bābu* of the modern type who shared jokes with each other while enjoying the fun and their cigar. Occasionally the Englishman burst out into fits of laughter at some sudden discomfiture of this or that fellow, and the Bengali *bābu* too followed suit.

After thus crossing a few stations Gora could bear no more. He came up and shouted in a thunderous voice, 'What is this? Don't you have shame!'

The Englishman stared hard at Gora from head to foot. The Bengali *bābu* replied, 'Shame, indeed! It should be shame for these beastly fools of the country.'

Gora flushed in anger, 'There is one beast who is more beastly than a fool. It is the heartless beast.'

The Bengali *bābu* angrily retorted, 'This is not your place—this is first class.'

Gora said, 'No, my place cannot be with you—my place is among those passengers. But I warn you don't force me to come back again to this your bloody class.'

Saying this Gora marched down. The Englishman tried to concentrate in a novel stretching his two legs on the two arms of the couch. His fellow passenger, the Bengali *bābu*, tried to resume the talk once or twice, but without much success. In order to send the message that he was not one of those average countrymen, he called the attendant and asked him if any chicken dish was on the menu.

The attendant said, 'No, only bread and butter.'

At this the Bengali said in English, 'Provisions for creature comforts in this ship are hopeless altogether.'

The Englishman said nothing. His newspaper was blown away to the floor. The *bābu* got up from his chair to go for it and pick it up, but received no thanks.

As he was about to get down at Chandannagar, the Englishman suddenly came to Gora, and slightly raising his hat said, 'I am ashamed for my manners—hope you'll forgive me.'

Saying this he left hurriedly.

But, that an educated Bengali could invite a foreigner to share his amusement at the discomfiture of his own poor countrymen and boastfully enjoy his superiority, seemed to consume Gora with anger. His heart seemed to be on the point of bursting under the oppressive heaviness of the realization that the common people of the country had surrendered to all sorts of humiliation and injustice, that they would accept even beastly treatment, and this was taken for granted by all and sundry, and behind all this operated a pervasive, profound ignorance. But, what hurt him most was the reality that the educated people were indifferent to this perennial humiliation and suffering perpetrated upon fellow countrymen—that they could even boast of their superiority by thus ruthlessly disowning their kin. Gora, therefore, as a deliberate gesture of defiance against the bookish and mimicking postures of the elite, had come today to visit a Brahmo family with forehead besmeared by Ganga sediment, feet in new absurd *Katki* slippers, and head held high in an aggressive mood of challenge.

Binoy knew at once what this meant—that Gora had donned on his warrior's cuirass. His costume today signalled a declaration of war. Binoy grew apprehensive—thinking of what Gora might do, he felt scared, uneasy and on the defensive.

So long as Baradasundari had been talking with Binoy Satish had been amusing himself at one corner of the balcony by swirling a tin top. Seeing Gora he stopped his play and slowly drawing up alongside Binoy gazed at Gora with unblinking eyes; he whispered into Binoy's ears, 'Is he that friend of yours?'

Coming up to the balcony Gora had glanced at Binoy just for the fraction of a second, and then he seemed not to see him at all. Folding his hands towards Paresh he smartly drew a chair a little away from the table and sat down on it. He considered it improper to notice that some women were around.

Baradasundari was about to leave taking her daughters away from the proximity of this unmannerly creature, when Paresh told her, 'Here is Gaurmohan, son of my friend Krishnadayal.'

It was only then that Gora turned in her direction and folded his hands. Although Sucharita had heard about Gora from Binoy she had never guessed that this very visitor was that friend Binoy spoke about. At the very first sight she felt a kind of hostility towards Gora. Sucharita did not have the kind of training or tolerance needed to accept a person who pursued orthodox Hinduism in spite of having English education.

Paresh enquired of Gora about his old pal, then reminisced about their own student life and said, 'In those college days we two made a perfect duo—both were known iconoclasts—we didn't obey any convention or taboo; and thought it was our noble duty to eat at hotels. Day after day we would take *kābāb* at some Muslim-run shop around Goldighi in the evening, and then would talk till late at night regarding our plans to reform the Hindu society.

Baradasundari asked, 'What does he do now?'

Gora said, 'Now he observes Hindu rites.'

Baradasundari was aghast: 'Doesn't he feel ashamed?'

She was disgusted like anything.

With a faint caustic smile Gora said, 'Shame is the symptom of weak nature. There are some who would be ashamed to acknowledge their parents.'

Barada. 'Wasn't he a Brahmo in the past?'

Gora. So was I.

Barada. Now you have come to embrace idol-worship!

Gora. I do not have any such superstition that I should disrespect the idol without any reason. Does the icon become contemptible just because you happen to abuse it? Who has ever been able to plumb the mystery of manifest form?

Paresh mildly suggested, 'But isn't the form constricted by limits?'

Gora said, 'How can you express a thing without the constriction of limits? It is the Infinite who takes the form of the Finite in order to express himself. How can he find manifestation otherwise? Without manifestation there is no completion. As idea informs language, the Infinite is manifested in the finite form.'

Barada shook head in disagreement, 'Do you mean concrete form is more complete than abstract idea?'

Gora. It does not matter in the least whether I mean it or not. The authenticity of form in this world does not wait for my confirmation. If the idea contained the real fulfillment then there would have been no place for form in this world.

Sucharita felt a strong longing that someone would come up and squash this arrogant youth, completely defeat and humiliate him by counter argument. She felt resentful at Binoy for sitting silently through all this. Gora had been speaking so forcefully, that Sucharita sought to gather strength to thwart that force, to make it bend.

At this point the attendant came with a kettle of hot water for tea. Sucharita got up to prepare tea. Binoy occasionally stole glances at Sucharita's face. Although Binoy had no difference with Gora regarding the form of prayer, it pained Binoy that Gora should thus storm into a Brahmo home uninvited and so freely express his disagreement with them. Comparing Gora's aggressive stance to Paresh's expression of self-contained placidity, his profound benignity that transcended all disputes, filled Binoy with admiration. He thought, —'Opinions were not important. The rarest and most precious attainment was the feeling of fulfillment, quiet, and benign contentment. You may debate a lot regarding what is true and what is false, but the real truth is what you attain within yourself.' During the heated argument going on around him Paresh was time and again closing his eyes and taking a plunge within his own self—it was a habit with him—at those moments Binoy looked fascinated at the peace of that self-absorbed face. Binoy felt quite hurt that Gora should fail to feel reverence for this elderly man and restrain his speech accordingly.

Making a few cups of tea Sucharita looked askance at Paresh. She was hesitant whom to offer tea and whom not to. Baradasundari looked at Gora and blurted out, 'Perhaps you are not going to take tea with us!'

Gora said, 'No!'

Barada. May I know why? Are you afraid of losing your caste status?

Gora said, 'Yes.'

Barada. Do you believe in the caste system?

Gora. It is not my making that I can choose between accepting or rejecting it. Since I accept my society, I accept its systems too.

Barada. Should the society be obeyed in everything?

Gora. Disobedience means subverting the society.

Barada. What's wrong in subverting it?

Gora. What's wrong in axing off the branch on which we are all sitting?

Feeling deeply irritated Sucharita intercepted, '*Mā*, What's the use of arguing? He won't take food touched by us.'

Gora turned his piercing eyes on Sucharita for a second. Sucharita turned to Binoy and asked with a slight hesitation, 'Would you...?'

Binoy never takes tea; he has also stopped eating bread or biscuit made by Muslim bakers for quite some time, but today it became a must. He forced himself to look up and said, 'Oh, yes, certainly....' Instantly he also glanced at Gora's face and noticed a faint grim flicker at the corner of his lips. The tea went stale and bitter on the tongue; still Binoy did not give up. Baradasundari thought to herself, 'Aha! What a nice boy!'

Now she turned completely from Gora and paid her full attention to Binoy. Seeing this Paresh slowly drew his chair closer to Gora and carried on conversation in low voice.

At this point the seller of hot and fried peanuts could be heard hawking around the end of the road. Leela at once clapped her hands and cried, 'Oh Sudhirda, call the nut-wallah please!'

Instantly Satish leaned over the railings of the balcony and called out to the nut-wallah.

In the meantime another gentleman arrived. All addressed him as Panubabu, although his actual name was Haranchandra Nag. He had earned the reputation of being an intelligent and knowledgeable man in the *Samaj*. Though it had never been mentioned in so many words by either of the parties, a rumour was afloat regarding the prospect of his marriage with Sucharita. That Panubabu was attracted towards Sucharita was obvious, and the girls never lost a chance to tease Sucharita about this.

Panubabu used to teach in a school. Since he happened to be a mere schoolteacher, Baradasundari did not have any great respect for the man. She did not conceal her attitude that it was only in the fitness of things that Panubabu did not dare to approach any of her own daughters; the prospective bridegrooms for her own daughters had to be at least deputy magistrates in order to be eligible for the match.

As Sucharita poured a cup of tea for Haran, Labanya smiled mischievously. Binoy did not miss it. Within a very short time Binoy had acquired a sharp and alert perception—although till the other day he enjoyed no reputation for being a connoisseur in the art of watching.

He guessed that Haran and Sudhir must have been known to the girls of this house for a long time, and had become so involved in their domestic affairs that they could even be the cause of the girls' mutual teasing. This seemed to strike Binoy as a sort of divine injustice.

In the meantime Haran's arrival heartened Sucharita a little. She could not get over her annoyance until somehow Gora's arrogance received a thrashing from some corner. At other times she had often felt irritable at Haran's quarrelsome argumentation, but today she welcomed this debater and gladly reinforced him with the supply of tea and bread.

Paresh said, 'Panubabu, here is our—'.

Haran said, 'I know him very well. He was once an enthusiastic member of our Brahmosamaj.'

Saying this Haran completely turned his back on Gora, and concentrated on his tea.

Recently just one or two Bengali youths had returned home after passing the civil service examination. Sudhir was referring to the reception of one of them. Haran remarked, 'Bengalis may pass this and that exams. But they are good for nothing.'

In order to prove that no Bengali can properly discharge his duties as a magistrate or a judge Haran cited various flaws and weaknesses of the Bengali character in general.

Within seconds Gora's face was all flush. Controlling his thunderous voice as best as he could, Gora said, 'If this is the reality then how can you chew your bread with such pleasure, so comfortably relaxed at this table!'

Haran raised his brows in surprise, 'What would you advise me to do instead?'

Gora. 'Either go and do something to remove this stigma of the Bengali character, or hang yourself. You say our race will accomplish nothing. Is it a matter of amusement! Is it such a light thing! How come the bread did not get stuck in your throat while saying this!'

Haran. Can't I tell the truth?

Gora. Don't mind. But if you really felt this to be the truth you could not sit here and boast of it so happily. Because you know it is not true you can mention it so casually. Haranbabu, falsehood is sin, false abuse is greater sin, and perhaps there is no greater sin than falsely abusing your own race.

Haran was furious. Gora continued, 'Are you alone superior to all the rest of your race? Do you suppose you have the sole right to take offence, and we shall humbly bear with all the offence hurled against all our ancestors!'

After this it was impossible for Haran to retrace. He launched a fresh volley of abuses against the Bengali race; after citing various evil customs of the Bengali society he emphatically concluded, 'Given this situation there is no prospect for the race.'

Gora hit back, 'It is your bookish knowledge of English culture that determines your identification of what you call evil custom. You yourself have no first-hand knowledge of the thing. It is only when you can denounce all the evil customs of the English that you get the right of talking on the issue.'

Paresh tried to stop the heated debate, but Haran, enraged as he was, could not to be stopped. The sun went down; an exquisite crimson radiance through the clouds filled the whole sky with a mellowed beauty; above all the noise of arguments a fine inaudible melody seemed to take possession of Binoy's mind. Paresh got up from the balcony for his evening prayer at the small praying corner under the huge *campā* tree in the garden.

Turned against Gora as Baradasundari was, she did not have much love to lose for Haran either. When the debate between the two became altogether unbearable, she took Binoy apart and invited him, 'Come on Binoybabu. Let us go indoors.'

As result Binoy had to give in to this affectionate partiality of Baradasundari and follow her indoors. Barada also called in her daughters. Seeing the trend of the debate Satish had already secured his share of peanuts and disappeared with Khude.

Baradasundari now launched her programme of introducing Binoy to the various accomplishments of her daughters. She asked Labanya, 'Won't you show that exercise book of yours to Binoybabu?'

Labanya had grown accustomed to display this book to all the newcomers to the house. Indeed, she waited for the invitation. Today she was feeling depressed at the distraction caused by the debate.

Binoy opened the exercise book to find copies of English poems by Moore and Longfellow. The handwriting showed care and neatness. The title and the first letter of each poem were in the Roman script.

Seeing this Binoy was genuinely surprised. It was a matter of no small credit for girls in those days to be able to copy Moore's poems in exercise book. Seeing Binoy adequately impressed Baradasundari now turned to her second daughter, 'Lalita, my darling girl, please that poem you—.'

Lalita stiffly said, 'No, *Mā*, I can't. I don't quite remember.'

Saying this she went up to the window to watch the street.

Baradasundari convinced Binoy that she remembered undoubtedly, but being very reserved she was not willing to display her learning. She cited a few instances from Lalita's childhood days in support of her claim regarding Lalita's extraordinary intelligence and scholarship. She also informed Binoy in this connection that Lalita was such a girl who would not shed tears even if she felt like crying, and that in this she resembled her father.

Next was Leela's turn. On being requested she giggled for a while, and then breathlessly repeated the poem 'Twinkle twinkle little star' like some programmed organ.

Guessing that the time had arrived to display musical talents Lalita left the room.

Outside on the balcony the arguments had become uproarious by this time. Losing his temper Haran had started abusing. Being embarrassed and annoyed by Haran's conduct Sucharita had taken Gora's side. This again had been no cause for comfort or peace to Haran.

Gradually darkness and monsoon clouds gathered in the sky. The hawker selling small garlands of *beli* flower finished his rounds for the day. Fireflies began to send their sparkling glints through the thick leaves of the wayside jacaranda trees. A dense darkness descended on the neighbouring pond.

Paresh came back to the balcony after offering his evening prayer. On seeing him both Gora and Haran felt ashamed and stopped. Gora stood up and said, 'It is already quite late. Allow me to leave.'

Binoy too took leave from Baradasundari and emerged on the balcony. Paresh told Gora, 'Look here, drop in whenever you feel like it. Krishnadayal was like my own brother. Now our religions are different. We have not met long since. Neither do we write to each other. But still, you know, friendship struck in one's childhood gets into the blood stream. I consider you very close to me on account of Krishnadayal. May God bless you.'

The calm affectionate voice of Paresh seemed to absorb and soothe the heat generated in Gora during the argument. At his first appearance Gora did not care to show much respect to Paresh. Now on the eve of leaving he touched the old man's feet with real reverence. He did not take leave from Sucharita. Indeed he considered it improper to acknowledge the very fact that Sucharita was physically present there before him. Binoy bent low to touch Paresh's feet, folded his hands towards Sucharita and then bashfully hurried out following Gora.

Haran avoided this leave-taking episode and went inside where he picked up a copy of the book of Brahmo prayer songs from the table and turned its pages.

As soon as Binoy and Gora had left Haran hastened back to the balcony and addressed Paresh, 'Look here, I don't think it desirable that girls of the family should be introduced to anybody and everybody.'

Sucharita had been fuming inside; she could not contain herself any longer and burst out, 'If *Bābā* maintained that attitude then you also stood no chance of knowing us.'

Haran replied, 'It is better that knowing and socializing is kept confined within one's own community.'

Paresh smiled, 'So you want to extend the domestic confine just a bit so as to make it a social confine. But in my opinion girls should mix with people of various opinions and mindsets. Otherwise we enforce a curb on their intelligence. I don't find any cause of fear or shame in this.'

Haran. I don't say that girls should not mix with people holding different views. But some people do not seem to know how to behave with ladies.

Paresh. Oh no, no, don't say such things. What you call lack of manners is but an indication of shyness. Until one gets used to female company one may not be able to overcome this.

Sucharita haughtily said, 'Listen Panubabu. Today during the argument it was the behaviour of our people that made me feel ashamed'.

In the meantime Leela had run in calling 'Didi, Didi', and holding Sucharita by the hand drew her inside.

11

That day Haran had particularly wanted to humble Gora in debate and thereby flaunt his own triumphant flag before Sucharita; initially Sucharita had also hoped for the same. But, as fate would have it, what took place was exactly its opposite. Sucharita and Gora did not see eye to eye regarding matters relating to religious faith or social issues. But both had an innate love for motherland and sympathy for their countrymen. Although she did not always discuss such matters, but that evening when Gora suddenly exploded like thunder at the abuse of countrymen, Sucharita at once responded to it with her whole heart quivering in unison. She had never before heard anyone else speaking of the country with such courage of strong conviction. Usually when our fellow citizens discuss the country and its people a shade of snobbery and insincerity informs their discourse; it was obvious that they did not genuinely believe what they spoke with such energy. That is why they do not have any real faith in, or hope for, the country, howsoever they might be poeticizing it. But Gora could clearly envision some noble truth through and beyond all the misery and flaws of motherland—and thereby without disowning the deficiencies of his country he could still place her on the altar of a strong reverential faith. His faith in the innate strength of the country was indeed so firm, that whoever came close to him—even if he was a skeptic—was bound to be moved by his total devotion to the country. Compared to this unimpeachable devotion of Gora, Haran's arguments of contempt seemed to hurt Sucharita like stinging insult. She could not restrain herself from getting over her shyness and joining in the protest that also sprang up from the core of her heart.

Afterwards when Haran, stung by petty jealousy, accused Gora and Binoy of lack of manners in their absence Sucharita was compelled to stand by them against such an unfair attack and meanness.

Yet it was not that Sucharita could altogether get over her antipathy towards Gora. Gora's aggressive arrogant Hinduism continued to hurt her long afterwards. Somehow she could feel there was an element of aggressiveness in this pronounced Hinduism—it was not spontaneous, natural, peaceful; it was not content with its own faith and devotion; it was ever and fiercely ready to hit others.

That evening an undefined sadness continued to haunt her in everything,—be it talking with others, or taking dinner, or telling story to Leela—the nagging pain could not be got over by any means. If one knew where it pinched one could spot the thorn and throw it out. In order to search for that thorn Sucharita sat up alone in the open balcony that night.

She tried as if to wipe out the vague uneasiness of her mind by the soothing darkness of night, but in vain. She felt like weeping under the undefined heaviness of her heart, but could not.

Some strange young man had come with *tilak*-marked forehead, and his pride could not be crushed by argument. But was Sucharita suffering so long for just this? What could be more ridiculous? She dismissed this as the most absurd idea. Then suddenly she remembered the real reason and blushed. Today she had been sitting face to face with that youth for more than three hours at least, and had even joined in his support on occasions, yet he did not seem even to notice her presence at all. Even on the eve of taking leave he did not look at her for once. It was this complete indifference that had hurt her so deeply; Sucharita had no doubt about it now. The lack of experience of social interaction with women outside the family can lead to a kind of shyness; this could be seen in Binoy's behaviour—it was marked by a charming modesty. But there was no trace of such a thing in Gora's conduct. She felt like dying in shame at her own garrulity that in face of such indifference she should have joined the debate without restraining herself. When Sucharita had been once extremely provoked by Haran's unreasonable argument, Gora had just glanced at her face. There was no sign of shyness in that glance—but what was there in it? She could not guess. Had he been thinking, 'What a shameless girl! Or, did the glance mean, 'What a haughty girl, that could join uninvited in the debate of menfolk!' Well, even if he thought this, what does it matter to her? It does not concern her at all. Still Sucharita could not pull up the thorn. She could not forget, or erase this from her mind howsoever she might try. She felt resentment towards Gora. She tried to despise Gora as a superstitious haughty youth. But still she felt very small before the straight glance of that big-boned man with thunderous voice as she recalled the scene. By no means she could hold on to a sense of self-superiority.

Sucharita had grown accustomed to receive special attention and love from everybody. Not that she herself was very keen about this attention. But why did the indifference on Gora's part become so unbearable to her today! Sucharita thought over the whole thing for a long time, and then persuaded herself to think that it was because she had so strongly wanted Gora to get defeated that his indifference was wounding her so much.

As she thus probed and analysed and dissected her own mind the night rolled on. All the other inmates had switched off light and retired to bed. She heard the front-door being closed—that meant the attendant had finished his cooking and night meal and was going to retire for the night. At this time Lalita came out to the balcony. She was in her night dress. Without saying a word she passed by Sucharita and stood at one corner of the balcony, her hands on the railing. Sucharita smiled a little. She knew Lalita was sulking. She had completely forgotten that tonight she was supposed to sleep with Lalita. But, saying 'I forgot' was no excuse for Lalita; because the very fact of forgetting was to be considered the most serious offence in the case. She was not one to remind of the promise at the appropriate hour. So long as she had been lying stiffly in her bed her resentment grew with every passing minute. At last when she could not bear it any longer she left the bed and came out only to signal the message, 'I am still waiting.'

Getting up from her chair Sucharita slowly came up and embraced Lalita, saying, 'Lalita, my dear sweet girl, please don't be angry.'

Lalita pushed off Sucharita's hand and said, 'No. Why should I! You linger here as long as you please!'

Sucharita grasped her hand and implored, 'Come on dear, let us go to bed.'

Lalita did not answer and stood on silently. At last Sucharita dragged her to the bedroom.

Lalita said tearfully, 'Why did you make it so late? Do you know it is already eleven? I have heard all the hours struck by the big clock. And now you will fall asleep within minutes.'

Sucharita held her close and said, 'It has been my fault, dear.'

As soon as she admitted her fault Lalita's resentment subsided. She grew soft like anything and asked, 'What had you been thinking Didi sitting alone till such late hours? Is it about Panubabu?'

Sucharita gave her a push with her forefinger, saying, 'Oh nonsense!'

Lalita could not stand Panubabu. It was impossible for her to even tease Didi about Panubabu like her sisters. When she remembered that Panubabu desired to marry Sucharita anger swelled within her.

After a brief silence Lalita raised the issue, 'Well, Didi, how did you like Binoybabu: He seems to be a nice man, doesn't he?'

I cannot be sure if she asked this with an intention to find out the true attitude of Sucharita.

Sucharita said, 'Yes, of course. He seems a nice man—quite a good soul.'

However, Lalita had perhaps expected another tenor in her voice which she could not detect in this reply. Then she ventured again, 'But whatever you may say to the contrary, I did not like Gaurmohanbabu at all. What bleached complexion, and rough appearance; looks as if he does not care for anybody in the world.'

Sucharita said, 'Seems too obsessed with Hinduism.'

Lalita said, 'No, no, it is not just that. If you speak of Hinduism our uncle too is an orthodox Hindu, but that is different. This is—I cannot exactly define what this is like—.'

Sucharita agreed smiling, 'Indeed, so odd it is!' Saying this Sucharita worked herself up into anger by recalling Gora's *tilak*-marked broad white forehead. The reason of her anger was, Gora had used that *tilak* as a script which inscribed in large letters the message, 'I am different from you.' Only if she could shatter that tremendous ego of exclusivism, perhaps she would have been at peace.

The talks stopped; eventually the two dropped off into sleep. When it was two o'clock, Sucharita woke up amidst sounds of heavy rainfall outside. The flash of lightning pierced through the curtain. The small lamp at the corner had gone out. In that stillness of night, in the darkness, amidst the ceaseless sound of thick rain, Sucharita felt an ache piercing her through. She turned this side and that, tried many ways, but had no sleep. Seeing Lalita soundly sleeping by her side she felt envious, but still could get no sleep herself. Exasperated she got up and came out. Standing at the open door she stared at the long balcony in front—occasional gusts of wind drenched her with rain. She turned about in her mind every detail of the evening. The glowing face of Gora on the balcony afire with the crimson hue of setting sun came back to her distinctly; and all the minute detail of the argument which she had heard and forgotten at the moment reverberated in her ears in the deep strong voice of Gora. It seemed to resound in her ear, 'I am on their side whom you call uneducated—my belief is what you call superstition. Until and unless you can love the country, and can stand by them as their own, I won't allow you to utter a single letter of abuse against them.' Panubabu had ventured to counter this: 'How can you thus reform the country?' Gora had exploded, 'Reform! Reform comes much later. Much more important than reform are love, respect. First we have to be united; reform will automatically follow. If you want to hold aloof and break up the country into fragments—if you highlight on what you call superstition then well—we will stand apart holding on to those 'superstitions'. I say this much that I won't separate myself from others by claiming superiority to any one—this is my greatest desire—after that which custom to retain or which to reject will be decided by my country and the destiny ruling my country. Panubabu said, 'there are many such customs and superstitions that have not been allowing us to get unified'. Gora said, 'If that is what you think then you would first try to uproot all those customs and superstitions one by one, and only after that the way to unity is cleared; it is like crossing the sea by pumping out the entire sea-water. Rather try to shed your own contempt and pride, and connect with others in humility and love. Thousands of blemishes and deficiencies will be compensated for by that love. Defects and deficiencies are there in every land, every society, but so long as the countrymen remain united under the bond of love for their compatriots, the poison does not work. The cause for disintegration is in the air. But as long as we live, we can resist it. The moment we die the rot sets in. I warn you I won't stand your reformist venture, be you a missionary or a Brahmo. Panu challenged, 'Why not!' Gora said, 'Precisely for this reason: one can accept correction from one's parents, but not from the jailor. In the Jailor's correction reform is lost under the weight of insult—if you have to accept that reform it would be at the cost of human dignity. Unless you be a kin first, a reformer next—even your lip-services can cause great damage to us.' As the entire discussion thus came back to Sucharita bit by bit she also seemed to suffer an undefined pain. Exhausted at last, Sucharita came back to bed, and pressing her palms on the eyes tried to push back all the thoughts and get some sleep. But her face and ears seemed to burn and bits and pieces of the discussion continued to float through her wakeful brain.

12

As Binoy and Gora came out from Paresh's house and stepped onto the road, Binoy said, 'Gora, please slow down a little—you have a pair of legs much longer than ours, if you do not slacken them a little how can we catch up with you?'

Gora said, 'I prefer to go alone, I am preoccupied today with many a thought.'

Saying this he strode off in his usual quick pace.

Binoy felt hurt. He had rebelled against Gora today, violated his laws. He would have been happy if Gora scolded him for this. With one squall the sky of their perennial friendship would have cleared and he would have felt relieved.

Another thought was also disturbing him. Today Gora had suddenly dropped in at Paresh's house and found Binoy there sitting like a family friend; this might lead Gora to assume that Binoy was a regular visitor here. Of course, that did not amount to any crime. Whatever Gora might say to the contrary, Binoy considered it a special privilege to get intimately acquainted with this cultured family. If Gora found fault with this it only proved his rigid orthodoxy. But earlier he had told Gora that he had not visited Paresh's house; today it might strike him that he was not told the truth. Gora's sharp eye could not fail to notice particularly when Baradasundari specially called Binoy indoors, and started entertaining him along with her daughters. No doubt Binoy felt proud and elated at this special attention from Baradasundari and the free interaction with the girls. But at the same time the difference in their respective reception of Gora and himself pained Binoy. Till date nobody had come up between the deep friendship of the two pals. Only once during Gora's enthusiastic Brahma days a thin veil had briefly come down upon the relationship. But as we have told earlier, for Binoy ideology has never been the big issue; howsoever he may fight over issues, the human factor is much more important to him than abstract idea. Today he was apprehensive about some barrier coming up to throttle their friendship. Binoy considered his connection with Paresh's family as a precious experience, because never in his life did Binoy get the taste of such joy. But

Gora's friendship was an integral part of Binoy's life. He could never imagine a life without it.

So far Binoy had allowed nobody to come so close to his heart as Gora had done. So far he has only read books, argued with Gora, quarreled with Gora, and loved him alone. He found no time for any other person in this world. Gora too—though he had no dearth of admirers—had no other friend than Binoy. There was an embedded loneliness in Gora's nature—on the one hand he did not ignore the common man, on the other it was impossible for him to get intimate with anybody and everybody.

Today Binoy realized that he felt deeply attracted by the members of Pareshbabu's family. Yet he had not known them long. On this account he felt a sort of guilt towards Gora.

Binoy could clearly imagine Gora's contempt had he known about Baradasundari's motherly pride at demonstrating her daughters' skills. Indeed this was quite ridiculous. Again, Baradasundari's insistent repetition about her daughter's English smatterings, the certificate from the English *Mem*, a moment of patronizing pat from the Lieutenant-Governor's wife,—all these indicated an approach of servility. But in spite of realizing all this Binoy could not despise them as Gora's ideology demanded. Rather he enjoyed this on the whole. A girl like Labanya—the fact that she was quite pretty could not be disputed—apparently felt proud to show Binoy her own handwritten copy of Moore's poems, and this seemed to offer Binoy a kind of ego satisfaction. Baradasundari failed to imbibe modernity in the true sense, and yet she was too pronouncedly eager to show her modernity; it is not that Binoy could not see through this anachronism, but still he liked her on the whole. Binoy had come to like the naiveté of her pride and intolerance. The girls kept the house sweetly resonant with their laughter; they made tea by their own hands and served it, decorated the walls with their own craft, besides reading English poetry and enjoying it too. However, trifling this might be, Binoy had been charmed by it. In his lonely life-style Binoy had never come across this kind of company. He imagined so many sweet pictures about these girls' costume, their talks and laughter, their ways and work. So long he had only read books and argued; he did not know when in course of this he had attained youth. Now this ordinary family in their small house seemed to reveal to him a new and wonderful world he had never imagined before.

Binoy could not blame Gora that he left Binoy's company in a sulk. At last a real division was on the way to part the duo who had been friends for years.

The silent darkness of the rainy night occasionally quivered to the tune of the roaring cloud. Binoy sat up with a heavy heart. He felt as if he had arrived at a turning point; so long he had been traveling straight in one direction, but now his life was going to change course. In this gathering darkness where was Gora, and whither was he himself going?

Love would only further swell up when facing the threat of separation. Binoy could feel today, when separation was imminent,—how strong, how immense his love for Gora was.

On returning to the flat the darkness of the night and the loneliness of the room seemed to oppress Binoy with profound intensity and vacuity. He came out once to set off towards Gora's place. But then he understood there was no hope of a hearty meet with Gora tonight. So he came back again and threw his tired body on the bed.

Next morning he woke up with a light heart. During the night he had unnecessarily intensified his anguish owing to an unusually activated imagination. In the morning it did not seem contradictory to him to carry on friendship with Gora and mixing with Paresh's family at the same time. 'What is so serious about this after all', he told to himself; he was even amused at remembering his suffering last night.

Throwing a *cādar* around the neck Binoy briskly walked straight to Gora's house. At that time Gora had been in his ground floor room reading the newspaper. In fact he had already spotted Binoy on the road before he reached, but did not raise eyes from the paper at Binoy's arrival. Without saying a word Binoy snatched the paper.

Gora said, 'I am afraid you are making a mistake. I am but Gaurmohan, just another superstitious Hindu.'

Binoy said, 'I am afraid the mistake is yours. I am Mr Binoy, a superstitious friend of the said Gaurmohan.'

Gora. But Gaurmohan is so shameless that he never feels ashamed of his superstitions before any one.

Binoy. Binoy is also exactly alike. The only difference is that Binoy does not rush out to fiercely pounce upon others for the sake of his superstition.

Within minutes they were engaged in uproarious debate. The neighbourhood had to remember that Gora and Binoy were together that morning.

Gora said, 'What was your great compulsion to disown the fact that you have been visiting that family?'

Binoy. No compulsion and no cause for disowning at all. I said I didn't because in fact I didn't. Yesterday was the first time I ever went to that house.

Gora. I have the hunch that perhaps, like Abhimanyu, you know only the entrance, and not the exit route.

Binoy. May be—perhaps that is my innate nature. I cannot abandon one whom I respect or love. I think you should know better than anyone about this side of Binoy.

Gora. So you are decided to maintain your connection there?

Binoy. Why must I go alone? You have also the capacity for walking; I am sure you are not an immobile matter.

Gora. Well, I go in and subsequently come out. But the symptoms I detected in you indicate you are on the verge of going in forever. By the by how did you enjoy the hot tea?

Binoy. Slightly bitter.

Gora. Then?

Bora. But if I refused that would have been more bitter.

Gora. That means sociability amounts to mere formality!

Binoy. Not always. But look here Gora, if the dictates of the heart clash with the strictures of society, it is for me—

Gora was too impatient to let Binoy finish. He thundered, 'Heart! It is because you consider society a trifling matter that your heart clashes with it at every little chance. But do you have any idea of the extent of the wound when you hit your society? If you had any awareness of this you wouldn't have talked about your heart. You feel great pain to give the least cause of hurt to Pareshbabu's daughters—but I feel tormented when you can hurt your whole country without a qualm for the sake of a mere trifling cause.'

Binoy replied, 'Then let me speak the truth Gora. If taking a cup of tea means hurting the whole country, then such a hurt may but benefit the country. If you have to go on protecting the country from even such trifling things then it will only leave her feeble like a baby.'

Gora. Oh Sir! Do you think me such a fool as not to anticipate this sort of reasoning? But that is not the thing at all. When a sick child refuses to take medicine, the mother, even if she herself be in perfect health, would take the same medicine in order to signal the message, 'my dear, I am with you in your sickness and health'. This is not the way of logic, but this is the communion of love. If this love is not there a whole world of arguments cannot help to sustain the bond between mother and child. Your activities become futile. Don't think it is my favorite habit to raise storm in teacups—and over teacups—but I can't bear alienation from my country. It is far too easier by comparison to refuse tea or hurt the feelings of Pareshbabu's daughters. Our primary duty now in the present situation is to get merged into the country. When the union is consummated it will be automatically decided whether to drink tea or not to drink.

Binoy. Seems it should be long before I have the chance of a second cup.

Gora. No, it need not be too long. But, Binoy, do you need me any more? I have the hunch that the time has come for you to leave me along with many an undesirable junk of Hindu society. Otherwise the daughters of Pareshbabu may feel hurt.

At this point Abinash entered the room. Abinash was Gora's disciple. What he hears from Gora, he prunes it down according to the limits of his intelligence, and then preaches a distorted version of it in his own language. Those who fail to follow Gora's talk, can quite understand and appreciate Abinash's teaching.

Abinash nursed an acute envy for Binoy. So, at the least chance he would try to challenge Binoy like a fool. When Binoy lost patience at his stupidity Gora would pick up the baton and start contesting Binoy's arguments. Abinash likes to imagine it was but his arguments that were pouring out of Gora's lips.

As Abinash arrived the friendly teasing of the two had to be suspended. Binoy then went upstairs. Sitting on the balcony in front of the store-room Anandamoyee was cutting vegetables.

Anandamoyee said, 'I have been hearing your voices for quite some time. Come so early today? Did you have your breakfast in the morning?'

If it were another day Binoy would have said, 'No, had no time for breakfast'—and at once get started with a good meal. But today he said, 'No *Mā*, no more breakfast today. I had something in the morning.'

Today Binoy did not want to launch yet another offensive against Gora. Binoy could feel that Gora had not yet forgiven his connection with Pareshbabu, and was apparently holding himself a little aloof. This acted as a kind of strain on his mind. He took out his pocket-knife and started peeling potatoes.

After some fifteen minutes he went down to find that Gora had already left with Abinash. He sat there silently for a long time. Then picking up the newspaper scanned the advertisements with an absent mind. Finally he heaved a sigh and left.

13

Around midday Binoy felt restless again and longed to meet Gora. Binoy had indeed never hesitated in the past to surrender to Gora. But though he did not have a personal pride, it was difficult to ignore the proud claim of friendship. True, Binoy had been feeling slightly guilty as if by responding to Pareshbabu he had fallen a little short in his loyalty to Gora. But he thought Gora would just taunt and scold him on that account; he had never imagined that Gora should thus keep him at a distance. Even after going a little way towards Gora's house Binoy came back again; he could not bring himself to go there lest his friendship is belittled or insulted.

After lunch Binoy sat down with pen and paper to write a letter to Gora; but before starting he found fault with the pen—apparently for no reason—and started sharpening it meticulously with the edge of a knife, when somebody called his name from downstairs. Putting down the pen Binoy came down in a hurry and warmly greeted, 'Mahim dada! Come in, come in please!'

Mahim came up, took his seat squarely on Binoy's bed, and after taking a good note of the furniture in the room said, 'Listen, Binoy, it is not that I don't know your apartment. Indeed I often feel like dropping in and see how you are. But I know, you are one of those goody boys of these days, and there is no chance of a good smoke here,—it is only on that account that unless it is very urgent—.'

As Binoy got fidgety Mahim said, 'Perhaps you are planning to go to the market and buy some brand-new hookah for your dada. Never mind. I can forgive you for not offering tobacco, but I can't stand the tobacco stuffed in by a novice, and that too in a new hookah.'

Saying this Mahim picked up the palmleaf fan lying on the bed and while fanning himself broached the subject. 'You see how I have spoilt my special post-lunch sleep of a Sunday afternoon for visiting you. But there is a special reason for this. You must do me a favour.'

Binoy wanted to know what the 'favour' was. Mahim said, 'Give me your word, first. Only then I can go on.'

Binoy. I can do so only if it is possible for me. Shoudn't I?

Mahim. It is possible for you alone. Just say, 'Yes'; you have to do nothing more.

Binoy. Why should you plead so much with me? Don't you know I consider myself as one of your family—is it possible that I won't help you if it is within my power or ability?

Mahim searched his pocket for a bunch of spiced betel leaf, offered a pair to Binoy, pushed three into his own mouth; then he spoke between his chewing, 'I think you know my Shashimukhi. She is not quite ugly, that is, not like her father. She is nearly ten, and it is time we had found a bridegroom for her. God knows, what wretch of a husband is waiting for her; I have been spending sleepless nights on that account.'

Binoy said, 'Why should you be so worried? You have enough time.'

Mahim. If you had been father of a daughter yourself you could appreciate my anxiety. With every passing year the girl grows taller, but the bridegroom does not drop from the sky. So with every passing day I have been feeling more and more anxious. Now, if you give me the assurance, of course I can wait a little more.

Binoy. I don't know many people—indeed in Calcutta I practically know no other family than yours—still as you are requesting I shall try.

Mahim. I think you know a little about Shashimukhi's character and conduct.

Binoy. Certainly. I know her since infancy—a nice girl.

Mahim. Then why must you take the trouble of looking here and there? I shall give the girl to you in marriage.

Binoy was stunned, 'What do you say!'

Mahim. What's wrong in my saying? True, I admit your family is superior to ours—but, Binoy, if you—being such a highly educated youth—obey the rules of family hierarchy, then what's the use of all this education?

Binoy. Oh no, hierarchy is not the point, but consider the age—

Mahim. Age! I must say I am surprised. Do you think Shashi is not sufficiently aged for marriage. Don't forget she is no memsahib, and comes of a Hindu family. How can we ignore the society?

Mahim was not one to give up easily. He insisted like anything. At last Binoy said, 'Please give me a little time to think over it.'

Mahim. Why not? I am not going to fix the date to-night!

Binoy. Moreover, my family members—

Mahim. Yes, yes, certainly. Their consent must be sought. Since your uncle is still alive nothing can be done without his consent.

Saying this he searched his pocket for a second bunch of betel leaf, inserted the lot into his mouth, and left as if the whole thing was finalized and clinched off altogether.

Some time ago Anandamoyee had once tried to broach the proposal of a marriage between Binoy and Shashimukhi. But Binoy paid no heed to it. Even today it did not seem a very appropriate idea, still somehow it seemed to nudge into Binoy's mind and settle into a corner of the same. The consideration that appealed to him was—in case this marriage took place then Gora, because of the very kinship, would not be able to reject him altogether. Since so far he has ridiculed the attitude that mixed up marriage with love as a mimicry of the English, the idea of marrying Shashimukhi did not appear altogether absurd to his thinking. Moreover, the hope that this proposal of Mahim offered a chance of interaction with Gora rather pleased him for the time being. Binoy wished Gora would come to him and try to persuade him in this matter. Binoy had no doubt that in case he did not readily give in to Mahim, the latter would employ Gora to bring him round.

The speculations boosted him up. Immediately he got ready for setting off towards Gora's house, and throwing a *cādar* on shoulder he came out. Before long he could hear someone calling from behind, 'Binoybabu'!

It was Satish. Binoy again came back to his apartment with Satish. Satish brought out a small knotted handkerchief from his pocket and challenged, 'Can you tell what's there inside?'

Binoy made wild guesses like 'skull of a dead body', 'a puppy' and various other unlikely articles, and was appropriately scolded by Satish. Then Satish untied the knot and revealing some five blackish fruits challenged again, 'Now tell me, what is this?'

Binoy again acknowledged defeat. Satish said, an uncle of Satish lived in Rangoon, who had sent this Burmese fruit to his *Mā*—*Mā* has sent five of them as gift to Binoybabu.

The mangosteen fruits of Burma were not readily available in Calcutta at the time. So Binoy turned them in his hand, observed and felt, and then asked humbly, 'Satishbabu, how to eat them?'

Satish was amused at Binoy's ignorance, and warned him, 'Take care. Don't bite into it. It is to be taken by cutting with knife.'

In fact, Satish himself had attempted a bite in vain and was thereby ridiculed by relatives—therefore his misery was now alleviated by laughing like the knowledgeable at Binoy's inexperience.

Then followed a jovial conversation between the two friends of unequal ages, at the end of which Satish said, 'Binoybabu, *Mā* has requested you to come to our house this evening if you can spare the time—it is Leela's birthday.

Binoy said, 'Today,—no dear, I cannot go today. Today I am going somewhere else.'

Satish. Where are you going?

Binoy. To my friend's.

Satish. *That* friend?

Binoy. Yes.

Satish could not understand the logic behind this decision—that Binoy could go to his friend's house, and yet could not go to their's,—especially since he did not like this friend. He seemed to be more stern than the headmaster of his school; it was not likely that anybody could impress him by playing a toy organ. That Binoy should feel the urge of going to see such a man did not please Satish at all. He implored, 'Oh no Binoybabu. You please come to our house.'

Binoy had silently boasted to himself on this decision—'In spite of invitation I will not go to Pareshbabu and go to Gora instead.' He had resolved that he would not allow his resentment to alienate his friend, that he would hold his friendship high above all else. But it did not take him long to forget the resolve. Though hesitating, equivocating, arguing with himself all the time, eventually Binoy took the road to number Seventy-eight, holding the child's hand. The way they had remembered Binoy specially for sending a portion of the rare fruits arrived from Burma evidenced such a genuine feeling that was impossible for Binoy to ignore.

While close to the house Binoy saw Panubabu and a few others he did not know coming out. Apparently they had been invited to lunch on the festive occasion. Panubabu went by as if he had not noticed Binoy.

The moment he entered the house Binoy could hear the sound of noisy laughter and chase inside. Sudhir had hidden Labanya's keys. Not only that; this robber was threatening to expose to public view Labanya's exercise book in the drawer which carried evidence of her secret pursuit of the poetic muse. When the fighting between the two camps had reached its height Binoy entered the stage.

Instantly the whole lot disappeared. Satish ran after them not to miss the fun. After a while Sucharita came into the room and said, '*Mā* has requested you to wait a little. She will be coming before long. Baba has been to Anathbabu's place, he too will return any moment.'

To help Binoy overcome shyness Sucharita mentioned Gora. She asked with a smile, 'Do you think he will ever come here again?'

Binoy asked, 'Why not?'

Sucharita said, 'I am afraid he has been taken by surprise at seeing us appear before the menfolk. Perhaps he cannot respect women anywhere else except within the four walls of domestic work.'

Binoy could not readily reply. He would have been happy if he could deny this. But how could he? That would mean telling a lie. Binoy said, 'According to Gora, if women did not apply their whole mind to domestic work, their duty suffered from lack of concentration.'

Sucharita said, 'But is it desirable to break the whole thing up into mutually exclusive compartments of the home and the world? According to this kind of logic we can say with no less validity that—because men are allowed to enter home, this affects their duty in the world outside. May I ask if you too subscribe to your friend's opinion?'

Regarding the issue of women's status, Binoy had so far consistently lent his support to Gora. He has even written in papers on the subject. But now he did not bring himself round to confess precisely that was his own opinion as well. He said instead, 'Look here. Regarding such matters as this we are actually slaves of habit. That is why we receive a jolt at seeing women come out—not that it is wrong or bad in itself—but we try to make it out that way. Reason is just an excuse in such cases; the real root is our inhibitions.'

Sucharita said, 'It seems the inhibitions are rather firmly rooted in your friend's psyche.'

Binoy. Apparently it may seem so to a casual observer. But I would request you to remember one thing; that he so deliberately clings to the customs of our country is not because he considers them ideal or desirable. It is because we have started blindly to denounce our heritage that he has stood up to resist this destruction. He says, first we have to know our country through reverence and love, to know and accept it wholly; then automatically the process of cure will start working according to the rules of natural health.

Sucharita retorted, 'Then why didn't it happen earlier?'

Binoy. It did not happen because never before did we perceive the entire country and race as a total whole. Perhaps we did not disrespect our own race, but neither did we revere, that is we did not have the very awareness—so the strength too was not stirred up. For a long time the patient was left alone, neglected, without medicine or nutrition. Now at last he has been carried into the hospital; but the doctor holds him in such contempt that he has no patience for some long-term treatment and nursing; instead he prescribes chopping off the sick limbs one by one. In this situation my friend the doctor has declared,

'I won't allow this treatment which will finish off my dear one. I must stop this chopping operation altogether, and slowly revive the life-energy within him first with compatible medicine and food. If I operate after that the patient will stand the ordeal; even without the surgery he may get cured.' Gora says, deep reverence is the best nutrient for our country today—it is because of this lack of reverence that we cannot know the real country—and because we do not know her, whatever we do for her becomes damaging in its turn. If you do not love the country you cannot have the patience to know her; if you do not know her you cannot do good to her even if you want to.

Sucharita continued her mild provocation so that the talk could continue to veer round Gora. Binoy too, on his part, waxed eloquent on whatever he had to say in Gora's support. He felt he had never before spoken so well, so logically with such illustrative examples on the subject. It is doubtful if Gora himself could have so clarified his own stand. Binoy felt so elated at discovering his own intellectual and expressive ability that his face became radiant with the joy of an exquisite excitement at this self-discovery.

Binoy said, 'Just consider, what the scripture says; it says '*ātmānanam bidhvi*'—know thyself. There is no emancipation without self-knowledge. I tell you my friend Gora has emerged as manifestation of that self-realisation of India. I can never think of him as just another average person. When all of us are distracted by the temptation for some trifling objects, by the fascination for the new, Gora stands apart as the sole exception to tower above all this chaos and confusion and chant that ancient mantra in his voice of thunder—*ātmānanam bidhvi*.

Binoy could continue in this vein much longer,—Sucharita too was listening with avid attention—when suddenly Satish started reciting from the next room at the highest pitch—

"Don't say pitifully without considering once
Life is like a dream, the world, an abode of illusions..."

Poor Satish used to get no chance of self-demonstration before guests and visitors to the family. Even Leela was allowed to carry the day by reciting English poems, but Baradasundari did not invite Satish to show his skills. Yet Satish and Leela were always on competitive terms. Somehow shattering Leela's pride was considered by Satish to be the greatest happiness of his life. Leela had passed her test before Binoy the previous evening. At that time Satish—uninvited as he was—got no chance to supersede her. Even had he tried Baradasundari was sure to snub him there and then. Therefore, today he had engaged himself in practicing recitation—as if solely for his own amusement—in the adjoining room. At this Sucharita could not restrain herself from exploding into laughter.

Right then Leela ran in—her hair loose and waving—and clasping her arms around Sucharita's neck whispered something into her ears. At once Satish too rushed in and shouted from behind, 'Well, Leela, can you tell us the meaning of the word, "attention"?'

Leela said, 'I won't tell.'

Satish. Pooh! Won't tell! Rather say you don't know.

Binoy drew Satish close to him and smiled, 'Well, you please tell us the meaning of "attention".'

Giving proud shake of head Satish said, '"Attention" means applying one's mind.'

Sucharita asked, 'What is meant by applying one's mind?'

Who else can land one into such traps unless it be one's own kin! Satish scampered out of the room as if he had not heard the question.

Binoy had resolved to take his leave early today and go to Gora. Moreover, as he spoke about Gora the longing to see him also rose increasingly stronger within him. So, as soon as he heard the clock striking four he got up from his chair.

Sucharita said, 'Are you leaving so early? *Mā* is preparing a dish for you. Is it not possible to wait a little longer?'

For Binoy it was more a command than a question. He sat down again. Labanya appeared in the room, dressed up in colourful silk, and said, 'Didi, snacks are ready. *Mā* asks you to come along on the balcony.'

Coming to the balcony Binoy was obliged to eat the snacks. Baradasundari sat down beside him and entertained him with the life and works of her children one by one. Lalita called Sucharita indoors. Labanya sat on a chair and bent on a piece of knitting she was doing with two iron sticks. Somebody had told her on some occasion that while knitting wool the movement of her soft fingers looked nice; since then knitting unnecessarily in presence of visitors had become her habit.

Paresh came. The evening drew on. It was Sunday and the scheduled hour for going to the temple for offering prayers. Baradasundari addressed Binoy, 'If you have no objection, would you come along with us to Samaj?'

After this no protest was possible. Taking two carriages all went to the temple. On the way back as they were boarding the carriages Sucharita cried out excitedly, 'Look there is Gaurmohanbabu; there he is—striding ahead—.'

There was no doubt in anyone's mind that Gora had seen the team; but he strode by with big steps as if he had seen nothing. Binoy felt deeply embarrassed before Pareshbabu's family at this show of arrogant impoliteness of Gora. But he knew deep within that it was because he noticed Binoy in this team that he turned back so abruptly and left in such great haste. The joy that had been radiating within Binoy so long, was suddenly snuffed out. Sucharita instantly understood Binoy's mood and also the cause behind it, and again she felt the resentment against Gora surging back in her mind at this injustice to a friend like Binoy in particular, and at his unreasonable disrespect towards the Brahmos in general. She once again wished Gora to be defeated and snubbed somehow.

14

As Gora sat down to his midday meal Anandamoyee broached the topic tentatively, 'Binoy came in the morning. Did he meet you?'

Without looking up from the plate Gora said, 'Yes, he did.'

Anandamoyee lapsed into silence for a long time before she ventured again, 'I told him to stay back, but he went away in such a preoccupied manner.'

Gora remained silent. Anandamoyee said, 'I have a hunch he is not happy Gora. I have never seen him like this before. I feel so depressed.'

Gora kept on eating silently. Because she loved Gora so excessively Anandamoyee was also a little diffident with the boy. If he did not come out himself she never insisted with him on any matter. Normally she would have stopped here; but since her heart was bleeding for Binoy today, she continued, 'Listen to me Gora, please don't take it otherwise. God has created many men, and he has surely not given only one road for all of them to follow. Binoy loves you like his own soul, so he adjusts with you in all respects—but if you force him to take the road of your choice, I am afraid, that may not lead to happiness.'

Gora said, 'May I have a little more milk, *Mā*?'

The conversation was squashed. After finishing meal Anandamoyee sat at the end of her bed silently sewing something. Lachmya tried in vain to engage her in some discussion regarding the rudeness of some particular servant and eventually fell asleep on the floor.

Gora spent quite some time writing letters. Binoy was clearly given to understand in the morning that Gora had been angry with him; it was not possible that he would not come to approach Gora to shake hands. Gora knew it only too well. Amidst all his work he expected and waited for the sound of Binoy's footsteps on his stairs.

The day rolled on, but Binoy did not come. As Gora was on the point of getting up from his desk, Mahim entered, slumped his weight upon a chair, and started immediately, 'What are your plans Gora regarding Shashimukhi's marriage?'

Since Gora had in fact never given a thought to the subject for once, he stood silent like the guilty offender.

Giving a long speech on the high cost of bridegrooms in the market and the lack of financial solidity in the family Mahim appealed to Gora to think of some way out of it. When poor Gora failed to think out a solution, Mahim came to his rescue and proposed the name of Binoy as the possible saviour in the situation. There was no need of so much beating around the bush before coming to the point; but whatever Mahim might brag, at heart he was a bit scared of Gora.

It had never occurred in Gora's remotest dream that Binoy's name could figure in this discussion. Furthermore, Gora and Binoy had resolved not to marry and instead dedicate themselves to the service of the country. Gora, therefore, expressed his amazement: 'Why should Binoy get married at all!'

Mahim taunted, 'So, this is then your brand of Hinduism! Indeed you may flaunt a thousand *tikis*, or put *tilak* on forehead, but the innate Anglophilia is bound to surface when the test comes. Do you have any idea that getting married is, according to the scriptures, a must for a Brahmin youth?'

Mahim does neither defy customs like some of his contemporaries, nor does he care for the scriptures. He considers it unnecessary fuss when someone boasts of having dined at some hotel. At the same time he also does not look upon excessive regard for and preoccupation with scriptures—as seen in Gora—as the symptom of sanity.

If such a proposal was broached a few days ago, Gora would have paid no heed to it. But today he thought perhaps it was not altogether a bad idea. At least he got an excuse to rush to Binoy's apartment right now.

At last Gora said, 'Well, let me sound Binoy.'

Mahim said, 'Oh, that'll be no problem. If you request he will never be able to turn down. It is now as good as settled. You have just to blurt it out.'

Gora knocked at Binoy's door that very evening. He stormed into the room to find it empty. He called the servant to receive the information that the master had been to number Seventy-eight. Gora felt mortified. The whole day since morning he had no peace, and Binoy, who was the cause of all this disturbance, had no time to spare for Gora! Whether Gora was resentful or sad, did not seem to affect Binoy's peace or happiness!

Gora's whole heart turned against the members of Pareshbabu's family, against the Brahmosamaj itself. He rushed towards that house in a state of great mental turmoil. His intention was to throw before them such challenging utterances that would annoy the Brahmo family like anything, while Binoy too will be greatly embarrassed.

Reaching Pareshbabu's residence he learnt that no one was at home, and all had left for the temple. For a flicker Gora hoped perhaps Binoy had not gone with them, perhaps he was at this very moment set for Gora's house.

Gora could not wait. In his natural stormy pace he at once started in the direction of the temple. At the gate he saw Binoy following Baradasundari into their carriage—in the midst of the public road before the public view he was shamelessly sitting up in the carriage alongside women who were not his relatives! The fool! Must you get trapped like one surrendering to the python's coiling! So quickly! So easily! Then what is the meaning of friendship! Gora sped off like a real storm,—and, in the darkness of the carriage Binoy sat silently staring at the darkness outside.

Baradasundari thought perhaps the *Acārya*'s recent speech had been doing its work on Binoy's mind—she, therefore, did not disturb.

15

Coming home Gora went up to the roof top and restlessly walked from end to end. He felt annoyed with himself. Why did he allow the Sunday to be so wasted? Gora had not come to this world to neglect his work just on account of some personal relationship. Binoy was now headed for his target. If Gora tried to draw him back from that course it would only lead to waste of time and heaviness of heart. Gora had only one friend in this world; by discarding even that single friend Gora will dedicate himself completely to the pursuit of his faith. Saying this Gora waved his hands about energetically as if he were shaking off all connections with Binoy by this gesture.

At this time Mahim climbed up on the roof top. While still gasping for breath he started in accusatory tone: 'When man got no wings why build these multi-storied houses? The gods whose abode is the sky do not look well upon this undue desire of an earthy creature for a place in the sky.' Then in the same breath he blurted out, 'Did you have the chance to talk to Binoy?'

Without directly addressing his query Gora said, 'This marriage cannot take place.'

Mahim was stumped, 'Why? Doesn't he agree?'

Gora. I don't agree.

Mahim threw up his hands in exasperation, 'Fine! Here is a new twist to the tale. So you don't agree. May I know the reason, Sir?'

Gora. I've come to the conviction that we can't hold him back within the fold of our community for long. It's not desirable that a daughter of our family is given away in marriage to Binoy.

Mahim. I've seen whole hordes of orthodox Hindus, but never one like you. You seem to surpass even the Kashi-Bhatpara Brahmins. It seems you have started predicting future and planning your actions accordingly. One of these days you may very well cry out one fine morning, 'Oh, I dreamt last night you have converted to Christianity; therefore, you must consume cowdung in order to get restored to the community!'

After rambling thus for a long while Mahim appealed to Gora, 'Look here, can I hand over my daughter to an ignorant fool? One who has been educated, who has cultivated his intelligence, is bound to have occasions of aberrations from the scripture-approved routes. For that you can argue with him, you can scold him, but why stop his marriage and thus punish my poor girl? It's all your angularity.'

Mahim came down with his appeal to Anandamoyee, '*Mā*, you please stop your Gora.'

Anandamoyee anxiously asked, 'What happened, my boy?'

Mahim. I had nearly settled the matter of Shashimukhi's marriage with Binoy. Had even got the consent of Gora. In the meantime Gora has come to 'clear' conclusion that Binoy is not sufficiently Hindu—he slightly differs from Manu-Parashar on occasions. Therefore, Gora has got adamant—and you know very well how adamant Gora can be when he chooses so. If a king Janak of Kaliyug happened to promise Sita as reward for bringing round an adamant Gora, I can stake any claim to declare that even Lord Ramchandra would have to admit failure. After Manu-Parashar it is you alone in the whole world whom Gora obeys. Now it is up to you to see my daughter through this. We shall never find another such suitable boy.

Saying this Mahim repeated his dialogue with Gora on the roof top. That a clash was imminent between the friends was clear to Anandamoyee, and she was deeply worried.

Coming to the roof top Anandamoyee saw Gora had stopped strolling on the roof and instead was reclining on a chair with his legs stretched upon another while reading a book. Anandamoyee drew another chair near him and sat down. Gora took down his feet from the other chair and sat up looking straight at her face.

Anandamoyee said, 'Gora, my son, you must comply with my one request—please don't break up with Binoy. To me you are like two siblings—if you two part ways I shall not be able to bear it.'

Gora said, 'When a partner wants to part ways I cannot waste my time pleading with him.'

Anandamoyee said, 'Son, I don't know what has taken place between you, but do you really believe that Binoy wants to move away from you? What sort of friendship is this then?'

Gora. *Mā*, I like to go the straight way. I won't have any compromise. Those who seek to balance opposed ways cannot have any truck with me. If somebody wants to hunt with the hound and run with the hare then he must leave me, this particular hare, alone—whether it be painful for me or tormenting for him, is immaterial.

Anandamoyee implored, 'Can't you tell me in so many words what exactly happened? I guess his only offence is he visits some Brahmo family; am I right?'

Gora. It is a long story, *Mā*.

Anandamoyee. Let it be as long as it may—but let me put one small question. In everything you are obstinate; nobody can dissuade you from what you fix your mind upon. Then how come you are so passive only in the case of Binoy? If your friend Abinash wanted to leave the party would you have allowed him? Is it because of his friendship for you that he figures least in your consideration?

Gora thought silently. Anandamoyee's observation helped him to look back into his own mind. He realized clearly that so long he had been assuming that he was sacrificing friendship for the sake of duty but actually it was just the opposite. It was because he was pained by the resentment of his wounded ego as a friend that he was on the point of punishing the friend with rejection. Deep within his heart he knew that to hold back Binoy friendship was enough, and any other device only amounted to an insult to their love.

Anandamoyee guessed that her appeal had gone home, and without saying anything more she was slowly getting up when suddenly Gora sprang up at a bounce, and snatched a *cādar* from the rack.

Anandamoyee asked, 'Where are you going, Gora?'

Gora said, 'To Binoy's flat.'

Anandamoyee. Dinner is ready. Take it before leaving.

Gora. I am bringing Binoy along; he too will dine here.

Without saying anything more she started for the stairs but stopped suddenly at the sound of footsteps on the stairs and announced, 'Look, there he comes.'

Before she could finish Binoy had arrived. Tears moistened her vision. Affectionately she touched Binoy and said, 'Binoy, my son, did you have your meal?'

Binoy said, 'No, *Mā*.'

Binoy glanced at Gora. Gora said, 'Binoy will live long. I was just setting off for you.'

A weight lifted off her mind; Anandamoyee quickly went down.

When the two friends entered the room Gora mentioned this and that thing—the new gymnastic teacher, for example, who had been doing fine—

Neither dared to venture deeper, within the mind.

When the two sat down at dinner Anandamoyee understood from their talk they were still a bit stiff—the curtain was not yet fully drawn up. She said, 'Binoy, it is already late. Better you stay back. I am sending message to your apartment.'

Stealing a quick glance at Gora Binoy said, '*Bhuktwā rājabadācaret.* After dinner relax like a king. Walking in the streets is not desirable after a heavy meal. Therefore, it is decided I sleep here tonight.'

After finishing meal the two friends rested on a mattress on the roof. Autumn had already set in. The sky was flooded with moonlight. Light white cloudlets were floating across casting their light shade on the moon occasionally like some brief spell of a drowsy numbness. All around roofs of various shapes and height, mingled with treetops in between, lay like some huge unreal useless whim in the chiaroscuro of light and shadow.

The church clock struck eleven. The ice-vendor's last call faded away at the end of the street. There were fewer horns of passing vehicles. There was no symptom to indicate wakefulness, except the sound of hooves on the wooden floor of the neighbouring stable now and then and the dogs barking out in response. The two were silent for a long time. Then Binoy, after a slight hesitation, released his heart in an outpouring stream. He said, 'My dear Gora, my heart is full; it aches in joy. I know you are not interested in such things, but I must speak it out to you. I don't know if this is right or wrong, but I know that I cannot take it lightly. I have read books and thought so long I knew everything. It's like one who sees picture of water and assumes he can swim. But today after a real plunge I know it is no illusion.'

Binoy tried with all his heart to hold up before Gora the extraordinary experience that had arrived in his life.

Binoy went on to describe how all the emptiness of his day and night had been filled up; as if there was no chink in the entire sky, the universe, everything had been full to the brim, like the beehive in springtide nearly bursting with its overflowing honey. Previously, a large part of the universe was outside the periphery of his life—his attention was confined to only that part which was necessary for him. Now the whole world, as it were, knocked at his door, everything was embracing him, everything seemed to have been imbued with a new meaning. He did not know he loved the earth so much, that the sky was so wonderful, that sunlight was so exquisite, that even the stream of strangers along the road was so deeply moving. He felt he wanted to do something for all, to offer his entire energy perennially for all, like the sun in the sky.

One could not initially guess that Binoy was referring to some particular person in this spontaneous overflow. It was as if he could not mention the name, he even shied away from the slightest suggestion. It was as if he would be offending someone by such disclosure—it should be unfair, it should be insult—still he could not deny himself the pleasure of this overflow, in this lonely night, under the silent sky, with the dearest friend sitting beside.

What a face it was! How delicately the cheeks glowed with the radiance of the soul within! How the smile cast the luminosity of a heart that scintillated like some wonderful star! How the forehead shone with intelligence! And the eyes—how deep and exquisite the eyes were under the shadow of thick lashes! And the hands—seemed to be ever ready to offer care and affection, seemed to be eloquent. Binoy felt his youth had found its meaning, and his heart was brimming over with the joy of it. Most people in this world lived and died without ever having a glimpse of the vision which Binoy had seen manifest before him, and what could be a greater wonder!

Was it madness? Was it wrong? Be that as it may, it could not be resisted any more. If this flood carries him over to some distant shore, he won't mind; nor did he care if it just carried him along indefinitely, or drown him; he had no choice. The problem was that he didn't even want to be rescued—as if thus being carried away on the crest of the flood beyond all convention, stability, belonging was the only appropriate fulfillment of one's life.

Gora listened in silence. On this very roof top they had spent so many sleepless nights in the past under the same lonely moonlit sky hanging over the slumbering city—literature, human nature, social welfare, plans about their own future, everything had figured in those nightlong exchanges. But never before did they talk this way. Gora had never been made to realize before this night how true the truth of the human heart was, and how intense its expression could be. So far he had just ignored this as poetical junk—but today he had such a close view of it that he could not disown any more. Not only that, he felt its thrill upon his own mind; its exquisite ecstasy flashed through his whole body like lightning. The curtain over a heretofore unrecognized chamber of his youthful mind was lifted for a moment by a sudden breeze, and the room, closed so long, was instantly flooded by the magic moonlight of the autumn night.

Eventually, the moon disappeared behind the neighbouring roofs. A chink of light just appeared in the eastern sky like the flicker of a smile on a sleeping face. At last Binoy felt relieved and also a little shy. After a brief silence he said, 'I know all this I said is of no significance to you. You may feel contempt for me. But what can I do? I have never hidden anything from you in the past—nor did I tonight, whether you understand or not.'

Gora said, 'Binoy, I cannot claim that I quite understand your experience. Perhaps you too could not do either a few days ago. Neither can I deny that this aspect of emotion and rapture in life seemed to me trivial matter till today. But that should not necessarily mean it is really trifling. As on my part I did not have a first-hand experience of its strength, its profundity, it appeared like an unsubstantial illusion to my perception; but how can I dismiss what has been such a magnificent revelation to you as unreal! The crux of the problem is that one cannot work within one's own sphere unless he pays an exclusive attention to it at the cost of his inattention to the rest of the world outside its periphery. This is precisely the reason why God has imposed limits to our perception—the distant is made to look small—to save us from the great danger that might result from perceiving all the truths equally. We must select and pick up some particular aspect, must get over the temptation of grasping everything together; otherwise we shall never be able to get at the truth. You have perceived a manifestation of truth from a specific vantage point. I cannot greet that manifestation from that perspective—in that case I shall have to abandon the truth of my own life. I have to choose one at the exclusion of the other.'

Binoy said, 'Either Binoy or Gora. I seek to fulfill myself. You are set for self-sacrificing.'

Gora lost patience, 'Binoy, don't talk bookish. On hearing you today I have clearly understood one thing. Your life has now arrived at a turn where you stand face to face with an irrevocable truth—you cannot ignore it. Once you realize the truth you must surrender to it. There is no other way. I have my own sphere of life and work; may I be granted similar realization of my truth, this is my desire now. So long you were satisfied with the account of love in books. My love of my country too is no less bookish. Only when love came to you in manifest form you recognized its unmistakable authenticity beyond and above all books. The joy of this discovery has come to possess your whole existence, you have no respite from it. The day my love of the country will appear before me in such a real manifest form I too will be left with no choice. Then that form will conquer at ease my life and all its possessions, my bones-flesh-blood, my sky, my light, everything. How indescribably beautiful that true form of my country must be, how unmistakably visible, stirring one with what exquisite joy, what excruciating pain that can flood over life and death in a moment like some gigantic tidal wave—today while hearing you I can imagine a little of it. Your experience has given me a jolt today—I don't know if I shall ever be able to understand what you have gained. But it seems through you I get a taste of what I want to acquire.'

While saying this Gora got up from the mattress and started walking on the roof. The first signs of the dawn on the eastern sky appeared to him like a message; it seemed to resonate like some Vedic mantra chanted in an ancient *tapovan*; he was thrilled—and stood motionless; for a second he felt as if a lustrous ray burst out from deep inside him and trembled upwards like some fine stem into the sky where it opened into thousand petals of a luminous lotus that blossomed till the whole sky was covered. It seemed to fill his entire entity, his whole consciousness, all his energy with the ecstasy of a supreme joy.

At last when he slowly came back to himself, Gora suddenly exclaimed, 'Binoy, you must transcend even this love. It is my conviction you must not stop there. One day I shall show you how supremely true is the great energy that summons me. I feel so happy today—I shall never allow you to abandon me for some other course.'

Binoy got up from the mattress and came close to where Gora stood. Gora spread out both the hands in immense enthusiasm and held him close to his bosom, saying, 'Binoy, my brother, if we have to die, we shall die together—we two are one! Nothing can separate us, nobody can resist us.'

The surge of this enthusiasm of Gora also sent its waves into Binoy's heart; without saying a word he allowed himself to be carried away along the crest of the waves.

Gora and Binoy strolled silently side by side. The east turned crimson. Gora said, 'My brother, I envision my goddess,—but it is not amidst beauty. I envision her place amidst famine and poverty, suffering and degradation. Music and flowers are not enough for her worship; it is to be done by offering your life, your blood. I feel that should be my greatest joy. No lure of happiness waits for me there; it is through my own strength alone that I have to arise and dedicate myself completely. Hers is not a soothing charm; it is an irresistible, unbearable revelation—it is cruel, it is terrible—its music arises from that merciless blow at which all the chords explode in turbulent symphony only to be torn into pieces. Thinking of this my heart bounces up in a wild dance—I think this is the right joy for the male—this is the *tāndava*, the ruthless dance of destruction—this is the worship of the male for envisioning the manifest form of the new in the ritual flame lit to consume the old. On the crimson canvas of the sky I can envision a glorious future—I can see it right now through this imminent dawn—feel here Binoy, don't you hear a *damaru* beating here!'

Saying this Gora took Binoy's hand and pressed it on his bosom.

Binoy said, 'Gora, my brother, I will come with you. But this is my appeal to you, don't allow me the chance for dithering. You pull me along like some ruthless destiny. Our course is the same, but our strength is not the same.'

Gora said, 'I know there's difference in our temperaments, but a great elation will wash away those differences. We two love each other—but a love, greater and higher, will unite us. Until that greater love is attained we may clash on many a trifle, but ultimately we shall forget all, we shall forget our differences, we shall forget even our friendship, and meet in indomitable strength amidst a great ruthless self-effacement. That hard-won happiness should be the final reward of our friendship.'

Holding Gora's hand Binoy said, 'Let it be so.'

Gora said, 'But in the meantime I shall make you suffer a lot. You'll have to bear with many an oppressive demand from me; because I cannot see our friendship as the final thing of life, and therefore, won't dishonour it by trying to save it anyhow. If the friendship collapses at this let it be so; but if it survives that will be our fulfillment.'

At this moment they started at footsteps behind them; Anandamoyee had come up. She took their hands and directed them towards the room, saying, 'Come boys, have some sleep.'

Both said, 'Can't sleep now, *Mā*.'

Saying 'You must', Anandamoyee forced the two to lie down side by side on the bed and shutting the door sat down at the head of the bed, waving a palmleaf fan.

After they sank into sleep Anandamoyee came out softly. While getting down the stairs she saw Mahim going up. Anandamoyee intercepted, 'Please not now—They did not have a wink of sleep last night. Just now I persuaded them to go to bed.'

Mahim exclaimed, 'Oh my goodness! This is called friendship! Anyway, did the marriage figure in their talk?'

Anandamoyee. 'I don't know.'

Mahim. I hope something has been decided. When will they get up? Unless the marriage is arranged shortly many problems will crop up.

Anandamoyee was amused, 'In any case their falling asleep will not lead to any problem—I hope they will get up before midday.'

16

Baradasundari asked, 'Have you decided not to take any initiative for Sucharita's marriage?'

Pareshbabu in his habitual quiet dignified manner caressed his grey beard for a while; then replied in mild voice, 'Where is the bridegroom?'

Baradasundari said, 'Why? Her marriage with Panubabu is already settled—at least we know this to be so, I think Sucharita too knows.'

Paresh remonstrated, 'I don't think Sucharita quite likes Panubabu.'

Baradasundari was annoyed, 'Listen, I don't like this sort of attitude. Of course I never make any difference between Sucharita and my own daughters, but you must also allow me to say,—is she really that extraordinary! If an educated pieteous man like Panubabu takes a liking for her is it to be dismissed contemptuously? Whatever you may say against it, I do believe my Labanya is much better-looking than her. But I can bet she will marry whoever we choose for her like a good girl. If you thus inflate Sucharita's pride then eventually it will be difficult to get a groom for her.

Paresh said nothing after this. He never argued with Baradasundari, especially in matters related to Sucharita.

When Sucharita's mother died after delivering Satish Sucharita was just seven. Her father Ramsharan Haldar joined the Brahmosamaj after his wife's death, and as a result was so persecuted by the neighbourhood that he left the village to settle in Dhaka. While working at the post office there he became an intimate friend of Paresh. Since then Sucharita has all along looked up to Paresh like her own father.

Ramsharan met a sudden death. Prior to this he had divided all his savings into two equal shares and appointed Paresh as the trustee to his deed. Since then Sucharita and Satish have been members of Paresh's family.

However, if people—within the family or outside—showed any special attention or affection towards the girl, Baradasundari did not like it. Yet, whatever be the reasons, Sucharita attracted attention and regard from all. Baradasundari's daughters were always vying with each other for Sucharita's attention. Especially the second daughter, Lalita, almost clung to Sucharita day and night with her possessive jealous love.

Baradasundari secretly nursed the ambition that her daughters should surpass all the educated girls around. The prospect that Sucharita too might reap the same benefit by virtue of growing up with her daughters did not gladden her. Therefore, many hindrances used to come up for Sucharita around the hour for school.

Paresh guessed the roots of these hindrances, and stopping her schoolgoing himself took up the responsibility of teaching her. Not only that, Sucharita became a special companion of Paresh. He used to discuss various subjects with her, took her along wherever he went; when forced to be out of station he would write letters to her raising various issues and discussing them elaborately. Thus Sucharita grew mature beyond her age and circumstances. The expression on her face as well as her conduct carried such dignity that no one could dismiss her as a mere girl; and although Labanya was almost the same age still she considered Sucharita superior to herself in every respect; even Baradasundari too, in spite of her inclinations, could not ignore her by any means.

Readers have already come to learn that Haranbabu was a very enthusiastic Brahmo; he was involved in all activities of the Samaj—be it teaching at night school, editing paper, or secretaryship of girls' school—he was indefatigable. It was the common expectation that one day this young man would risc to the top of Brahmosamaj. Especially his reputation for command of English language and philosophy had spread beyond the periphery of Brahmosamaj through his students.

For these various reasons Sucharita too quite respected him like all other Brahmos. While coming from Dhaka to Calcutta she was indeed keen to know this man.

At last she not only got acquainted with the famous Haranbabu, but before long Haranbabu unhesitatingly expressed his attraction towards Sucharita. Not that he had knelt before Sucharita to pour out his love in so many words; but he grew so attentive to correct her faults, to increase her enthusiasm for the Samaj, in short to improve her in all possible ways, that his desire to mould this girl specially into a suitable partner became apparent to everybody.

At this Baradasundari lost her previous respect for Haranbabu, and tried to feel contemptuous toward him as a mere schoolmaster.

Although no proposal came from the party concerned, everybody had taken it for granted that marriage of the two was certain. Sucharita too mentally accepted the idea, and how to become suitable through education and effort, for the way Haranbabu dedicated his life towards the betterment of Brahmosamaj, was a matter of anxious concern for her. Indeed she did not get the feeling that she was going to marry a real human, but rather as if she were going to marry the noble cause of the Brahmosamaj itself. That 'cause' was made absolutely grave by means of philosophical knowledge and highly erudite reading of countless books. In her imagination this marriage was like a stone castle constructed with fear, reverence and an extremely demanding responsibility—it was not meant for living happily inside, but rather for the purpose of fighting—it was not familial but historical.

If the marriage had been over in this situation then at least the bride's party would have considered itself lucky. But Haranbabu envisioned the responsibilities of his dedicated noble life so seriously that marrying just for the sake of love seemed to him unbecoming for a man like himself. He could not take the plunge without taking a full account of the extent of possible gain that might accrue to the Brahmosamaj through this marriage. Therefore, he continued to test Sucharita from this standpoint.

Anyway, when one is set for such evaluative schemes, one himself too, in due course, cannot evade evaluation. Haranbabu became a familiar figure in Pareshbabu's household. His other name—Panu—by which he was addressed among the kin, got currency in this family as well. It was not possible to see him any more as mere storehouse of English knowledge, or vehicle of philosophical information and incarnation of Brahmo faith—he began to be measured as a human. As a result he ceased to be the repository of respect and regard only, and it seemed possible to see him as an object of liking or disliking.

Strangely, the very approach of Haranbabu which had attracted Sucharita from distance, began to hurt her when she faced it from close quarters. As Haranbabu took over the charge of protecting all the truth and good and beautiful elements in Brahmosamaj as its self-appointed guardian, he looked absurdly small in proportion. Man's relation to truth is the relation of admiration—it automatically makes one humble. If it makes one arrogant and proud instead, then the person concerned appears too obviously small in comparison to the truth. At this point Sucharita could not fail to notice the difference between Pareshbabu and Haran. Pareshbabu seemed to be ever humble in reverence to the truth he had received from the Brahmosamaj; there was no trace of vulgar show in him; rather he seemed to have taken a deep plunge into its profundity. Looking at Paresh's quiet expression one could feel the sublime nobility of the truth he had been carrying within his own heart. But Haranbabu was a different type. His aggressive self-assertiveness in the name of Brahmoism seemed to condition all his activities and find vulgar manifestation in all his speech and conduct. This had helped his reputation with the community, but since Sucharita—thanks to Paresh's teaching—could not be clannish, this orthodox Brahmoism of Haranbabu was a strain on her natural humanism. Haranbabu used to think that religious pursuit had endowed him with such extraordinary transparency of vision that he could at ease understand what was good or bad, right or wrong, for all others. The mundane materialistic people also enjoy gossip and abuse of others a lot. But when the same thing is done in the name of religion, then the cocktail of abuse and spiritual arrogance leads to a very pungent nuisance. Sucharita could not stand it at all. Not that Sucharita felt no pride about Brahmosamaj; yet on many occasions she would contest Haranbabu's claim that those who were eminent people within the Brahmosamaj were so precisely on account of being Brahmo, and the hapless fellows outside the periphery of the Samaj were specially lacking in integrity and prospect because of the precise reason that they were non-Brahmos.

It was particularly on those occasions when Haranbabu—with the benefit of the Brahmosamaj in his mind of course—did not restrain from castigating even Pareshbabu, that Sucharita lost her patience and reacted fiercely like some wounded female snake. Those were the times when the *Bhāgavatgītā* did not figure in the discussion among English-educated Bengali elite. However, Pareshbabu sometimes used to read the *Gītā* with Sucharita. He had also read out to Sucharita nearly the whole of the *Mahābhārata* as translated by Kaliprasanna Singha. Haranbabu did not like this. He was in favour of banning these books in a Brahmo household. He himself too had not read them. He held the *Rāmāyaṇa-Mahābhārata-Gītā* as exclusively Hindu material and therefore to be kept at a distance. Among all the Scriptures the Bible alone was his choice. That Pareshbabu did not care for the boundaries between the Brahmo and non-Brahmo in his studies as well as in many small daily matters annoyed and provoked Haran to any extent. Sucharita, on the other hand, could never stand the arrogance of any one who could go to the extent of blaming Pareshbabu, verbally or silently. It was precisely because of exhibiting such arrogance that Haranbabu's stock had fallen in Sucharita's mind.

Thus day by day Haran had been losing his glamour before Pareshbabu's family. Although Baradasundari did not fall behind Haranbabu in her enthusiasm to maintain the line of distinction between the Brahmo and non-Brahmo, and though she too found many a cause for embarrassment in her husband's conduct, still she did not consider Haranbabu an ideal man either. She in fact noticed many blemishes in Haranbabu.

Although day by day Sucharita's mind was turned more and more against Haranbabu, thanks to his oppressive communal enthusiasm and withering narrowness, still neither of the parties had any uncertainty regarding the marriage. When someone displays in the market of a 'religio-society' a high price tag printed in very large letters upon himself others also eventually come to believe in its preciousness. That is why Haranbabu, and for that matter, none other, had the least doubt that once Haranbabu, following his noble commitment, approved Sucharita after appropriate examinations everybody would accept it in grateful humble assent. Even Pareshbabu too did not think of contesting Haranbabu's claim in this matter. All thought of Haranbabu as the prospective leader and prop of Brahmosamaj, and he too did not question it. Indeed, he was worried by the anxiety whether Sucharita could be sufficiently suitable for a man of Haranbabu's stature; it never occurred to him to probe if Haranbabu could be desirable for Sucharita.

As nobody thought it quite necessary to consider Sucharita's feelings on the issue of this marriage, Sucharita herself too did not think otherwise. Like all others of the community she too took it for granted that the day Haranbabu came out with the announcement, 'I am ready to receive this girl', she too would at once accept this marriage as her noble duty.

Things were going on this way. Then Gora came and from the tone of the little bits of the heated exchange between Haranbabu and Sucharita on the occasion, that reached Paresh's ears, he gathered that perhaps Sucharita did not sufficiently respect Haranbabu; perhaps there were some deeper reasons behind their difference. That is why at Baradasundari's insistence for the marriage he could not respond as he used to do in the past.

The very same day Baradasundari took Sucharita apart and complained, 'It seems you have been worrying your father!'

Sucharita was startled; nothing could be more painful to her than giving cause for anxiety to Pareshbabu. Turning pale she asked, 'Why do you say this, *Mā*? What have I done?'

Baradasundari. How do I know, girl! He has the feeling that you do not like Panubabu. All in the community know that your marriage with Panubabu is as good as settled—now, in this situation, if you—

Sucharita. But *Mā*, I have never mentioned anything about this to anybody.

Sucharita had reasons to be surprised. True that she had been annoyed again and again by Haranbabu's behaviour, but never for once did it occur to her to reconsider the idea of this proposed marriage. The thought—if this marriage should make her happy or not—simply did not occur to her; because, she had all along assumed that this marriage was not to be considered in terms of happiness or unhappiness.

Then she remembered that she had clearly expressed her annoyance with Panubabu that evening in the presence of Pareshbabu. She felt guilty at the thought that this had worried him. Never before did she react with such lack of restraint; she resolved not to repeat such a thing in future.

In the meantime the very same day Haranbabu too arrived before long. He too felt restless. So long he was confident that Sucharita worshipped him. The offerings of this worship could be more complete though, if Sucharita had not nursed an absurd instinctive blind devotion to the old man. Even though he could point out the various deficiencies of Pareshbabu, Sucharita still continued to look up to the old man as if he were a deity incarnate. Haranbabu had silently laughed at this, resented too, but hoped that eventually with appropriate chance he should be able to redirect this misled devotion into the right channel. Anyway, so long as Haranbabu assumed himself the object of Sucharita's admiration, he continuously criticized her action and conduct in every small matter and was engaged in moulding her in the right shape by means of endless instructions; he did not make any clear offer of marriage. That evening, at a few utterances of Sucharita, it suddenly flashed upon his mind that Sucharita had started criticizing him, and after this it became difficult for him to retain the posture of inviolate reserve and poise. In the meantime the few occasions when they met did not allow him to feel or express self-glory as before. His speech and behaviour with Sucharita were marked by an element of acrimony. He has been fastidious at finding faults on small or no excuses. He had to acknowledge defeat to himself at Sucharita's unperturbed indifference to all this, and repent at leisure at this loss of his self-prestige.

Anyway, after observing one or two symptoms of disrespect on the part of Sucharita, it became difficult for him to stick to his posture of the examiner for long. Previously he did not use to visit the family so frequently; lest people suspect that he had been restive with love, Haranbabu used to come only once a week, and maintained his gravity as if Sucharita was his disciple. But, who knows what has happened in the last few days—Haranbabu has been knocking more than once a day on any small excuse—and has been trying to enforce his presence on Sucharita on even smaller excuses. During this period Pareshbabu too thus got the chance to watch them closely and his misgivings thickened.

As soon as Haranbabu arrived today Baradasundari took him aside and asked, 'Well, Panubabu, everybody says you will marry our Sucharita. But I never hear any mention of it by you. If you do really have some such intention then why don't you come out with it in so many words?'

Haranbabu could not let it go. Indeed he was now eager to capture Sucharita somehow—the test of her regard for him or her suitability for benefiting the Brahmosamaj could wait for some later time. Haranbabu replied therefore, 'I did not speak out because that needed no saying. I was just waiting for Sucharita to be eighteen.'

Baradasundari said, 'I must say you are a bit too fussy. We, on our part, believe fourteen is enough.'

During tea that evening Pareshbabu was taken aback at Sucharita's behaviour. Indeed it had been long since Sucharita paid such attention to Haranbabu. And when Haranbabu was about to leave, she even requested him to stay on a little while for having a look at some new piece of handicraft by Labanya.

Pareshbabu was relieved. He thought he had been mistaken earlier. He was even amused a little at the thought that it was just a lovers' tiff between the two for some unknown reason and now it was over.

That evening before taking his leave Haran broached the proposal of marriage before Pareshbabu. He told Paresh in so many words that he did not want to delay it any longer.

Pareshbabu was a bit surprised, 'But don't you maintain that it was wrong to marry girls before they reached eighteen. In fact, you have even gone in print regarding this your opinion.'

Haranbabu said, 'This does not apply to Sucharita; because she has attained such mental maturity which may not be found even in an elderly woman.'

Pareshbabu asserted with a quiet firmness, 'Let it be. Since there is no apparent problem in waiting, we should wait till Radharani reaches the appropriate age according to your declared opinion.'

Haranbabu was ashamed at having disclosed his own weakness, and said, 'Of course, of course. My only wish is to confirm the engagement in the name of God, and in the presence of all.'

Pareshbabu agreed, 'That's a fine idea.'

17

On waking up after two to three hours of sleep Gora saw Binoy was still sleeping by his side, and his heart was filled with joy. Gora had the feeling of one who had lost something dear in dream and then waking up finds it has not been lost. Today, seeing Binoy by him on waking up, Gora realized how crippled his life would be if he had to shut out Binoy. The joy of the realization made him restless and he noisily pulled Binoy out of sleep, calling, 'Come along, we have some work there.'

Every morning Gora had a regular appointment. He used to visit the homes of the low-caste people in the area. It was not for doing some good turn or showering advices—he just went to meet these people. He had no such social relation with the elite.

They used to address Gora as '*Dādāthākur*' and welcomed him with the offer of a special hookah. It was just to honour this reception that Gora had forced himself to take tobacco.

Among this team Nanda was Gora's first disciple. Nanda was the son of a carpenter. He was just twenty-two. Nanda used to help his father at his shop by making wooden boxes. Among the hunting party at the marsh of Dhapa Nanda had no peer in rifle-shooting. In the cricket field too he was the top bowler.

In his hunting party and cricket team Gora had included these children of blacksmiths and carpenters alongside the upperclass boys. In this mixed team Nanda was the topper in all sorts of sports and exercises. Some of the upperclass boys were envious, but under Gora's ruling all had to accept Nanda as the team leader.

For the last few days Nanda was absent from the playground owing to a leg injury caused by an accidental slip of the hammer. Since Gora was not in the right shape of mind because of his problems with Binoy in the last few days, he had not been able to inquire about Nanda. This morning he lost no time and at once arrived at the carpenters' colony along with Binoy.

Before they reached Nanda's house they could hear the wailing of women. Neither Nanda's father nor any other male guardian was to be seen around. There was a tobacco shop by the house; the shopowner came out to inform, 'Nanda died this morning, they have gone for his last rites.'

Nanda dead! Such excellent health, such strength, such courage, such a wonderful heart, and so young—Nanda died this morning! Astounded, Gora stood motionless. Nanda was the son of a mere carpenter. The small gap caused briefly by his death would be noticed by few. But to Gora this morning Nanda's death appeared horribly unreasonable, absurd, unbelievable. Did he not see how full of life the boy was! So many people were alive; but where was the one with that overflowing abundance of life!

On inquiring they were told Nanda died of titanus. Nanda's father wanted to call a doctor, but Nanda's mother insisted that her son was under the spell of some evil spirit. Through the whole night the witch-doctor had burnt holes into the body, beaten up the poor boy and chanted mantras. At the start of the attack Nanda had once requested to send for Gora—but lest Gora should insist on medical treatment, Nanda's mother did not allow them to inform Gora.

On the way back Binoy said, 'What enormous ignorance, and how terrible its punishment!'

Gora burst out, 'Binoy, don't seek any consolation by condemning this ignorance and thinking you're above it. If you could perceive the terrible degree of the enormity of this ignorance and its punishment, you wouldn't have tried to dismiss it just by that one exclamation of yours.'

In proportion to the growing excitement Gora's footsteps quickened every minute. Without answering Binoy applied his energy to catch up, while Gora continued, 'The entire race has surrendered to falsehood. So many kinds of fear—fear of gods, demons, evil spirit, fear about sneezing, about Thursdays, about planetary positions, and what not—have trampled them down. How can they know how to face truth and with what courage! You and I—the moment we have read one or two pages of the science book—assume that we are of a different category. But take it for sure—when things all around you are pulling downwards—just a few people cannot survive by means of their bookish knowledge. So long as this vast mass does not come to believe in the rule of natural laws, so long as they remain vulnerable to false fears, our elite too will not be able to outgrow its influence.'

Binoy said, 'Even if the elites succeed how does it matter! How many are educated? It is not for the sake of the elite that others have to be uplifted—rather it is the effort to uplift the rest that should constitute the glory of the elite's education.'

Gora took Binoy's hand, 'That is precisely what I want to say. But with your pride in genteel status and education you can isolate yourself from the common people and rest happily thereafter—I have seen it so many times. That's why I want to warn you all that unless you rescue the people below, you can't survive either. If there is hole in the keel of the boat the mast cannot hold for long, however highly it may have been placed.'

Without answering Binoy walked alongside Gora.

Gora fell silent for a while and then suddenly exclaimed, 'No Binoy, I cannot give in so easily. When I think of that witch-doctor, the scoundrel who sneaked in and tortured my Nanda to death,—Oh Binoy, I cry out in misery—it is my suffering, it is the suffering of my whole country. I cannot view these things as small isolated events by any means.'

Still finding no response from Binoy Gora burst out, 'Binoy, I can very well read your mind. You are thinking there is no remedy to this, or even if there is one it will take long to arrive. You are thinking,—Oh this Himalayan weight of fear and falsehood trampling the whole of India—who can move it by an inch even! But I cannot think that way. How could I live if I thought that way. I believe whatever be hitting my country, however strong the attack is, there must be some remedy as well,—and it is with us that the remedy lies, in our own hands. It is only this firm belief in my mind that enables me to bear so much misery-degradation-humiliation around us.

Binoy said, 'I don't have the courage to hold on to my faith in the face of such enormous immeasurable pervasive misery.'

Gora said, 'Darkness is vast and the flicker of the lamp is small. I place greater trust in that small flicker over and above the vast darkness. I cannot accept by any means that misery will be eternal. I feel all the energy of knowledge, of life from the vast world is continuously striking it from both outside and inside. However, small we may be individually, we must stand by that force of knowledge, of life. If we die as result, we shall die with the certitude that it is our force that will overcome. I won't accept the stagnation of my country as the most powerful insurmountable reality upon which to spread my bedroll and repose. You know what I always say—reposing your trust in devil and fearing ghosts amount to the same thing; both result in the same inertia against proper treatment of the disease. The ignorant fear and the ignorant witch-doctor kill us equally. Binoy, I am telling you again and again, never for a single moment think it impossible that our country will be free one day, that ignorance will not keep coiling round our neck like python, and the British will not be able to drag her in chains behind its trade-ship for ever. Holding on firmly to this vision in our mind we have to get ready right now. On what uncertain date in what unknown future the freedom struggle of India may be launched—reposing your responsibility on that flimsy anticipation you lie relaxed. Now take it from me,—the struggle has started, it is going forward every moment; if you can remain unconcerned at this hour, nothing can be worse cowardice than that.'

Binoy said, 'Look here Gora. The basic difference between you and the rest is that the things which take place daily in the streets and squares around us, and indeed have been taking place for ages, strike you everyday as something remarkable. We take these casually, without being conscious, just as we go about without being conscious of our own breathing—these do neither encourage us, nor dishearten. Neither do we have joy in them, nor grief. Day after day pass by in vacuity; we do not get the least feel of ourselves or of our country in the life flowing by us.'

Suddenly Gora's face turned crimson, the veins on the forehead swelled up—clenching his two fists he chased a carriage in the middle of the street while startling people along the road with thunderous roar: 'Stop! Stop it, I say!' A fat babu, dangling a gold watch from golden chains, who was atop the carriage, just turned once and lashed the pair of strong horses to disappear within a minute.

An old Musalman was going along the road towards the kitchen of some English boss, carrying a cane basket of fruits, vegetables, eggs, bread, butter and such other edibles on his head. The chain-dangling babu had shouted to him to make way for his carriage. As the old man could not hear, the carriage stumbled almost upon his neck. Death was marginally averted, but the basket along with its contents rolled down on the road, and the angry babu, coming back to the coach-box, lashed out on the old man's face, while shouting, 'the damn'd swine!' Instantly a line of blood appeared on the forehead. The old man said, 'Allah!', heaved a sigh and turned to recover the articles that were not completely spoiled and gather them back in the basket. Gora came back to collect the scattered things himself and replace in the basket. The Muslim porter was deeply embarrassed at this manner of a gentleman passer-by; he pleaded, 'Why do you take so much trouble, Babu? This will come to no use.'

Gora knew the uselessness of his gesture, and also understood the man being so helped was himself ashamed at it—indeed, considered in material terms this sort of assistance was practically useless. But somebody had been nastily insulted by a 'gentleman', and another gentleman was trying to reach out to him as man to man and thus somehow restore a minimum sense of fairness to humanity; how could a man in the street understand such subtleties? When the basket was refilled Gora invited him, 'I can understand compensating the damage is beyond you. Come along to my house, I shall buy the whole lot at full price. But, Baba, allow me to tell you one thing—you bore with the insult without a single word of protest, and Allah won't forgive you for this.

The old man was surprised, 'It is for Allah to punish the guilty, why should He punish me?'

Gora said, 'One who fails to protest against wrong is also guilty; because, by his acquiescence he helps crime. You perhaps do not follow me, but still remember humility is not the last word in religion. It can help the evil to flourish. Your Mohammed knew this, that's why he didn't pretend to be a soft man while preaching his religion.

Since Gora's house was not close to the spot he took the old man to Binoy's apartment. Standing before Binoy's safe he commanded, 'Give me some money.'

Binoy said, 'Why are you getting so worked up? Take your seat, I am giving him the money.'

Then suddenly he failed to trace the key. Gora in his impatience pulled at the handle and the creaky safe opened at once to expose a large group photograph of the whole family of Pareshbabu. Binoy had collected this from his young friend Satish.

Gora took out the money, sent off the old man with it, but made no mention of the photograph. As Gora remained mum on the subject Binoy too could not raise the issue—yet he would have felt relieved if there were some exchange.

Suddenly Gora said, 'Bye.'

Binoy remonstrated at once, 'Bah! How can you go alone! *Mā* has asked me to lunch at your place. Therefore, I too come along.'

The two came out into the street. For the rest of the walk Gora said nothing. The photograph in the desk again jolted Gora into remembering that a main stream of Binoy's mind was now following a particular course which had no relevance in Gora's life. An unexpressed apprehension—that eventually the original stream of friendship may wither up with the main stream taking that other course—oppressed Gora like some undefinable weight crushing the deepest core of his heart. So long there had been no separate spheres of thought or activity that could divide the two; now it was growing difficult to retain that empathy. Binoy was turning an individual in a sphere of his own.

Binoy could read Gora's sudden lapse into silence. But he felt shy to interfere and forcibly push down this barrier of silence. Binoy himself felt that it was a real barrier before which Gora came to halt.

On reaching home they found Mahim at the door watching the road. Seeing the two comrades he said, 'What's the matter! Last night you had no sleep—I had been wondering in case you had been snatching some sweet sleep on the roadside footpath. Already it's quite late in the day. Come along, Binoy, go in and finish your bath.'

Sending Binoy off for bath Mahim himself engaged Gora, 'Look here Gora. Consider once again what I had been telling you the other day. If you disapprove of Binoy for not being orthodox enough, then please tell me where to find the right up-to-the-mark Hindu bridegroom in the market these days? What am I to do with a pure Hindu unless there's a touch of education! Indeed the mixture of Hinduism and education—

though not strictly in accordance with the scriptural dictates—is not bad either. I think if you had a daughter of your own, you would have come to see eye to eye with me in this regard.'

Gora said, 'Yes, indeed, why not? I don't think Binoy will object.'

Mahim was exultant, 'Hear, hear! Who cares about Binoy's objection? All my anxiety is about your objection. You just request Binoy once, I want nothing more. If that does not work then nothing else will.'

Gora said, 'O.K.'

Mahim thought to himself, 'Now I can safely place my order with the caterers for the feast.'

In course of the day Gora broached the topic, 'Binoy, Dada has been insisting so much for marrying Shashimukhi to you. Now, what do you suggest?'

Binoy. Let me know first what do *you* wish?

Gora. If you ask me I would say—not a bad idea.

Binoy. But in the past you would find it bad. Didn't we more or less agree that both of us should remain bachelors?

Gora. Now let us agree you'll marry while I won't.

Binoy. May I ask why? Why this bifurcation of courses after starting off together?

Gora. This arrangement is being made particularly to prevent that prospect. God creates some to be weighed down with responsibility, while some others are born to be light—if these two have to be yoked together, then the latter one is to be made heavier with extra weight imposed from outside. If you become a bit heavier with responsibility through marriage, then we two will be able to step together.

Binoy smiled a little and said, 'If that is the idea then you may put the weight on this side of the balance.'

Gora. Are you sure that you have no objection about the particular weight in this case?

Binoy. If balancing is the aim then you can use whatever you may lay your hands on; be it a chunk of stone, or a clod of earth, as you like it.

Binoy had no doubt about the reason behind Gora's interest in this marriage. Binoy smiled to himself at guessing Gora's apprehension that he might one of these days marry some girl of Pareshbabu's family. But the thought of such a resolve or even the possibility had never for once occurred to him. It was so impossible. Anyway, once he marries Shashimukhi such apprehensions will be completely weeded out, and thereby their normal, healthy friendship will be restored; furthermore he will have no reasons for any hesitation regarding his social interaction with Pareshbabu's family. Thinking this way Binoy readily gave his consent to the proposal of marriage with Shashimukhi.

After lunch they had to compensate for the deficit of sleep last night, and thus the day was over before the two friends could have another round of talk. At last the time came when at the fall of the dark curtain over the visible world another curtain lifts between lovers. At such a time, sitting on floor of the roof, Binoy looked up straight to the sky, and started talking: 'Listen, Gora. I want to tell you one thing. I have a feeling that there is a serious shortcoming in our patriotism. We see only half of the country.'

Gora. Why do you say so?

Binoy. We envision Bharatbarsha as a land of males only; women do not seem to exist in our perception.

Gora. Do you want to see women as the British do—at home and in the world outside, on land, water and in air, in work, pleasure and entertainment, everywhere? Of course as result of such a desire you will notice the women more than men—and thereby lose the balance of perception as well.

Binoy. Oh no, you must not trivialize my argument. What is the point of dragging in the analogy of the British? Can you deny that we do not give due consideration to the place of women in our country? For example, you—I can claim you never for a moment think about women—as if your country is an exclusive zone for men where women don't exist. This kind of approach never helps to arrive at the truth.

Gora. Since the day I have seen my mother, have known my mother, I have also seen and known all the women of my country as her replica.

Binoy. That is your self-delusion; you have persuaded yourself to think that you believe in this deliberately imagined notion. When women are merely seen as negligible objects within the four walls of domestic life and work exclusively amidst family members, it is not a proper perspective to see them. If we could envision them beyond our daily mundane domestic need then we could get a glimpse of the beauty and completeness of our country; we could envision the country in terms of such exquisite beauty for which sacrificing one's life should seem worthwhile. I know you'll flare up this moment if I draw an analogy from the British society—so I won't do that. Indeed I don't claim to know the exact limits, extent, or border line—how far and in what form women should come out in our society so that their dignity is not impaired. Anyway, you must admit that our system of pushing women behind the purdah has been responsible for our lack of a true vision of India—it remains only half of the truth which cannot energise us with the fullness of love and strength.

Gora. How come that you happened to stumble across this wisdom only recently and suddenly, if I may ask?

Binoy. Yes, indeed I have discovered this truth only recently and only by a sudden stroke of luck. Prior to this I didn't know how magnificent this truth was. I really consider myself blessed that this has been revealed to me at last. As we see the farmer in terms of his farm work, or the weaver in terms of his weaving we ignore them as lowly people, they do not appear as complete individuals to our perception—and this separation of the 'lowly' from the 'genteel' folk has only weakened the country. In exactly the same way we keep our women yoked to cooking-grinding and domestic chores and then contemptuously look down upon them as some very insignificant creatures—with the result that the country itself becomes reduced to insignificance in our mind.

Gora. As day and night mark the two divisions of time, so do the male and female constitute two compartments of the society. In a normal society women should be invisible like night—all her activities remaining invisible, obscure, private. We keep the night out of our working hours. But that does not mean the job of the night is less important. From behind the curtain of sleep she invisibly compensates for the loss we suffer during the day, helps to regain energy through nourishment. In an unnatural situation society forces the night to mimic the day, machines are run in gas light, nightlong carnivals are held in candle light. But what does all this lead to? As a result the natural intimate activity of night is affected, fatigue mounts, loss suffered during the day is not compensated, man grows wild. In the same way if we drag women out into the public spheres of activity then the system of their intimâte private operation is impaired—it leads to the collapse of peace and well-being of the society, yielding place to excitement. Initially that excitement may delude you as strength, but that strength leads only to destruction. Energy can be seen in its two aspects: manifest and unexpressed; enterprise and rest; application and restraint. If you disturb this balance of energy, it becomes wild and that wildness brings no good. Man and woman are the two faces of this social energy. Of course it is the male who is vocal, though that should not mean he is magnificent; woman is silent. Now if this silent energy continuously tries to secure voice, that would lead to a self-consuming process which in its turn will leave the society bankrupt in no time. That is why I prefer to stick to the opinion—let us, the men, perform the *yagna* in public fora, while the women guard the storeroom. Then the *yagna* will be performed without a hitch even if women remain invisible. Those who want to engage all forms of energy in the same direction and on the same cause, are just mad.

Binoy. Gora, I don't want to counter your remarks. But neither have you countered my logic. The real thing—.

Gora. Look here Binoy, if we carry on this way it will end up in a quarrel. I admit I have not grown so sensitive and conscious about women as you have recently—therefore if you try to make me feel what you have felt yourself, you stand no chance of success. So why don't we agree to differ on the issue?

Gora thus dismissed the point. But, as the seed—be it blown along by the wind or thrown away in a casual fling—eventually lands on the earth, and once it falls on the earth sprouting is a matter of time. So far Gora had kept women quite at bay from his life. Never even in dream did he feel this to be a lack or loss. At seeing the recent change in Binoy he realized for the first time the reality of women's existence and impact in one's life. But he is still confused regarding its role or place—that's why he does not like to be drawn into debate with Binoy on the subject. He cannot altogether ignore it, nor can he fully comprehend it—and so he prefers to keep it outside the pale of their discussion.

As Binoy was about to leave after dinner Anandamoyee took him aside and asked, 'Binoy, is it true that your marriage with Shashimukhi has been finalised?'

Binoy blushed, 'Yes *Mā*—Gora is the match-maker behind this auspicious agreement.'

Anandamoyee said, 'Shashimukhi is a nice girl—but still you must remember my son, this is no child's play. I can read your mind Binoy—It is because you are mentally a bit disturbed that you have so hastily decided on the matter. There is still time for reconsidering. You are now grown up. Please don't take such a vital decision so casually.

Saying this she ran her hand on Binoy's face and arms affectionately. Binoy slowly walked away without a word.

18

While walking homewards Anandamoyee's affectionate words followed him. Never before did Binoy ignore a single plea or command from Anandamoyee. That night he seemed to feel a weight on his mind.

Waking up next morning, however, he got the feeling of a great relief. He felt that he had paid off a great price for Gora's friendship and thus his account with Gora was settled. On the one hand by agreeing to marry Shashimukhi he had accepted a life-long bondage, and in exchange had gained a sort of freedom in another direction. Gora had indulged in the very unfair suspicion that Binoy was about to desert society for the lure of marrying into a Brahmo family; Binoy had bailed himself out from this unfair suspicion by offering marriage to Shashimukhi as his life-long ransom. After this Binoy began to visit Paresh's house frequently, and without any compunction or constraint.

It was no problem for Binoy to get chummy with people he liked. Now that he got over his compunctions related to Gora, he became close to Pareshbabu's family within a few days and was before long accepted by all the members as another member of the family.

Only Lalita was hostile to Binoy initially for those few days when she had a hunch that perhaps Sucharita's mind was a bit inclined towards Binoy. But when she was convinced that Sucharita had no special partiality for Binoy she too got over her rebelliousness and felt quite comforted; she had indeed no hesitation to accept Binoy as an extraordinary human being.

Even Haranbabu had no reservation against Binoy—rather he conceded, almost emphatically, that Binoy was a polite man. The obvious suggestion behind such admission was that Gora was not so.

Binoy never raised any controversial issue in Haran's presence—Sucharita too saw to that—thus Binoy's presence caused no storm in the tea-cups at Pareshbabu's table.

But in Haran's absence Sucharita herself drew Binoy into discussions on social issues. She could never get over her wonder at the fact that Gora and Binoy, in spite their education, continued to support the age-old superstitions of the society; how indeed could they? If she did not know Gora and Binoy, and if somebody else held these opinions she would have dismissed them as contemptible. But since she had seen Gora she could by no means dismiss this man from her thoughts with contempt. So, at every chance she steered her talk with Binoy to the subject of Gora's thoughts and life, and by her tone of protest provoked Binoy to speak out at length. Pareshbabu believed right education came from listening to the opinions of all communities; therefore he felt no worry at such discussion nor did he try to stop them.

One day Sucharita asked Binoy, 'Well, can you tell me if Gaurmohanbabu really believes in the caste system or is it an exaggerated expression of his patriotism?'

Binoy replied, 'Do you accept the steps in your staircase? Those too indicate division—some being higher, some lower.'

Sucharita. That has to be accepted for going up; otherwise it was unnecessary. If it is on the same plane then steps are redundant.

Binoy. You are perfectly right. Our society is a staired system; it had a purpose,—to help a movement upwards—to lead human life to some ulterior goal. If I took family and society as the ultimate end then no division was necessary—and we could go along in the competitive spirit that is so fiercely operative in the European societies. The fittest survive, and the unsuccessful get lost. It is because we want to overcome this earthly life by means of passing through it, that we have not founded our daily duties on the basis of desire and competition; we have seen our daily duties as part of religion, since our ultimate goal is not success through work, but liberation of the spirit. Therefore, taking into account our daily duties on the one hand and their ultimate goal on the other, our society has instituted the system of caste or professional division.

Sucharita. I am afraid I do not get you very clearly. Anyway I would like to know one thing: you claim some purpose behind the caste system; do you think that purpose has been achieved?

Binoy. It is very difficult to recognize the manifest form of success on this earth. The success that the ancient Greece achieved is no longer there now. But can we say that all the ideas of Greece therefore were wrong and futile? India had addressed the problem of social divisions by its caste system; that solution has not yet died out; it is still there before the world. Europe too has not yet been able to address its social problems satisfactorily; fierce competition is going on there. The solution offered by India is still awaiting a trial by mankind. Don't assume that it will be thrown to the winds just because we seek to dismiss it in our narrow communal blindness. We, the small communities, will disappear in due course like drops of water in the ocean; but this immense solution that has risen from the innate genius of India will stand like a rock till its purpose is served.

Sucharita asked a little shyly, 'Don't take it otherwise, but do you really believe all this from your heart, or are you just echoing Gaurmohanbabu?'

Binoy smiled, 'I must admit to you I do not have his strength of conviction. When I perceive the nastiness of caste division and perversions of society I frequently have my doubts. But Gora says, it is the wrong perspective that is the source of distrust—taking broken twigs and withered leaves for the real tree is the evidence of impatient intelligence—I don't tell you to admire broken branches, but try to envision the great tree as a whole and understand its significance.'

Sucharita. Well, let us agree to ignore the dry leaves. But what about the fruit? What has been the fruit or result of the caste system for our country?

Binoy. What you call the result of caste division is but the result of the particular situation. It pains if you chew with the loose tooth; it is not the fault of teeth as such, but of the particular loose tooth. Because various perversions and infirmities have set in thanks to many a reason, we have distorted India's ideals instead of realizing them. But the ideas are not necessarily accountable for this distortion. All this will be cured once we acquire abundant health and energy. That is why Gora says again and again, 'you cannot chop off the head in order to get over headache—you have to be healthy, to be strong'.

Sucharita. Does it follow then that you want us to bow down before the Brahmins as demigods? Do you really believe that by touching the dust on a Brahmin's feet one gets blessed or sanctified?

Binoy. Is it not true that many of the notions of honour in this world are but subjective? So long as the king is relevant people look upon him as someone extraordinary. Yet, actually the king is but just another human. Yet it is his compulsion to surmount his ordinariness and emerge as an extraordinary icon; otherwise he cannot rule. It is we who create this extraordinary image of the king so that we can get from him the right kind of rule—the king has to honour our demand of acting honourably, he has to evolve into extraordinariness. This make-believe is there in all human relationships. Even the ideal of parenthood that we have agreed to set up goes a long way to make the parents act parent-like; mere natural affection would not have been enough. In a joint family an elder brother accommodates and sacrifices a lot for the sake of the younger brother—why does he do this? It is because our society had made '*Dādā*' a very special elder brother, which is not found in other societies. Similarly if we can make the born Brahman evolve into a Brahman in the real sense of the term isn't it a great benefit for the society? We want demi-gods; if we can desire a demi-god intelligently and sincerely we will get him; if we desire him foolishly, mechanically, then it will be only adding up to the demons who indulge in all sort of criminal misdeeds, and sustain themselves by getting on our heads with dirty feet.

Sucharita. This demi-god of yours—does it really exist anywhere?

Binoy. It is there—as the tree is there in the seed—within the deep longings and needs of India. Whereas other countries celebrate generals like Wellington, scientists like Newton, millionaires like Rothchild, our country wants Brahman,—such a Brahman who does not fear, hates greed, conquers suffering, does not fear poverty, who is the supreme yogi, unperturbable, quiet, free—India celebrates that Brahman—India can win her freedom only when she has that kind of Brahmanas. We want the Brahman not just for cooking or ringing the *puja* bell,—we want him to provide the right tune of fulfillment to every division of work in society, we want him to represent the manifest form of fulfilled society. The honour of Brahman will rise proportionately with our respect for this ideal of Brahmanism. That honour is far higher than the honour of the king. It is reverence that gods deserve. When the Brahman in our country evolves to deserve that status no one will dare to insult our country. Is it the king before whom we kneel? Is it the oppressor whose collar we hang around the neck? Our heads are bowed down before our own fear, we are enmeshed in the trap of our own greed, we are the bondslaves to our own stupid ignorance. Let the Brahman do his *tapasyā,* and liberate us from the fear, greed, stupidity. We don't want help from him in war, in commerce, in any other need; let him only realize the pursuit of truth in the heart of the society.

So long Pareshbabu had been listening silently. Now he slowly said, 'I cannot say I know India. I am sure I don't know what India had really aspired after and whether she had ever attained it. But can we ever go back to the times which are now gone? We should pursue what is possible, attainable in the present times. Is it any use wasting your time by reaching out to the past?'

Binoy said, 'I have also thought like that as you say; have also expressed my doubts. But Gora says, is it 'past' just because we have stamped it that way and thrown to the bins. It is not 'past' merely because it eludes our ken, thanks to the sound and fury of the uproarious present, it is flowing in our veins. That's why its truth has started to hit us. If even a single one among us recognizes and accepts it as truth it will open doors for us into immense resources of strength, the storehouse of the past will become the most useful house for the present. Do you think such a man has not been born anywhere in India?'

Sucharita said, 'The way you have been putting it is not the common man's perception. So they feel hesitant to accept your ideas as the opinion of the whole country.'

Binoy continued, 'Look here, the phenomenon of sunrise is explained by the scientists in one way; again common people explain it in other ways. It does not affect the sun's rising. Of course, it is always desirable to know the truth. The truth of the country appears in our vision in fragmented pieces; Gora can see them as an integrated whole, Gora has that strange gift of vision. How can we assume that his is the confused vision whereas our fragmented perception is the right one?'

Sucharita remained silent. Binoy said, 'Please don't take my friend Gora as just another proud Hindu snob, the kind we find so abundant around us. If you saw his father Krishnadayalbabu you would have known the difference between father and son. Krishnadayalbabu is always anxiously busy with the job of keeping himself sanctified by means of changing clothes, spraying Gangawater, consulting almanac and other strictures. Regarding cooking he does not trust a Brahmin even with the best pedigree, lest there be some flaw in the cook's lineage. He does not allow Gora within the periphery of his living room. In case he has to enter his wife's suite he would perform self-cleansing rites afterwards. He carefully tiptoes on this dusty world, lest knowingly or unknowingly he is touched by the contamination of rules-breaking. It is like some super-fop Babu who is ever busy to avoid sun, evade dust, and somehow maintain the shine of his complexion, the curl of hair, the creaseless suit. Gora is not at all like this. Not that he disrespects the conduct-rules of Hinduism, but he does not follow them so fastidiously. He looks at Hinduism from inside and as something much more vast and magnificent. He never holds that it is something as fragile as to wither up at the slightest touch, or fall dead to the least blow.'

Sucharita. But he himself appears to obey these 'touch-don't touch' strictures quite meticulously.

Binoy. Yes. It is a strange fastidiousness in his case. If asked he would instantly retort, 'Yes. I believe all this. Losing caste through touch, or committing sin through eating—all these are indisputably right.' But I am sure this is only a facade; the more irrational the idea is the louder bangs his emphatic voice. Lest rejection of the least item of *Hinduānī* leads to dishonour of its noble aspects by foolish people and those who are irreverent to *Hinduānī* consider it a triumph, Gora prefers to observe all the rules without question—he does not want to betray any sign of laxity even before me.

Pareshbabu said, 'This kind of people is there among the Brahmos too. They seek to reject *Hinduānī*—lock, stock and barrel, lest any outsider mistakes that they are carrying on some residual features of *Hinduānī*. Such people are never easy in their ways; either they pretend or they overdo; they assume truth is too fragile a thing and it is part of their duty to defend truth by force or trick. Those who think—"Truth depends on me, I don't depend on truth", are called orthodox. Those who trust in the strength of truth restrain their own imposition towards strengthening truth. It is a small loss if outsiders fail to understand you for some time. It involves much greater loss if you fail to recognize and accept truth under duress of some petty consideration. I always pray to God that I may be able to humbly kneel and surrender before truth anywhere and everywhere—be it at the prayer-meeting of Brahmosamaj or in the Hindu temple; let no external obstacle stand in my way to this acceptance.'

Saying this Paresh fell silent and seemed to probe within his own mind. These few words uttered in his mild voice imparted a noble tuning to the whole discussion. The melody derived not from the mere words, but from some deep inner peace that informed the music of Paresh's own life. The expression of Sucharita and Lalita became radiant for a moment with the luminosity of a joyous devotion. Binoy fell silent. He too knew deep within himself that there was an element of oppressiveness in Gora's conviction—that Gora lacked the unstrained, simple peace which should be there in the messiahs of truth. Listening to Pareshbabu, once again the realization came back to him with all the force. True, Binoy had so long tried to persuade himself in support of Gora's stand by the logic that when a society was in turmoil, when clash with the outside world was imminent, then the crusaders of truth cannot afford to retain norms—then truth may also suffer some damage at the onslaught of the moment's need. Today, listening to Paresh a doubt flashed through his mind; if it was normal for ordinary people to compromise on truth under the temptation of serving momentary needs, then was his Gora too of the same category? Was Gora too just another ordinary human?

When Sucharita retired at night Lalita came to sit at the end of her bed. Sucharita guessed Lalita was disturbed by something. She could also guess it concerned Binoy.

Sucharita therefore broached the subject herself, 'Binoybabu seems to me a quite nice person.'

Lalita. Naturally, since he speaks only about Gaurbabu. Right!

Sucharita caught the hint but did not show. She continued in an apparently innocent tone, 'Indeed you are right! I enjoy hearing about Gaurbabu from him. It seems as if I can clearly envision the man.'

Lalita. I don't enjoy at all—I feel irritable.

Sucharita was surprised, 'But why?'

Lalita burst out, 'Gora, Gora, Gora, day and night only Gora! May be his friend Gora is a big guy, O.K. let him be,—but he too should be an individual human!'

Sucharita laughed, 'Yes, of course. But what prevents him being so?'

Lalita. His friend seems to have overpowered him so much that he cannot become himself. It is like the cockroach being caught by the beetle; at such a state of things, I feel angry with the beetle, and I feel no respect for the cockroach either.

At the pungency of Lalita's remarks Sucharita could not control her laughter.

Lalita said, 'Didi, you are amused. But I tell you in so many words,—if any one tried to rule me that way I could not stand him for a single day. For example, here you are—whatever others may say, you have never dominated me—it's not in your nature—that's the reason I love you so. Actually you have got this from Baba—he allows every one his/her own space.'

Among the family members Sucharita and Lalita were the two great admirers of Pareshbabu. The very mention of 'Baba' seemed to make their heart rise in love and admiration.

Sucharita said, 'Baba! Can there be any comparison with Baba? But whatever you may say, Binoybabu is at least a fine orator.'

Lalita. It is precisely because the things he says are not his own feelings, that he can speak them so beautifully. If he expressed his own feelings he would have spoken with ease and simplicity; one would not get the idea that he was straining his imagination to speak artificially. I prefer simple genuine expression to superb artificial oratory.

Sucharita. Even so, why do you resent? It seems he has appropriated Gaurbabu's ideas as his own.

Lalita. If that is the situation then it must be quite bad; did God give us intelligence only to justify others' opinions, and gave voice only to repeat others' observations in superb language? I have no business with such superb language.

Sucharita. But why don't you understand that Binoybabu loves Gaurmohanbabu? Here's a real affinity of heart.

Lalita shook her head in impatience, 'No, no, no, there is no real affinity. It has become his habit to obey Gaurbabu—this is slavery, not love. Yet he wants to persuade himself that they are of the same opinion. That's the reason why he strains to articulate another's opinions so superbly and thereby delude himself and others. All the time he is seeking to suppress the dissent within himself lest this involves disobedience to Gaurmohanbabu. He does not have the courage to disobey him. If love is there, one can accommodate without surrendering—one can accept without being blind. This is not the case here. Perhaps he accepts Gaurmohanbabu out of love, but he won't admit this by any means. It is clear from his speeches. Well, Didi, didn't you perceive this yourself? Come on. Tell me the truth, please!'

Sucharita, in fact, did not think this way at all; because, she was eager to know about Gora; regarding Binoy she had no curiosity at all. Sucharita avoided a direct reply to Lalita's question and said instead, 'Well, let us agree—but then what is to be done?'

Lalita. I feel like making him free by releasing him from the shackles of his friend.

Sucharita. Why don't you try?

Lalita. My trying won't be enough. But you can do it easily if you so desire.

Though Sucharita could feel Binoy's fascination for her, she tried to dismiss Lalita's suggestion by laughing it away.

Lalita started again, 'I like him because he comes to surrender to you in spite of Gaurmohanbabu's guardianship.

Anyone else in his position would have written abusive plays on Brahmo girls—but he still has an open mind—that he loves you and admires Baba are the evidence. Didi, you must install the individual in him. His continuous publicity of Gaurbabu's views is beyond my endurance.'

At this point Satish rushed into the room shouting 'Didi, Didi'. Binoy had taken him to the Maidan today. Though the night had already advanced he could not wait, so excited as he was at the first experience of a circus in his life. After describing the circus he said, 'I requested Binoybabu to drop in and share my bed tonight. He had entered but then went away saying, he would come tomorrow. Didi, I have asked him to take you all to the circus one of these days.

Lalita asked, 'What was his response to your suggestion?'

Satish replied, 'He said women will get creeps at seeing the tiger. But I did not feel any fear.'

Saying this Satish puffed up his chest thus demonstrating manly pride.

Lalita said, 'Indeed! I can well guess the extent of your friend's daring. Oh Didi, he must take us to the circus.'

Satish tried to dissuade, 'But tomorrow it will be the day shift.'

Lalita said, 'All the better. O.K. We shall go to the day-shift performance.'

The following day Binoy's arrival was instantly followed by Lalita's exclamation. 'Oh Binoybabu. You are just in time. Let us start.'

Binoy. Where to, if I may ask?

Lalita. To the circus.

To the circus! Taking women to circus in broad daylight in front of a tent full of spectators! Binoy was perplexed.

Lalita innocently ventured, 'Perhaps Gaurmohanbabu may not approve.'

Binoy flushed a bit.

Lalita said again, 'I am afraid Gaurmohan may have some distinct opinion on the subject of taking women to circus.'

Binoy replied, 'Of course he has.'

Lalita. 'May I request you to explain that to us. Wait a minute, I am also bringing Didi along; she too will hear.'

Binoy laughed at this taunt. Lalita challenged, 'Why do you laugh Binoybabu? Last night you had told Satish women were scary of tiger—what are *you* scary of?'

The following day Binoy took the women to the circus. Not only that, he continued to ponder on the possible projection of his relationship with Gora in the perception of Lalita and possibly of the other girls in the family.

The first time they met after the circus Lalita, apparently in the tone of innocent curiosity, asked Binoy, 'Did you tell Gaurmohanbabu about the circus that day?'

The shot hit its target sharply; because, Binoy had to admit, while blushing from ear to ear, 'No, not yet.'

Labanya entered the room and invited Binoy, 'Oh Binoybabu, please come along.'

Lalita said, 'Whereto? Is it circus again?'

Labanya remonstrated, 'Bah! Don't you know there is no circus today? I am calling Binoybabu for drawing a border in pencil on the four sides of my kerchief. I shall embroider on it. How finely he draws!'

Labanya, led Binoy indoors.

19

Gora had been working in the morning. All of a sudden Binoy entered to make the abrupt announcement, 'I had taken Pareshbabu's daughters to the circus the other day.'

Without stopping his writing Gora said, 'I know.'

Binoy was surprised, 'How did you?'

Gora. From Abinash; he too went to the circus.

Without saying anything more Gora continued to write. So Gora knew this all the time, that too again from Abinash, thereby lacking nothing in the way of description and commentary—at this Binoy shrank within himself. He felt he would have been happy if no circus episode along with its subsequent publicity had ever taken place.

At this point he remembered last night he had a long imaginary quarrel with Lalita till he slipped into slumber. Lalita thought he was scared of Gora and obeyed him like a small schoolboy fearfully obeying his domineering teacher. How unfair to misunderstand like that! How could she know that Gora and Binoy were inseparable souls. True, he nursed a sort of admiration for Gora because of his extraordinary qualities; but the way Lalita looked at it was unfair to Gora, unfair to Binoy too. Binoy was not a minor, and nor was Gora the guardian of that minor either.

Gora wrote on silently, and the few sharp questions Lalita had hurled at him haunted Binoy; he could not just dismiss them.

Within minutes a rebellion started stirring in Binoy's mind. 'What does it matter if I go to circus? Who cares for Abinash? How does he dare to discuss me with Gora? Furthermore, why should Gora discuss my movements with that nincompoop? Am I an internee under Gora's police! Why must I justify to Gora my social interactions or my whereabouts! Is it not too much to interfere thus in the name of friendship!'

Binoy would not have been so aggrieved against Gora had he not suddenly realized his own inhibitions only too clearly. That he had to suppress something to Gora even for a little while, made him try to put Gora on the dock. If Gora had kicked up a row with him over the circus episode, that would have been within the right of equal friendship, while Binoy could also feel better. But this attitude of Gora—this show of silent contempt towards Binoy by assuming the posture of a Daniel—brought back to his mind Lalita's sharp taunts remembering which he flinched.

At this time Mahim entered the room holding his hookah. Lifting the wet cloth over his betel-box he picked up one betel leaf and offering it to Binoy started, 'Binoy, my son, it is all settled on our side. Now only one thing remains to be done—a letter from your uncle; once the letter arrives we can rest assured. Did you really remember to write to him?'

Today this kind of pressure for marriage disgusted Binoy; yet he knew Mahim was not to be blamed—it was Binoy who had promised him. But this very act of promising seemed to fill him with a sense of compunction. Wasn't it true that Anandamoyee had practically warned him against it? Neither did he himself ever feel really interested in this marriage. Then how come that the whole thing got settled so quickly amidst confusion! It could not be blamed on Gora that he had hurried him up in any way. In fact had Binoy disagreed a little bit seriously, Gora would not have insisted at all. But still—. The remembrance of Lalita's taunts did not allow him to forget this 'still'. The developments of that particular day were not so special, but at the back of it was a long history of domination. It was out of sheer love and goodness that Binoy had become used to accepting this domination as a matter of course. And that's why this domineering has eventually come to enslave friendship. So long Binoy did not feel it, but now it could not be ignored any more. Why should he be forced to marry Shashimukhi!

Binoy said, 'No, the letter to uncle is yet to be written.'

Mahim hastily rejoined, 'Indeed it is my fault. It is not your responsibility—leave it to me. Please give me the full name, sonny.'

Binoy said, 'What's the great hurry? No marriage can take place in the coming two months—*Āświn* and *Kārtik*. So there remains only *Agrahāyaṇ*, but that too will not do. Some mishap had occurred to somebody in our family in the past during *Agrahāyaṇ*; since then no auspicious ritual is performed in our family during this month.'

Carefully laying down his hookah to rest in a corner Mahim said, 'Binoy, what's the use of all your education if you persist in observing such fads. Did you just learn by rote? While already it is difficult to find an auspicious day in this damn'd country, you start introducing private almanacs for every family; how can we carry on this way?'

Binoy countered, 'Then why must you adhere to the ban on the months of *Bhadra-Aswin*?'

Mahim protested, 'I adhere! Who told you that I adhere? Never. But what can I do my son? We live in such a domain where it does not matter if you disobey God, but they will make it a hell for you if you defy these multiple bans on months and days, stars and planets, etc. Moreover, I must also admit that—although I say I don't believe in this trash, still any departure from them in practical life fills the mind with uneasiness. Like malaria the virus of fear too is in the air around us; therefore, I admit my failure to overcome fear.'

Binoy. My family too fails to overcome the fear of *Agrahāyaṇ*. At least my aunt will never agree.

Thus somehow Binoy managed to evade the issue for the time being.

Listening to the tone of Binoy's talk Gora had a hunch that Binoy was in two minds. For some days Binoy had become nearly inaccessible. Gora guessed that Binoy was going to Paresh's house more frequently than before. Then this attempt to avoid the clinching of the marriage proposal—Gora felt alarmed.

When a python starts swallowing a creature it can never stop halfway through the act. Similarly, Gora was altogether unable to leave a job halfway through, or compromise on it in any way. Any sign of resistance or laxity from the other side made him even more determined. Gora was now fully roused to hold back the wavering friend with all his strength.

Gora looked up from his writing and said, 'Binoy, since you have once promised Dada, why do you make him suffer unnecessary tension?'

Suddenly Binoy lost temper and even before Gora could finish retorted peevishly, 'Did *I* make the promise or was I pressurized to commit in a hurry?'

Gora was stunned at this unexpected gesture of rebellion from Binoy; he stiffened and asked sternly, 'What do you mean? Who pressurized you to commit?'

Binoy said, 'You.'

Gora. I! I did not exchange more than five or seven words with you on the issue. Do you call this pressurizing!

Binoy indeed had no clear evidence in favour of his accusation. Gora was right. They had spoken very little on the subject, and that too did not involve any such insistence which can be called pressurizing, or even pleading. Still it was also true that Gora somehow seemed to snatch his consent at ease. When one fails to muster enough external evidence in support of an accusation, it proportionately increases his grievance in connection with the same. Therefore, Binoy said in a tone of disproportionate anger, 'It does not take many words for forcing one's promise.'

Immediately Gora sprang up pushing the table aside and roared back, 'Here, take back your word. It is not that precious for which I can beg or rob you.'

Mahim was in the adjoining room. Gora called out to him thunderously, 'Dada!'

Mahim anxiously rushed in and Gora burst out instantly, 'Dada, didn't I tell you at the very start that Shashimukhi cannot be married to Binoy—that I don't have consent!'

Mahim. Of course you did. Who else could have said like that. Any normal uncle would have rejoiced and eagerly joined in settling his niece's marriage.

Gora. Why did you make me request Binoy?

Mahim. Just because I thought this would help; for no other reason, dear.

Gora flushed crimson and declared, 'I refuse to be bothered in any such matter. Brokery for marriage is not my vocation; I have other preoccupations.'

Saying this Gora stormed out of the room. Before the stunned Mahim could ask Binoy a thing about it Binoy too had stepped out into the street. Mahim picked up the hookah from the corner and silently drew meditative puffs of smoke.

Gora and Binoy had quarreled on many occasions in the past, but never had there been such a sudden violent explosion. Binoy was stunned at first at what he had done. Then on reaching home he became conscious of an unbearable remorse piercing his heart, as it were, from end to end. The thought that he had hurt Gora so deeply in those few minutes tormented him so much that he could not eat or sleep. He was especially mortified at realizing how completely absurd and unfair it was to blame Gora on the issue. He murmured to himself again and again, 'Unfair! Unfair! Unfair!'

Around two in the afternoon Anandamoyee had just finished her meal and settled down to her sewing when Binoy came to sit down at her feet. She had learnt a little about the morning's episode from Mahim. Seeing Gora's expression during lunch she had further confirmation of her guess—that a stormy showdown had taken place.

Binoy said at once, '*Mā*, I am guilty. The trash I have spoken to Gora this morning regarding my marriage with Shashimukhi is all nonsense.'

Anandamoyee said, 'Let it be, Binoy—when you want to suppress some pain in the mind it surfaces unexpectedly in some other direction like this. It is better that it came out. After a day or two both of you will forget today's tiff.'

Binoy. But, *Mā*, I have come specifically to tell you that I have no objection to the marriage.

Anandamoyee. My son, don't get enmeshed in some new trouble in your haste to make up for the quarrel. Marriage is a life-long affair, whereas the quarrel is but a passing phenomenon.

Binoy could not be brought to listen to any argument. He could not of course approach Gora right at the moment. Anyway he met Mahim to inform that there was no obstacle to the marriage, and it will be held in the month of Magh, and Binoy himself will see to it that his uncle does not raise any objection.

Mahim tentatively suggested, 'Then let's have the *Pānpatra* part over.'

Binoy immediately agreed, 'That's fine. But do this in consultation with Gora.'

Mahim looked anxious, 'Again consultation with Gora!'

Binoy was firm, 'No, that's a must.'

Mahim conceded, 'O.K. if it's a must it is a must, but—'; the unfinished sentence was stopped with a betel leaf he pushed into his mouth.

20

Mahim did not tell anything to Gora that day; he ventured into Gora's room the following morning. Mahim had apprehended a lot of trouble in bringing Gora back to the track. But when at last he summoned the courage to blurt it out—that Binoy had come yesterday and confirmed the engagement and asked him to consult Gora about *pānpatra*, Gora instantly assented, saying, 'O.K., let the *pānpatra* be arranged then.'

Mahim was knocked off. 'Now you say "O.K." Hope you won't give trouble again?'

Gora said, 'But I think I caused trouble by requesting rather than by opposing.'

Mahim. 'Therefore, this is my appeal to you, please do not bother either to oppose or to request. I need neither the Narayani Sena on the Kaurava side, nor Narayana in the Pandava camp. It is better to go by myself. It was my blunder indeed,—I had no idea that even your help could be so self-defeating. Anyway, I hope you approve this.'

Gora. Yes, I do.

Mahim. Then the approval is enough; but I think it is better to forego your active assistance.

True that Gora was prone to anger and could do anything under the impulse of an angry moment; but it was not his nature to ruin his own resolve by nursing that anger. He now wanted to hold back Binoy, to make him commit by any means; it was not the time for resentment. Recalling that the marriage proposal was confirmed as a consequence of yesterday's quarrel Gora felt happy at the development of the previous day. He did not wait to resume his lifelong natural bond with Binoy. But still there was a slight departure this time from their normal easy relationship.

This time Gora understood—it will be difficult to retain a remote control on Binoy, and the defence should be installed in the potentially most vulnerable zone. Gora thought to himself, 'If I start visiting Pareshbabu's house regularly I shall surely be able to keep Binoy confined within the limits.'

That very day, that is one day after the showdown, Gora appeared at Binoy's flat in the afternoon. Binoy did not expect in the least that Gora should come to him that very day. His surprise was as great as his delight. What was even more strange,—Gora himself started talking about Pareshbabu's daughters, and that too without the least acrimony. Of course Binoy did not need much encouragement for waxing eloquent on the subject.

Today Binoy told Gora about his discussions with Sucharita in detail. Binoy tried to enthuse him by describing how Sucharita herself used to raise the issues with particular eagerness, and in spite of her counter-arguments an assent was growing deep within her.

In course of their talk Binoy mentioned, 'As I had been telling her how Nanda's mother virtually killed her son by calling the witch-doctor, and about your reaction to this, she said, "You think it enough to keep women confined withindoors, and doing the daily chores of cooking, scrubbing, cleaning. On the one hand you cripple them intellectually; yet when, as consequence of that very crippling they send for the witch-doctor you do not hesitate to place the blame squarely on them. This is the irony. One can never be a complete human if one's entire world is confined to one or two families—and if women are not allowed the chance to be complete humans they are bound to undermine all the noble projects of men, and pull them downwards by their own burden; this is nature's revenge.

You have moulded Nanda's mother in such a fashion and kept her imprisoned within such a fort, that even if you want to appeal to them for the sake of your own survival the appeal won't reach its target." Although I tried hard to counter this, frankly speaking, Gora, I could not argue with conviction, because mentally I agreed with her position. Again, though it is possible to argue with her I do not dare to be drawn into a debate with Lalita. When Lalita said, "You assume you'll serve the big causes of the world, whereas we should be there to serve you! But that won't do. Either we too take up the big causes, or we shall hang round your neck like millstones. Then—when we are reduced to millstones—you denounce us, saying, *pathi nārī bibarjitā*, women must be excluded from your ventures along the paths of the wide world. But if you let the women the right to venture,—be it in the world or at home—then there remains no need to exclude women anywhere"—I kept mum. Lalita does not speak out often, but when she does one has to answer very carefully. Whatever you may say against it Gora, I have come to the firm conviction that so long our women are forced to remain cramped and crippled like the Chinese girls' feet, we shall never be able to forge ahead.'

Gora. But I never say women should not receive education.

Binoy. Yes, indeed. Teaching upto *Dhārāpāt* and *Chārupāth* should be considered enough education. Isn't it!

Gora. O.K. From now on we shall introduce *Binoybodh*, Volume One.

That day the two friends' talk repeatedly veered round the daughters of Pareshbabu till afternoon rolled into night.

On his way home Gora continued to ruminate on the subject, and even after going to bed he could not drive away the daughters of Pareshbabu from his mind until he lapsed into sleep. Such symptoms had never visited Gora in the past. He had indeed never spared a thought for women as such. That this too was one of the vital issues of life was brought home to him through Binoy. It could not to be ignored any more; either he had to sign a pact or fight it outright.

The next day Binoy suggested to Gora, 'Why don't you come along to Pareshbabu's house at least once more? It has been long since you last visited them; he frequently asks about you too.' Gora agreed instantly without any argument. Not only did he agree, he also lacked that indifference which marked his attitude so long. Initially Gora was completely indifferent to the existence of Sucharita and the daughters of Pareshbabu; subsequently he had developed a contemptuous hostility; now a new curiosity had stirred in his mind. He was particularly keen to know what attracted Binoy so strongly.

As the two reached Paresh's residence the evening had already set in. In a first-floor room Haran was reading out a piece of his English composition to Pareshbabu in the light of an oil-lamp. In fact Pareshbabu was a mere excuse—his real target was Sucharita. Sucharita was sitting at the far end of the table, silently holding a palm-leaf fan before her eyes as shade against the light. With her habitual obedience she tried to concentrate on the essay, but felt distracted again and again.

At this time the servant came to announce the arrival of Gora and Binoy; Sucharita started. She was about to rise and leave when Pareshbabu called back, 'Radhe, where are you going? It is only our Binoy and Gaur.'

Sucharita shyly sat down again. She felt relieved at this interruption to Haran's long recital of his English essay. It cannot be denied that she felt a certain excitement at the news of Gora's visit; but at the same time she felt very uneasy and uncomfortable at this appearance of Gora in the presence of Haranbabu. It is difficut to say if this was owing to the apprehension of an imminent showdown between the two, or owing to some other reason.

At the very mention of Gaur's name Haranbabu went stiff. Somehow returning his greetings briefly he sat glum and silent. On the other hand as soon as he spotted Haran Gaur's aggressive instinct was astir.

Baradasundari had been out along with her three daughters on an invitation; as per arrangement Pareshbabu was to go and bring them home. It was time for Pareshbabu to start, but he was delayed by the sudden arrival of Gora and Binoy. But, as he could not wait any more he whispered into the ears of Haran and Sucharita, 'Please sit with them for a while, I shall come back as soon as possible.'

Before long Gora and Haranbabu locked horns. The issue was as follows. During their stay at Dhaka Pareshbabu's family had come to know a British magistrate named Brownlow, who happened to be in charge of some district adjacent to Calcutta. As Pareshbabu's wife and daughters did not observe 'purdah' the Englishman and his wife held them in special regard. On his birthday every year the magistrate used to hold an agricultural fair. When Baradasundari met Mrs Brownlow last she had mentioned her daughters' skill in English language, literature, etc., at which the British lady came out with an unexpected suggestion, 'This time the Lieutenant-Governor, along with his wife, will grace the fair, and it should be very nice if your daughters present some brief verse drama in English before the guests.' Baradasundari got euphoric over the proposal. Today she took her daughters to a friend's house for rehearsal. On being asked if it should be possible for Gora to attend the fair, Gora refused with a certain degree of excessive aggressiveness, emitting a strong 'No'. This led to the issue of impediments in social interaction between the English and the Bengali in this land, and very soon it turned into a fierce debate.

Haran said, 'It is the fault of the Bengali. We carry such a junk of superstition and evil custom that we do not deserve to be socially treated at par with the English.'

Gora retorted, 'If that be the truth then it must be shameful for us to hanker for their company in spite of such unsuitability on our part.'

Haran said, 'But those who have become suitable get adequate attention from the English—take this family for example.'

Gora. When reception of one involves humiliation of others then I would consider such reception a deliberate insult.

Before long Haranbabu was beside himself in anger, and Gora continued to pierce him with his volley of sharp remarks.

When the two were so locked in their debate Sucharita was watching Gora from behind the shade of her handfan. The arguments were entering her ears no doubt but she did not really register them. Perhaps she would have felt ashamed if she were conscious that she was staring at Gora so absorbedly; but she was gazing at him as if she had forgotten herself. Gora had been sitting slightly bent forward with his two strong arms planted on the table. The light from the lamp fell on his broad white forehead; the face was eloquent with an occasional smile of contempt or a raised eyebrow denoting hatred; every expression on that face reflected a grandeur of self-respect. That his remarks did not mean just a casual debate or repartee, that every statement he made carried a mark of conviction which was moulded through long years of thought and action, that he suffered from no hesitation, weakness or inconsistency, was evident not only in his voice but was also writ large on his face and the whole body. Sucharita continued to gaze at him in amazement. This was the first occasion in her life when she at last perceived someone as a special person, as a very special man. She could not see him as one in the crowd, or just another acquaintance. He was incomparable. In his attempt to confront this Gora Haranbabu paled to insignificance. The shape of his body and face, his gestures and postures, his mannerisms, even his shirt and *cādar* seemed to mock him. So long Binoy's frequent evocations of Gora in their talk had led Sucharita to envision Gora as an extraordinary personality with a particular set of opinions and belonging to a particular organization; she had imagined this much that this person was born to serve some great beneficial or noble cause for the country. Today while looking at him intently she started to see Gora apart from all organizations, opinions, purposes, as only Gora the person. As the sea perceives the moon—beyond all necessity, all practical use—and rises towards the moon without any reason, so Sucharita's heart surged, forgetting all, overflooding all her reasonings and inhibitions, all her life, it seemed to spread all around on the crest of exuberant waves on a high tide. This was the first time she saw what a man could be, what a man's soul could be and she forgot herself under the surging tide of this exquisite ecstasy.

Haranbabu, however, had noticed her absorbed look. As a result the force of argument failed him. At last, getting extremely restless, he stood up and addressing Sucharita like some very close relative called her, 'Sucharita, please come inside, I have something to tell you.'

Sucharita winced. It seemed somebody had suddenly thrashed her. Indeed the relationship between them allowed this kind of address. Perhaps she would not have minded it either at another time. But today, before Gora and Binoy, she felt insulted at it. Moreover, Gora suddenly looked at her face with such a curious expression that she could not forgive Haranbabu. At first she sat silently as if she had not heard anything. Then Haranbabu, with an added dose of annoyance in his voice, called again, 'Do you hear Sucharita? I want to have some words with you. You have to come inside for a while.'

Without looking at him Sucharita said, 'Leave it now—let Baba come back first.'

Binoy got up and suggested, 'We can go now, in any case—.'

Sucharita hurriedly stopped him, 'Oh, no, Binoybabu, please don't go. Baba has told you to wait. He will come back any moment.'

A note of desperate appeal dripped through her voice; as if there had been a suggestion to leave the doe at the mercy of the hunter.

'I can't wait any longer, so, bye',—saying this Haranbabu left the room with quick steps. After coming out under a momentary impulse of anger Haranbabu repented it instantly. But he could not think of any appropriate excuse there and then for re-entering the stage.

After Haranbabu had left Sucharita sat silently lowering her flushed face in some unfathomable shame; she could not think of anything that she could say or do at the moment. During that brief moment Gora had the chance to look at her face freely and scrutinize it. Where was the least trace of the kind of arrogance, the sort of garrulence that Gora had imagined in association with the figure of an educated girl—in the features of Sucharita?

The luminosity of intelligence unmistakably lent a radiance to the face, but how delicately mellowed it looked today with the softening glow of modesty and coyness. What an exquisite face! Above the pair of brows the forehead was clear and transparent like a piece of autumnal sky. The lips were still, yet the sweetness of unspoken words seemed to rest between those lips like a soft flower-bud. Gora had never before paid any attention to the dress up of modern young ladies, and without having a look at it he had been prejudiced against it. But today the unfamiliar fashion in which the *sārī* wrapped round Sucharita's body struck Gora as particularly beautiful. One of her palms was laid on the table. That palm blossoming out of the curled frill of her sleeves appeared before Gora's eyes like some message of benediction flowering out of a kind soul. In the lamplit quiet evening the room around Sucharita, along with its light, its wall-paintings, its furniture, its neatness, appeared to Gora as a manifestation of some unique image of beauty. The perception that it was a home, imbued with the beauty, care, love of an accomplished nurturing woman, that it was much more than mere brick and mortar, flashed upon Gora's mind in a moment of revelation. Gora felt the presence of a new life in the air around him. Ripples from another heart curled in from all sides, and stroked his own heart again and again; some undefined sensation seemed to embrace him. He had never gone through this exquisite experience in his life. Within seconds, the entire image of Sucharita—from the loose curl of hair on her forehead to the border of her *sārī* encircling the feet—became very real and very special to him. The whole of Sucharita and every minute detail about her seemed to attract Gora's vision simultaneously.

For a while no one could speak and this made them feel a little shy. Then Binoy turned to Sucharita and said, 'The other day we had been talking of—', and thus he initiated a discussion.

He said, 'As I told you earlier, there was a time when I believed that we had nothing to hope for regarding our country, that we shall always be like juveniles and the British will ever remain our self-appointed trustee—everything in society will remain stagnant—we had no means to move the enormous power of the British or the enormous stagnation of the society. The majority of our countrymen think like that. In such a situation one could either get preoccupied with his own interests or drift along callously. It is precisely because of this that our middleclass people have no other target than promotion in service, and the rich consider a title from the government the supreme achievement of one's life. Thus the course of our life is covered by just so little; consequently we cannot imagine of some distant target, nor do we think it necessary to mobilize resources towards such a venture. I had also decided once that with the recommendation of Gora's father I would manage some government service. But at that time Gora stopped me; he declared, 'Never, you must not join government service.'

Noticing a faint surprise in Sucharita's expression at this, Gora came forward to explain, 'Don't think that I have said so in order to vent any grievance against the government. Those who are in the government service imbibe a peculiar pride assuming the government's power to be their own personal power, and eventually they emerge as a different class. This attitude is on the rise with every passing day. I have a relative who was a deputy in the earlier days of the Raj; now he has resigned. Once the District Magistrate asked him, 'Babu, why are so many people acquitted by your court?' He replied, 'Saheb, there is a reason. Those whom you throw into the prison are mere cats and dogs in your perception; but those whom I have to send to jail are but my own brothers.' There were this kind of Deputies still then; there were also British magistrates who were ready to listen to them. But with time the chains of service are being increasingly celebrated as precious ornaments, and the present day Deputy considers his fellow-countrymen no better than cats and dogs. Mounting on others' shoulders I would look down upon my own people and consequently perpetrate injustice on them—such an approach cannot lead to any good.'

Saying this Gora struck his fist on the table. The oil-lamp shivered.

Binoy said, 'Gora, I am afraid this table is not government property, and this lamp belongs only to Pareshbabu.'

Gora let out a loud guffaw. The whole house resonated with that strong sound of uproarious laughter. That Gora could laugh so unrestrainedly like a child at jokes surprised Sucharita and thrilled her with a deep joy. She did not know before that those who thought of big things could also laugh so heartily.

Gora said many things that evening. Although Sucharita kept silent, still Gora found such a wave length in her expression that his heart was filled with enthusiasm. At the end he said, as if addressing Sucharita alone, 'Look here. Please remember one thing. If we develop the wrong notion that since the British has become all-powerful we too must mimic the British in order to gain power, then the aim will never be fulfilled, and with continuous mimicry we shall be neither here nor there. Please know this for sure that Bharat has a unique nature, unique strength, unique truth; only if we can fully develop it India will attain her fulfillment, she will be saved. If we have not learnt this by studying British history, we have learnt nothing. To you I have an appeal—Please come and step into the heart of India, come down amidst all its good and evil. If there is deformity correct it from within—but look at it, understand it, think, turn your face toward it, be one with it. If you stand apart and look at it from the perspective of your foreign initiation inculcated since childhood, then you would be only wounding her, but will come to no help.'

Although Gora said, 'my appeal', it was more a command than an appeal. His words carried such a tremendous force that they did not wait for another's consent. Sucharita listened to everything with bent head. That Gora's last few words, voiced with such tremendous energy and appeal, were specially addressed to her deeply moved her. She had no time to define the nature of that turbulence. Sucharita had never for a moment thought that there was such a vast ancient identity called Bharatbarsha. This identity pervaded obscure past and remote future and was invisibly weaving a unique pattern with a unique thread in the vast web of human destiny. While listening to the exposition in Gora's bass voice this was suddenly revealed to Sucharita; she came to realize how fine the thread was, how varied, and yet how intimately related to some distant fulfillment.

In the flash of an epiphanic moment Sucharita had a glimpse of this vast identity that embraced and pervaded every Indian's life; she realized how small and impercipient we are without having an awareness of this magnificent belonging. Carried along the crest of that sudden spontaneous surge of a joyous heart Sucharita forgot her shyness and said with very simple, uninhibited modesty, 'I have never thought of the country in this way, so sincerely, on such a magnificent scale. But may I ask one thing? What is the connection between religion and motherland? Isn't religion a matter of the past?'

This question in Sucharita's soft voice struck Gora as inexpressibly sweet. It appeared sweeter as it became eloquent in the look of her large eyes. Gora said, 'The past of the country belongs to something much more magnificent than the country itself, and it is this that finds manifestation in the country. This is God's way to express his infinite truth through varied forms. Those who claim there is only one truth, and only one religion is true, only one form of a religion is true—they accept that truth is one, but they fail to see that truth is also infinite. The Infinite One expresses himself in infinite pluralities—this is the joy of the world we see around. That's why there are so many religious faiths, which help us to see that great divine king from various angles. I assure you, you can see the sun through the open window of Bharatbarsha; it won't be necessary to reach the window of some Christian church across the seas for that.'

Sucharita said, 'It seems you want to say that the religious ideology of India directs one to God along a unique route. But what is that uniqueness?'

Gora said, 'It is this—Brahma, who is abstract, and yet gets manifested in the concrete and the specific. But there is no end to these specificities. These include the water, the land, the air, life, intelligence, love, everything—you can never count them up, however much science may try to. In other countries they have tried to confine their God within some specific form—in India too such attempts are seen, but India does never consider a particular form as the only possible one, or the supreme one. No devotee in India would ever deny that God is more than any particular form by virtue of His infinity.'

Sucharita said, 'The wise men do not; but the ignorant?'

Gora said, 'I have already said, the ignorant will distort truth everywhere.'

Sucharita said, 'But has not that deformity spread too far in our country?'

Gora said, 'May be. Since Bharatbarsha wants to fully acknowledge both the crude and fine forms, the external and the internal, the body and the soul of religion, those who do not go for the fine, opts for the crude, and ignorance leads to strange deformities in that concrete. But at the same time India has made the enormous effort to realize Him who is true both in the concrete and the abstract, crude and fine, imagination and reality; we must not irreverently turn away from this to follow a narrow, dry, monolithic religion in the model of eighteenth century Europe's scepticism and faith. Perhaps you are not getting me because of your way of thinking since childhood. You may think that this man has learnt nothing in spite of his English education. But if some day you come to evolve respect towards the true nature and pursuit of India, how India has been trying to be and become herself in spite of all these obstacles and deformities,—if you can gain access into the heart of the matter, then—how can I express it—then you shall attain your fulfillment by being restored to your inborn Indian nature and strength.'

Sucharita was silent for a long while. Observing this Gora said, 'Don't take me as an orthodox person, please! Don't count me as another of those who are orthodox Hindus, or especially those who have recently emerged as orthodox champions of Hinduism. I have seen a profound and vast unity in the various diverse expressions and efforts of India, and the joy of that discovery is maddening. It is for that joy of unity that I don't have the least hesitation to take the same rank as the most ignorant, to share the dusty seat with them. Some understand this message of India, some do not. Let it be. For myself I can say I am at one with all Indians. All are my own kin. I do not have the least doubt that through all of them the great Indian heritage is doing its own work.'

At these words of Gora, uttered in his strong voice, even the walls, the table, the furniture seemed to quiver in resonance.

These were not clear enough for Sucharita to follow; but the force of newly-stirred emotion can be turbulent. The feeling that life was not confined within four walls, or one institution, seemed to oppress Sucharita with its very intensity.

At this time sound of quick footsteps on the staircase came up, along with loud giggles. Pareshbabu returned with his wife and daughters. While climbing up the stairs Sudhir was teasing the girls somehow, and hence this hilarity.

Labanya, Lalita and Satish entered the room and seeing Gora, restrained themselves immediately. Labanya went out. Satish took position by Binoy's chair and started some intimate talk in whispers. Lalita drew a chair up behind Sucharita and became nearly invisible.

Paresh stepped in apologetically, 'I have been late. I am afraid Panubabu has left?'

Sucharita did not reply; Binoy said, 'Yes, he could not wait any longer.'

Gora stood up, saying, 'So let us call it a day.'

Saying this Gora bent low to greet Pareshbabu.

Pareshbabu said, 'I am sorry that I missed the chance of conversing with you this evening. My son, drop in now and then when you can spare a little time.'

As Gora and Binoy were about to leave, Baradasundari arrived. Both bowed to her. She asked, 'Are you leaving right now?'

Gora said, 'Yes.'

Baradasundari turned to Binoy, 'But Binoybabu, you will not be allowed to go. You must stop for dinner tonight. Besides I have something urgent to discuss with you.'

Satish jumped up to hold Binoy by the hand and said, 'Yes, *Mā*, don't let Binoybabu go. He will sleep with me tonight.'

Seeing Binoy hesitating Baradasundari turned to Gora, 'Do you want to take him along? Do you need him?'

Gora replied, 'Oh no. Not at all. Binoy, why don't you stay on? I am off.'

Saying this Gora left with quick steps.

The moment Baradasundari sought Gora's permission for retaining Binoy, Binoy could not but steal a quick glance at Lalita. Lalita turned her face, as if suppressing a caustic smile.

Binoy could not protest against these small jeers and taunts from Lalita, yet they hurt him like thorn-pricks.

As Binoy came back to the room and sat down again, Lalita said, 'Binoybabu, perhaps it would have been better if you escaped tonight.'

Binoy. Why?

Lalita. *Mā* has a plan to trap you. The producers of the proposed play to be presented at the magistrate's fair have fallen short of one actor. *Mā* has decided to have you there.

Binoy was anxious, 'Oh God! No, no, I can't do it.'

Lalita smiled more broadly, 'I have already told that to *Mā*. I know that your friend will never allow you to join.'

Binoy caught the hint, and said, 'Leave my friend alone. I have never acted in my last seven incarnations—why me of all persons?

Lalita retorted, 'Perhaps we have been acting for so many incarnations.'

At this time Baradasundari entered. Lalita said, '*Mā*, it is no use trying to involve Binoybabu in the play. If you can persuade his friend first, then perhaps—.'

Binoy remonstrated pathetically, 'It is not about friend's consent. Everybody cannot act—I don't have the aptitude at all.'

Baradasundari assured him, 'For that you needn't worry. We shall train you. These small girls are performing; how can you say that you won't be able?'

So Binoy got no chance to escape.

21

Unlike his normal brisk pace Gora was walking slowly towards home with a preoccupied look. Leaving the short route to home he took the longer path along the bank of Ganga. Ganga and her banks by Calcutta in those days were not yet so thoroughly mauled by the greedy ugliness of commercial civilisation, and had not yet put on the shackles of railway tracks on the land, and iron bridges on water. In those days winter evenings did not suck in the blue sky with its foul sooty breath. The river then used to carry the message of lonely peaceful Himalayan peaks down to the dusty busy banks of Calcutta.

Nature as such had not much attraction for Gora. His mind was ever turbulent under the force of its own active energy. He had no time to notice the spaces—on land, water, or air—which were not immediate spheres of his activity.

Tonight, however, the sky above the river silently touched his heart again and again with its star-studded darkness. The river was unruffled. At the *ghāt* on the side of Calcutta lamp-lights could be seen in a few boats, while others rested quietly in darkness. On the other bank it was dense dark among the leafy trees. Above them the Jupiter watched with unblinking stellar vision that pierced through the dark void like some god of darkness.

Tonight this vast silent nature seemed to overwhelm his body and mind. The immense darkness of the sky seemed to pulsate through his veins to the beat of his own heart. So long nature had been waiting patiently—today she spotted some chink and immediately took over the undefended fortress. So long Gora had been a very distinct individual with his learning, thoughts, activities. But what happened today! Tonight he recognized nature and at once this deep dark water, this dense black shoreline, that vast dark sky closed up to embrace him. Somehow he had been caught unaware by nature tonight.

The mild soft fragrance of some unknown flower on an alien creeper wafted in from the wayside garden of some merchant office and seemed to comfort his disturbed heart with its fragrant fingers. The river seemed to point at some indefinite distance far away from the restless workfield of human habitation; who knows what flowers had been sprouted by the trees bending over the water along lonely shore-line; what shadows were playing on the river! There the days under clear blue sky were like the gaze of someone's beautiful eyes; the nights wore the coy shadow cast by the dark lashes of someone's lowered eyes. A sensation of charming sweetness seemed to close in from all directions and swept him along the strong current of some bottomless, timeless force about which he had no idea till this day. This seemed to lap his mind from end to end with synchronic waves of unknown joy and unknown pain. This autumn night by the river, with indistinct sounds from the city, under the faint starlight Gora stood enraptured before some veiled charming beauty who pervaded the world. As he had never surrendered to this queen in humility, tonight the spell of her charm suddenly captivated Gora and fastened him with her magically powerful billion-shaded thread to the land-water-sky from all directions. Overwhelmed, Gora sat down on a step of the lonely *ghāt* by the river. Again and again he asked himself, 'What is this, what does this new revelation mean for me.' Where was its place in his plan of an organized systematic dedicated life of action? Would it clash with his commitments? Must he fight it down? Saying this Gora firmly clenched his fist, and at once the fingers of an exquisitely beautiful palm swam up into his vision, evoking the untasted ambrosia of a tactile ecstasy. A thrill of joy seemed to electrify his entire body. This intense sensation silenced all hesitations in the lonely darkness; he joyously surrendered to it body and soul. For a long time he did not feel like stirring.

When Gora reached home it was already late. Anandamoyee asked, 'So late, my son! Your dinner has become cold.'

Gora replied, 'I don't know *Mā*, what happened to me today—I had been sitting by the Ganga bank for a long time.'

Anandamoyee said, 'I can guess, Binoy was there with you.'

Gora said, 'No, *Mā*, I was alone.'

Anandamoyee was a bit surprised. Gora sitting alone by the river so late into the night—such a thing had never happened before. It was indeed not in his temperament to think in silent passivity. As Gora started taking his meal, still looking preoccupied, Anandamoyee noted the glow of some strange wistfulness in his expression.

After a while Anandamoyee slowly ventured, 'Did you go to Binoy today?'

Gora said, 'No, today we went together to Pareshbabu's place.'

Anandamoyee fell silent at this. Then she asked again, 'Did you meet all the members of the family?'

Gora said, 'Yes, I did.'

Anandamoyee. I think their daughters do not maintain Purdah.

Gora. No. They do not have to.

At other times such a reply would have also carried a suggestion of excitement or resentment, but today no such sign was there. Anandamoyee again lapsed into her own thoughts.

On waking up in the morning Gora did not immediately get ready for the day's work as was his normal routine. He opened the door to the east of the bedroom, and stood absentmindedly for a time. The lane before the house ended in a street towards the east. A school stood at the eastern end of the street. A patch of white fog floated above an old Jam tree in the plot adjacent to the school, and behind it a faint golden line emerged indicating the imminent sunrise. Gora silently watched the scene for a long time until the thin mist disappeared, bright sunlight sprang out from behind the trees like a host of shining bayonets piercing through the leaves, and within minutes the Calcutta street was filled with crowd and noise.

At this moment Gora suddenly spotted at the turn of the lane Abinash coming up along with a few students. At once Gora's trance was shattered as if a fine lace was torn apart by some strong jerk. He thrashed his own mind, fiercely warning himself, 'No, no, all this is nonsense; this cannot do, no, by no means.' Saying this he rushed out from the bedroom. Gora's followers had arrived, and yet he was not ready to receive them ahead—such a thing had never happened before. This small lapse made him feel very bad. He resolved, henceforth he will never visit Pareshbabu's house, and will try to stop any discussion about them by evading Binoy for some time.

After he went downstairs that morning it was decided that Gora, along with two or three of his team will set out on a walking tour along the G.T. Road; they will take no money or provisions with them and instead will seek hospitality in the wayside homes.

In launching this amazing project Gora displayed excessive enthusiasm. He was obsessed with idea of setting out on the open roads by severing all ties. He thought that this very project of setting out should mark a release from the mesh in which his heart was getting tangled. He repeated to himself with great insistence the idea that all such fine charming sensations and emotions were but illusions, and work constituted the only reality. Thus spurring himself he rushed out of the sitting room, almost running like a schoolboy at the day's end, towards preparing for the journey. At the very same moment Krishnadayal, after having his dip in Ganga, was on the way to his own room, carrying a bowl of Ganga-water in one hand, a *nāmābalī* on the shoulders, silently chanting some 'mantra'. Gora nearly stumbled against him. Instantly he was ashamed and bent down to touch his feet. 'Leave it, leave it', he anxiously tried to stop Gora and shrank away. Gora's touch, on the eve of sitting down for puja, ruined all the benefit he might have reaped from his Ganga-dip. Gora did not quite understand that it was especially his touch that Krishnadayal was anxious to avoid. He assumed that because of Krishnadayal's fastidiousness about touch and 'purity', meticulous avoidance of all sorts of touches was his single daylong pursuit. In fact he kept Anandamoyee always at arm's length as a heathen or *mleccha*; Mahim was a busy man, and rarely a chance occurred for meeting him. Among the whole family it was only Mahim's daughter Shashimukhi who got any attention from him.

Krishnadayal taught the little girl to memorise Sanskrit hymns, and perform various rites and rituals related to puja.

As Krishnadayal shrank from Gora's gesture of touching his feet and hastened to escape Gora guessed the cause of his reaction and felt amused. In this way day by day Gora's alienation from his father had been nearly complete; and however much he might criticize his mother's disregard for custom, it was this rebel *Mā* whom Gora worshipped with all the devotion of his soul.

After lunch Gora made a bundle with a few dresses, and fastening it on his back like European tourists he came to his mother. '*Mā*, I am going out for a few days.'

Anandamoyee asked, 'Where are you going, son?'

Gora said, 'About that I have no definite idea.'

Anandamoyee asked again, 'Is it on some mission?'

Gora said, 'It is not exactly what we can call a mission or work—you may say this very setting out itself is a sort of mission.'

Anandamoyee was silent for a while. Gora noticed this and said in an appealing tone, '*Mā*, please, don't stop me. You know me, don't you? There is no chance of my turning into an ascetic monk. I can never stay away from my *Mā* for long.'

Gora had never expressed his love for his mother thus in so many words. So, instantly he felt embarrassed.

Anandamoyee was elated, but to cover up his shyness added, 'I hope Binoy too is going with you.'

Gora quickly replied, 'No, no, *Mā*. Binoy is not going. Look there, you have already started worrying, who will save your Gora from the hazards of the big world. If you look up to Binoy as my saviour that's but a superstition of yours—you'll get over this superstition once I come back safe and sound.'

Anandamoyee asked, 'Shall I have some news now and then?'

Gora replied, 'Be prepared for not getting any. If some message arrives in spite of that won't it be a pleasant surprise? There's absolutely no cause for worry, *Mā*; no one will kidnap your Gora. *Mā*, nobody should think him so precious as you imagine. Still if anyone is allured by this bundle I shall surely surrender it as alms; certainly I shall not give my life for saving this bundle.'

Gora touched Anandamoyee's feet, she blessed him by touching his head and then kissing her hand that touched it, but she made no attempt to hold him back. Anandamoyee never forbade any one to do something on account of her own suffering or of the apprehension of harm it might cause to others. In her own life she had gone through many a crisis and ordeal, the big world was not unknown to her. Fear was alien to her nature. She had not been worried about the possibility of hazards on the trip; but she had a hunch of some radical change taking place within Gora, and since last night this was bothering her. On learning about Gora's sudden and intriguing tour plan this morning her uneasiness on that account only increased.

Just the moment Gora had stepped out on the road with his backpack, Binoy appeared before him holding carefully a pair of crimson red Turkese roses. Gora said, 'Binoy,—whether seeing you on the eve of a trip means an auspicious sign or inauspicious for the journey will now be tested.'

Binoy asked, 'Are you going somewhere?'

Gora said, 'Yes.'

Binoy asked, 'To where?'

Gora replied, "The echo answered, 'where'."

Binoy. 'Is there no better answer than an echo?'

Gora. 'No. Go to *Mā*, you will learn everything. So, now I shoot off.'

Saying this he immediately set off in big strides. Binoy went inside and touching Anandamoyee's feet placed the pair of roses there.

Anandamoyee picked up the roses and asked, 'Where did you get them, Binoy?'

Avoiding a straight answer Binoy said, 'When I get something fine I feel like offering it first to *Mā* as worship.'

Then Binoy sat down by Anandamoyee on her plain wooden plank, and said, '*Mā*, you are preoccupied today.'

Anandamoyee asked, 'Why do you think so, son?'

Binoy said, 'You have forgotten to give me the betel leaf which is my quota.'

Anandamoyee was ashamed and immediately brought a pan for Binoy.

Then they got engaged in a long talk.

Binoy could furnish no clear explanation about Gora's sudden decision to go on an indefinite tour.

In course of the talk once Anandamoyee asked, 'Did you take Gora to Pareshbabu's house yesterday?'

Binoy then described the previous evening in detail. Anandamoyee listened with full attention to everything he said.

Before leaving Binoy said, '*Mā*, now that my worship is over, may I take those flowers at your feet and carry them on my head as your *Prasād*.'

Anandamoyee smiled and returned the flowers to Binoy; she thought to herself, perhaps this fondness for the pair of roses is not just due to their beauty, and some special fond associations must have been attached to them which are necessarily far above and beyond the domain of the botanist.

After Binoy had left in the evening she continued to brood on so many things. She prayed to God again and again to save Gora from unhappiness, and to sustain the friendship of Gora and Binoy in face of all adverse situations.

22

The roses had a brief history.

The previous night Gora left Pareshbabu's house. But after that Binoy had to suffer a lot in connection with the proposal of his acting in the play to be produced at the magistrate's residence.

Not that Lalita felt any particular enthusiasm about the drama; indeed she positively disliked these things. But she seemed to have developed a kind of obstinate desire to involve Binoy somehow in this acting episode. To force Binoy willy-nilly to do just those things which were disapproved by Gora had become her fixation these days. Lalita could not herself explain why should she feel so exasperated with Binoy's loyalty to Gora. She felt she had no peace until she could snap off all the chains and release Binoy from that bond.

Swinging her tresses, shaking her head, Lalita pounced upon him, 'Why Sir, may I know? What's the great crime in acting a part in a play?'

Binoy protested, 'Acting itself is no crime; but I don't feel like going to that magistrate's residence for performing.'

Lalita. 'Is this your own feeling, or are you speaking on behalf of somebody else?'

Binoy. 'It is not my responsibility to speak on behalf of others; it is difficult as well. You believe or not, what I say is my own opinion.'

Without a reply Lalita just curled her lips into a caustic smile. Then after a while she resumed, 'Perhaps your friend Gaurbabu would consider refusal to a magistrate's invitation something heroic; perhaps he would think it as good as fighting the British in an open battle.'

Binoy excitedly countered, 'My friend may or may not think that way. But I must say I think that way. What else is it than a challenge? If the person who cares a damn for me thinks that I should feel gratified at the slightest signal from his smallest finger, and I don't fight back that contempt with my own contempt, then how can I retain my self-respect?'

Lalita herself was a proud nature, and these proud words from Binoy pleased her. But for that very reason she realized the weakness of her own points of attack, and this again led her to mount repeated assaults on Binoy with the shafts of her taunting remarks.

At last Binoy said, 'Look here, why do you argue? Why don't you say, "It is my wish that you join the acting." Then I can have the pleasure of sacrificing my conviction for the sake of your request.'

Lalita protested, 'Aha! Why should I say that? If you really have a conviction why must you sacrifice that at my request? But that must be truly *your* own conviction.'

Binoy acquiesced, 'O.K. That's done. Well, I have no real conviction. And it is not at your request, but being defeated by your logic, that I agree to join.'

At this point Baradasundari entered and Binoy went up to her saying, 'Please let me know what preparation I have to make for my part.'

Baradasundari proudly said, 'You needn't worry at all. Leave that to us. We shall surely manage you alright. Only you have to attend the rehearsal daily.'

Binoy said, 'Alright. So allow me to leave now.'

Baradasundari protested, 'How can you say such a thing! You must have dinner with us tonight.'

Binoy said, 'Must I? Why not have it another day?'

Baradasundari insisted, 'No, no, that cannot be.'

Binoy ate, but he was not in his natural jovial mood. Sucharita too seemed absentminded and kept silent. When Lalita was fighting with Binoy Sucharita was walking alone in the balcony. The conversation did not click tonight.

Binoy noticed Lalita's serious expression and before leaving told her, 'I courted defeat, but still could not please you.'

Lalita left the room without a word.

Normally Lalita did not weep, but today she felt like weeping. What happened! Why had she been hurting Binoy thus again and again and yet feeling so miserable at this!

So long as Binoy did not agree to join their play Lalita's obstinacy too was on the mount, but the moment he agreed she lost all her interest. All the arguments against his joining seemed to grow stronger in her perception. She felt miserable, and thought, 'Binoybabu should not have agreed just to honour my request. Request! Why should he honour my request! He assumes he is being polite with me by honouring my request; as if I had been hankering for this bit of politeness on his part!'

But how could she maintain her hauteur? Wasn't it true she has all along insisted on involving Binoy in their team of actors? Now that Binoy, out of sheer politeness, had complied with her request, could she afford to be angry? There was no apparent reason for the sharp pang of remorse and disgust with herself that Lalita felt at this upshot. Had it been another day, she would have approached Sucharita in this mood of mental restiveness; but today she did not go to Sucharita, and could not clearly understand why she felt such a weight on her heart, which pressed up and welled out in streaming tears.

The following morning Sudhir had brought a bouquet for Labanya. There were two blooming rose buds in the bouquet. Lalita loosened these from the bunch.

Labanya protested, 'What are you doing?'

Lalita replied, 'I feel saddened at seeing nice flowers fastened along with a junk of twigs and flowers in the bouquets; it is indeed barabaric to bind up all categories into one single cluster by force.'

Saying this she released all the flowers from the string and arranged them in separate bunches in the different corners of the room; she herself took only the two roses.

Satish ran in asking, 'Didi, where did you get the roses?'

Instead of answering him Lalita asked, 'Won't you go to your friend's house today?'

Until then Satish had not thought of Binoy, but at the very mention he sprang up, 'Yes, certainly.'

He at once became impatient for starting off towards Binoy's house.

Lalita caught hold of him and asked, 'What do you do there?'

Satish briefly answered, 'Talking.'

Lalita asked again, 'He gives you so many pictures, why don't you give him anything in return?'

Binoy used to keep clippings of various kinds of picture from English magazines and papers for Satish. Satish had started keeping an album where he pasted these pictures with gum. Thus he had become so obsessed with the hobby that he could hardly restrain himself from tearing off pictures even from fine books. On account of this greediness he was often scolded by his sisters too.

Being suddenly faced with the reality that there was a practice called 'return' in human transaction Satish was thoroughly puzzled. It was not easy for him to part with a single item among the various treasures he had accumulated over years in a broken tin box. Watching his worried expression Lalita laughed and patting his cheeks assured, 'Leave it, don't worry; here, give him these roses.'

He was beside himself with joy at such an easy solution to the problem. He at once took the flowers and trotted off to pay his friend's dues.

He met Binoy on the way. Shouting at the top of his voice,—'Binoybabu, Binoybabu'—Satish ran up to him and hiding the flowers under his shirt challenged, 'Can you guess what I have brought for you?'

Binoy admitted defeat. Then Satish brought out the pair of roses. Binoy said, 'Oh, how wonderful! But still, Satishbabu, I am afraid this is not your own property. Suppose I take this and then the police apprehend me for carrying stolen goods?'

Satish was jolted a bit; he could not instantly decide if these flowers could really be claimed as his own property. He thought a little and then said, 'No, not like that exactly; because it was Lalitadidi who gave me these flowers to give you.'

Thus the problem was sorted out, and assuring him about his visit in the afternoon Binoy sent the boy back.

Binoy had been suffering a pain since last night; this was caused by Lalita's volley of taunts and sharp remarks. Normally Binoy did not run into clash with any one. Naturally he did not expect this kind of sharp attack from anybody. Earlier Lalita was part of the backdrop of Sucharita in his perception. But for the last few days Binoy's situation could be compared to that of the goaded elephant which gets no chance of forgetting its keeper. How to keep Lalita a little pacified and thus earn himself a little respite had become his main concern. On coming home in the evening scraps and bits of Lalita's caustic, incisive, sharp remarks, her taunting laughter continued to surface in his consciousness and made dents into his sleeping hours. 'Lalita detests me because she thinks I am like a shadow of Gora, I have no real identity of my own, which is again not true at all.' He mustered all sorts of counter-arguments in his mind. But these arguments came to no avail since Lalita had never made any explicit accusations against him—had indeed given him no chance to broach a debate on the issue. Yet, given the chance, Binoy could have said so much; therefore the lack of chance to use his shafts made Binoy feel more and more restive. Last night, when even after accepting defeat to her at last he did not see her happy, Binoy returned home feeling really bad. He went on thinking, 'Am I really as contemptible as that!'

Therefore, when he learnt from Satish that it was Lalita who had sent these flowers to him through Satish he was quite elated; he assumed it was as a token of peace that Lalita had sent these roses, because his consent to join the play had finally appeased her. At first he thought, 'Let me go back and leave these in my room.' Then he thought, 'No, this is the flower of peace, and therefore I shall sanctify them with the blessed touch of *Mā*'s feet.'

When Binoy went to Pareshbabu's house that evening Lalita was assisting Satish in his home task. Addressing Lalita Binoy said, 'Red is the colour of war; therefore the flower of truce should have been white.'

Lalita could not follow his meaning and looked askance at him. Binoy took out a bunch of white oleander and offering it to Lalita, said, 'Your flowers are beautiful, but still the shade of anger remains; this humble flower of mine can bear no comparison to its beauty, but it offers itself humbly in the white colour of peace.'

Lalita blushed to the lobe of her ears, 'My flowers! What do you mean!'

Binoy was a bit nonplussed, and said, 'Then perhaps I got it wrong. Satishbabu, whom did you give whose flowers?'

Satish protested loudly, 'Baah! It was Lalitadidi; she sent the flowers.'

Binoy. Sent to whom?

Satish. To you, of course!

Lalita went crimson and slapped Satish on the back, 'Never seen a fool like you! Didn't you want to give the flowers to Binoybabu in exchange of his pictures?'

Satish was thoroughly puzzled, 'Yes, yes, indeed; but it was you who gave me the idea. Didn't you?'

While trying to refute Satish Lalita got herself more and more enmeshed. Binoy got it clearly that it was Lalita who had sent the flowers, although her plan was to do it incognito. Binoy said, 'O.K., I give up the claim that these were sent by you, but regarding my flowers there is no such confusion. May I offer these to mark the auspicious occasion of our ceasefire—.'

Lalita shook her head, 'I don't know what do you call fighting and how can it end?'

Binoy. 'Is it all an illusion then? Since the fighting is an illusion, the flowers a confusion, the end too must be delusion. It is not only taking the oyster for silver, even the very oyster seems an illusion. Then is that play in some magistrate's house also—.'

Lalita. 'No, that's no illusion. But why should there be any fight over it? Why should you assume that I have launched a great war just to persuade you to join this small thing, and have been gratified by your consent? If acting seems wrong to you then why should you agree to it at anybody's request?'

Saying this Lalita left the room. Everything seemed to have got upset. Today Lalita had planned to admit her defeat to Binoy, and request him not to participate in the play. But the talk took such a turn that it led just to the opposite direction. Binoy thought Lalita still nursed resentment at his initial stand of strong opposition. The thought that Binoy had only formally accepted defeat, but was not mentally reconciled to it, did not allow Lalita's grievance to subside. Binoy was pained at the idea that Lalita should have been so hurt in the matter. He decided that he won't discuss it even as joke, and instead would perform his part with such sincerity and excellence that none should be able to accuse him of indifference.

Since morning today Sucharita has been trying to concentrate in the privacy of the bedroom on an English religious book, *Imitation of Christ*. Today she has not been able to take up her daily chores. Nor can she concentrate on the pages and the printed words have been repeatedly turning into so many vague shadows though she would at once force herself back to the study.

At this time she heard the voice of Binoybabu from another end of the house; instantly she stood up to fold the book and was about to rush for the drawing room, when feeling annoyed at this eagerness in herself she again sat down on the chair and resumed her reading. She even pressed her palms on the ears lest the sound of talk there should distract her.

Then Lalita entered her room. Looking up at her Sucharita said, 'What's the matter, sister! Please tell me!'

Lalita vehemently shook her head, 'Nothing.'

Sucharita asked again, 'Where were you?'

Lalita. 'Binoybabu has come. Perhaps he wants to talk to you.'

Today Sucharita could not bring herself to ask, if someone else had come with Binoybabu. If somebody had come Lalita would have certainly mentioned. Still she could not be sure. Giving up the effort to restrain herself she started for the drawing room ostensibly to discharge her duty towards a visitor in the house. She asked Lalita, 'Won't you come too?'

Lalita said with a tinge of impatience in her voice, 'You go. I am following later.'

Coming to the drawing room Sucharita saw Binoy gossiping with Satish.

Sucharita said, 'Baba has gone out—he will return shortly. Ma has taken Labanya and Leela to the tutor's house for rehearsing their parts in that play—Lalita could not be persuaded to join them by any means. Ma has told you to wait—today is your test.'

Binoy asked, 'Aren't you going to take part in this?'

Sucharita replied, 'If everybody acted then who would be the audience in this world?'

In such matters Baradasundari tried to avoid Sucharita as best as she could. As usual, this time too she was not called to exhibit her accomplishments.

Normally, when these two persons were thrown together they never ran short of words or ideas. But today each was disturbed in his or her own way and the conversation could not get going. Sucharita had resolved not to mention Gora. These days Binoy could not wax eloquent on Gora as he used to do earlier. He feels inhibited at imagining that perhaps Lalita along with all the other members of this family, looked down upon him as just another satellite of Gora.

On some previous occasion Binoy had arrived earlier and Gora dropped in later on. Thinking of such a possibility Sucharita continued in a kind of tension. She feared that Gora might come; she was also apprehensive that he might not and the anxiety made her miserable.

After some casual exchanges with Binoy Sucharita found no other way to drag on the conversation and picking up Satish's picture album started discussing it with the boy. Occasionally she teased Satish to a temper by pointing out some anomaly of the arrangement. Thus being provoked to great excitement Satish loudly refuted all criticism, while Binoy occasionally stole glances at the rejected bunch of his Karabi flowers, and was filled with shame and resentment; he thought, 'at least for the sake of politeness Lalita should have accepted these flowers from me.'

Sucharita started at the sound of footsteps behind and saw Haranbabu entering the room. Since her startling was too obvious Sucharita blushed deeply. Haranbabu took a chair and asked, 'Where is your Gaurbabu today?'

Binoy was annoyed at this kind of unnecessary query, and asked, 'Why? Do you want to meet him for some reason or other?'

Haranbabu said, 'You are here, yet he is not here. This is indeed a rare phenomenon. That's the reason of my humble query.'

Binoy felt a seething anger—and lest it becomes apparent he replied curtly, 'He is out of Calcutta.'

Haran. Is he on some campaign?

Binoy became angrier, and offered no answer. Sucharita too got up and left without a word. Haranbabu quickly followed her but could not catch up. He called out to her, 'Sucharita, I have something to tell you.'

Sucharita's reply could be heard, 'I am not well today.'

Before she had hardly finished she shut her bedroom door.

At this point Baradasundari came to call Binoy inside for rehearsal. Before long the flowers on the table also suddenly disappeared. That night Lalita too remained absent from Baradasundari's rehearsal programme, and Sucharita, with *Imitation of Christ* folded on her lap, pushed the lamp into a corner of the room and sat staring at the dark night outside the door long into the midnight. A strange unknown exquisite land had, as it were, flashed on her vision like some mirage; there was a wide gulf separating the world she had seen or known so far from that other land; so the lamps burning on the window-sills there thrilled her with the fearful mystery of their remoteness like the garland of stars on the neck of the dark night; yet she felt, 'my life is futile, what I have known so long is confused and what I have been doing everyday is meaningless—perhaps, only if I can reach there, my knowledge will achieve completeness, my work will attain nobility, and life will find its fulfillment. Who called me out there to stand in front of the unknown liongate of that exquisite, strange, fearsome land! Why does my heart quiver so! Why do I fail to take a single step and stand still as if under a spell!'

23

Binoy comes daily for rehearsal. Sucharita just looks at him once, and then turns to the book in her hand or retires into her own room. The incompleteness of Binoy's visits without Gora hurts her everyday, but she asks no question. Thus days followed one after another. A cloud of resentment against Gora seemed to gather in her mind and grow stronger day by day. It seemed as if Gora had promised her to come again; at least that day it had seemed so.

When at last Sucharita came to learn that Gora had, for no apparent reason, left for some unplanned trip, she tried to ignore the information as just another unimportant news item. But still the fact got stuck in her mind like some painful shaft. In course of daily chores suddenly she would remember it; she would apply her mind to some preoccupation and then suddenly realize that so long she had been preoccupied precisely with this pain.

Indeed Sucharita had not expected Gora to thus disappear suddenly after their conversation that day. In spite of the wide gulf between her own thoughts and Gora's opinions there was no rebellious wind of hostility blowing that day to drift them apart. It is not clear if she got Gora's ideas, but she somehow had a glimpse of Gora the person. Whatever be Gora's ideology, that ideology did not make the man inconsequential, or contemptible; instead it had brought out the robust vigour of Gora's mind. Sucharita had felt this with strong conviction that evening. She could not stand such ideas if voiced by someone else; she would have been vexed, would have thought the speaker ignorant, and would have felt excited to correct him at once. But that day she felt nothing like this towards Gora. Reinforced by Gora's personality, his sharp intelligence, the firmness of his unwavering faith, the heart-rending intensity of his thunderous voice, Gora's speech came alive, and with the unmistakable ring of truth. Sucharita herself might not subscribe to these opinions, but if somebody else accepted them so completely with all his reason and belief and life, then it was not a matter to be denounced; rather it could be respected in spite of his subscribing to a different faith. It was such an approach that had taken complete possession of Sucharita. This state of mind was a new experience for Sucharita. So long she had been quite intolerant about a contrary opinion. In spite of the living example of a quiet detached meditative life as set by Pareshbabu Sucharita had been enveloped by a kind of communal ethos since childhood and thereby opinion or ideology was all-important for her. This was the first time that she could see the human person and the abstract opinion in reconcilement within a whole living mysterious entity. She had been able to overcome the divisive vision that breaks up human society into two distinct camps of ours and theirs, good and bad, and thereby could perceive someone even with a different ideology as primarily a human; thus difference of opinion had become unimportant.

That evening Sucharita had clearly felt that Gora was experiencing a thrill of joy in conversing with her. Was it just the joy of articulating one's ideas? Did she herself play no role behind this outpouring of joy? Or did she have really any role? Perhaps no individual had any special value for Gora; with his idea and commitment he maintained distance from the rest of the world, and other humans were perhaps just objects to him for applying his ideas.

For the last few days Sucharita has been specially applying her mind to meditation. She seemed to need the mental support of Pareshbabu even more than before. One day as Pareshbabu was reading alone in his room, Sucharita came in and sat down near him in silence.

Pareshbabu put down the book on the table and asked, 'What's the matter Radhe!'

Sucharita said, 'Nothing as such, Baba.'

Saying this she started rearranging his table though it was quite tidy and in order; after a while she suddenly came out, 'Baba, why don't you read books with me any more as you used to in the past?'

Smiling affectionately Pareshbabu said, 'My pupil has completed that stage of her schooling. Now you can follow a book yourself.'

Sucharita said, 'No, I cannot follow anything. From tomorrow again I shall read with you.'

Pareshbabu said, 'Alright. We shall resume our joint reading from tomorrow.'

After another spell of silence Sucharita suddenly said, 'Baba, the other day Binoybabu spoke at length in support of caste system. Why don't you enlighten me on the subject?'

Pareshbabu replied, '*Mā*, as you know I have always tried to bring you up in such a way that you would think for yourself instead of thoughtlessly repeating what other people said. Offering advice on a question until it stirs in your own mind is like offering food before the appetite is whetted; both lead to loss of appetite and indigestion. As soon as you come forward with your question I shall try to meet it to the best of my ability.'

Sucharita said, 'I am asking you the question, Baba,—why do we denounce caste system?'

Pareshbabu said, 'A cat can eat near your table; that is not forbidden; yet a man enters the room and at once the rice in your plate is spoilt; the caste system generates such inhumanity and hatred in man for another man. How can I call such a system anything but irreligion? Those who can so despise a fellow human can never achieve greatness or nobility in this world. They must bear with the contempt of others.'

Sucharita echoed what she had heard from Gora, 'The perversion of today's society is evident in its many blemishes; perhaps those are percolating through all the facets of the society. But does that justify an attempt to forego the real thing?'

Paresh said in his habitually quiet tone, 'I would answer this if I could have known where that 'real' thing resides. I can see with my own eyes man's unbearable hatred of man in our country and that has been driving the wedge of separation among us; in such a situation what's the consolation in thinking of some imaginary concept of the "real" thing?'

Sucharita again spoke as if like an echo of Gora, 'But wasn't the vision of equality our supreme philosophy?'

Pareshbabu said, 'perception of all as equal involves the brain, not the heart. The perception implies neither love nor hatred—it is beyond anger or envy. The human heart cannot function in such an emotional void. That's why in spite of our heritage of such an equality principle the low caste has no entry to temples. If we don't observe equality even in the vicinity of God, then what avails at all if equality exists only at the theoretical level in the domain of philosophy alone?'

Sucharita was silent for a long time trying to follow Paresh's argument. At last she asked, 'Well, Baba, why don't you try to make Binoybabu and others see this way?'

Pareshbabu smiled a little, 'It is not on account of any dearth of intelligence or understanding that they do not grasp the point; rather it is precisely their remarkable intelligence that renders them impatient; they seek to make others understand instead. When they will genuinely seek to understand these things from the perspective of religion, that is the highest truth, then they will not have to wait for your Baba's guidance. At present they are looking from another perspective, and my speeches will fall flat upon them now.'

Although Sucharita had listened to Gora and Binoy with due respect, still Gora's assertions clashed with her convictions and thereby pained her. She was not at peace. Today, while talking to Pareshbabu, she gained a brief respite from that painful conflict. Sucharita could never for a moment allow herself to think that anybody—be it Gora or Binoy or any other person—could understand a thing better than Pareshbabu. Whenever anybody differed from Pareshbabu, that was sufficient cause for inviting her wrath. Recently after coming to know Gora she could not altogether dismiss his opinions either angrily or contemptuously, and that was at the back of her anguish. Also for that very reason a yearning had come over her to seek the shelter of Pareshbabu like the shadow clinging to the shelter of the tree. Getting up from the chair she went up to the door, but again came back, stood behind his chair, placing her palms on its back, and said, 'Baba, I shall join you during your evening meditation today.'

Pareshbabu said, 'Alright.'

Then Sucharita went to her bedroom, closed the door, and tried to ignore all Gora had spoken. But she simply could not erase his face, glowing with intelligence and conviction, from her vision. She felt Gora's speeches were not mere speeches, they were Gora himself. They had shape, motion, life—they were brimming with the strength of conviction, throbbing with the pain of an intense patriotism. It was not just an opinion which you could dismiss by disagreeing—it was a complete individual, and that too not an average one; you could not bring yourself round to push him back. Caught in an agonising conflict, Sucharita felt like weeping. The thought that somebody could thus land her in such an excruciating uncertainty and easily sail out thereafter with complete indifference, seemed to rend her heart apart; at the same time the very thought that she was suffering for this filled her with annoyance and a feeling of self-chastisement.

24

It was decided that Binoy should recite a poem by Dryden on music with appropriate emotion and expression while the girls would appear on the stage in costume and present a dumb show on the subject of the poem. In addition to this, the girls were also to recite English poems and sing some songs.

Baradasundari had assured Binoy time and again that somehow they would manage to train him for the performance. She herself knew very little English, but she had faith in one or two scholars in her team.

But when the rehearsal started, Binoy surprised the 'scholars' of Baradasundari by his recitation. Baradasundari was thus deprived of the happiness of training this person who was an outsider to her community. Those who had not paid much attention to him earlier, now could not hold back their admiration at hearing his English. Even Haranbabu requested him to write occasionally for his paper. And Sudhir began to pester Binoy for delivering English speeches to their students' gatherings.

Lalita was placed in a strange situation. That Binoy did not need any support from any one made her simultaneously happy and displeased. The realization that Binoy was inferior to none among them, rather the best of the lot, and thereby could feel his superiority to the rest to whom he won't turn for any assistance, hurt her in a strange way. She could not herself understand what she wanted regarding Binoy, what could put her mind at ease. As a result her annoyance targeted Binoy and found frequent sharp expression on small issues. She knew this was not fair, nor even decent; she felt bad about it afterwards, and tried hard to control herself—but she failed to make out why an unreasonable vexation burst through the bars of such control at the slightest provocation. Earlier she had ceaselessly provoked Binoy towards joining the programme; now she could not rest until she dissuaded him against it. But how could Binoy abandon the team at this stage for no reason and thus ditch the whole preparation? Not much time was left either. Furthermore, on discovering his own skill, Binoy himself had become enthused.

At last she declared to Baradasundari, 'I am not going to be in this.'

Baradasundari knew her second daughter well enough, so she was reasonably apprehensive, 'But, why?'

Lalita replied, 'Because I just can't.'

In fact, since the time Binoy ceased to be considered a novice, Lalita refused to rehearse, either recitation or acting, in his presence. She said, 'I shall do it by myself.' This affected the rehearsal of the others, but Lalita was unmanageable. Eventually, they had to accept defeat and carry on the rehearsal without Lalita.

But when she declared total abstinence at the eleventh hour it came like a crash on Baradasundari. She knew she could not persuade her. So she sought Pareshbabu's help. Normally Pareshbabu did never interfere in his daughters' personal affairs. But, this time they had already promised the magistrate, the host party had also made some arrangements accordingly, time too was very short; so, considering all this Pareshbabu called Lalita, affectionately touched her head, and said, 'Lalita, it would be wrong to fall back at this stage.'

Lalita replied in choked voice, 'Baba, I cannot. It does not come to me.'

Pareshbabu said, 'If you do not perform well that is no offence. But if you do not perform at all that will be wrong.'

Lalita lowered her face. Pareshbabu said, 'Ma, since you have accepted a responsibility you must fulfil it. There is no time to run away in the fear that your pride may receive a jolt. Let there be a jolt, still you have to ignore it for doing your duty. Can't you do it, Ma?'

Lalita looked up to her father and said, 'Yes, I will.'

That evening she got over all her diffidence on account of Binoy's presence, and started to do her duty with an additional will, which almost verged on haughtiness. So far Binoy had not heard her recitation. Today he was surprised. What clear strong pronunciation, devoid of the least trace of hesitation! What unambiguous force of expression! Listening to her Binoy was thrilled by an unexpected pleasure. The voice continued to resonate in his ears long afterwards.

A fine recitation of a poem can charm the auditor in a very special way and put him under a spell of the performer. The poem lends its own nobility to the reciter which emerges through her voice, her features and personality. Like a flower on the branch, the poem seems to blossom inside the reciter and thus enrich her beauty.

Lalita too began to be enveloped by the beauty of the poem in Binoy's perception. So far she had kept him tense and excited by her sharpness. As one cannot forget an ache, Binoy too, for the last few days, could think of nothing else besides her biting words and caustic smile. He was preoccupied with the riddles,—why did Lalita say this or do that; the more he failed to pierce through the mystery of her displeasure, the more Lalita came to obsess him. On waking up at dawn he would suddenly remember her. Everyday on his way to Pareshbabu's house he anxiously conjectured—who knows how should Lalita behave today. On occasions when she showed the least sign of approval Binoy had felt a surge of relief, and his immediate thought was how to retain this mood. But he could never really find out a means of doing so.

After such a turmoil day after day, the charm of Lalita's recitation moved him like anything and carried him away. He could not find the adequate words for expressing his appreciation. Indeed he did not dare to say anything good or bad; because although it was a common law of human nature to be pleased at appreciation, it might not work in Lalita's case. Therefore, Binoy enthusiastically praised Lalita's talents to Baradasundari. This only further confirmed Baradasundari's opinion regarding Binoy's knowledge and intelligence.

Another strange thing happened. When Lalita herself felt that her recitation and acting were excellent, that she could smoothly tide over the supposedly difficult duty like a fine boat riding along the crest of waves, she also got over her aggressiveness towards Binoy. No effort on her part to dissuade Binoy was visible any more. Instead she showed increasing interest in the programme and regarding rehearsal a good rapport was struck between Binoy and Lalita. Indeed, she didn't even refuse to take suggestions from Binoy regarding recitation or other related matters.

At this change in Lalita Binoy felt as if a weight was lifted off his chest. He felt so happy that every now and then he went over to Anandamoyee to play pranks like a small child. Many things arose in his mind which he would have poured out to Sucharita, but these days Sucharita had become nearly inaccessible. At every chance he would sit down to talk with Lalita, but while talking to Lalita he could not be quite off guard. Since he knew Lalita was a sharp judge of his words and him, Binoy could not speak to her relaxedly with natural unrestraint. Occasionally Lalita would say, 'Why do you speak like this, as if you have just read these lines in some book?'

Binoy replied, 'All these years the only thing I have done is reading books. So my mind has turned into a printed book.'

Lalita said, 'Please don't try to speak impressively—just speak out your own say in your own words. You speak so finely, that I have the hunch you are dressing up other people's thoughts.'

For this even when an original idea automatically came to him clothed in fine words, he deliberately simplified and curbed the expression. If by chance he happened to drop a sophisticated expression he felt instantly shy.

It seemed a cloud had lifted from Lalita's mind leaving it shining and radiant. Even Baradasundari was taken aback at this change. Lalita was no more aggressive or withdrawn as earlier; instead she got involved in all the details. Everyday she landed upon fresh ideas regarding the costume and other details of the play, and with these she bothered everybody. In spite of all her enthusiasm about the programme, Baradasundari could not ignore the expense; therefore, just as she had been anxious earlier at Lalita's non-participation so she was worried no less at her recent enthusiasm. But she did not dare to dampen Lalita's roused imagination; because once she was interested in something she must go the whole hog and at the slightest obstacle she would be too depressed to carry on.

During this period when her mind was in effusion Lalita had eagerly approached Sucharita many a time. Sucharita had smiled, talked, but Lalita had felt a distance between them. Vexed, she had come back.

One day she approached Pareshbabu, 'Baba, we go to the programme, but Suchididi keeps on reading her books sitting alone in a corner. This won't do. She too must join us.'

Pareshbabu too had been wondering for some time if Sucharita was getting somehow distant from the other girls. He felt anxious that this might adversely affect her personality. Lalita's words prompted him to think that this staying away from little entertainments might further enhance her alienation. Pareshbabu told Lalita, 'Convince your Ma first.'

Lalita said, 'I shall manage Ma. But you have to persuade Suchididi.'

When Pareshbabu broached the proposal Sucharita could not refuse. She responded dutifully.

As soon as Sucharita came out of her exclusive corner to join them Binoy tried to kick up conversation like earlier days. But what had happened during these few days? Binoy could not make any headway. Such a distance was manifest in her expression, in the looks of her eyes, that made one shrink from approaching her. Earlier too Sucharita's sociability and movements were marked by a certain degree of detachment. Now that element had surfaced distinctly. Even after joining the rehearsal her aloofness was not lost. She attended just that much which was essential for the work, and left immediately after that was over. Binoy was sociable by nature. It was hard for him to bear indifference from the dear ones. So long he had received special attention from Sucharita in this family; now this sudden inexplicable avoidance pained him. But, when he realized that Lalita too was resentful towards Sucharita for the same reason he got some consolation and this helped to draw them even closer to each other. True, he did not give Sucharita any excuse to avoid him; however he gave up attempts to build bridges and thus before long Sucharita drifted far far away from Binoy.

Thanks to Gora's absence this time Binoy could freely mix with all the members of Pareshbabu's family without inhibition. The family also was very pleased at this free play of Binoy's personality. Being able to reach this uninhibited natural relationship Binoy himself was so happy as he had never been before. On feeling that they all liked him, his ability to be liked only increased.

However, it was during such a time of natural expansion, of attaining self-assurance as an individual, that Sucharita drifted miles and miles away from Binoy. At any other time this loss, this wound should have been unbearable, but now he took it in his stride. What is no less strange is that Lalita too did not express her resentment at Sucharita's change as she would have in earlier times. Is it because the euphoria over recitation and acting had so completely possessed the two?

In the meanwhile, seeing Sucharita join the programme Haranbabu too got enthused all of a sudden. He announced his decision to recite a passage from *Paradise Lost* in addition to delivering a brief speech on the charming attributes of music as prologue to the play. Baradasundari was deeply annoyed at this; Lalita too was not very pleased. But Haranbabu had already seen the magistrate and clinched the issue there. When Lalita suggested that thus lengthening the programme might invite objection from the magistrate, Haranbabu stopped her by flashing his ace card,—a letter from the magistrate 'gratefully' accepting his proposal.

Gora had set out on an indefinite trip. Nobody knew when he would return. Although Sucharita had resolved not to think about it, still everyday an expectation flowered within her, perhaps Gora would return today. She could not crush out this hope. When she was miserable at this indifference of Gora and at the disobedience of her own mind, when she was longing to escape somehow from this mesh, one day Haranbabu renewed his request to Pareshbabu—particularly in God's name—to confirm his betrothal with Sucharita.

Pareshbabu said, 'There is still some time for the marriage to take place. Is it desirable to have the engagement so soon?'

Haranbabu insisted, 'I consider it essential for the mental preparation on both the sides to spend a period prior to marriage in this state of engagement. Such an ethereal relationship in between first acquaintance and marriage proper—in which there is no domestic responsibility and yet there is a kind of tie—is particularly beneficial.'

Pareshbabu said, 'Anyway, let me seek her opinion first.'

Haranbabu said, 'Hasn't she already given consent?'

Pareshbabu still had his doubts about Sucharita's attitude to Haranbabu. So he called Sucharita and told her about the proposal. Sucharita was desperate to get over her torment somehow. So she gave her consent so instantaneously and unambiguously that Pareshbabu was relieved of his doubts. Nevertheless he requested Sucharita to consider if entering an engagement so much ahead of the scheduled marriage was advisable; but in spite of his suggestion Sucharita expressed no objection to the proposal.

It was decided that after the family came back from Mr Brownlow's party a day would be fixed for finalizing the engagement in a public programme.

For a brief moment Sucharita felt as if her mind had come out of an eclipse. She resolved to herself that she would sternly prepare her mind to join the work of the Brahmosamaj by marrying Haranbabu. She further resolved to take a daily lesson from Haranbabu in English on theology and follow his guidance henceforth. She felt a swelling pride within her at resolving to do what was difficult and even unpleasant for her.

It was for some time that she had not read the English paper edited by Haranbabu. Today a copy of that paper fresh from the press came to her hand. Probably Haranbabu himself had sent it specially for her.

Sucharita took the paper to her room, sat down quietly and started reading from the very first line as a holy duty. She sought to receive instructions from this paper like a devoted disciple.

The smooth-sailing ship of obedient devotion suddenly struck against a rock and tilted. The issue contained an essay titled, "Obsessed with the Past". The essay attacked those who, in spite of living in the present kept their faces turned back toward the past. Not that the arguments were illogical. Indeed Sucharita herself was on the lookout for some such arguments. But as soon as she started reading it was transparent to her that the target of this attack was Gora. Yet neither was his name mentioned nor his essays. As a trigger-happy soldier is supposed to gloat while killing one life per bullet so each sentence seemed to reflect a gloating envy at wounding a living object.

The essay was too much for her. She wished to tear every argument into shreds. She told to herself, 'Gaurmohanbabu can grind it to dust if he so wishes.' At once Gora's bright face surfaced with radiant glow before her vision while his roaring voice resonated in the innermost core of her heart. Before that extraordinary face and voice the essay and its writer were reduced to such mean insignificance that she threw the paper on the floor.

After so many days Sucharita came to take her seat by Binoy, and in course of casual talk said, 'Well, this is just to remind—you had assured me you would lend me all the published articles of you two for reading. Did you forget?'

Binoy did not confess that he did not dare to carry out his promise in view of Sucharita's recent change. Instead he said, 'I have collected them into a bunch. I shall surely bring them tomorrow.'

The following day Binoy handed over a bundle of booklets and papers. Sucharita, however, did not plunge into them, instead she put them aside in a box. She did not read precisely because she felt such a strong longing to read. She resolved not to allow herself any distraction and sought peace by surrendering her rebellious soul once again to Haranbabu's stern rulings.

25

It was Sunday. Anandamoyee was preparing spiced betel-leaves; squatting by her side Shashimukhi was chipping betel-nuts into a small mound when Binoy entered the room. Shashimukhi at once threw down the nuts on her lap and ran away in a hurry. Anandamoyee's lips curled into a smile.

Binoy could make friends with all. With Shashimukhi he was on reasonably good terms. They teased each other quite a lot. Shashimukhi had devised a means to hear stories from Binoy: this was by hiding his shoes. By using a few small events in the child's small life as source material Binoy had added a lot of color and this was highly effective for the purpose of leg pulling. Initially the girl would loudly protest accusing the speaker of falsehood; finally she left the spot. She too had tried to foist parallel tales on Binoy's life, but being inferior to Binoy in creative art she did not meet much success that way.

Anyway whenever Binoy came to the house Shashimukhi would rush in and loud noise and fun would follow. Some days she was so uncontrollable that even Anandamoyee scolded her. But it was not her fault alone. Binoy provoked her so much by leg pulling and teasing that she could hardly restrain herself. The very same child today ran out of the room at Binoy's arrival; noticing this Anandamoyee smiled, but this was no smile of happiness.

Binoy too was so touched by this small incident that he sat silent for a while. From such small things it became evident how absurd it was for Binoy to marry Shashimukhi. When Binoy gave his consent his only consideration was Gora's friendship; he had not applied his mind to the whole issue and its possible implications. Besides, marriage in our country is viewed primarily as a family affair and not as an individual's personal concern. Binoy too had written quite a number of essays in papers extolling the approach. Neither did the thought of personal likes or dislikes in the matter occur to him. But as Shashimukhi ran out of the room today Binoy had a sudden glimpse of the form of his future relationship with the girl. At once his whole heart rebelled. He felt angry with Gora remembering how Gora was about to drag him against his nature; he also felt like denouncing himself. Remembering that Anandamoyee had been against this marriage from the beginning he was filled with surprise and admiration at her fine insight.

Anandamoyee could read Binoy's mind. To distract him she said, 'Gora's letter came yesterday.'

Binoy asked in a still preoccupied tone, 'What does he say?'

Anandamoyee said, 'Not much about himself; has expressed sadness at the miserable condition of the poor of the country; also described the injustice of a magistrate in some village called Ghoshpara.'

Out of his previous mood of resentment against Gora Binoy spoke out impatiently, 'Gora is obsessed with the outsiders. But for the kind of wrong we are perpetrating on our own society he has only forgiveness; you must say nothing can be better than this!'

By thus suddenly accusing Gora Binoy seemed to present himself as his opponent. Seeing this Anandamoyee smiled.

Binoy said, '*Mā*, you are laughing. Perhaps you are wondering why should Binoy be so angry all of a sudden? Let me explain to you why I feel vexed. The other day Sudhir had taken me to his friend's garden at Naihati. As soon as we left Sealdah it started raining. When the train stopped at Sodpur, a Bengali babu in European costume holding the umbrella on his own head got down along with his wife. The poor lady stood under the pouring rain somehow covering the baby astride her lap with the thick chadar—stiff in shame and cold—while the umbrella-holding husband fussed over the luggage, the porter and what not. In a flash I remembered that across the length and breadth of Bangladesh no woman uses an umbrella—be it in sun or in rain, or be she rich or poor. I saw the husband shamelessly holding the umbrella on his own head, and his wife silently standing in the downpour with only a chadar to cover her body; she did not blame this treatment even silently, and the whole crowd in the station found nothing wrong with the scene. Since then I have resolved never to repeat the false, pretentious, nice claims that we respect our women greatly, or we look up to them as deities, etc. We invoke the country as "motherland". But if we fail to perceive the nobility of this female icon in its manifested form in our women, if we do not envision the possibility of their full blossoming into intelligence, strength, sense of duty, magnanimity, the vision of country will never come alive—full and bright—in our perception.'

Then feeling suddenly embarrassed at his own enthusiasm Binoy reverted to a natural tone, '*Mā*, perhaps you are thinking Binoy has the habit of delivering longish speeches on occasions—and today he is in such an oratorial mood. True, thanks to my habit, what I say sounds like oratory. But today this is no public speech. Never before did I realize what a part of the country is constituted by its women. *Mā*, no more today. Because I speak too much nobody takes my words seriously as expression of my own conviction. From now on I shall try to curb my talkativeness.'

Saying this Binoy did not wait any more but left in an excited mood.

Anandamoyee sent for Mahim and told him, 'My son, give up the plan of marrying off our Shashimukhi to Binoy.'

Mahim. But why! Do you have any objection?

Anandamoyee. I disagree because this negotiation will not materialize; otherwise why should I object?

Mahim. Gora has agreed. Binoy too is agreeable. Then why should it not materialize? Of course, if you object Binoy will never go ahead, that I know well.

Anandamoyee. I know Binoy better than you know him.

Mahim. Better than Gora?

Anandamoyee. Yes. Better than even Gora. That's why, considering all the aspects of the situation I cannot say that I agree.

Mahim. O.K. Then let Gora return.

Anandamoyee. Mahim, please listen to me. If you insist too much on this it may lead to some serious trouble. I don't want that Gora says anything to Binoy about this.

'Well, let us see', saying this Mahim pushed a *pān* into his mouth and angrily left the room.

26

When Gora set out on the trip he had four companions—Abinash, Matilal, Basanta and Ramapati. But they could not catch up with Gora's pace. Within four to five days Abinash and Basanta left for Calcutta on the pretext of illness. Out of sheer loyalty to Gora Matilal and Ramapati carried on. But their condition was miserable; because Gora was never tired of walking, and again he was not bored if he got stuck up in one place for long. As a Brahmin Gora was welcome to every household in the village, and he would stay on with his host without caring for any inconvenience. All the villagers used to gather to listen to him and did not want him to leave.

This was the first time Gora saw what the country was like beyond the pale of the genteel elite circle of the Calcutta society. This remote, vast, rural India—how fragmented it was, how narrow, how weak, how completely unaware of its own strength, ignorant and indifferent to betterment—how different it was at the interval of every ten to fourteen miles, how debarred from the big world by its own self-imposed imaginary obstacles, how obsessed with trivialities and rigidly resistant to any change or reform; what stagnation of mind, paucity of life, feebleness of effort! Gora could not have imagined this India if he had not lived thus among the villagers. During his stay in the village once a fire broke out in a particular area. Gora was stunned at seeing how little was their ability for organized effort even in the face of such a crisis. It was all chaos with confused noise, wild rush, and loud lamentation, but nothing was done systematically. There was no water tank in the vicinity; women carried water from a distant area to serve the household need; yet nobody, not even the moneyed ones had ever thought of digging a low-cost well towards removing this daily hardship. In the past, too, there had been occasional fires in the area; people accepted it as the work of destiny and took no initiative to arrange for some water resource nearby. It seemed a mockery to Gora to discuss the whole country before those who were so insensitive to the bare necessities of their own small area. What surprised Gora most was the reaction of Matilal and Ramapati; they were not at all disturbed by the scene or events, rather they thought his reaction as absurd. Their assumption was that lowclass people have always been like that, lived like that, and this was no suffering for them. It seemed absurd to them to imagine that anything else than this could be the lot of the lowclass people. How terrible, how enormous was this burden of ignorance, stagnation and misery, and how it was weighing down alike upon the elite and the subaltern, the rich and the poor, thereby pulling them backwards! Gora realized this clearly and his heart bled day and night.

Eventually Matilal too bade good-bye, supposedly on receiving some bad news from home. Only Ramapati remained to accompany Gora.

In course of their journey one day they reached a Muslim village on the sandbank of a river. Their search for a possible host led them to the single Hindu house in the village—that of a barber. Reaching the house the two Brahmin youths discovered that the old barber and his wife were bringing up a Muslim child. Ramapati, who was a staunch orthodox, was agitated. On being scolded by Gora for heresy, the barber replied, 'Thakur, we call Hari, they call Allah. There is no real difference between the two.'

The sun had already touched meridian over the vast sandbank; the river was far away. Choking with thirst, Ramapati asked, 'Where can I get some drinking water appropriate for a Hindu?'

There was an earthen well in the barber's house, but Ramapati could not drink from that heretical water; therefore he had no choice but to squat with a depressed look.

Gora asked, 'Who are the parents of this child?'

Barber said, 'They are there. But it is as good as being dead.'

Gora. How's that?

The barber told him a long story the summary of which is like this—

The land on which they were living was leased to British indigo planters. There were endless disputes between the planters and tenants on this bank over the land for indigo planting. All the other tenants had eventually surrendered. Only the tenants of this bank—called Char-Ghoshpur—had not surrendered to the British planter as yet. All the tenants on this bank are Musalmans, and their leader Farusardar does not fear anybody. Twice he has seen the inside of prison for beating up policemen who acted as the henchmen of the planters. He is reduced to the condition of near starvation, but still he knows no surrender. This time the villagers cultivated the low land close to the river and harvested some cheap rice. But about a month ago the manager of the indigo farm himself came flanked by armed guards, and looted that rice. During the plunder Farusardar had dealt such a blow with his stick to the manager that he had to get his right arm amputated by a surgeon. Such a daring thing had never happened before in this area. Since then the police have been after us like licking fire—they have plundered every house, violated women, imprisoned Farusardar along with a lot of people, while many others have fled from the village. Faru's wife is starving. Even her only sari has become so tattered that she cannot venture out of doors; her only child, Tamij calls Barber's wife auntie. Seeing the child starving, the barber's wife brought him over to her own place and has been looking after him since. There is an indigo farm within three miles of this place. A sub-inspector of the police is camping there with his contingent. You never know when they come down and what they do on the pretext of investigation. Yesterday the police had landed at the house of the barber's neighbour, old Najim. Najim's young brother-in-law had come from a distant village to see his sister. Without any reason the sub-inspector exclaimed, 'Ah! A hero indeed! Look at the chest!', and dealt such a blow with his baton that broke his teeth and drew out blood. As his sister rushed out at this torture she was instantly thrown to the dust with another blow. Earlier the police did not dare to perpetrate such barbarism here, but now that all the strong young men are either in prison or gone underground, the police are torturing the villagers on the pretext of searching for the escapees. One does not know when this terror will end.

Gora listened spellbound. In the meantime Ramapati was dying of thirst. Even before the barber could finish his account he came out impatiently, 'How far is it from the Hindu area?'

Barber said, 'There is an indigo farm some three miles from here. The book-keeper of that farm is a Brahmin, Madhab Chatterjee by name.'

Gora asked, 'What kind of a man is he?'

Barber said, 'You could call him a constable of Yama. Such a combination of cruelty and cleverness is rare. Rest assured that he will squeeze out from us the entire cost he has incurred by playing host to the sub-inspector in addition to some cut money for himself.'

Ramapati called, 'Gaurbabu, let us move. I cannot take any more.'

Especially when the barber's wife started bathing the Muslim boy with bowls of water from the well in the yard he felt thoroughly disgusted and did not feel like lingering for another moment in this unholy house.

Before leaving Gora asked the barber, 'How come that you stay on here in spite of all this trouble? Don't you have relatives elsewhere?'

Barber said, 'I have been here for a long time. I am a Hindu barber, and I have no land. So the indigo people do not care about me. Today there is practically no other male in the area excepting me. If I desert them the women will die out of fear.'

Gora said, 'O.K., I shall come back after lunch.'

This long account of the oppression of indigo planters delivered at an hour of keen hunger and thirst made Ramapati averse to the very villagers. The scoundrels wanted to raise their heads in defiance of the powerful; this seemed to him but another good evidence of the audacity and idiocy of adamant Musalmans. He did not have the least doubt that this audacity was better crushed by appropriate thrashing. Ramapati subscribed to the notion that it was only normal that police should give such worthless creatures a good thrashing now and then—it is bound to happen, and it is these people who are themselves responsible for such police action. Why not come to an understanding with the ruler? Why must they invite trouble? What did the audacity avail for them? Indeed Ramapati's sympathies lay rather on the side of the British planters.

Gora was completely silent while walking the long stretch of hot sand under midday sun. At last when the thatch of the indigo farm was visible through the trees Gora suddenly stopped and told Ramapati, 'You go for lunch. I am going back to that barber.'

Ramapati was surprised, 'What do you say? Won't you eat? Have your meal first with Chatterjee and then you can go there at leisure.'

Gora said, 'I will do my duty. After food and rest you pack off for Calcutta. I think I have to stay back for a while on that Ghoshpur bank. I don't think you can join me there.'

Ramapati had goosebumps all over his body. He could not make out how a staunch pious Hindu like Gora could mention the idea of living with that heretic. He tried to guess if Gora had resolved to abdicate food and drink and end his life in 'fast unto death' like the ancient *rishis*? Anyway, it was no time for guessing. Every second hung upon him like an age. He did not need much persuasion to desert Gora and rush for Calcutta. For a fraction of a moment Ramapati looked back to see Gora's tall body trudging back alone, along the hot deserted sand bank under the scorching midday sun, with only a dwarfish shadow following behind.

Gora was dying with hunger and thirst. But must he save his caste by taking food at the criminal Madhab Chatterjee's table? The more he thought of this the more unbearable it appeared. A fierce rebelliousness reddened his face and eyes while sending fiery signal to the brain. He thought, 'We have made purity an external thing, and what an aberration this is from religion. My caste is saved by eating with one who is playing host to criminals for torturing Musalmans. And I shall ruin my caste status by eating with the very man who protects a Musalman child in the face of threats and is ready to run the risk of social censure for the poor child's sake! Anyway, I shall think of this matter of do's and don'ts at some other time. Now I can bear no more.'

The barber was surprised to see Gora coming back alone. Gora took the barber's bowl, scrubbed it clean and then scooping up a bowl of water from the well, gulped it down. Then he told the barber, 'If you have a handful of rice and pulse to spare please give me; I shall cook it.'

The barber quickly arranged for the cooking. After having his meal Gora declared, 'I shall stay with for a few days.'

Barber was scared. Folding his hands he said, 'You to stay with this humble man! Nothing can be more welcome. But, look here, we are now under the surveillance of the police. If you stay on, who knows what kind of trouble may take place.'

Gora assured, 'If I stay here the police will not dare to harass you. And even if they do I shall protect you.'

Barber pleaded, 'For God's sake, don't. If you try to protect us we shall be ruined. Those devils will think I have somehow hatched a conspiracy and smuggled you in for witnessing their misdeeds. So long I have somehow managed to survive, but after this I won't. If I am compelled to shift then the rest of the village will go to the rots.'

Gora has grown up in cities all along. It was difficult for him to understand why the barber was so scared. He believed if one stood firmly on the just side it automatically removed injustice. His sense of duty did not allow him to leave the endangered village behind to its own helplessness. Then the barber fell at his feet, 'Please try to understand me. You are a Brahmin. It is my great fortune that you have come as a guest to me. But I know you are kindly disposed toward us. That is why I tell you this. If you oppose the police torture while staying as a guest with me, that will be landing me in great danger.'

Gora was a bit vexed at this fear of the barber which he put down to unreasonable cowardice. In the afternoon he set out. A certain annoyance also stirred within him at remembering that he had taken his meal in the house of this heretic. With an irritated mind and tired body he reached the office of the indigo farm in the evening. As Ramapati had lost no time after lunch to start for Calcutta, he was not to be found there. Madhab Chatterjee ceremoniously invited Gora to accept his hospitality.

Gora flared up instantly, 'I won't take even a drop of water here.'

Surprised, Madhab begged for the cause and in reply Gora accused him as the perpetrator of injustice and oppression. He stood firm without taking the offered seat. The sub-inspector was resting against a pillow on the bed while puffing at a *gurguri*. He sat up and asked rudely, 'Who are you? Where do you hail from?'

Without answering his query Gora came forward, 'Oh, you are that sub-inspector, I think! I have got all the information regarding your misrule on the bank of Ghoshpur. Take care before it is too late, otherwise—.'

Sub-inspector. Yes! What would you do? Hang me from the scaffold? Indeed, here is an audacious one! I thought some one had come for alms, but he seems to threaten! Heigh, constable!

Madhab anxiously pulled at his hand, 'Oh, what are you doing! Here is a gentleman. Don't insult him.'

The sub-inspector was peevish, 'Gentleman indeed! And he has abused you too like anything. Isn't that an insult?'

Madhab said, 'But what he says is not untrue; so, how can I afford to be offended? I, a man who earns his living by serving indigo planters? Don't take it otherwise my brother—you are a police inspector, and if somebody calls you a footman of Yama, can you really say this is abuse? It is common knowledge that the tiger lives by killing men, he is not a vegetarian Vaishnavite; what can the poor tiger do? He too has to survive.'

Nobody had ever seen Madhab unnecessarily losing temper; because who knows how you can squeeze benefit from others or may suffer at the hands of another if things go awry? When he harmed or insulted one it was only after an elaborate calculation; he did not believe in wasting energy on hitting people under an angry impulse.

The sub-inspector then turned to Gora, 'Look here, Mister, we are here on governmental work—if you interfere or create obstruction you'll land in trouble.'

Without saying a word Gora left the room. Madhab hurried up behind him, 'Sir, what you say is absolutely right. Our job is the butcher's job. And that scoundrel of a sub-inspector—it is sinful to share a seat with him. I cannot mention in so many words the volume of misdeeds that I have done through him. But it will not be many more days; within two to three years more of this service I shall earn enough to marry my daughters off; then we, husband and wife will seek the reclusion of Varanasi. I am disgusted Sir—sometimes I feel like hanging myself from the ceiling! Anyway, where will you go at this hour of nightfall? Please stop here for tonight, have your food and rest. You needn't be bothered at all by that sub-inspector; I shall make completely separate arrangement for you.'

Gora had a stronger appetite than an average youth. Furthermore, he had no square meal since morning. But his entire body and soul seemed to flare up in anger. He could not halt here. He left saying, 'I have some urgent work.'

Madhav said, 'Then wait a bit. Let me send you a lantern.'

Without answering him Gora left in long quick strides.

Re-entering the room Madhab called, 'Brother, that man went to the town. You immediately send a messenger to the magistrate.'

Sub-inspector. But why? What is to be done?

Madhab. Nothing much. Only inform the magistrate a gentleman outsider has sneaked in from somewhere and is trying to mislead our witnesses.

27

At the end of the day Magistrate Mr Brownlow was enjoying a walk along the road by the riverside. Haranbabu was giving him company. A little ahead his wife was out with the ladies of Pareshbabu's family to enjoy a ride in the carriage.

Mr Brownlow used to occasionally invite select Bengali gentlemen to his garden parties. He also used to preside over the annual prize distribution ceremony of the district entrance school. If some prosperous man invited him to social occasions like marriage, etc., he accepted the invitation. Being invited to *jātrā*-opera and similar functions he even patiently tried to listen to the music for a while, reclining on a huge chair. During the last puja held at the house of the government pleader at his court, he had particularly enjoyed the performance of two youths in the role of water-supplier and sweeper woman; indeed, at his special request they had to repeat that part of the play several times before him.

His wife was the daughter of a clergyman. Sometimes missionary ladies used to gather at her house for tea. She had established a girls' school in the district, and took enough initiative to ensure an adequate number of girls in the school. Noticing the educational pursuits of Pareshbabu's daughters she always encouraged them. Even while staying far away she wrote letters to them and used to send them bibles as Christmas gifts.

The fair had started. On the occasion Baradasundari and her daughters had come along with Haranbabu, Sudhir and Binoy. They had been accommodated in the inspection bungalow. Pareshbabu did not feel at home in this kind of noisy milieu, so he had stayed back at Calcutta alone. Sucharita had tried to stay back with him so that he was not left all by himself; but Pareshbabu sent her off with special advice to perform her part of the duty in responding to the magisterial invitation. The day after tomorrow Pareshbabu's daughters will present their cultural programme before the Commissioner, the Lieutenant Governor and his wife at the evening party following dinner. Many British friends of the magistrate have been invited from Calcutta and the districts on the occasion. Some select Bengali gentlemen too are supposed to attend. It was reported that a Brahmin cook would prepare snacks for them in a separate tent in the garden.

Within a very short time Haranbabu had been able to highly please the magistrate by his high-toned discussions. The Englishman was astonished to see Haranbabu's extraordinary knowledge of Christian theology. He even asked Haranbabu why he was still delaying to embrace Christianity.

This afternoon, while walking along the riverside road, Haranbabu was engaged in a profound discussion with the Englishman about the procedures of Brahmosamaj and the reform of Hindu society when suddenly Gora appeared before them saying, 'Good evening, sir.'

Yesterday, while trying in vain to see the magistrate, Gora had realized that he had to bribe the Saheb's peon before he crossed the threshold of his office. Refusing to yield to this pressure and humiliation Gora came today to take this chance of meeting him outdoors. During this meeting no sign of prior acquaintance was shown either by Haranbabu or by Gora.

Seeing the man the magistrate was a bit surprised. He could not remember ever having seen such a tall man in Bengal—more than six feet indeed—with such strong bones, and stout build. His complexion too was not like that of the average Bengali. He wore a loose grey cotton shirt, a thick and shabby dhoti, holding a bamboo stick in one hand, while the *cādar* was wound around the head like a *pāgrī*.

Gora told the magistrate, 'I am coming from Char-Ghoshpur.'

The magistrate whistled a surprised note. He had already received the news the day before that an outsider had come to the Char to obstruct investigation work. So this was the man! He sharply scrutinized Gora from head to foot once and asked, 'What is your caste?'

Gora replied, 'I am a Bengali Brahmin.'

Saheb asked, 'Ah! I see. Do you have any connection with newspapers?'

Gora said, 'No'.

Magistrate asked, 'Then why have you come to Char-Ghoshpur?'

Gora said, 'In course of my travel I stopped there for rest. But seeing evidence of the misery of the village under police oppression and apprehending the possibility of further torture, I have come to you seeking some redress.'

Magistrate said, 'Do you have any idea how notorious the people of the Char are?'

Gora replied, 'They are not notorious, they are fearless freedom-loving souls—who refuse to silently accept unjust oppression.'

The magistrate was ruffled. He told himself, 'Here is a new generation Bengali—learnt some cliché from history textbooks—insufferable indeed!'

'You know nothing of the situation here', the magistrate howled out to Gora.

Gora replied in his thunderous voice, 'You know even less than I of the situation here.'

The Magistrate was furious, 'I warn you, if you interfere in the Ghoshpur case there will be no easy respite for you.'

Gora said, 'Since you have decided not to make any redress for the torture, since you are biased against the villagers then I am left with no other choice. Now I shall go back to encourage the villagers to stand up on their own against the police action.'

The magistrate's walk suddenly came to a halt and quickly turning like a flash to Gora he roared out, 'What! How do you dare!'

Without uttering another word Gora slowly walked away with firm dignity.

Magistrate said, 'Haranbabu, what are these symptoms appearing among your countrymen?'

Haranbabu said, 'Sir, it is the lack of genuine education. Especially the absence of spiritual and moral education has been leading to such phenomena. Virtually these youths do not have the ability to receive the best gift of English education. This ungrateful lot won't admit that British rule in India is willed by God. Actually they have only read books, but their religious sensibility is yet to be formed.'

Magistrate said, 'Until you convert to Christianity this religious sensibility will never blossom in India.'

Haranbabu dittoed, 'It's true in a sense.'

After this Haranbabu kept the magistrate so engrossed with his fine discourse on the semblances and differences between the respective opinions of a Christian and of himself, that when the Saheb's wife, on her way back from seeing off Pareshbabu's daughters to the bungalow called her husband,—'Harry, it's time we went home'—he started and taking out the wristwatch exclaimed, 'By Jove, it is already eight twenty!' Before boarding the carriage he shook hands with Haranbabu, bade him good-bye and said, 'I had a nice time talking with you.'

Returning to the bungalow Haranbabu elaborately reported his conversation with the magistrate but carefully avoided any mention of Gora.

28

Without any pretence of a trial forty-seven people were thrown into the prison just to repress the village.

After his encounter with the magistrate Gora set out in search of a lawyer. Somebody told him about one Satkari Haldar who was a good pleader in the locality. As soon as he entered Satkari's house the latter exclaimed, 'Bah, what surprise. Gora here! What are you doing here!'

Gora's guess was correct. Satkari was Gora's classmate. Gora said, 'You have to bail out the prisoners arrested from Char-Ghoshpur and fight their case.'

Satkari asked, 'But who will stand security?'

Gora said, 'I will.'

Satkari said, 'How can you alone stand security for all the forty-seven prisoners?'

Gora said, 'If the advocates together stand security I will pay their fees.'

Satkari said, 'It will cost a lot.'

The following day bail petition was moved in the magistrate's court. The magistrate glanced once at the heroic figure in turban and dusty clothes, and rejected the petition. The prisoners—from the boy of fourteen to the old man of eighty—were left to rot behind the bars.

Gora appealed to Satkari to fight for them. Satkari said, 'Where to get witnesses? Those who could give evidence are all accused. Besides, people of the locality have been quite harassed by the investigation work of the Saheb-beating case. The magistrate has got the idea that there must be some upperclass boys behind it. They may even suspect me, who knows? The English papers are continuously campaigning—if the natives become so audacious how can the undefended helpless English officials work in the mofussils? In the meantime things have come to such a pass that the natives cannot carry on in their own country. I know oppression is there, but nothing can be done.'

Gora thundered, 'Why not?'

Satkari laughed, 'You are still the boy you were at school. Nothing can be done, because we have wife and children—if we don't earn daily many have to go starving. There aren't many people in the world who would be ready to die for the sake of other people—especially so in a country where a family is not a small affair. Those on whom ten people depend get no chance to look beyond that ten to others.'

Gora intercepted, 'Then won't you do anything for these people? Suppose we moved the High Court—.'

Satkari lost patience, 'Don't you see it is a case of beating an Englishman? Every Englishman is a king—even if you thrash a petty Briton that would amount to sedition on a small scale.

Fighting this case will be futile; on the other hand this will antagonise the magistrate. Excuse me, please. I can't help.'

Gora had set out to catch the ten-thirty train for Calcutta with the intention to probe the possibility of getting legal assistance at Calcutta, when there came up an obstacle. On the occasion of the fair a group of Calcutta students had come to play cricket-match against a local team of students. The Calcutta team was practicing when the ball injured a boy on the leg. There was a big tank by the field. Two of the students carried the injured boy close to the tank and tearing a piece of their *cādar* soaked it in the water to bandage the leg, when a guard rushed in and rudely pushed a boy by the neck while hurling filthy abuses. The tank was reserved for drinking water, and getting into it was forbidden. But the Calcutta boys did not know it. Even if they knew they were not accustomed to this kind of insult from a guard; they had physical strength too. Therefore, they started to hit back. Seeing this four or five constables rushed in. Just at the very same moment Gora arrived at the spot. The students knew Gora. Gora had often played cricket with them. When Gora saw the students being beaten and dragged along he could not stand silent. He shouted, 'Hei! Don't beat them.' The guards hurled filthy abuses at him too and at once Gora kicked up such a row showering blows with his fists, and wildly kicking, that before long a crowd gathered in the street. Meanwhile other students too had come up. Encouraged and led by Gora they attacked the police and instantly they were seen fleeing. The spectators thoroughly enjoyed the scene. But it needs no mention that this did not prove to be much of an amusement for Gora.

By afternoon, around three o' clock, Binoy, Haranbabu and the girls were rehearsing for the evening when two students, who knew Binoy, came to inform him that Gora, along with a few students, were arrested and remanded to police custody, and that they would be presented to the magistrate in the first hour tomorrow.

Gora was under arrest! Hearing this everyone was shocked excepting Haranbabu. Binoy rushed out to meet his classmate

Satkari Haldar and together they went to meet Gora in the police custody.

Satkari offered to bail him out and act as his defence. Gora refused, 'No, I won't have any lawyer, nor do I want you to bail me out.'

What does he say! Satkari turned to Binoy, 'See! Who will say that Gora has crossed the school threshold! He is still that volatile boy.'

Gora said, 'I don't want to be released from the handcuff just because incidentally I have the money, I have friends. According to the ethos of India it is the duty of the ruler to deliver justice; perpetrating injustice on the people is against the principles of kingship. But under the present rule in this state people may rot in the custody, or die in the prison if they do not have the money to procure a lawyer; they have to go insolvent for purchasing justice; in such a situation I refuse to pay a single penny for securing such justice.'

Satkari pleaded, 'Consider the times of the *Kāzīs*; one could be ruined just by the bribes one had to pay.'

Gora replied, 'Bribing was not the king's law. A bad Kazi used to take bribes, which practice is still in vogue. But, now if you seek justice before the king, whether you are the accused or the accuser, guilty or innocent, you are forced to eat the dust. The poor is ruined both ways, be it loss or win in the case. Furthermore, when the king himself is the accuser, and people like me are on the dock, then the whole pack of advocates and barristers will be on his side. If I can procure one, well and good. If I can't, leave it to my fate! If lawyers are redundant in the system, then what is the point of having a government pleader? And why in case of need the non-government party should be forced to find its own pleader? Isn't this injustice towards the people? What kind of ruler's principle is this?'

Satkari said, 'Brother, what's the use of getting angry? Civilization is not easy to understand. If you need fine judicial system you need fine laws, for framing fine laws you require professional lawyers, professionalism will involve market rules of buying and selling—therefore the court of a civilized state is bound to become a market for sale and purchase—so that one who lacks money runs every possibility of being doomed. Tell me what you would have done if you were the ruler?'

Gora said, 'I would have framed such laws as would defy the probing of judges earning four figures, and then I would have appointed pleaders for both the defence and the accuser at government expense. I would not have passed on the burden of expense towards good judiciary to the people and then boast of fine legal system comparing it to the damned system of the Pathans and Mughals.'

Satkari said, 'Encore! But since that auspicious condition is yet to take place—since you have not been king—since you are an accused in the court of a civilized king, your choice is limited; either you have to spend from your own pocket or you have to seek assistance from your lawyer friends, and the third remaining choice is no good.'

Gora was adamant, 'Let me go the way of those who are totally helpless; don't make any exertion for my sake.'

Binoy pleaded a lot, but Gora paid no heed. He asked Binoy, 'How come that you are here at this juncture?'

Binoy blushed a little. If Gora was not in police custody today Binoy would perhaps announce the reason of his presence here in a rather rebellious tone. But today he failed to blurt it out. Instead he said, 'Don't bother about me—now it's your—.'

Gora said, 'Don't you see I am the royal guest today? The king is my host. The king himself is looking after me; you needn't worry.'

Binoy knew it was not possible to make Gora budge an inch. So they had to give up on legal assistance. Binoy said, 'I know you cannot take their food. I am bringing some food from outside.'

Gora lost his patience, 'Binoy, why are you wasting your energy? I don't want anything from outside. I don't want anything more than what others get in police custody.'

Binoy returned to the bungalow, sad and depressed.

Sucharita had closed the door of a street-facing bedroom from inside, and opening a windw on the road was waiting for Binoy to return. She could by no means stand the company or talk of others.

When Sucharita saw Binoy—worried and dejected—approaching the bungalow her heartbeat quickened in anxiety. She quietened herself with great effort and came to the drawing room with a book in her hand. Lalita did not like sewing normally. But today she sat silently in one corner with a piece of embroidery. Labanya was playing English scrabble with Sudhir, while Leela watched on. Haranbabu was discussing the next day's festival with Baradasundari.

Binoy described all about the encounter between the police and Gora in the morning. Sucharita sat motionless. The embroidery slipped off from Lalita's lap, and her face reddened.

Baradasundari said, 'Have no worry Binoybabu—in the evening I shall personally appeal to the magistrate's wife about Gaurmohanbabu's case.'

Binoy hastily implored, 'Please don't—in case Gora comes to learn this he will never forgive me for the rest of my life.'

Sudhir said, 'But some arrangement must be made for his defence.'

Binoy then told them everything about Gora's objection to their effort to bail him out or appoint a lawyer. At this Haranbabu impatiently commented, 'All unnecessary fuss!'

Whatever Lalita's attitude to Haranbabu was, so far she had shown him respect, and never joined in argument with him. Now, vehemently shaking her head she protested, 'It's no fuss at all. Gaurbabu has done the right thing. The magistrate will oppress us, and we have to save ourselves! We have to pay tax for ensuring their fat salary packet, and at the same time we have to pay court-fee for saving ourselves from them! It is better to court imprisonment than seeking this "justice".'

Haranbabu had seen Lalita since she was a mere slip of a girl. That she too could have her own opinions was beyond the pale of his imagination. He addressed her in a scolding tone,

'What do you understand about such matters! You get dizzy at listening to the irresponsible mad delirium of those people who have just passed through the college by memorizing a few books, and have no religion, no idea.'

Then he described the encounter between Gora and the magistrate last evening, and also gave an elaborate account of his own dialogue with the magistrate on the subject. Binoy did not know about the developments at Char-Ghoshpur. Now he felt really anxious and certain that Gora was going to get a really rough deal from the magistrate.

Haran's purpose in telling the story was completely defeated. So far he had maintained complete silence about his meeting Gora last evening, and the meanness of this hurt Sucharita to the very core. Every comment of Haranbabu regarding Gora expressed such a personal jealousy that it stirred a revulsion in all during this hour of crisis for Gora. Sucharita was silent so long; it seemed she longed to say something, but then she checked herself and opening the book turned the pages with trembling fingers. Lalita haughtily exclaimed that Haranbabu might agree with the magistrate as much as he liked, but the Ghoshpur case only proved the nobility and high-mindedness of Gaurmohanbabu.

29

Since the Lieutenant Governor's visit was scheduled today the magistrate arrived at the court at ten-thirty on dot for having the court-work over as early as possible.

Satkaribabu stood on the side of the students and took this chance to have a try at saving his friend. He had already guessed from the trend of things that it should be the better strategy to admit offence in the present case. He pleaded for the boys on the ground that kids are naturally mischievous on account of their immaturity and ignorance and sought forgiveness on their behalf. The magistrate gave his verdict to take the boys inside the prison and deal them five to twenty-five lashings according to their age. There was no lawyer for Gora. As soon as he started saying something about fighting his own case and about police oppression the magistrate stopped him with sharp rebuke; he gave the verdict of rigorous imprisonment for one month as punishment for obstructing police work, and also delivered a brief speech describing this 'light' punishment as a special kindness.

Sudhir and Binoy were present in the courtroom. Binoy could not look at Gora's face. He felt claustrophobic and hastened out of the courtroom. Sudhir requested him to come back to the bungalow for taking bath and lunch. He seemed not to register. He walked aimlessly through the fields for some time and then suddenly slumped down under a tree. He told Sudhir, 'You please go back to the bungalow. I am following a little later.'

Sudhir left.

Binoy did not know how long he sat like that. When the sun was past the meridian and tilted towards the West a carriage drew up in front of him. Binoy looked up to see Sudhir and Sucharita who had come down from the carriage and were walking towards him. Binoy got up in a hurry. Sucharita came close and called out to him in a tone moist with affection, 'Binoybabu, come along.'

Binoy suddenly became aware that the public in the street were being amused at the scene. He quickly got into the carriage. None could say a word for the rest of the road.

Reaching the bungalow Binoy found things quite in a mess. Lalita has put her foot down; she will by no means join the magistrate's party today. Baradasundari has been landed in a tough situation. Haranbabu is beside himself in fierce anger at this absurd rebellion from a slip of a girl like Lalita. He has been exclaiming the same observation over and over again,—'What perversion is this among the young people these days? They won't follow any discipline. All this is due to their connection and interaction with undesirable people.'

As soon as Binoy entered Lalita came forward, 'Binoybabu, please forgive me. I have greatly wronged you. I could not understand your point earlier; it is because of our lack of experience of the outside world that we make such blunders.

Panubabu says this magistrate's rule in India is willed by God. If that be true, then flaring up the desire to curse this rule with all my heart and soul should also be the will of the same God.'

Haranbabu was furious, 'Lalita, how can you—.'

Lalita turned and facing Haranbabu cried, 'You shut up. I am not speaking to you. Binoybabu, please don't bother about anybody's request today. The play must not be held today.'

Baradasundari hastened to distract, 'Lalita, what kind of a girl you are! Won't you let Binoybabu take bath and lunch? Do you remember it's already half past one? Look at his face, how exhausted he looks.'

Binoy said, 'Here we are guests of that magistrate. I cannot take my bath or food here.'

Baradasundari pleaded a lot to persuade Binoy. Seeing all the girls silent she was angered, 'What happens to all of you! Suchi, please make Binoybabu understand. We have promised—people have been invited—we must somehow have it through—don't you guess what they'll think of us! It will be such a loss of face for me!'

Sucharita lowered her face and remained silent.

Binoy left for the steamer waiting on the river close by. Within two hours the steamer, with passengers on board, will be off for Calcutta—where it will reach by eight next morning.

Haranbabu got excited and began to speak abuses against Gora and Binoy. Sucharita quickly got up from her chair and entering the adjoining room closed the door with a loud bang. Before long Lalita pushed the door and entered. She found Sucharita lying on the bed, her face covered with her palms.

Lalita shut the door from inside and slowly sitting down by the bed ran her fingers through Sucharita's hair. When at last Sucharita recovered after a long time Lalita pushed off the cover from her face, and whispered into her ears, 'Didi, let us go back to Calcutta; I cannot attend the party.'

Sucharita did not answer for a long while. When Lalita insisted she sat up on the bed and said, 'How can we do it, sister? I did not have the least wish to come. But since Baba has sent me how can I go back without completing the job?'

Lalita said, 'Baba does not know all this. If he knew he would never have asked us to stay on.'

Sucharita said, 'How do I know that, sister?'

Lalita. Didi, can you really do it? Just tell me how you would go, and moreover dress up, appear on the stage lisping poetry? My tongue will crack and bleed before I utter a single word.

Sucharita said, 'Don't I feel the same, dear? But, there are times one has to stand the ordeal of hell. There is no choice now. I shall never forget this day.'

Angered at this complaisance of Sucharita, Lalita left the room. She went up to her mother and asked, 'Ma, won't you start?'

Baradasundari said, 'Are you mad! We have to start after nine at night.'

Lalita said, 'I mean, starting for Calcutta.'

Baradasundari, 'Hear! Just hear the girl!'

Lalita approached Sudhir, 'Sudhirda, will you too stay on?'

Sudhir had been mortified by Gora's punishment, but he could not overcome the temptation of demonstrating his talents before the big British officers. He vaguely said something—which indicated that he was feeling embarrassed, but still he would stay on.

Baradasundari exclaimed, 'Oh, it is already late! No, no more of dilly-dallying. No one will leave the bed from this minute till five-thirty in the evening. You must take rest. Otherwise you will look tired and ugly at night.'

Saying this she forced everyone into the respective bedrooms and made them lie down. All fell asleep except Sucharita. In another room Lalita was sitting up straight on her bed.

The siren of the steamer hooted on.

As the steamer was about to embark, the crew were getting ready for drawing up the connecting plank, Binoy spotted from the deck a lady briskly coming up towards the steamer. Her costume, gait etc. seemed to suggest Lalita, but Binoy could not believe it at first. But soon he had no doubt. Once he thought perhaps Lalita was coming to persuade him back; but how could that be? Was it not Lalita herself who had declared her non-cooperation with the magistrate's party? Lalita boarded the steamer. The crew took off the plank. Binoy anxiously clambered down from the upper deck and appeared before Lalita. Lalita said, 'Please take me upstairs.'

Binoy was surprised, 'But the steamer is about to start!'

Lalita said, 'I know that.'

Saying this she did not wait for Binoy but climbed up the ladder before her. The sirens hooted again and the steamer sailed off.

Binoy made Lalita take a chair on the first class deck and looked askance in silent query at her face.

Lalita said, 'I will go to Calcutta. I could not stay on by any means.'

Binoy asked, 'But what about the others?'

Lalita said, 'Nobody knows as yet. I have left a letter, when they read it they will know.'

Binoy was stunned at this extraordinary courage of Lalita. He hesitantly started, 'But...'

Lalita quickly stopped him, 'The ship had already left the bank behind. What's the use of your "buts" in this situation? Must I bear with everything just because I happened to have been born a female? I don't understand the point. We too may have certain convictions about what is right and what is wrong, what is possible and what is impossible. It is easier for me to commit suicide than joining the party and perform on the stage tonight.'

Binoy realized the irreversibility of what had happened, and recognized that it was useless to fret over its desirability or otherwise.

After a brief silence Lalita started, 'I had done great injustice to your friend Gaurmohanbabu. I don't know why, from the very start his appearance, his speech somehow antagonized me. He seemed to speak too emphatically, too imposingly, and all of you seemed to ditto in support. I felt a seething anger at this. This is indeed in my nature—I cannot stand it if anybody tries to impose upon others by words or deeds. But now I know Gaurbabu forces not only others, but also himself—and this is real force—I have never seen another such personality.'

Lalita went on rambling thus. Not that she was talking so much just because she felt remorseful about Gora. Actually she had acted on a moment of impulse, and now an uneasiness within was about to raise its hood; a hesitation that perhaps she had been too rash. She had never envisioned the embarrassment of sitting face to face with Binoy alone on the steamer deck. But if she allowed her uneasiness to surface that would be even more embarrassing; it was in order to avert that possibility that she desperately talked on. On the other hand, Binoy could hardly speak. On the one hand the suffering and humiliation of Gora, on the other the shame of having come to this holidaying at the magistrate's residence here, and then the sudden crisis precipitated by Lalita on the top of it,—all this together had rendered him speechless.

In the past Binoy would have felt reproachful at this kind of rash and daring action of Lalita. But today he could not criticize her by any means. Not only that, the surprise he felt at this was tinged with admiration; there was an added joy that among the whole team it was only Binoy and Lalita who had done something at least, however little it was, towards protesting against Gora's humiliation. Binoy will not have to suffer for this, but Lalita will have to pay much and for long in consequence of her defiance. Yet all along Binoy knew Lalita to be hostile to Gora. The more he thought about this the more he admired Lalita for her genuine uncalculating courage and unequivocal hatred toward injustice. He could not think out a way to express his admiration. He thought again and again that Lalita had been right in detesting him all along as one lacking independence and courage. He could never thus defiantly ignore blame or praise from friends and relatives to assert his own opinion in any such matter. Many a time he had betrayed his own nature lest Gora be hurt or lest Gora think him weak; many a time he had tried to delude himself by assuming Gora's opinions as his own, and weaving fine web of arguments in favour of that delusion. Today he admitted to himself that Lalita was many times superior to him in independence of spirit, intelligence, strength. In the past he had many a time denounced the girl in his mind; today remembering that he felt ashamed. Even he felt like seeking her forgiveness; but how to? He could not think of a way. The delicate feminine figure of Lalita acquired, in Binoy's vision, a radiant dignity which derived from the glow of her spirited nature; Binoy felt his own life attained a fulfillment by coming in contact with this superb woman. Today he completely surrendered all his pride and smallness before this exquisite embodiment of charm and strength.

30

Binoy reached Pareshbabu's house along with Lalita.

Before boarding the steamer Binoy did not know his own mind regarding Lalita. All the time he was busy resisting her assaults. How to come to a treaty of peace with this unmanageable girl had become a matter of his daily concern in recent times. Sucharita was the first to appear on the horizon of his life like the first evening star, with the pure lustre of feminine charm. Binoy felt that the exquisite joy of this experience had contributed to the blossoming of his nature. But Binoy was not aware that other stars had emerged and he did not notice when, after initiating the stellar festival, the first star had imperceptibly started setting down beyond the horizon.

The day Lalita, the rebellious girl, came up on the steamer deck Binoy felt, 'Lalita and me together on one side are defying the whole hostile society mobilized on the other side. He could not get over the consciousness that on this occasion Lalita had left all her friends behind to come up and stand by him alone. Whatever be the reason, and whatever the occasion, to Lalita Binoy was no more just another of the crowd—he was the only one to stand by Lalita, the very special one; while all the friends and relatives were far away at the moment. The thrilled pulsation of that feeling of proximity resonated within his heart like thunder clouds. When Lalita retired to sleep inside the first class cabin Binoy could not go back to his own berth for sleeping; putting off the shoes he silently strolled on the deck outside the cabin. There was not much of a chance that anybody should disturb Lalita on board; but Binoy longed to get a thorough feel of his newly gained sudden responsibility, and therefore could not restrain from rendering the unnecessary service.

It was deep into the night; there was dense darkness around; the cloudless vault of the sky was strewn with stars; on the banks rows of trees stood motionless like pitch black pillars of the night sky; down below the gorgeous river was silently flowing in strong current. Amidst all this Lalita was sleeping. It was nothing more; but this beautiful, trustful sleep that Lalita had presented to Binoy tonight as a supreme gift. Binoy had taken charge to protect this sleep as a most precious jewel. There was no one by her side, no parents, no siblings; reposing her beautiful body on a strange bed she was sleeping peacefully; even her breathing, very mild and calm, seemed to follow the rhythm of this poetry of sleep; not a single tress of the fine knot of her hair was disarrayed; the two hands, manifesting the benign tenderness of the feminine heart, were lying relaxed on the bed; the pair of feet, delicate like petals, were spread on the sheet, their charming mobility stilled for a while like music stilled at the end of a fiesta. This vision of repose filled Binoy's imagination to the brim. Like the pearl inside the oyster, this slumber of Lalita under this vast sky surrounded by this silent darkness scinctillating with the splendour of countless stars and planets—this beautiful, perfect, complete repose—appeared to Binoy as one such unique treasure. 'I am here', 'I am watching'—this message of assurance seemed to burst the seams of his heart and tremble up to the heavens like some benign conch-call to meet the silent message of some unblinking watchful spirit pervading the vast space.

In this moonless night another thought also haunted him. Gora was in prison tonight! So long Binoy has shared all the joys and sorrows of Gora. This was the first exception. Binoy knew that prison could not affect Gora's spirit. But this time from the first to the last he had no connection with Gora. In this major event of Gora's life Binoy was completely out of the picture. Here was a point where the streams of their two lives had suddenly parted ways; when will they converge again and will that convergence ever fill up the void caused by the present separation? Didn't the wholeness of their friendship receive a crack this time? Such a whole unique friendship was theirs—so rare to be found in this world! Facing simultaneously the void before, and the memory of fullness behind, Binoy stood motionless at the juncture of the new and old, creation and destruction, staring into the darkness.

If it were true that only incidentally Binoy could not join Gora on his trip and only incidentally he could not share his misery of imprisonment, then it would not have impaired their friendship. But it was no accident that Gora had set out alone while Binoy was enjoying himself with the trivia of rehearsing and amusement. The course of Binoy's life had taken such a turn from which the old familiar tracks of their past friendship had already receded too far. It was precisely for this reason that eventually this external separation also became possible. But he had no choice now; he could not evade truth any more. It was no more right for Binoy to follow Gora's ways with unflinching loyalty. But what about their lifelong love? Will it be over with this change of courses? The thought sent a shiver through his heart. He knew Gora followed a single track and must have all his friendship and all his duties directed to a single goal. How indomitable Gora was! What tremendous will he commanded! He would forge ahead by committing all his ties, all relationships of life to that one will. God had moulded Gora's nature with that extraordinary royal grandeur.

The coach stopped at Pareshbabu's door. Binoy could distinctly feel that Lalita's steps were slightly hesitant while getting down, and that she deliberately stiffened herself before entering the house. Lalita could not guess the exact degree of her offence owing to what she had done under the impulse of a moment. Lalita knew that Pareshbabu wouldn't say a single thing to her in the way of scolding; and precisely for that very reason she feared his silence most.

Noticing her hesitant mood, Binoy could not decide what should be his duty in the situation. To test if his presence added to her embarrassment, Binoy ventured hesitantly, 'So, may I go now?'

Lalita hurriedly interposed, 'No. Please come in to see Baba.'

Binoy felt elated at this eager appeal of Lalita. Then his duty did not end just by safely dropping her at home; this sudden development then had established a special bond between Lalita and himself. Assuming this Binoy stood by her side with a slightly added confidence. This idea of Lalita's dependence on him seemed to electrify his entire body. His male ego was gratified at the imagination. He thought to himself in case Pareshbabu is annoyed at this unthinking rashness of Lalita, if he scolds her, then Binoy will shoulder the entire responsibility, share the rebuke without hesitation, and protect Lalita from all attacks like a cuirass.

Binoy, however, did not understand the exact state of Lalita's mind. That she detained Binoy was not because she wanted to use him as a shield against possible chiding. The real reason was that Lalita did not like secrets. Pareshbabu should know everything she did, and then let him pass his verdict; whatever the verdict be she would accept it in full. Such was Lalita's approach.

Since morning Lalita has been vexed with Binoy. She knows fully well that the vexation is unreasonable; but because of its very unreasonableness the anger was increasingly on the mount instead of gradually cooling down.

So long as she was on the steamer her attitude was different. Since childhood she had perpetrated many a big or small crisis through anger or obstinacy. But this time it was a serious case. With Binoy too getting involved with her in this crucial situation, she was feeling simultaneously shy and strangely elated. The very fact that it was an act of nonconformity, seemed to churn up the joy the more wildly. There were such reasons for embarrassment—the way she had sought help from a male outsider, had come so close to him without the mediation of any relative or friend; and all the time Binoy's innate politeness had helped to maintain such a fine veil of restraint between them that pleased Lalita greatly by revealing Binoy's delicate sense of propriety and decency. This Binoy manifested another personality than the one she knew,—who indulged in amusement and fun, who talked non-stop, who could freely interact with anybody, including the servants of the house. Binoy could have taken the chance of intruding into her privacy under the excuse of guarding her; yet he took such meticulous care to maintain respectful distance that she could only feel him getting closer to her heart. During the night on the steamer her sleep was disturbed by the hang-over of a traumatic day. After lying restless for a time she thought perhaps it was already morning; slowly opening the cabin door she looked out. The dewy darkness of the small hours was still holding in embrace the open sky hanging down on the river and the rows of trees along the banks. Just then a cool breeze came up, stirred the ripples and raised a lisping sound of the river waking up to the breeze. There were small sounds downstairs indicating the first stirring of the crew before the daybreak. On stepping out of the cabin Lalita at once saw Binoy a little ahead; he had fallen asleep on a cane-chair with a shawl wrapped about him. Her heartbeat quickened at this sight. So he had guarded her sitting there through the night! So near, yet so far! Lalita at once came back to the cabin with trembling steps. Standing by the cabin door she stared at Binoy sleeping alone amidst the strange river-scape under the darkish twilight of the autumn dawn. The stars on the horizon in front of her appeared to her vision as if they fondly threw a ring round Binoy's slumber. Her heart was filled to the brim with the sensation of an unspeakable grandeur and sweetness. She could not understand why tears filled her eyes. She had learnt from her father to meditate on God; she felt that God touched her with His right hand this morning. It was the hour when the dark night on the river banks, spangled with dense leaves and twigs, was rising to meet the emerging young light of dawn in a first mysterious consummation; in that holy moment of union the full galaxy of stars seemed suddenly breaking out into a divine music on some invisible inaudible great lyre in an unbearable ecstasy of exquisite pain.

Binoy moved his hands just a little in sleep, and Lalita at once closed the door and went back to bed. Her palms and feet went cold. For a long time she could not stop the throbbing of her heart.

Darkness receded. The steamer was moving on. Lalita washed, got ready and came out to stand on the deck holding the railing. Binoy too had been up at the hooting of the ship, and after getting ready he was waiting for the first sign of dawn on the eastern bank.

As Lalita came out he was about to withdraw, but Lalita called, 'Binoybabu!'

As soon as Binoy came near her Lalita said, 'I'm afraid you did not get much sleep last night.'

Binoy said, 'Not bad.'

After this there was no other exchange between the two. Beyond the shrub of white *Kāś*, moistened with dew, there appeared the golden glow of the imminent sunrise. The morning sun had never touched them like this before—this was the first time they knew that the sky was not an empty void, but it was ever watching the creation silently in wondrous delight. The two had become so sensitized that the embedded consciousness at the core of existence seemed to hug them in a close embrace. Neither did speak a word.

The steamer reached Calcutta. Binoy hired a coach from the river bank and making Lalita take an inside seat, himself got up to sit by the coach-driver. Who knows why an adverse wind began to rise in Lalita's mind while she rode along the Calcutta roads of daytime. Binoy was on the steamer during the hour of crisis; Lalita had become thus involved with Binoy; Binoy was escorting her to her house like a guardian in a hired carriage; all this seemed to oppress her. The thought that incidentally Binoy had earned a kind of controlling right over her seemed unbearable to Lalita. Why did it so happen? Why did that exquisite music of the night come to an abrupt halt at the advent of the busy world of daytime?

When Binoy stopped at the door and bade good-bye, Lalita felt even more vexed. She thought, 'Binoybabu assumes that I shrink from facing my father in his company.' She did not like Binoy to take leave at the doorstep like some guilty person precisely because she wanted to prove emphatically that she had no hesitation about this, or to reveal everything before her father.

She wanted to shake off all shyness, all illusory charms in their relationship so that she did not have to feel inferior to him.

31

Satish had spotted Binoy and Lalita and ran in to stand between them; holding the hands of both in his two small hands, he asked, 'Where is Baradidi?'

Binoy slapped his pockets and looked around, 'Baradidi! Indeed, where is she? Seems she has got lost!'

Satish pushed him back, 'No, never! Oh Lalitadidi, please tell me what happened?'

Lalita said, 'Baradidi will come tomorrow.'

Saying this she started for Pareshbabu's room.

Satish dragged them by the hand saying, 'Come in to see who has come to our house.'

Lalita pulled back her hand and said, 'Let anybody come, but leave me now. I am going to meet Baba.'

Satish said, 'Baba has gone out. He won't return soon.'

At this both Binoy and Lalita felt a sort of relief for a brief moment. Lalita asked, 'Who has come?'

Satish said, 'That's a secret. Well Binoybabu, can you tell? I am sure you can't. Never, never.'

Binoy went on citing impossible and absurd names—names like Nabab Siraj-ud-daullah, King Nabakrishna, even king Nandakumar. Satish loudly challenged the probability of having such guests in the house. Binoy admitted defeat and said humbly, 'Yes, of course, there are some practical difficulties regarding Siraj-ud-daullah's coming to this house, I had not thought about it earlier. Anyway, let your Didi first investigate the matter, then if necessary call me; I shall run up at once.'

Satish said, 'No, both of you must come.'

Lalita asked, 'Which room do we proceed to?'

Satish said, 'To the second-floor room.'

There was a small room at one corner of the roof top; its tiled roof sloped towards the south as protection against sun and rain. The two followers of Satish went up there to find an elderly woman in spectacles sitting on a small mat under that projectile and reading Krittibas's Bengali version of *The Rāmāyaṇa*. The frame of the glasses was broken and held with a string, the end of which was wound round her ear. She seemed to be around forty-five. The hair had thinned in the front part of the head; but the fair face was still nearly round like a ripened fruit. There was a tattoo mark between the eyebrows, no ornament on her body, and she wore the costume of a widow. She first saw Lalita and quickly laying aside her glasses and book, scanned her face with a special eagerness. The very next moment she saw Binoy behind her and hastened to stand up, pulled the sari over her head, and was about to withdraw into the room. Satish quickly went up and encircled her with his arms, saying, 'Auntie, why do you run away? This is our Lalitadidi, and this is Binoybabu. Baradidi will come tomorrow.'

This brief introduction seemed to suffice for Binoybabu. Apparently lots of information about Binoybabu had already been passed on. Indeed Satish lost no chance to wax eloquent on the very few things in the world which were close to his heart, and apparently he had left little unsaid on those topics.

Lalita could not guess the exact identity of the 'auntie', and stood a bit surprised. As Binoy greeted the lady by bending low and touching her feet, Lalita too followed suit.

Auntie brought out another mat from the room and spreading it on the floor invited them, 'Baba, take your seat; *Mā*, please sit down.'

After they took their seats she sat down on her own mat and Satish slumped close to her. She encircled Satish with her right hand and said, 'You do not know me, I am Satish's *māsi*. His mother was my own sibling.'

This was not much in the way of introduction; but something was there in her face and voice which seemed to reflect a pure expression of some deep tear-drenched sorrow. When she pressed Satish close to her bosom saying, 'I am Satish's *māsi*', Binoy was filled with a sad compassion though he knew nothing about her life history. Binoy said, 'It won't do being only Satish's *māsi*. Then after all these days I shall have a fight with Satish on this very issue. Firstly he calls me Binoybabu, and not Dada; then if in addition to this offence, he deprives me of a *māsi* that can't be accepted by any means.'

Binoy did not take long to win over a stranger. Before long this handsome pleasant-spoken youth acquired a share of Satish's kingdom in *māsi*'s mind.

Māsi asked, 'My son, where is your mother?'

Binoy said, 'I have lost my own *mā* long ago. But I can't say that I don't have a *mā*.'

Saying this he remembered Anandamoyee and at once his eyes were moist with emotion.

The conversation between the two parties clicked fine. None had a feeling this was their first meeting. Satish continued to throw in occasional and quite irrelevant comments during the talk, while Lalita sat silently.

Lalita could not easily come out of her shell even if she tried. It took her long to cross the barrier of non-acquaintance. Besides, she was not in mood today. She did not like this easeful rapport that Binoy instantly struck with this unknown woman. Lalita was facing a crisis, and yet Binoy seemed to be so unconcerned, paying no attention to its seriousness; at this she silently accused Binoy as light-hearted. Indeed, even if Binoy sat silently pulling a long face he would not have evaded Lalita's displeasure. In that case too Lalita would have thought angrily, 'Whatever showdown takes place that should be between Ma and Baba; yet Binoybabu is so presuming as if it is his responsibility!' The core of the matter is that the stroke that had stirred music last night was causing only pain in the daylight today—and nothing seemed to work as it should have done. So Lalita was silently quarrelling with Binoy at every step since morning. No behaviour of Binoy could stop this quarrel; correction at what level could at all alleviate this was known only to the omniscient God.

Alas! What is the point of blaming women for irrational behaviour since their prime concern was matter of the heart! If it was installed at the right place at the beginning, the heart could sail on so easefully and beautifully, that all reasoning and argument would have courted defeat; but if some dislocation takes place in the beginning, then no amount of intelligence can set the machine right—then it becomes useless to probe the source of any anger or attachment, laughter or tears.

On the other hand, neither was the machine of Binoy, i.e. his heart, was functioning quite normally; if things were exactly like they had been in recent past, he would have this instant rushed off to meet Anandamoyee. Who else could inform *Mā* of the news of Gora's imprisonment! Who else was there to console *Mā*! This pain was weighing down on his mind and oppressing him; but how could he leave Lalita right now? He was persuading himself to the notion that it was his responsibility to defend Lalita against the whole world today, and he could not leave before completing his duty towards Pareshbabu in this regard. It did not require much effort for this self-persuasion; the poor mind had no power to protest. In spite of his genuine pain for Gora and Anandamoyee, the very proximity of Lalita seemed to thrill him with a strange joy this morning. He felt such an expansiveness, such a special glory, such a unique distinction of his own identity that the pain at the bottom of his mind could not surface and take over. He could not look straight at Lalita—the occasional bits that caught his eye—a portion of the sari, a motionless palm resting on the lap—thrilled him again and again with shivers of delight.

It was getting late. Pareshbabu was yet to return. An inner urge to get up was growing strong—to repress this he plunged into conversation with Satish's aunt. At last Lalita could not hold back her irritation any longer. She suddenly interrupted their talk—'Who are you waiting for? Baba's return is uncertain. Won't you go to see Gaurbabu's *Mā*?'

Binoy was startled. Binoy was quite familiar with Lalita's tone of vexation. He looked once at Lalita's face and got up instantly—he stood up in a flash like the bow snapping up when suddenly unstrung. For whom had he been lingering here! He didn't stop here with any such ego that he was specially needed by somebody; wasn't it Lalita herself who had requested him to step in,—and then at last this from her!

So quickly did Binoy get up from his mat, that Lalita looked at him in surprise. She saw that the natural radiance of his face was suddenly put out like a lamp extinguished by a blow of breath. Lalita had never noted before this kind of sad expression on Binoy's face, such sudden change of appearance. Instantly she was lashed by intense remorse which seemed to pierce her heart from end to end and burn her through.

Satish hurriedly jumped up and hung on his hands pleading, 'Binoybabu, please sit down; please don't leave right now. Please have your meal with us today. O Masima, why don't you ask Binoybabu to have his lunch here? O Lalitadidi, why did you ask him to leave!'

Binoy said, 'Satish, dear, not today please! Some other day, if Masima remembers me, I shall come and take *prasād*. I am already late today.'

The words were not remarkable as such, but his voice seemed to be drenched with tears; the sadness of it struck even Satish's aunt. She stole a glance at Binoy and Lalita, and guessed destiny was at some game.

Soon afterwards Lalita left for her room on some small excuse. So many times she had thus caused herself such miserable tears.

32

Binoy set out at once for Anandamoyee's house. A mixed feeling of shame and pain seemed to crush him. Why didn't he start earlier for *Mā*! What a great lapse indeed! He had assumed Lalita specially needed him. Why didn't he ignore all needs to hasten for *Mā* immediately on reaching Calcutta? Yes, God has rightly punished him for such a lapse. At last he had to hear from Lalita of all persons, 'Won't you see Gaurbabu's *Mā* for once?' How to account for such a confusion, even if for a single moment, when the thought of Gaurbabu's mother receives greater priority in Lalita's mind than in the concern of Binoy! Lalita knows her just as Gaurbabu's mother; but wasn't she the only manifest image of *Mā* in Binoy's world?

Anandamoyee had then just taken her bath and was sitting still on a mat on the floor; possibly she was citing God's name to herself. Binoy at once fell at her feet, saying, '*Mā*!'

Anandamoyee fondled his prostrate head with both her hands and called, 'Binoy!'

Who else could have such a voice as his mother had! The very voice seemed to soothe his whole body with a touch of compassion. He struggled to resist tears and said in a low voice, '*Mā*, I have been late!'

Anandamoyee said, 'I have heard everything, Binoy.'

Binoy was surprised, 'Everything!'

While in police custody Gora had written a letter to her and sent it through a lawyer. He had certainly guessed the possibility of imprisonment. Towards the end of the letter he wrote,—

"Prison will not affect your Gora in the least. But it won't do if *you* suffer. Your suffering should be my only punishment. It is beyond the magistrate to punish me in any other way. *Mā*, don't think of your own son alone. There are many sons of many more mothers who have to endure the prison for no fault of their own; I long to be at par with them in suffering for once. If this wish of mine is fulfilled this time, don't fret or lament for me.

"*Mā*, I don't know if you remember an event. During famine the other year I had left my moneybag on the table of our roadside room and went indoors for five minutes. But on returning I found it gone. The bag contained eighty-five rupees which I had saved from my scholarship money. My aim was to save a little more and then order a silver bowl for washing your feet. As the money was stolen a futile anger against the thief was consuming me, when God sent me a nice idea. I told to myself, 'Let me make a gift of this money to the person who has stolen it during this famine.' As soon I could say this all the futile fretfulness of my mind calmed down. Today, again, I persuade my mind to say, 'I am courting the prison of my own choice. I have no grievance, no anger against anybody. I am going to seek the hospitality of the jail. There I may meet some discomfort regarding food and other things—but during the trip this time I stopped at various homes, where I did not get the necessary or accustomed comfort. The suffering I accept of my own choice ceases to torment. Today I am going to jail of my own choice, and I assure you nobody can force me to stay for one single day more than I wish.'

"So long as we had been enjoying at ease the security and comfort of our own homestead, we could not feel what a great right it was to move about freely under the open sky amidst profuse light and air; at that very moment so many people were deprived, for their fault or for no fault, of the divine gift of this right and instead suffering bondage and humiliation. I have never thought of them so long, have never kept any touch with them; now I want to be branded alongside them with the same misery before I go out. I don't want to protect my prestige by joining the ranks of the majority of so-called nice people who hypocritically pose as gentlemen.

"*Mā*, I have learned a lot this time through my direct exposure to life. God knows most of those who have assumed the role of justice-givers are pitiable themselves. The prisoners are bearing punishment for the sins of those who do not receive verdicts, but issue them. Others together commit the crime and the poor prisoners have to expiate for it. Those who live outside the jail in comfort and dignity—when and how will they be made to pay for their sins, I don't know. I will denounce that comfort and dignity, and come out with the imprint of the shame of mankind inscribed on my chest. *Mā*, you give me your blessings; don't shed tears. Lord Krishna has carried the imprint of Bhrigu's feet on his chest till the end. All the arrogance, all the injustice assaulting the world anywhere are but sharpening that imprint on God's bosom. If that imprint can be carried by God like an ornament, then what should I care, or why should you grieve at all?"

On receiving this letter Anandamoyee had tried to send Mahim to Gora. Mahim remonstrated that he had his office, that the white boss won't sanction leave; he also said, 'It seems a matter of time only when I may also lose my job thanks to my illustrious brother.' Anandamoyee thought it redundant to say anything about the case to Krishnadayal. She had a deep resentment towards her husband regarding Gora; she knew that Krishnadayal had never really accepted him within his heart as a son; not only that, he even nursed a hostile attitude towards Gora. Gora stood in their middle like the mounts of Bindhya, dividing Anandamoyee's conjugal life into two different compartments. On one side was Krishnadayal alone with his over-meticulous ritualistic purity; on the other was Anandamoyee alone with her *mleccha* Gora. It seemed that all the channels of communications between the only two persons who knew the history of Gora's life had become blocked. For these reasons Anandamoyee's affection for Gora was a totally exclusive treasure of her own. She tried to accommodate and make light of Gora's unrightful position in this house in all possible ways. Lest some say, 'This happened because of your Gora', or 'Thanks to Gora we receive this blame', or 'Through your Gora we suffer this loss'—Anandamoyee was always on tenterhooks. Wasn't it entirely her responsibility for whatever Gora might do? Again, her Gora too was no ordinary nice goodboy type. It was not easy to hide his presence wherever he was. She had brought up this extraordinary, peerless Gora from an infant in arms to the defiant youth of today by guarding him, protecting him in face of a hostile family and society day after day, night after night for so many years. She has heard so many accusations but did not reply; had endured so much pain without being able to share a fraction of it with any one.

Anandamoyee sat by the window in silence. From there she saw Krishnadayal returning from his morning bath at Ganga, his arms, chest, and forehead smeared with the holy sediments from the river bank, chanting mantra as he stepped indoors. Anandamoyee could not go near him. It was forbidden. Forbidden, forbidden, forbidden, forbidden everywhere! At last she sighed and got up for Mahim's room. Mahim was reading newspaper, squatting on the floor, and his servant was giving him a pre-bath oil massage. Anandamoyee told him, 'Mahim, please arrange for an escort to go with me, I shall see Gora once before he is thrown into the prison, about which he seems to have been determined.'

Whatever Mahim might show in his outward behaviour, he had a kind of affection for Gora. He made a lot of noise, shouting, 'Let the hopeless vagabond go to jail—indeed, why did he not go there earlier, I wonder', etc. Yet the very next moment he called his loyal friend Paran Ghoshal and giving him some money for engaging lawyer immediately sent him off; he further decided that he would seek leave from his office boss, and in case the leave is granted he too will follow Ghoshal.

Anandamoyee also knew Mahim could not rest without taking some action towards Gora's help. Being assured that Mahim had taken measures to the best of his ability, Anandamoyee went back to her own room. She did not have the least doubt that there was no one in this family who would take her to that unfamiliar place where Gora was at the moment and thereby dare to face public raillery, curiosity and gossip at this hour of crisis. She remained silent with compressed lips, while the shadow of a voiceless sadness hung over the look of her eyes. When Lachmya burst in loud tears she rebuked and sent her off to another room. It had been her habit all along to absorb all anxiety without fuss. She could accept both happiness and unhappiness calmly; the turbulence of her heart could be perceived only by the omniscient God.

Binoy did not know what to say to Anandamoyee. But Anandamoyee did not depend on others' consoling. Her very nature shrank from any discussion of a grief for which there was no remedy. She preempted any further conversation by hurrying Binoy, 'Binu, I think you have not yet taken your bath. Go this minute, and take a quick bath—it is already quite late.'

When Binoy, after taking bath, sat down for his meal, the empty place of Gora by him seemed to crush her heart and tear it asunder. Gora had to take the prison food today, a food made bitter by ruthless law, and not sweetened by mother's affection; remembering this Anandamoyee too had to leave the spot on some excuse.

33

On returning home and finding Lalita already arrived before scheduled time Pareshbabu knew at once that this wild daughter of his had kicked up some unprecedented row. As he looked askance Lalita at once blurted out, 'I have come back. I could not stay on there, by any means.'

Pareshbabu asked, 'But why? What happened?'

Lalita said, 'The magistrate has thrown Gaurbabu into prison.'

How Gaur came into the picture, and from where, and what exactly happened: Paresh could not make any head or tail of it. On hearing all from Lalita he fell silent for a while. At once he remembered Gaur's mother, and his heart ached. He thought, what a cruel punishment could be dealt to a number of innocent people by sending one person to jail; if the judge could feel this he could not send people to prison so casually as a routine matter. The magistrate could at ease pass the same verdict for Gora as for a burglar; such barbarism was possible only due to an insensitised conscience. How much more terrifying was man's inhumanity to man compared to all other forms of violence in the world, how enormously monstrous it has become with the support of organized power of the ruler! On hearing about Gora's imprisonment this became apparent to his perception.

Seeing Pareshbabu thus silently pondering Lalita felt encouraged and asked, 'Well Baba, don't you think this is very grave injustice?'

Paresh replied in his habitual quiet tone, 'I don't know exactly what Gaur has done and what is the extent of his offence. Anyway, even if he transgresses his jurisdiction under the impulse of his strong conscientiousness, I am absolutely certain of this much that committing anything that can be called crime is completely against his nature. But what can you do, Ma? The laws of the times have not yet reached an adequate level of conscientiousness. The same punishment is dealt out for both crime and fault; both have to undergo the same rigours of prison life. You cannot blame just any particular person for this. The collective sin of all men is responsible for this.'

Suddenly Pareshbabu stopped midway through this subject and asked, 'With whom did you come back?'

Lalita seemed to straighten herself up a bit self-consciously and said, 'With Binoybabu.'

Although she threw up a careless and emphatic posture, there was weakness within. Lalita could not say it very smartly that she had come with Binoybabu—a tinge of shyness suddenly intervened and got spilled over into her facial expression. The consciousness of this only increased her embarrassment.

Pareshbabu had a special affection for this whimsical uncontrollable daughter. It was precisely because her behaviour used to draw censure from others that Pareshbabu admired the element of genuineness in her conduct. He knew that her faults would be apparent to people whereas her qualities, however precious they were, won't find appreciation. Pareshbabu, therefore, had tenderly and carefully indulged and nurtured that quality; he had not wanted to maul that nobility of her nature by suppressing her wild ways. His other two daughters were instantly recognized by all and sundry as beautiful girls; they had fair complexion, and perfect features. But Lalita was darker than them; there could also be difference of opinions regarding the prettiness of her features. Baradasundari would frequently express anxiety to her husband regarding the prospect of finding a suitable groom for her. But Pareshbabu used to see a special beauty in her face; it was not the beauty of complexion or features, but it was the profound beauty of the mind. It was constituted not by delicate grace alone, but rather by the spirit of distinction and firmness of strength—a firmness which did not appeal to all. That might attract some particular people, but would keep most at bay. Lalita would not be popular with people but she will be true; this foreknowledge made Pareshbabu draw Lalita closer to himself with a certain tinge of sadness. As he knew none else was to forgive her he always judged her with special compassion.

When Pareshbabu heard that Lalita had suddenly come back alone with Binoy, he knew in an instant that Lalita will have to suffer much and long for this. She will receive punishment disproportionately heavier than her offence. As he was considering the idea silently for a brief minute Lalita said again, 'Baba, I plead guilty. But this time I have come to realize clearly that in view of the relationship between the magistrate and the common people of our country his hospitality means no respect but just condescension. Should I have stayed back in spite of that?'

Pareshbabu did not find it easy to answer the question. Instead of attempting a reply he softly stroked Lalita's hair with his right hand and said, 'My mad girl!'

In the evening that day Pareshbabu was strolling outside his house and thinking of this when Binoy came up and touched his feet. Pareshbabu discussed Gora's imprisonment with him for a long while, but made no mention of his steamer journey with Lalita. When it became dark he said, 'Come in Binoy, let us go inside.'

Binoy said, 'Excuse me. I shall now proceed to my apartment.'

Pareshbabu did not request him a second time. For the fraction of a second Binoy looked up at the first floor and then slowly walked away.

Lalita had seen Binoy from upstairs. When Pareshbabu came in alone she thought perhaps Binoy would follow a little later. But Binoy did not follow a little later. Then she unnecessarily fiddled with a few books and the paperweight upon the table and then left the room.

Pareshbabu called her back. Looking affectionately at her sad face he said, 'Lalita, please sing a Brahmo devotional song to me.' Saying this he drew the shade on the lamplight.

34

Baradasundari and the rest of her team returned the following day. Haranbabu, being unable to control his annoyance with Lalita, landed along with them straight at Pareshbabu's door instead of proceeding towards his own apartment. Baradasundari was so angry and resentful that she made straight for her room without once looking at or talking to Lalita. Labanya and Leela too were very angry with Lalita. On account of her withdrawal their recitation and acting had flopped so badly that they were put to shame as anything. Sucharita had kept herself completely detached from Haranbabu's angry and caustic excitement, Baradasundari's tearful lamentations, or Labanya-Leela's shamefaced dampness, and maintained a stony silence. She just mechanically did her part. Today too she entered the last of all, like some machine set on motion. Sudhir shrank in shame and remorse and taking leave at Pareshbabu's door instantly headed for his own apartment. Failing to persuade him to come indoors in spite of her repeated requests, Labanya decided not to speak to him again.

Immediately on entering the room Haranbabu announced, 'Some serious offence has been committed.'

Lalita was in the adjoining room. The moment this reached her ears she came in and stood firmly behind Pareshbabu's chair, holding the back of it with her two hands, and watched Haranbabu's face without blinking.

Pareshbabu said, 'I have heard everything from Lalita. It is no use discussing what is *fait accompli*.'

Quiet, restrained as Paresh was, Haran used to imagine him to be a weak-natured person. So he said with a touch of contempt in his tone, 'An event takes place and is over in due course, but what remains is the issue of character; that's why it's necessary to discuss even what is *fait accompli*. What Lalita has done would never have been possible if she did not get indulgence from you all along. If you hear the whole thing you shall clearly realize the extent of harm you have done to her.'

Pareshbabu felt a slight tremor at the back of his chair and quickly drew her close to his side; then tightly holding her hand, addressed Haranbabu with a little smile, 'Panubabu, when the time comes you will realize that for bringing up children affection is also essential.'

Lalita encircled her father's neck with one hand and bent down to bring her lips to his ear, saying, 'Baba, the water is getting cold, please go for your bath.'

Pareshbabu looked at Haran and said in a low voice, 'The bath can wait a little. It is not very late.'

Lalita said softly, 'No Baba, you please finish your bath—till then we are keeping company to Panubabu.'

As Pareshbabu left the room Lalita drew a chair, sat down firmly, and fixing her gaze at Haran's face said, 'You assume you have the right to say anything to anybody!'

Sucharita knew Lalita. If it were another day she would have been anxious at such a mood of Lalita. Today she just went over to a window-side chair and opening a book stared at a page. Restraining herself was Sucharita's perpetual habit and temperament. As pain had been accumulating in her mind from various injuries for the last few days, she was getting concomitantly more silent and withdrawn until the weight of this silence had become nearly unbearable today. Therefore, when Lalita started to take on Haran Sucharita seemed to get a chance at last to unburden the pressure of her repressed emotion.

Lalita went on, 'You assume that you know better than Baba about his duties towards us! You seem to be the self-appointed headmaster of the whole Brahmosamaj!'

Haran was at first stunned at this audacity of Lalita. Then he was about to come down on her with a very heavy rebuff when Lalita interrupted him, 'So long we have endured your posture of superiority, but if you presume to be superior to even Baba, no one in this house will bear with you—not even our bearer.'

Haranbabu was beside himself, 'Lalita, you—'

Lalita cut him short with sharp reprimand, 'Shut up. We have listened to you long enough; now it is time you listened to me. If you don't believe me ask Suchididi—however tall you may imagine yourself to be, our Baba is many a cut above that height. Know this and then pour out what strictures you may have in store for me.'

Haranbabu's face became dark. He got up from his chair and called, 'Sucharita!'

Sucharita looked up from the pages of her book. Haranbabu asked, 'Will you allow Lalita to insult me in your presence!'

Sucharita said calmly, 'It is not her intention to insult you. She only wants to tell you to remember that you should behave respectfully to Baba. We do not know any one else who is worthy of better respect than he.'

It seemed for a brief moment that Haranbabu would at once push back the chair and rush out of the doors. But he did not actually do such a thing. Instead he continued there with a very sullen expression. He had been losing his position in this house by degrees; the more he felt this the keener he grew to retain the same. He did not remember that when the shelter has been fragile, the more one attempts to cling to it the more it comes crumbling down.

Haranbabu sat wordless in sullen anger. Seeing this Lalita went up to Sucharita, and sitting down beside her began conversation in low voice as if nothing special had happened.

In the meantime Satish entered the room and started pulling Sucharita by the hand while imploring, 'Baradidi, please come along.'

Sucharita inquired, 'Where?'

Satish said, 'Follow me first. I shall show you a thing. Lalitadidi, have you divulged our secret?'

Lalita assured, 'No.'

The agreement with Satish was that Lalita wouldn't disclose the Masi-episode to Sucharita; Lalita had kept her word.

Sucharita could not leave the visitor alone; she implored, 'Bakhtiyar, wait a little please—let Baba finish his bath first.'

Satish fidgeted. If it were within his power he would not have spared any effort towards erasing Haranbabu from the vicinity. Since he was terribly scared of Haranbabu he could not address him. Indeed, apart from occasional flings at correcting Satish's ways, Haranbabu paid no attention to the boy.

The moment Pareshbabu reentered the room after having his bath Satish nearly pulled away his two sisters.

Haran said, 'You remember that proposal regarding Sucharita; I don't want to have it delayed any more. I wish, it is clinched off by next Sunday.'

Pareshbabu said, 'I have no objection—if Sucharita agrees, of course.'

Haran. 'Hasn't she already given her consent?'

Pareshbabu. 'O.K., then it is decided.'

35

On returning home that day Binoy felt that an uncertainty had entered his mind and continued there like some thorn pricking every now and then. He thought, 'I am frequenting Pareshbabu's house like an intruder without ascertaining whether somebody wishes it or not. Perhaps this is not desirable. Perhaps I have bored them many a time in season and out of season. I don't know the ways of their community. I have no idea of the extent of my rightful place in this house. Perhaps like a fool I have been encroaching into an area which is forbidden for non-relatives.'

While pondering like this suddenly it occurred to him that perhaps Lalita had noticed something in his face, its expression, which offended her. So long Binoy was not aware of the exact nature of his feeling towards Lalita. But today it was no mystery any more. He dit not know what to do with these new feelings arising in his heart. What was its connection with the big world, what was its implications for the society? Was it humiliating for Lalita? Was it a kind of treachery towards Pareshbabu? All these doubts continued to torment him. Imagining that he had been exposed to Lalita and precisely for that very reason Lalita was vexed with him, he felt like eating the dust.

It became impossible for Binoy to go to Pareshbabu's house, while the emptiness of his own apartment too seemed to oppress him like a crushing weight. Early in the morning the following day he went to Anandamoyee and announced, '*Mā*, I shall stay here with you for a few days.'

Binoy also longed to be with *Mā*, to console her during these days of her separation from Gora. Anandamoyee got the message and her heart went out to the boy. Without saying a word she affectionately ran her hand over his back.

Binoy started a lot of fuss over his food and other demands. Occasionally he would launch a mock quarrel with *Mā* accusing that he was not getting the right care or attention here. All the time he would raise such a hue and cry, make such a fuss with his noisy demands and loud ramblings as to keep both Anandamoyee and himself distracted from their gnawing pains. During the afternoons, when it became difficult to control the mind, Binoy would interrupt Anandamoyee's household work and compel her to leave the chores for the time being. Then the two would spread a mat in the balcony outside the room and sit down. Binoy made Anandamoyee speak about her childhood days, about the days in her father's house—how she was a pet with the students of her professor grandfather's *tole*, and how the fatherless girl was spoilt by all of them, which was again a cause of particular anxiety to her widowed mother, and such other fond memories. Binoy used to say, '*Mā*, I cannot imagine a time when you were not our *Mā*. I have the feeling that the students at the *tole* knew you as their tiny cute mother, and it was you who took the charge of bringing up your grandfather.'

One such evening Binoy laid his head at Anandamoyee's feet, stretched on the mat and said, '*Mā*, I wish I could return all my learning and intelligence to God and come back to the shelter of your lap as an infant—so that there could be only you, you alone for me in this world, and no one else.'

Such a sadness dripped through Binoy's voice that Anandamoyee was pained and surprised at the same time. She came closer to Binoy and slowly ran her fingers through his hair. After a long silence she asked, 'Binu, are they alright at Pareshbabu's house?'

Binoy was startled and ashamed at this sudden query. He thought, 'Nothing can be concealed from *Mā*. My *Mā* is omniscient.' He answered in a faint voice, 'Yes, they are alright!'

Anandamoyee said, 'I wish so much that I could know the daughters of Pareshbabu. Initially Gora was not favorably disposed towards them; but since he too has been brought round recently, they are obviously no insignificant people.'

Binoy was enthused, '*Mā*, I too have longed many times if I could somehow introduce them to you. I did not broach the idea lest Gora took it otherwise.'

Anandamoyee asked, 'What is the name of the eldest daughter?'

When Lalita's case figured eventually in course of this question-answer session Binoy tried to gloss over it quickly. Anandamoyee did not allow him the chance. Smiling to herself she said, 'I have been told Lalita is very intelligent. Is she?'

Binoy asked, 'Who could have told you?'

Anandamoyee replied, 'Why? It was but you Binoy; who else could it be?'

There was a time when Binoy had no hesitation in his mind regarding Lalita. In those infatuation-free days he had freely discussed Lalita's sharp intelligence with Anandamoyee, which he forgot now.

Like the skilled boatsman removing all obstacles on the way, Anandamoyee guided the conversation so expertly that all the major episodes in the history of Binoy's acquaintance with Lalita came out. Binoy also kept no secret today about her pained reaction to Gora's punishment and her consequent singular escapade by steamer with him. While talking thus he felt a surge of energy—the depression that had got hold of him at the fall of evening dispersed. The very fact that he had come to know such an extraordinary character like Lalita and could thus speak about her, seemed a great stroke of luck to him. When the call for dinner came and the conversation stopped Binoy seemed to wake up from a dream and realise that whatever he had to say was said. Anandamoyee listened so attentively, with such total acceptance, that gave Binoy no chance to feel ashamed. Till the other day Binoy had nothing to conceal from *Mā*; every trivial detail he would share with her. But since his acquaintance with Pareshbabu's family a kind of veil had come down somewhere. That distance had not been healthy for Binoy. Today his feeling towards Lalita had become fully exposed before the fine perception of *Mā*, and this filled Binoy with elation. Until he placed this major affair of his life before *Mā* it would not be sanctified; it would continue to stain his thoughts.

At night Anandamoyee thought over this for a long time. She seemed to light on the possibility of a solution to the problem at the heart of Gora's life, a problem that was escalating with time; she thought she must somehow meet these girls.

36

Mahim and the other inmates in the house were behaving in such a manner as if the marriage of Shashimukhi with Binoy was already settled and confirmed. Shashimukhi never appeared in Binoy's presence these days. Shashimukhi's mother was as good as unknown to Binoy. Not that she was exactly what can be called shy; but she was extraordinarily secretive. The door to her room remained closed most of the time. Apart from the husband, all other articles belonging to her were kept carefully under lock and key. Not that the husband got a very long rope; under the strict rule of his wife the poor man's movements were very much restricted while the radius of his movements too was severely circumscribed. Thanks to this precise limitedness of her nature Lakshmimani, the mother of Shashimukhi, had her narrow world completely under her thumb. There was no chance of an outsider crashing into, or an insider taking flight from, that world. Even Gora too had not much of an access to Lakshmimani's suite. The rules of her kingdom were completely monolithic; because here Lakshmimani was the sole law-giver right from the lower court to the supreme court. There was no separation of the executive from the judicial departments either, while the legislative too was joined to those Siamese twins. Although Mahim appeared to be quite a tough guy in his dealings with outsiders, in the domain of Lakshmimani he stood no chance of having his own way in anything; not even in the smallest matter.

Lakshmimani had measured up Binoy from behind the curtains; she had approved him too. Mahim had seen Binoy so much since boyhood as Gora's friend, that because of the very over-familiarity the possibility of envisioning Binoy as prospective son-in-law did not occur to him. When Lakshmimani drew his attention to Binoy, Mahim's admiration for his wife's intelligence escalated. Lakshmimani resolved that Binoy must marry her daughter. She also impressed upon Mahim's mind one major advantage of this marriage: that Binoy won't be able to claim dowry from them.

Although Mahim came across Binoy inside the house he could not broach the subject of marriage for the last few days. He restrained himself as Binoy seemed too depressed at Gora's imprisonment.

Today was Sunday. Mahim's wife interrupted his weekly luxury of post-lunch sleep. Binoy was reading aloud to Anandamoyee from a fresh issue of Bankim's *Baṅgadarśan* journal when Mahim, holding his betel-box, entered and took his seat on the wooden bedstead. He started by offering Binoy a piece of spiced betel-leaf and then expressing annoyance at Gora's foolhardiness and lack of restraint. This led to the count of days,—how many days remained before his release, and this seemed to suddenly remind him that already it was half-way through the month of *Agrahāyaṇa*.

He said, 'Binoy, you said marriage was forbidden in your family in the month of *Agrahāyaṇa*. But I don't think this is worth considering. First, there is nothing else but a bundle of bans in your almanacs and scriptures; if you start constructing your own almanacs in every house in addition to this, how will a family survive!'

Sensing Binoy's dilemma Anandamoyee intervened, 'Binoy has been seeing Shashimukhi since she was the slip of a child—so he cannot get reconciled to the idea of marrying her; I'm afraid that's the reason why he is taking time under the ruse of *Agrahāyaṇa*.'

Mahim was petulant, 'He could have said so at the start.'

Anandamoyee said, 'One needs time in order to understand even one's own mind. Is there any scarcity of boys, Mahim? Let Gora return; he knows many good boys—he will certainly be able to settle the matter with a suitable boy.'

Mahim's face darkened; voicing a monosyllable, 'Hum!', he fell silent. After a while he said, '*Mā*, if you didn't ditch, didn't persuade Binoy against the marriage he wouldn't have backtracked.'

Binoy hastened to say something in denial. Anandamoyee stopped him and said, 'Yes Mahim, I must admit I could not encourage him in this case. Binoy is young; he might do something without realizing the implications of his act, but the consequences would not have been happy in the long run.'

Anandamoyee shielded Binoy to take the thrust of Mahim's anger on herself. Binoy understood this and felt ashamed at his own weakness. He was about to voice his disagreement in so many words when Mahim got up and left the room muttering to himself, a stepmother can never be a real mother.

Anandamoyee knew perfectly well that Mahim could think like that and as stepmother she always stood in the rank of the accused in the court of society. But she simply did not have the habit of moulding her action according to the consideration of possible public opinion or reaction. Since the day she had picked up little Gora into her bosom she parted ways with social customs, social opinions and developed as a distinct individual different and distant from all the rest. Since that day she has followed ways which invited public censure only. She suffered the pain of concealing a truth at the core of her life, and this public censure seemed to bring her a sort of relief from that nagging pain. When people criticised her as 'Christian-like', she would press little Gora tightly to her bosom and say, 'God knows "Christian-like" is not a word of blame for me.' Thus she had by degrees eventually detached herself, her own conduct, from all public criticism until this became her second nature. Therefore, when Mahim accused or abused her, silently or explicitly, as stepmother, she refused to be affected and did not budge from her own stand.

Anandamoyee said, 'Binu, it seems long since you have been to Pareshbabu's residence last time.'

Binoy said, 'Can you really call it long?'

Anandamoyee. 'At least not once since the day you came back by steamer.'

That too was not very long ago. But Binoy was conscious that prior to this his visits to that house had become so frequent that even Anandamoyee saw him rarely. By that standard of course it had been a long time, and people might notice it as well.

Binoy suddenly became preoccupied in silently pulling at a thread at one end of his dhoti and tearing it into bits.

At this time the bearer entered to announce, '*Māji*, some ladies have come from somewhere.'

Binoy got up quickly. Before they could ascertain who came and from where, Sucharita and Lalita stepped in. It was too late for Binoy to leave the room.

The girls greeted Anandamoyee by touching her feet. Lalita did not appear to notice Binoy's presence. Sucharita greeted him with a '*namaskār*' and asked, 'How are you?'

Then she turned to Anandamoyee and said, 'We are from Pareshbabu's house.'

Anandamoyee warmly received them and made them take their seats. She said, 'You need no introduction to me. I have not seen you, *Mā*, but I know you as my own.'

Soon the talk flowed fine. Seeing Binoy silently keeping to a corner Sucharita tried to draw him into the conversation; she asked softly, 'Why didn't you come once to our place all these days?'

Stealing a glance at Lalita Binoy replied, 'I am afraid lest I lose your affection by pestering too frequently.'

Sucharita smiled a little, 'Affection too longs for frequent pestering; don't you know this?'

Anandamoyee said, 'Indeed he knows that very well! How can I tell you *Mā*, the way he keeps me on tenterhooks the whole day with endless demands and orders.'

Saying this she watched Binoy with her soft look which was mellowed with affection.

Binoy said, 'God has bestowed patience on you, and has sent me thereafter to test it.'

Sucharita gave Lalita a slight nudge and said, 'Do you hear Lalita? So, should we presume our exam is over! And we have failed in the test, haven't we?'

Seeing Lalita did not join this raillery Anandamoyee smiled, 'This time our Binu is testing his own patience. You don't know what you are in his perception. Every evening we have no other topic than you. And, when Pareshbabu is mentioned, he seems to be carried away.'

Anandamoyee looked at Lalita; she tried her best to look up, but blushed unaccountably.

Anandamoyee resumed, 'He has quarreled with so many people about your Baba. The people of his team are about to ostracise him as a Brahmite!—Oh Binu, why be so restive, I am telling but what is fact. There is no cause for embarrassment in this. Is there any, my girls?'

This time Lalita had to lower her eyes as Anandamoyee turned to her. Sucharita said, 'We know very well how Binoybabu considers us as his own people,—but that is not just our credit, it is also because of his own ability to accept people.'

Anandamoyee said, 'I am afraid I have to differ, *Mā*! I know him since he was a little boy. But so long he had only one friend, that was my Gora. But since he came to know you things have come to such a head within this short time that he has become nearly inaccessible even to us. I had thought of quarreling with him on this, but now I see I too have to join ranks with him. You will make everybody admit defeat.'

Saying this Anandamoyee touched the chins of both by turn with her finger and kissed them.

Noticing Binoy's miserable condition Sucharita took kindness on him and said, 'Binoybabu, Baba has come; he is talking with Krishnadayalbabu outside.'

At this Binoy hurried out. Then Anandamoyee started her description of the extraordinary friendship between Gora and Binoy. That the pair of listeners were not indifferent was evident to her. It was these two lads whom Anandamoyee had offered the best affection of her motherly heart as if like a worship. No one else in the world was closer to her or more precious. True, she had moulded them like the little girl moulding her earthen Shiva; but it was they who received all her love, care, worship. This tale of the pair of small gods in her lap, washed in the nectar of affection, emerged so sweet and radiant that Sucharita and Lalita listened in charmed attention. They had considerable respect for Gora and Binoy, but today they had a glimpse of some other added dimension of the two through the prism of the affection of such a unique mother as Anandamoyee.

After coming to know Anandamoyee today Lalita's anger against the magistrate flared up even more than before. Listening to her heated observations Anandamoyee smiled. She said, '*Mā*, Gora is in prison today. Only God knows what torment this is for me. But I cannot be angry with the Saheb. Don't I know my Gora? He would defy all rules and laws for the sake of what he thinks right. But if he does not obey law then the law-giver or executor too cannot be blamed for sending him behind the bars. Gora has done his duty, they have done theirs—now those who have to suffer will suffer for this. If you read my Gora's letter, *Mā*, you will understand he has not feared suffering, neither is he angry. He has acted knowing the full implications of his action.'

Saying this she brought out Gora's letter from the box in which it was carefully treasured, and handed it over to

Sucharita; she said, '*Mā*, read it aloud. Let me hear it once more.'

After that extraordinary letter of Gora was read out, all three sat motionless for some time. Anandamoyee wiped the corner of her eyes with the end of her sari. The tears not only expressed the ache of a mother's heart, but also reflected a certain joy and pride. Her Gora! Was he just another boy! Was he such a Gora whom the magistrate could kindly forgive and release! Didn't he admit all his offence and embraced the prison term of his own choice? There could be no quarrel with any other human for such a suffering as his. As Gora has been enduring that suffering without complaint, Anandamoyee too will be able to bear it.

Lalita stared at Anandamoyee in amazement. The notions of a Brahmo family were firmly entrenched in her mind. Lalita had no respect for women who did not receive modern education and whom she knew to be the 'womenfolk of Hindu household'. In their childhood Baradasundari would occasionally scold them for some offences, saying that even 'womenfolk of Hindu houses' did not do such a thing; on such occasions Lalita felt specially ashamed. Today, while listening to Anandamoyee she was amazed again and again. What strength and what peace! And what extraordinary reasoning! Lalita, with her unrestrained impulsiveness, felt herself very inferior before this lady. Today she was restive with a feeling of grievance; for that reason she had not looked at Binoy, or talked with him. But while watching Anandamoyee's face—a face eloquent with affection, compassion, peace—she felt the heat of rebellion within her cooling down, and connecting with all the world seemed easy. Lalita told Anandamoyee, 'Today I understand the source from which Gaurbabu derives such enormous strength.'

Anandamoyee said, 'Not exactly. If Gora had been just another ordinary child where could I get my strength from? Could I then bear his sorrow in this way?'

Why was Lalita so unhinged today? That needs a little explanation.

For the last few days every morning she woke up to the thought that Binoybabu won't come today. Yet the whole day she could not give up the expectation for a single moment. Every now and then she thought, perhaps he has come, perhaps he is downstairs talking with Pareshbabu. This had made her go in and out of the rooms so many times a day. At last when the day ended and she retired to bed, she did not know what to do with this mind of hers. Tears welled up bursting the bosom, and at the same time anger stirred. What or who was the target of this anger? She could not define. Perhaps the anger was against herself. All the time a self within her seemed to ask, 'What has happened to me! How can I live now? Where is the way! I can find none as I look around. How long can I carry on like this!'

Lalita knows Binoy is Hindu; they cannot be married by any means. Yet she cannot control her heart howsoever she may try, and as a result shame and fear were draining her. She has known that Binoy is not indifferent to her; because she knows this it has become so difficult for her to restrain herself today. That is why even as she eagerly waits for Binoy to come, she is scared at the very same moment lest Binoy arrives. Thus wrestling with herself for all these days at last she broke down this morning. She persuaded herself to assume that she was feeling so restive only because Binoy was not coming; if he comes for once this restlessness will be gone.

In the morning she called Satish to her room. Recently Satish had earned an aunt and thereby had been more or less oblivious about cultivating his other friend. Lalita asked him confidentially, 'Have you quarreled with Binoybabu?'

He vehemently denied this charge. Then Lalita said, 'A friend indeed! All the time you are after Binoybabu, you are full of Binoybabu, but he never appears to think of you at all.'

Satish protested, 'Oh, no, it is not true, never!'

As the youngest inmate in the house Satish had to lodge such loud protests every now and then in order to save his own prestige. To ensure it further today he at once ran for Binoy's apartment. But before long he came back to report, 'He is not there; that's the reason of his not coming.'

Lalita countered his logic, 'Then why didn't he come all these days?'

Satish said, 'Because he was not there all these days.'

Then Lalita approached Sucharita, 'Didibhai, don't you think it's time we paid a visit to Gaurbabu's mother?'

Sucharita hesitated, 'But we don't know them.'

Lalita reminded her, 'Don't you recall Gaurbabu's father was a pal of Baba?'

Sucharita remembered, 'Yes, that's right.'

Sucharita too became quite enthused. She told Lalita, 'Lalitabhai, you please go and tell Baba about it.'

Lalita denied, 'No, that I can't. You do it.'

Finally Sucharita broached it with Pareshbabu and he at once responded, 'Of course. It is time we visited her.'

But as soon as the visit was fixed after lunch, Lalita felt uncertain. Again doubts and resentments stirred up and pulled her in the opposite direction. She approachd Sucharita again, 'Didi, you go with Baba. I won't go.'

Sucharita pleaded, 'How can that be! I can't go alone without you. My darling, my dear sister, oh my sister—please come along; no trouble please.'

Thus, after a lot of pleading, Lalita agreed at last. But the thought that she admitted defeat to Binoy, that Binoy could easily afford to avoid their house and yet she was eagerly rushing out for a glimpse of the man seemed humiliating and led to a deep resentment and anger. She tried to deny to herself the idea she had been so eager to visit Anandamoyee precisely because she expected to see Binoy here; in order to cling obstinately to that self-delusion she did neither look at Binoy, nor return his polite greeting, nor exchanged a single word with him. Binoy assumed that Lalita had seen through his secret, and thereby was denouncing him with her silent contempt. Binoy did not have enough self-confidence to guess that Lalita could love him as well.

Binoy appeared at the door from where he shyly announced, 'Pareshbabu wants to leave now; he sends the message to the ladies.'

Binoy stood at an angle where Lalita could not see him.

Anandamoyee intercepted, 'Oh no, that can't be. You can't leave without taking some sweets. It won't take much time. Binoy, please keep them company for a little while; let me see about the sweets. Why do you remain outside, please come inside.'

Avoiding the direction of Lalita Binoy stiffly took a seat. Lalita said with perfect naturalness—as if nothing had altered in her dealings with Binoy—'Binoybabu, have you deserted your little friend Satish altogether? Do you know he ran up to your apartment this morning in order to ascertain this?'

Binoy was visibly startled in delighted surprise like a man facing a sudden miracle. Instantly he blushed because his surprise became too obvious. He could not muster up an answer with his habitual smartness and finesse. Instead, blushing from ear to ear, he mumbled, 'Oh, did Satish come? But, I was not there.'

But these few mundane words from Lalita opened a floodgate of joy in his mind. An unbearable enigma, which had enveloped his world like some claustrophobic nightmare, was dispelled in a moment. As if he had nothing more to wish for on the earth. His mind seemed to repeat like a chant,—'I feel so relieved! So relieved indeed! Lalita is not angry with me, Lalita is not suspecting me.'

Within seconds all his stiffness disappeared. Sucharita teased him with a smile, 'It seems Binoybabu suspects us to be of some of those dangerous species,—wielding claws, teeth, horns or clubs!'

Binoy said, 'In this world those who cannot lodge their protest vocally, and remain silent, are put on the dock. Didi, this comment does not befit you. You yourself have become so distant these days, and yet you are accusing others of maintaining distance.'

This was the first time that Binoy addressed Sucharita as Didi. It pleased her. Since the day of their first acquaintance Sucharita had felt a warm regard for Binoy; today with this address, 'Didi', that response acquired a special affectionate dimension.

When Pareshbabu departed with his daughters the day was nearly over. Binoy told Anandamoyee, '*Mā*, today I won't let you do any work. Come along to the upstairs room.'

Binoy could hardly contain the surging wave of joy within his heart. Bringing Anandamoyee to the upstairs room he spread the mat on the floor and made her sit down. Anandamoyee asked, 'Binu, what is on thy agenda?'

Binoy said, 'I have nothing to say, I want to hear from you.'

Binoy was actually impatient to know how *Mā* found the daughters of Pareshbabu.

Anandamoyee said, 'Fine. So you called me up just for this. And I thought perhaps you had something urgent to tell.'

Binoy said, 'If I did not call you up, could you see such a wonderful sunset?'

Truly speaking the autumn sun that evening was going down behind the roof tops of Calcutta rather drably; there was no glamour of prismatic hues; a golden aura was only faintly visible through the smoke-gray fog at the horizon line. But even the grey drabness of the evening charmed Binoy. He felt the world around was gathering close to him from all sides, the sky was as it were touching him.

Anandamoyee said, 'The girls are very nice.'

Binoy did not allow her to shift from the subject. He kept it alive by comments, reminiscences. So many small details of so many days centering round the girls were called up; most of them were trifles, but thanks to Binoy's fervour and Anandamoyee's encouragement these obscure trifles of a small homestead attained a special grandeur in the quiet intimacy of that peaceful room in the darkening twilight of an autumn evening.

At one turn Anandamoyee sighed and suddenly said, 'If a marriage takes place between Gora and Sucharita I will be very happy.'

Binoy jumped at the idea; he said, '*Mā*, I have toyed with the idea so many times. She should be the right partner for Gora.'

Anandamoyee. But, will that ever be?

Binoy. Why not? I don't think Gora does not like her.

It was not unknown to Anandamoyee that Gora's mind had found a point of attraction somewhere. She had also gathered from her talks with Binoy that Sucharita was the girl. After remaining silent for a time she asked, 'But will she marry into a Hindu family?'

Binoy asked in reply, 'Well, *Mā*, suppose Gora marries into a Brahma family; will you oppose?'

Anandamoyee. He shall have every support from me.

Binoy repeated, 'Shall he?'

Anandamoyee said, 'Of course Binu! Marriage is ideally an understanding between two humans. How does it matter which particular mantra is chanted on the occasion, my son! It is enough to remember God.'

A weight was lifted from Binoy's mind. He said fervently, '*Mā*, when I hear you speaking thus I feel amazed. Where did you learn such magnanimity!'

Anandamoyee smiled, 'From Gora.'

Binoy said, 'Gora makes just the opposite claim.'

Anandamoyee. Let him! Whatever I learned was through Gora. How precious man is, and how insignificant all man's quarrels over doctrines—God has taught me that very day he bestowed Gora to me. My son, how to distinguish between a Brahmo and a Hindu! What is the caste of human heart? It is here that God reconciles all and makes himself available. If we throw him overboard and depend on mantra and ideology to unify people, can it work?

Binoy touched her feet and said, '*Mā*, I feel so soothed by what you say. It seems a great day to me.'

37

Recently domestic peace in the house of Paresh had been seriously affected on account of Sucharita's masi, Harimohini. Before we go into those details let us first recount briefly Harimohini's self-introduction to Sucharita.

'I was older than your mother by two years. There was no limit to the affection and indulgence that we enjoyed in our parental house. The reason was that except we two there was no other child in the family at the time. Our uncles loved us so much that they would hardly allow us to tread the ground.'

I was married into the famous Palchaudhuri family when I was just eight. They were highly placed in terms of both wealth and family line. But happiness was not my lot. There had been some dispute between my father and my father-in-law about my wedding expenses. My in-laws could not forgive my father for this offence for a long time. All of them used to say, "We will marry our son again; let's see what happens to that girl." On seeing my sufferings my father took a vow not to marry his other daughter into a rich family. That's why your mother was married into a poor family.

It was a large joint family and even at the tender age of eight or nine I had to run the kitchen; from fifty to sixty people used to eat. After serving all of them I had only the left-overs for me: sometimes only rice, sometimes rice and dal. It was only around two o'clock when I was allowed to have my lunch; sometimes I had to wait till afternoon. I had to start cooking for the night meal immediately after I had my lunch. At night I could find time for eating only around eleven or twelve. I had no fixed place for sleeping either. I slept in the women's part of the house with whomsoever I had an opportunity to. There were days when I would sleep on the floor just with a wooden slab under my head.

My husband too subscribed passively to this treatment I received at their home. For long he used to keep me at a distance.

Around this time when I was seventeen my daughter Manorama was born. On account of giving birth to a daughter I became the butt of added insult and humiliation in my in-laws' family. Amidst of all this neglect and humiliation this daughter became my only solace and joy. Since Manorama did not receive proper affection from her father or other members of the family I showered all my affection on her and held her as the dearest object close to my heart.

My situation began to change when after three years a son was born to me. At last I was considered fit to be recognized as a daughter-in-law. My mother-in-law had died before my marriage and my father-in-law also died two years after the birth of Manorama. Immediately after his death my husband and the brothers of my husband entered into litigations over their respective claims to the family property. At last after wasting a lot of property in the process we became separate.

In the meantime Manorama was growing up into marriageable age. Out of fear that she might be taken far away, and I would not be able to see her often we gave her in marriage to a family in Simul which was about twelve miles away from our village, Palsa. The bridegroom was handsome like Kartik with fine complexion and fine figure. Moreover, they were quite well-to-do.

The sufferings that I had undergone for a long time was partly compensated for a few days by God before I was undone again. Towards the end of his life my husband used to hold me in great affection and respect, and he would never do anything without consulting me. But such a good fortune was not for me. Within a span of just four days both my son and my husband died of cholera. God left me alive only to teach me what unbearable and unimaginable sorrow can be borne by a human in this life.

Gradually I came to know what my son-in-law was like. Who could have imagined that such a poisonous snake lay hidden inside that beautiful flower? My daughter had never told me that under the influence of bad company he had become addicted to liquor. He would come to me at all odd hours and, pleading this or that exigency, collected money from me. Since I had no need to save up my money for anybody else in the family I really felt happy when my son-in-law endearingly insisted on a sum. Sometimes my daughter used to forbid me and accused me. "By giving money now and then you are spoiling him; you can't guess how he squanders it." I thought, Manorama forbids me possibly because of her apprehension that her husband's taking money from me could involve disgrace to the family of her in-laws.

At that time I had been so foolish as to start secretly giving money to my son-in-law without the knowledge of my daughter. When eventually Manorama came to know about it she came to me one day and, full of tears, told me everything about the misdeeds of her husband. In utter remorse I could only slap my own forehead! How can I tell you about my sorrow—it was actually a brother of my husband who had spoilt my son-in-law with his bad company and evil counselling.

When I stopped paying money my son-in-law suspected that my daughter had forbidden me and the mask fell off. Then he started to torture my daughter and humiliate her in the presence of everybody in such a way that to stop it I again started paying him money without the knowledge of my daughter. I knew I was bringing him to ruins but I could never remain at peace whenever I heard that he was putting Manorama to unbearable torture.

The last time he came—I remember the day distinctly—it was towards the end of the month of *Māgh*; that year the weather was prematurely warm and we were saying that 'In our backyard garden the mango trees are already in blossoms.' That afternoon a palanquin arrived to stop in front of our house. I saw Manorama stepping out and she smilingly touched my feet. I asked, 'Manu, what's the news at your end?' Manorama smilingly replied, 'Can I not come to my mother's house without some special news?'

My daughter's mother-in-law was not a bad person. She sent me the message that Manorama was pregnant and it was better that she stayed with her mother till the delivery. I thought that explained. But I never knew that my son-in-law had started beating her even in this condition, and it is out of the fear of a possible miscarriage that my daughter's mother-in-law had sent her to me! Thus I was completely kept in the dark by Manu and her mother-in-law about the grim reality of the situation. Whenever I wanted to anoint her body myself she would always avoid it on one or another pretext. Actually she did not want her mother to see the marks of bruise that she had been carrying all over her soft body.

My son-in-law sometimes came and insisted on taking Manorama back to their house. Since my daughter was with me it was difficult for him to ask for money. After some time he ignored this impediment and started pestering me for money in the presence of Manorama. Manorama strongly insisted, "You must not give him money. Under no circumstances you can." But my mind was weak and lest my son-in-law became too rude to my daughter I could not help giving him something out of fear.

One day Manorama said, "*Mā*, I shall keep all your money in my custody", and took possession of my cashbox and the key. When my son-in-law could not find any way to get money from me and also failed to soften Manorama he started a new tune, "I shall take my wife back home." I used to tell Manorama, "Give, *Mā*, give him some money and get rid of him—otherwise one doesn't know what he would do." But Manorama was as soft on the one hand as she was tough on the other. She would say, "No, there is no question of giving any money."

One day my son-in-law arrived without notice and said sternly—his eyes were bloodshot—, "Tomorrow I shall send the palanquin. If you don't send my wife you will suffer dire consequences." Next day when the palanquin arrived before evening I told Manorama, "*Mā*, there is no point in delaying; next week I shall send somebody to bring you back."

Manorama said, "Not today, *Mā*, I don't feel like going today; ask them to come after two days."

I said, "*Mā*, if the palanquin is sent back, do you think my cranky son-in-law would spare us? No, Manu, you better go today."

Manu said, "Please *Mā*, not today; my father-in-law has gone to Calcutta; he will be back around the middle of Falgun—then I shall go."

I still insisted, "No, *Mā*, it's better to comply."

Then Manorama started packing. I became busy in arranging food for the servants and the palanquin bearers from the house of her in-laws. I longed to make some special treat for her, to dress her up with my own hand or cook her favourite dish and feed her with my own hand before she left, but alas, I had no time for anything. Just before boarding the palanquin she touched my feet and said, "So, *Mā*, I leave then. Bye."

How could I know that she was actually leaving for ever? She did not want to go; I forced her—this pain has been consuming me ever since; nothing can cool the fire.

On that night itself Manorama died of miscarriage. When the news reached me her funeral rites were already over, performed secretly in great haste.

You can never understand the kind of sorrow when one cannot say anything, do anything, or think out any solution; may God never lead you into such a situation.

I lost everything, yet the trouble was not over. The brothers of my husband had been trying to grab my property since the death of my husband and my son. They knew that after my death they would inherit all my property; but they didn't have the patience to wait till then. You cannot really blame anybody for this; it is criminal for a hapless person like me to remain alive. How can those who have various needs in the society can tolerate a person who has lost any justification for her life and continues to live occupying their space without any reason?

As long as Manorama was alive I did not give in to the arguments of the brothers of my husband. I fought to the best of my ability for my share of the property. I was determined to save money as long as I would live so that in the event of my death it could go to Manorama. The fact that I was saving money for my daughter was unbearable to the brothers of my husband; they felt that I was virtually stealing their wealth. My only prop was Nilkanto, an old faithful servant of my husband. Whenever I thought of winning peace at the cost of a portion of my dues he strongly objected, 'Let me see who can take a farthing from our dues.' It was during this dispute over property that my daughter died. The very next day the second brother of my husband recommended renunciation for me: 'Boudi, after what God has brought you to, you should no longer lead a domestic life. You should go to some sacred place and devote yourself to religious rites and rituals for the rest of your life; we shall take care of your maintenance.'

I sent for our guru and told him, 'Baba, please tell me how I can survive this unbearable sorrow; I don't have a moment's respite of peace; I feel like being surrounded by fire—which way I go, which way I turn I find no way out of my agony.'

My guru took me to our prayer room and said, 'From now on this Gopiballabh will be your everything—your husband, your son, your daughter. Your life will be fulfilled by serving him.'

For the whole day and night I stayed in the prayer room. I tried to devote my whole mind to god alone. But how can I give if he does not take it himself!

I called Nilkanto and told him, 'Niluda, I have decided to give away all my property to the brothers of my husband. In exchange they will regularly give me some monthly allowance towards my maintenance.'

Nilkanto said, 'That can never be. You are a woman; you should not get involved in all these!'

I asked, 'What shall I do with property any more?'

Nilkanto said, 'You shouldn't speak like that. Why should we surrender our rights? Don't be insane.'

Nilkanto cannot see anything larger than rights. I was placed in a very difficult situation. Property tasted like poison to me, but how could I give pain to Nilkanto, the only trusted man in my world? After all he had always protected my rights in the face of great difficulties.

At last I signed a paper, keeping it secret from Nilkanto. I never properly understood what was written in that paper. I persuaded myself, why should I fear to sign? What is there for me to lose, or what loss can be too great to bear now? Everything originally belonged to my father-in-law. Let his sons get it!

After the registration was done I called Nilkanto one day and told him, 'Niludada, please don't be angry; I have legally foregone all my rights; I don't need anything any more.'

Nilkanto was agitated and cried, 'What! What have you done?'

When he read the document and saw that I had really given away all my rights, there was no limit to his disappointment. After the death of his master protecting my rights had become his concern. He devoted all his intelligence, all his strength to it. He found pleasure in running around for the lawyers, for finding suitable legal clauses and pursuing the legal suits; so much so that he had virtually no time to look after his own family. When those rights were thrown to the winds by one scratch of a foolish woman it was impossible to console Nilkanto.

He said, 'Now that my connection with this place is finally severed I wash my hands off. I shall not come back again.'

Was this the acme of my misfortune in my husband's house that Niluda too would leave me at last in anger and annoyance? I made earnest entreaty: 'Dada, please don't be angry with me. I have saved some money, out of that I am giving you five hundred rupees—when your son marries please make an ornament for the bride out of it as my blessing.'

Nilkanto said, 'I need no money. When everything of my master's rightful possession is squandered what shall I do with that five hundred? Keep it with you.'

After saying this the last true friend of my husband left me.

I sought refuge in the prayer room. The brothers of my husband said, 'You go to some holy place and live there.'

I said, 'The place of my father-in-law is the sacred place for me, and my shelter is where my deity is.'

But that I was occupying some part of the house also became increasingly intolerable to them. They had already brought their things to our house and had decided who was to use which room and how. At last they told me, 'You can take along your deity; we won't object to that.'

When they found me still hesitating they said, 'How can you meet the expenses of your maintenance here?'

I said, 'Whatever amount you have allotted for my maintenance will be sufficient for me.'

They said, 'But there is no mention about your maintenance in the deed.'

Then, just thirty-four years after my marriage I left my in-law's place with my deity. On enquiring about Niludada I learnt that he had already left for Brindaban.

I went to Kashi in the company of the village pilgrims. But I did not find peace anywhere because of my sinful mind. Everyday I began to pray to my god, 'My deity, please become as real to me as were my husband and my children.' But, alas, he did not pay heed to my prayer. My heart refused to cool off, my entire body continued to weep as it were! Oh God, how hard the heart of a human is!

I went to my in-law's place at the age of eight and could never come to my parents' place even for a day. I tried hard to attend the marriage of your mother, but in vain. Later I received the news of your birth from my father's letter; I got the news of the death of my sister also. Till now God did not give me the opportunity to gather you in my lap—you who have lost the lap of a mother.

In course of my pilgrimage when I realized that I still had strong attachment and my thirst to gather to my heart the object of my affection still remained unquenched, then I started enquiring for your whereabouts. I had heard that your father had left the place after forsaking his religion and his society. But what can I do? Your mother was my own sister.

I came here after getting information about you from a gentleman in Kashi. I heard that Pareshbabu does not believe in God, but that God is pleased with him is evident from his face. I know very well that God cannot be won over by offerings alone—I shall try to find out how Pareshbabu has won him over. However, my child, it is not yet time for me to live alone—I can't do it—I don't know when God will have mercy on me, but I can't survive if I cannot keep you close to my bosom.

38

Paresh had given shelter to Harimohini in the absence of Baradasundari. She was placed in the secluded room on the terrace so that she could continue with her rites and customs without being disturbed by anybody.

When Baradasundari found this development on her return she was furious. She told Paresh sharply, 'I can't stand this.'

'You can stand every one of us and can't you tolerate one poor, hapless widow?'

Baradasundari knew that Paresh had no practical wisdom, he never thought what could be profitable or unprofitable for the family—he acted on the spur of the moment. He could remain firm like a rock whether you felt angry, shouted or cried. Who can tackle such a man? Can a woman live with such a man with whom you cannot even quarrel when necessary!

Sucharita and Manorama were more or less of the same age. Harimohini began to imagine that Sucharita looked like Manorama; her conduct also resembled hers. So calm yet so firm. She would at times startle when she had a sudden rear view of Sucharita. Some days in the evening sitting in the darkness all alone she would be silently weeping, all of a sudden if Sucharita came near she would close her eyes and press her close to her bosom with both the arms and say, 'Oh I am feeling, as if it is she whom I have found again in my bosom. She had not gone herself, I had forced her to go. Shall I ever be sufficiently punished for this? I have been rightly punished—but now she has come back; look, she has returned; she has returned with the same smiling face; you are my *Mā*, you are my gem, my treasure!' Saying so she used to touch Sucharita all over her face, while kissing and drowning everything in tears. Tears too rolled down Sucharita's cheeks and, holding her endearingly she would say, "Masi, I too could not enjoy my mother's affection for long; now I've got my lost mother back. Many days, engulfed in grief, I did not have the power to call God, when everything inside me went dry, then I called my mother. That mother has answered my call at last."

Harimohini used to say, 'Don't say so, don't. I feel so elated hearing you that I feel a fear within. O Lord! Don't tempt me Lord! I don't want to be entrapped in the Maya of life—I try to make myself hard like a rock but I fail. I am too weak oh Lord, have mercy on me, don't beat me any more! O Radharani, go, go away from me. Don't entwine me, don't! O my Krishna (Gopiballabh), ruler of my life, my Gopal, my Nilmani, to what predicament have you put me in!'

Sucharita used to say, 'You cannot force me away, Masi! I will never leave you—I will be near you forever.'

Saying so she hid her head in her bosom remaining quiet like a child.

Baradasundari would get irritated even at this. 'Just see the conduct of this girl. As if we had never loved or cared for her. I say, where was the Masi so long! We nurtured her from her very childhood and today she responds as if she would faint in love for her Masi. I have repeatedly told my husband, this Sucharita whom you praise so much, is good only in her exterior, but one can never win her love. Whatever we have done for her so far has all gone in vain.'

Baradasundari knew that Paresh would never support her. Not only that, she also knew that if she expressed her irritation about Harimohini to him she would appear mean to him. So she was getting more and more furious. She did not care what Paresh would say, but in order to prove that her views were supported by most of the intellectual people, she tried to mobilise her support. She started discussing Harimohini with the important as well as unimportant members of the society. She started regretting and complaining about Harimohini's Hinduism, her idol-worshipping and its possible ill-effect on the children of her family.

Baradasundari did not rest content with lodging her complaints, but also started causing deliberate inconvenience for Harimohini in every possible way. The water-bearer of *Goala* caste, who was appointed to supply Harimohini's cooking water, was assigned different job exactly when Harimohini would need him. In the event of any query she would say, 'Why,

Ramdin is there!' Ramdin was *Doshad* by caste; she knew that Harimohini would not use the water supplied by him. If any one pointed out the problem with Ramdin she replied, 'If she wants to remain such a purist Hindu why did she come to stay in our Brahmo house? Such caste distinction cannot be maintained in our house. I will never support it.' On such occasions her sense of duty found very strong articulation. She would say that in Brahmo Samaj such social laxity was on the rise and that's why the performance of the Brahmo Samaj was not being up to the mark. As far as she herself was concerned she was against indulging such laxity. No, never. If someone misunderstands her for it then he too must have been its prey, if her relatives too went against her about this she would humbly accept it. She started reminding everyone that in the world all the great men, who had done something noble, had to face opposition and bitterness.

Inconvenience failed to affect Harimohini. She seemed to have vowed to raise herself to the level of tolerance that could absorb the maximum physical hardship. She had been deeply wounded at the core of heart and to bring her daily life at par with the inner scar, she seemed to observe her painful rigorous rites even more strictly than necessary. In this way she not only welcomed suffering but absorbed it as part of her being.

When Harimohini saw that water became a problem she almost stopped cooking. The fruits and milk she offered in prayer to her God was her diet afterwards. Sucharita felt hurt about it. Masi tried to make her see reason in it and said, '*Mā*, it is of a great benefit for me. This was necessary. I don't feel any pain in it, rather I am happy about it.'

Sucharita said, 'Masi, if I do not take food and drink, touched by people of other caste, will you let me assist you?'

Harimohini said, 'Why *Mā*, you should follow the practices of your religion—you don't have to follow the rules of any other religion for me. That I have you around, have held you close to my heart, can see you every day, is enough happiness for me. Pareshbabu is your guru, he is like your father, you should follow whatever he has taught you, and God will bless you.'

Harimohini adjusted to Baradasundari's treatment in such a way as if she had not noticed anything odd. Paresh Babu would come everyday and enquire—How are you, hope you don't feel any inconvenience—she replied, 'I am quite comfortable.'

But all the pettiness of Baradasundari deeply pained Sucharita every moment. She was not a girl to complain; furthermore, to complain to Paresh Babu against Baradasundari was unthinkable. She tried to bear up with every thing calmly—as even the idea of expressing grievance made her feel embarrassed.

As a result Sucharita eventually came to be more and more close to Masi. Though Masi forbade her, she started eating and drinking in her way. At last seeing that Sucharita was suffering on her account, Masi was compelled to resume her cooking. Sucharita said, 'Masi, I will follow every stricture that you lay down, but I will fetch the water for your cooking; about this I will not hear you under any circumstance.'

Harimohini said, '*Mā*, please don't mind, but my God can't drink the water brought by you.'

Sucharita replied, 'Masi, does your God also believe in caste? Can He be touched by impurity? Does He too have a *samāj*?'

Finally Harimohini was compelled to concede defeat to Sucharita's firm decision. She completely accepted Sucharita's service. Satish too, imitating his sister started fussing; 'I will eat what Masi is cooking', he declared. The three got harmoniously knitted together and formed a micro unit in one corner of Paresh Babu's house. Only Lalita remained as a bridge between the two units. Baradasundari never allowed her other daughters to mix with them—but she did not have the power to prevent Lalita.

39

Baradasundari started inviting her friends who supported the Brahmo Society. Sometimes their gatherings were held on the terrace. Initially Harimohini, with her rural simplicity, tried to greet the ladies affectionately, but before long she realized that they ignored her. Moreover, Baradasundari often started her scathing criticism of the rites of the Hindus in front of Harimohini and the other women folk zealously participated in the open castigation launched specially for Harimohini's consumption.

Sucharita stayed back with her Masi and absorbed all the attacks silently. Only she wanted to make it clear that she was on her Masi's side. Whenever there was a dinner party, Sucharita's quiet response to the invitation was: 'No, I won't eat.'

'What does it mean! You seem to have decided not to eat with us!'

'No.'

Baradasundari replied, 'Don't you know Sucharita has of late become a confirmed Hindu? She does not take the food touched by us.'

'Really! Even our Sucharita turned a Hindu! I just wonder what strange surprises are still in store for me!'

Harimohini would feel embarrassed and say, 'Radharani *Mā*, go *Mā*! Go and have your food with them!'

It was painful for Harimohini to see Sucharita being mocked by the members of her community. But Sucharita was determined. One day a Brahmo lady out of curiosity was about to step into Harimohini's room wearing her shoes. Sucharita obstructed her way saying, 'Please don't step into that room.'

'Why?'

'Her God is there.'

'God is there! Do you worship your God every day?'

Harimohini said, 'Yes *Mā*, I worship everyday.'

'Are you devoted to your God?'

'Alas! I wish I was blessed enough to have that devotion!'

Lalita was present there that day. Her face turned crimson and she asked the interrogator, 'Are you devoted to the one to whom you pray?'

'Yes, of course I am!'

Lalita violently shook her head and said, 'Not only do you lack the devotion but you do not even know that you lack it.'

Harimohini tried her best to dissuade Sucharita against abandoning the rituals and ways of her community, but in vain.

Prior to this Haranbabu and Baradasundari were not on the best of terms, but now they joined hands on this issue. Baradasundari said—Whatever people may say about Panubabu, if anyone really tried to preserve the pristine purity of the Brahmo Samaj it was he. Haranbabu too valorized Baradasundari's awareness as exemplary model for the Brahmo ladies. His praise of course implied a dig at Pareshbabu.

One day Haranbabu told Sucharita in the presence of Pareshbabu, 'I hear that nowadays you have started eating your food after offering it to God.' Sucharita's face reddened, but she pretended as if she did not hear and continued with her arrangement of the pens in the pen-stand on the table. Pareshbabu stole a quick glance at Sucharita and then quietly addressed Haranbabu, 'Panubabu, whatever we take is actually but God's *prasād*.'

Haranbabu said, 'But Sucharita is about to abandon our God.'

Pareshbabu replied, 'If such a thing really happens would it be of any use to create a furore over this?'

Haranbabu said, 'If one is seen being sucked off by flood shall we not even try to rescue the person?'

Pareshbabu replied, 'If everyone joins in throwing stones at her that cannot be exactly called rescuing. Panubabu, rest assured, I have been looking after Sucharita since she was a child. If she had been drowning, I should be the first person to know it and the last to remain indifferent.'

Haranbabu said, 'Sucharita is present here. Why don't you ask her? I hear that she does not take food touched by others. Is it untrue?'

Sucharita withdrew the unnecessary attention she was giving to the penstand and said, 'Baba knows I don't take the food touched by anyone. If he can bear up with this practice of mine that's enough for me. If you are not happy about it, you can say anything you like. But why disturb Baba? Do you have any idea of the extent of his forgiveness for all the mistakes of all of you? Is this the return?'

Haranbabu thought in stunned silence—Sucharita too has learnt to argue nowadays!

Pareshbabu was a peace-loving man. He had an aversion to discuss either himself or others. So far he had not held any important post in the Brahmo Samaj; he did not like to draw attention and had so long carried on a quiet withdrawn life. Haranbabu blamed this very approach of him as an evidence of indifference and unconcern; in fact he had even sought to bring him to books about this. In response Pareshbabu had said, 'God has created two kinds of creatures: dynamic and immobile. I am of the latter category. God will put me to whatever service I am capable of rendering, and there is no point in getting upset about the impossible. I am now old enough to know my limits, and nothing is to be gained by pushing me around.'

Haranbabu had a notion that he could inspire even an inert heart; that it was his natural talent to motivate the passive into the course of duty and melt a wayward life so as to flow into the channel of remorse. He had the conviction that no one could resist his strong and determined will for long. He had also no doubt about the fact that he was the driving force behind all positive changes in the personal lives of the members of his community. Neither did he have the least doubt about his own invisible influence working beneath the surface of all such developments. So far if any one had praised Sucharita in front of him he assumed it was he who deserved all the compliments. His great hope was that he would mould Sucharita's character in such a way by means of his sheer instruction, example, and spirited company that the society should eventually realize the wonderful impact of his wonderful influence through the live model of this girl's life.

Not that his pride and self-assurance did suffer any jolt at this miserable fall of Sucharita; he just passed the buck on Pareshbabu. Though Pareshbabu had been generally praised and admired, Haranbabu had always maintained a studied distance from such talks; he hoped that now at last people will come to realize how wise he was in not joining the chorus for Pareshbabu.

People like Haranbabu could tolerate everything, but if those for whom he had taken special care to guide in the right direction betrayed any tendency to walk independently in accordance with their own reason or conscience it amounted to an unforgivable crime in Haran's perception. It was unlikely for him, therefore, to dismiss the matter casually; the more he saw that his advice was going unheeded, the more stubborn and aggressive he became. Just as a machine cannot stop till it has completely run its course, he too could not stop himself in this regard; he was not ready to give up even after pouring for the thousandth time into unwilling ears.

Sucharita was deeply grieved at this—not for herself, but for the sake of Pareshbabu, who was being made the butt of criticism of the entire Brahmo Samaj. How to stop this unfortunate trend? On the other hand Sucharita's Masi too increasingly realized with every passing day that the more she tried to remain quietly invisible, the more she was posing a threat to the peace of the family. The consequent shamefacedness and embarrassment on Masi's part pained Sucharita like anything, and yet she could not think out any solution to this deadlock.

In the meantime Baradasundari mounted her pressure on Pareshbabu for marrying off Sucharita at the earliest. She argued, 'It is not desirable that we continue as Sucharita's guardians any longer. She has started having her own way. If you still put off her marriage then I may have no other choice than leaving this house and putting up elsewhere with my daughters; Sucharita, by her strange ways, has proved a very bad example for my daughters. I am certain you will have to repent for it sooner or later; you just wait and see. Was Lalita like this in the past? These days she has been so willful, so disobedient, so unpredictably perpetrating crises. Who is at the root of it all? Do you think Sucharita had nothing to do with what she did that day, for which I am almost dying of shame? You love Sucharita more than your own daughters, though I have never mentioned it; but I can't go on like this any more, I tell you plainly.'

Pareshbabu felt worried, though not on account of Sucharita, but for the imminent trouble on the domestic front. He did not have the least doubt that Baradasundari will now go to any extent on the latest issue, and the more she fails to achieve her target the more adamant she will become in her battle. It was also true that if Sucharita could be married off quickly, that would be conducive to the girl's peace as well. So he said to Baradasundari, 'If Panubabu can make Sucharita agree about it, I have no objection.'

Baradasundari exclaimed, 'How many times is the consent to be taken? It's amazing! What is the point of so much persuasion either! When shall she ever get a groom like Panubabu, I should like to ask. To tell the truth, you like it or not, I think it is Sucharita who is not a suitable bride for Panubabu.'

Pareshbabu replied, 'I don't understand what Sucharita actually thinks about Panubabu. So I cannot interfere till they reach a clear understanding through mutual interaction.'

Baradasundari exclaimed, 'You don't understand! So you come to admit at long last! It's not indeed easy to understand that girl. The reality is quite different from what she appears to be.'

Baradasundari sent message to Haranbabu. In that day's paper there was a discussion about the miserable condition of Brahmo Samaj. In it Pareshbabu's family had become a target and though no name was mentioned the identity of the target was obvious; and the writer too could be easily identified by the particular style of writing. Sucharita just ran her eyes over the paper and then began to tear them into tiny shreds. The way she was tearing them further and further into smaller and smaller bits it seemed she was determined to reduce them to atomic fragments.

All of a sudden Haranbabu stepped inside and pulling a chair sat down next to Sucharita. Sucharita did not so much as glance at him even for a moment and continued with her tearing of the paper into the smallest shreds.

Haranbabu said, 'Sucharita, I have an important matter to discuss with you today. You have to pay attention to what I say.'

Sucharita continued with her tearing. When it was no longer possible to tear with her nails she took out a pair of scissors from the bag and started cutting the pieces. Just at that moment Lalita stepped in.

Haranbabu said, 'Lalita, I have something to discuss with Sucharita.'

Lalita was about to leave the room when Sucharita caught the end of her sari. Lalita said, 'But Panubabu has something to discuss with you.'

Sucharita did not reply but continued to clasp the end of her sari firmly—then Lalita sat down at one end of the seat on which Sucharita was sitting.

Anyway, Haranbabu was not a person to be daunted by any obstacle. Without wasting time on introduction he plunged straight into the subject. He said, 'I don't think our marriage ought to be delayed any further. I talked to Pareshbabu about it; he said, if you agree there will be no further obstruction. I have decided, the very next Sunday after the coming Sunday—

Without allowing him to complete the sentence Sucharita said, 'No.'

Hearing this extremely precise, clear and arrogant 'No' from Sucharita, Haranbabu was nonplussed. He knew Sucharita to be very obedient. He had never imagined that Sucharita could shoot down his proposal half-way in an instant with a single sharp missile—'No'. Extremely irritated he shouted, 'No! what do you mean by No? Do you want to take even more time?'

Sucharita repeated, 'No.'

Haranbabu was astounded, 'Then?'

Sucharita replied with bent head, 'I don't agree to this marriage.'

Haranbabu fumbled like a blockhead, 'You don't agree? What do you mean?'

Lalita tauntingly remarked, 'Panubabu, have you forgotten Bengali today?'

Haranbabu looked at Lalita angrily and replied in harsh tone, 'It's easier to accept that I have forgotten my mother tongue, than to admit that I have misunderstood the person whose utterances I have always respected.'

Lalita replied, 'It takes a lot of time to understand a person; it may be true in your case also.'

Haranbabu said, 'From the beginning till today I have never contradicted my words or opinion or conduct—I have never given any opportunity to any one to misunderstand me and I can say so with full conviction—let Sucharita confirm whether I am saying the truth.'

Lalita was about to give some reply—Sucharita stopped her and replied, 'You are right. I don't blame you in any way.'

Haranbabu questioned, 'If you don't blame me then why are you doing this injustice to me?'

Sucharita firmly replied, 'If this is called injustice then I will do injustice—but—.'

Some one called from outside, 'Didi, are you inside?'

Sucharita was overjoyed and called out, 'Come in, Binoybabu, come in.'

'You are making a mistake Didi. It is not Binoybabu. I am only Binoy. Don't embarrass me by treating me with respect.' Saying so Binoy stepped inside and saw Haranbabu. He saw the displeasure in Haranbabu's face and smilingly asked, 'Are you displeased because I haven't come for a long time?'

Haranbabu tried to participate in the joke and replied, 'A cause of displeasure indeed! But I must say today you have arrived at an improper hour—a special conversation was going on between Sucharita and me.'

Binoy stood up at once saying, 'Just see, I have not even the idea of what is not the improper hour for my visit! That is why I cannot summon courage enough to come.'

Saying so Binoy was about to leave.

Sucharita said, 'Binoybabu, don't leave. Our discussion is already over. You please take your seat.'

Binoy understood that his arrival had rescued Sucharita from some special crisis. Gladly he sat down taking a chair and said, 'I can't restrain myself if I am given indulgence. If I am asked to sit I must sit; such is my nature. So, my request to Didi is that, she should consider all pros and cons before inviting me, otherwise she may land in trouble.'

Haranbabu did not comment and maintained a sullen silence like the lull before a storm. He seemed to be silently conveying the message, 'Okay, I can wait, I will leave only after I have finished saying what I have come to say.'

Lalita had felt a strange sensation in her blood on hearing Binoy's voice outside. She had tried her best to keep her composure, but in vain. When Binoy entered the room she could not speak quite easily like two good old friends. In which direction she will look, what she will do with her hand, became, as it were, a matter of great concern. Once she was about to leave but Sucharita had firmly gripped her sari.

Binoy talked only to Sucharita, about whatever he had to talk. Speaking fluently with Lalita today was difficult even for a good orator like him. It was for this that he continued to address Sucharita with redoubled energy, without allowing scope for any interruption.

But this new uneasiness between Binoy and Lalita did not escape the notice of Haranbabu. Haranbabu felt jealous by seeing Lalita, who had at present become too discourteous to him, hesitating before Binoy and he began to hate Pareshbabu all the more, for thus debasing his family by allowing the girls to mix with boys of other communities; he particularly longed to see Pareshbabu repenting some day for this. Thus Haranbabu silently cursed Pareshbabu with all the strength of his inflaming hatred.

After continuing in such a manner for a long time it became clear that Haranbabu would not leave. Then Sucharita told

Binoy, 'You have not met Masi for a long time. She often inquires about you. Could you see her once?'

Binoy stood up saying, 'Don't put such a blame on me that I forgot Masi entirely.'

When Sucharita took Binoy to her Masi, Lalita got up and said, 'Panubabu, I think you don't have any important business with me.'

Haranbabu replied, 'No. I think you are urgently required elsewhere. You may go.'

Lalita understood the hint. At once she raised her head defiantly and said, 'Binoybabu has come after a long time, I am going to have a talk with him. Meanwhile if you want to read what you have written then—oh no, it's not possible, Didi has converted it to tiny shreds. If you can stand things written by others you may go through these.'

Saying so she took the essays written by Gora from the corner table where they were carefully kept, and placing them in front of Haranbabu quickly left.

Harimohini was elated on seeing Binoy. It resulted not only from the affection she had for this handsome boy. All the outsiders who came to visit looked at her as if she were a strange creature. They were Calcuttans, almost all of them were well-versed in English and Bengali, much more articulate than she could ever be—she felt small at their aloofness and contemptuous behaviour. She found in Binoy a kind of refuge. Binoy too lived in Culcutta, she had heard that he too was quite educated—but he had never shown any disregard to her, he seemed to treat her like a close relative, and it gave a boost to her sense of self-respect. It was for this reason, primarily, that Binoy had secured the place of a kin in her mind. She began to feel that Binoy was like a shield protecting her from the general disrespect. She felt considerably exposed in this house—Binoy was like a garment which could help her as a cover.

Lalita would normally never go to Harimohini immediately after Binoy had gone to her—but today due to Haranbabu's sly taunting, she shed all her hesitations and forced herself to the room upstairs. Not only that, she also deliberately broached conversation with Binay. They soon became engrossed in lively exchanges; as a matter of fact, the noise of their laughter floated downstairs and reached the lone ears of Haranbabu sitting there to pierce his heart. He could not sit alone for a long time, and tried to calm his disturbed mind by talking to Baradasundari. Baradasundari learnt that Sucharita had not consented to the proposal of her marriage with Haranbabu. Hearing this she lost her patience. She said, 'Panubabu, leave your gentlemanly attitude. On all previous occasions she had always consented to the marriage and the whole Brahmo Samaj is eagerly waiting for it; and now everything cannot be turned upside down just because she refuses to give her nod. You are not to budge an inch from your proposal, let's see what she can do.'

Haranbabu actually needed little goading in this matter. Sitting stern as a log of wood with his head held stiff, he was reflecting at that moment—'The argument is not negligible; of course leaving Sucharita does not really matter much for me, but I can't put Brahmo Samaj to shame.'

In order to make his relation stronger with Harimohini Binoy had deliberately insisted for some food. Harimohini instantly busied herself and on a small plate she arranged some raw gram seeds, paneer, butter, some sugar, a banana, and some milk in a bronze bowl and offered it affectionately to Binoy. Binoy smiled and said, 'I thought I would catch Masi on the wrong foot by mentioning my hunger at this odd hour, but I admit my failure.' Saying so Binoy sat down to take his meal ceremoniously when Baradasundari entered. Binoy bent his head across his plate as much as possible in order to show his respect and said, 'I was downstairs for a long time, but I could not see you.' Baradasundari did not reply and addressed Sucharita directly, 'Oh, so she is here! Just as I thought! A meeting is on. She is reveling. On the other hand poor Haranbabu is waiting for her since morning, as if he is her servant. I have taken care of them since childhood—but believe me, I have never seen them behave in such a manner. I don't understand from where they are getting such ideas. Things that could never happen in our family are happening nowadays—how can we ever show our faces in the society! The training of so many years is just thrown to the winds in two days. What is all this, may I know?'

Harimohini hurriedly said, 'Sucharita, I did not know that someone was waiting for you downstairs. I have made a great mistake. *Mā*, please go downstairs quickly. I have made a great mistake.'

Lalita was about to protest instantly that Harimohini had not committed any wrong. Sucharita secretly caught hold of her hand and quietened her and went downstairs without protest.

We have already mentioned that Binoy had previously stirred Baradasundari's affection. She was sure that under the influence of her family Binoy would eventually become a member of Brahmo Samaj. She took great pride in thinking that she herself had moulded Binoy; she had also confided her pride to some of her friends. It can be guessed how she was inflamed to see the same Binoy comfortably installed in the camp of her opponent and the fire flared the more on sensing that her own daughter Lalita could be responsible for his relapse into barbarism. She rudely asked, 'Lalita, do you have any business here?'

Lalita responded, 'Yes, Binoybabu came; so—.'

Baradasundari said, 'Binoybabu has come to her, let her play the hostess. You come downstairs, there is some work.'

Lalita was sure that, Haranbabu had certainly said something about her and Binoy to her mother which should be none of his concern. Drawing such an inference she stiffened at once and replied with an extra curtness, 'Binoybabu has come after a long time, I shall be coming downstairs only after I have finished talking with him.'

Hearing the tone of her reply, Baradasundari understood that she would not be able to make her budge. Apprehending that her defeat will be revealed to Harimohimi she left without saying anything and without addressing Binoy further.

Lalita expressed her intention of talking to Binoy before her mother, but after Baradasundari left no sign of the interest was noticeable. The three sat embarrassed and silent for a while, and then Lalita went to her own room and shut the door.

Binoy understood clearly the kind of situation that had resulted due to Harimohini's stay in the house. By means of his tentative queries he gathered the story of Harimohini's sad past. Harimohini concluded her narration with the remark, 'Baba, for a destitute bereaved woman like me the society is not the right place. It would be better if I could pack off to some holy place and spend the rest of my life in worshipping God. I have a little money left which can sustain me for a while; subsequently, I can work as a cook in some family and thus manage to maintain myself. I visited Kashi, and saw many people who had been carrying on this way. But I am too big a sinner, so I failed to get reconciled to it. As soon as I am alone all the terrible memories crowd in to encircle me from all sides; they fence off even my God. I fear, I may go mad. Radharani and Satish have been to me like a floating raft to the drowning man—if I ever think of leaving them I feel nearly undone. So day and night I am haunted by the fear that perhaps I must leave them—otherwise after losing everything why did I start loving them so much within such a short time? Baba, I have no qualms to confess to you, since the day I got these two kids I have been able once again to worship my lord from the depth of my soul; if I lose them my Lord too will instantly relapse in my mind into mere hard stone.'

Saying so Harimohini wiped her eyes with the end of her *sāri*.

40

Sucharita entered into the room downstairs and stood before Haranbabu—saying, 'Now say what you have to say to me.'

Haranbabu said, 'Sit down.'

Sucharita however stood still.

Haranbabu said, 'Sucharita you are doing injustice to me.'

Sucharita replied, 'You, too, are doing injustice to me.'

Haranbabu said, 'Why, I have given you my word, and till now—.'

Sucharita interrupted and said, 'Do you think justice and injustice to be just a matter of words? Do you want to virtually torture me just on the excuse of those two words? Is not one single truth more precious than one thousand lies? If I have committed a mistake hundred times would you stick only to that with all the force? Today when I have realised my mistake I won't consider myself bound by the word I had uttered in the past—that will be doing a grievous wrong to myself.'

Haranbabu could not understand by any means how Sucharita could change so completely. Her general calmness and quietness seemed to have been shattered today; and he had neither the capacity nor the humility to realise that he himself could be responsible for this. While silently accusing all the new contacts of Sucharita he asked bluntly, 'What precisely is the mistake that you think you committed?'

Sucharita replied, 'Why do you ask me such a question? Previously I agreed, now I disagree. Isn't it enough?'

Haranbabu replied, 'But we are answerable to Brahmo Samaj. What will you or I say to the members of the Samaj?'

Sucharita said, 'I will say nothing. If you think you should account for it then you may say, Sucharita is young, she is unintelligent and fickle minded. You can say whatever you like. But for us the issue is finally clinched here and now.'

Haranbabu said, 'It cannot be final. If Pareshbabu—'

Even as he was saying this Pareshbabu arrived; he said, 'Well, Panubabu, did you mention me? What's the matter?'

Sucharita at that moment was about to leave the room. Haranbabu called her back, 'Sucharita, don't leave, let us have it over in the presence of Pareshbabu.'

Sucharita turned about. Haranbabu said, 'Pareshbabu, after all this long dilly-dallying Sucharita now says she does not consent to the marriage! Should she have taken such a serious matter so lightly all these years? Will you too not be held responsible for this nasty development?'

Pareshbabu ran his hand on Sucharita's head and affectionately said, '*Mā*, you are not needed here, you may please go.'

Hearing these few words Sucharita's eyes at once overflowed with tears and she quickly left the room.

Pareshbabu said, 'I had the apprehension long since that Sucharita had agreed to the marriage before properly probing her own mind. That's the reason why I could not comply with your request for confirming the engagement before the Samaj.'

Haranbabu retorted, 'Doesn't it occur to you that Sucharita might have understood herself better when she had given the consent, and now she is withdrawing on account of lack of understanding?'

Pareshbabu said, 'It can be either way, but a marriage cannot take place when there is the scope of such uncertainties.'

Haranbabu asked, 'Won't you give the right advice to Sucharita?'

Pareshbabu replied, 'You are well aware that it is simply beyond me to give Sucharita any wrong advice.'

Haranbabu said, 'If it had been so indeed, Sucharita would not have come to this. I can challenge you that everything that has started to take place in your family nowadays is due to your lack of foresight.'

Pareshbabu smiled slightly and said, 'You're absolutely right—if I don't take the responsibility of things happening in my family who else will?'

Haranbabu said, 'You will have to repent for it, I warn you.'

Pareshbabu replied, 'Repentance is but grace of God. I fear doing wrong, Panubabu, not repentance.'

Sucharita stepped into the room and holding Pareshbabu's hand said, 'Baba, it's time for your prayer.'

Pareshbabu asked, 'Panubabu, will you wait a little then?'

Haranbabu replied, 'No', and briskly walked away.

41

Sucharita was beginning to fear the conflict between her real self and her appearance. Her feelings for Gora had gained strength without her knowledge and after Gora was sent to prison she became aware of it and it was such an irresistible one that she could not understand what to do about it, or what will be its ultimate result; she could not convey it to anybody, and suffered from a feeling of diffidence. She did not even have the privacy of solitude either when she could weigh and consider the deep pain that she cherished secretly—Haranbabu standing on her very doorstep was trying to alert the whole Samaj against her; even the press was being roped in for the purpose. On the top of it all her Masi's problem came to such a pass that an immediate solution was a must. Sucharita felt that her life had reached a crucial turning; it was no more the balmy days when she could walk the trodden path with accustomed unconcern.

Pareshbabu was her only stay during this time of crisis. She did not seek any advice from him, nor consolation; there were matters which she could never directly discuss with Pareshbabu and there were matters which were too mundane to be brought to his notice. But Pareshbabu's very presence seemed to silently gather her to the lap of a father, to the bosom of a mother.

Now in winter Pareshbabu did not go to the garden in the evening. In the western side of his house in a small room he sat on a mat for his prayer, while the departing rays of the sun lit his tranquil face, his white-hair. During that time Sucharita would tiptoe to him and silently sit near him. She would, as if, immerse her pained turbulent heart in the soothing depth of his deep meditation. During his meditation Paresh could see this daughter of his, this pupil, sitting quietly beside him; then he could see her touched with splendor of unspeakable spiritual grace and would silently bless her with all his heart.

Pareshbabu's aim was to become one with the cosmic being and so he always aspired after the best and the truest. Family life thus was never a major concern for him. In this way he had earned an inner freedom; so he never imposed on anyone regarding one's belief or practice. Trust in goodness and patience in family matters were quite natural for him. This quality was so strong in him that people his society rebuked him, but he accepted rebuke in such a manner that it might have hurt him, but never affected his mind. 'I will no more take anything from anyone's hands, I will take everything from His hand', he would say.

Sucharita wanted to have a touch of this deep tranquility from Pareshbabu and so she frequently came to him on various pretexts. When in this stage of inexperienced girlhood her conflicting heart and a hostile society had made her totally perplexed she thought time and again, 'If, lying on the ground, I can hold the feet of my Baba onto my head for sometime, my mind will be filled with peace.'

Sucharita thought that she would awaken all the power of her mind and with unwavering confidence forestall all the miseries, and then the oppositions will be automatically defeated. But this did not happen; she had to tread untrodden grounds.

When Baradasundari saw that Sucharita could not be controlled through anger or rebuke and there was no question of getting the support of Paresh, then her rage against Harimohini was uncontrollable. The presence of Harimohini in her house became a thorn in the flesh for her.

It was the day she had invited Binoy to the annual prayer meeting on the occasion of the death anniversary of her father. The prayer would be held in evening; before it she was decorating her household; Sucharita and her other daughters were helping her.

Of a sudden her eyes fell on Binoy climbing up the stairs toward Harimohini's room. When a mind is obsessed even a small incident can assume huge proportion. Binoy's going upstairs became intolerable for her to such an extent that abandoning the decoration work she too flew upstairs. She saw Binoy sitting on the mat like a close kin and happily engaged in a conversation with Harimohini.

Baradasundari blurted out at once, 'See, stay here as long as you wish, I will treat you with love and care. But I tell you, you can't keep your idol here.'

Harimohini had spent all her life in villages. She thought that the Brahmos were only a sub-class of the Christians. So there was a point to be discreet about *their* contact. But that they too could have reservations about Hindus had begun to dawn on her during the last few days. She was thinking what she should do, and now hearing it from Baradasundari she understood that, there was no more time for thought—but a course had to be decided upon. First she thought she would rent a house in Calcutta, then she would be able to see Sucharita and Satish sometimes. But with the meagre amount that she had she could not afford to live in Calcutta.

During Baradasundari's sudden stormy arrival and departure Binoy sat quietly with bowed head.

After remaining quiet for sometime Harimohini said, 'I will go on a pilgrimage, can any one of you escort me to the place Baba?'

Binoy replied, 'I can do it very well. But the preparation will take two-three days' time; till then Masi, please come and stay with my *Mā*.'

Harimohini replied, 'Baba, my responsibility is a heavy burden. I don't know what Lord has loaded my fortune with, nobody can bear me. When my in-laws could not bear my burden I should have understood. But the mind never understands Baba—my heart has become empty, I am only roaming around to fill it up, my misfortune is also roaming with me. Leave it, Baba, I don't want to go to anybody's house again—I will take shelter in the lotus of his feet who bears the burden of the entire world. Now he will give me shelter—I can bear no longer.'

Saying so she began to cry and wipe her eyes repeatedly.

Binoy said, 'You cannot say like that Masi! You cannot compare my *Mā* with anyone else. Since she has surrendered all her burden to God, she does not feel any difficulty in carrying the burden of others. I will take you just for once to *my* pilgrim spot, then I will go to visit *your* pilgrim spot.'

Harimohini said, 'Then you should inform them—.'

Binoy replied, 'As soon as we go *Mā* will get the information—that will be the confirmed information.'

Harimohini said, 'Then tomorrow morning—.'

Binoy replied, 'Why tomorrow? We can go tonight.'

In the evening Sucharita came and said, 'Binoybabu, *Mā* is calling you. It's time for prayer.'

Binoy replied, 'I have something to discuss with Masi, I will not be able to attend today.'

The fact was that today Binoy could not bring himself by any means to accept Baradasundari's invitation. He felt that it was simply a farce.

Harimohini hurriedly said, 'Baba, you go. We can talk later. First finish your work, and then you come.'

Sucharita said, 'It will be better if you go.'

Binoy understood that if he did not attend the meeting the turmoil that had started brewing up in the family would become stronger. So he went where the prayer was conducted, but that too did not yield the desired result.

There was a party after the prayer. Binoy said, 'I have no appetite today.'

Baradasundari replied, 'Appetite can't be blamed. You have already taken your meal upstairs.'

Binoy smiled and replied, 'Yes, a greedy man commits such blunders. He loses his future by surrendering to the temptation of the present.' Saying so, Binoy turned to go.

Baradasundari intervened, 'Are you going upstairs?'

Binoy briefly replied, 'Yes' and left the room. Sucharita was standing near the door; he said to her in a low voice, 'Didi, will you come to Masi for once, there is an important matter to discuss.'

Lalita was attending the guests. She came once to Haranbabu and he unnecessarily blurted out, 'Binoybabu is not here, he has gone upstairs.'

On hearing this Lalita looked straight into his face without hesitation and replied, 'I know. He will not leave without meeting me. As soon as I finish my work here I will go upstairs.'

Not being able to create an awkward situation for Lalita the hidden raging flames began to spread further. That Binoy told Sucharita something and Sucharita followed him within a few moments, did not escape Haranbabu's notice. Today he was constantly looking for an opportunity to speak to Sucharita but could not succeed in his efforts. Once or twice Sucharita had disregarded his clear summons in such a way that he had felt insulted before the assembled guests. He had felt mentally ill after it.

When Sucharita went up she saw that Harimohini had packed her belongings and was sitting in such a way as if she was about to go somewhere. Sucharita asked, 'Masi, what is this?'

Harimohini could not reply to her query, broke into tears and said, 'Where is Satish? Call him for once *Mā*.'

When Sucharita looked at Binoy's face he replied, 'If Masi stays in this house every one feels inconvenienced, so I am taking her to my *Mā*.'

Harimohini said, 'From there I am planning to go on a pilgrimage! It looks odd if people like me stays in some one else's house. Why should people tolerate me like this for ever?'

Sucharita herself was thinking about it for some days. She had felt that it was degrading for her Masi to live in this house, so she could not reply. She sat quietly near her. It was night. The earthen lamp was not lit in the room. In the October sky of Calcutta the stars looked frosty. Whose eyes were shedding tears could not be seen in the dark.

From the stairs Satish's loud voice calling 'Masima' was heard. 'What Baba, come Baba,' Harimohini quickly stood up. Sucharita said, 'Masima, tonight you cannot go anywhere, tomorrow morning it shall be decided. Without informing Baba properly how can you go, tell me. It will be wrong.'

The idea had never occurred to Binoy: so excited was he by the disgrace that Harimohini faced from Baradasundari. He had determined that it would be improper for Masi to stay in that house even for a night—and to break Baradasundari's notion that Harimohini stayed there tolerating everything because she had nowhere else to go, he did not want to delay for a moment to take her away. Hearing Sucharita Binoy of a sudden was reminded, that it was not Baradasundari with whom Harimohini had primary and only relation in this house. It is improper to give so much importance to the person who had humiliated her and forget about the person who had magnanimously given shelter to her as a relative.

Binoy said, 'That's true. You cannot leave without informing Pareshbabu.'

Satish ran in shouting, 'Masi-ma, you know, the Russians have come to attack India? It will be great fun.'

Binoy questioned, 'Whom are you supporting?'

Satish replied, 'The Russians of course.'

Binoy said, 'Then the Russians have no more worries.'

As Satish enlivened the talk this way Sucharita slowly got up and went downstairs.

Sucharita knew, that before dozing off to sleep Pareshbabu read some part of any one of his favourite books. Many a times Sucharita would come and sit near him at that hour and on her request Pareshbabu had also read it out to her.

Today also in the silent room lighting the lamp Pareshbabu was reading a book by Emerson. Sucharita slowly pulled up a chair and sat beside him. Pareshbabu glanced at her face for once. Sucharita determination broke down—she could not bring herself to speak anything regarding family matters. She said instead, 'Baba, read it to me.'

Pareshbabu began to read and explain to her. It was ten o'clock when they finished reading. Then Sucharita was slowly departing without saying anything sensing that it might disturb Pareshbabu's peace before he went off to sleep.

Pareshbabu called affectionately, 'Radhe!'

She returned. Pareshbabu asked, 'Did you come to talk about your Masi?'

She was surprised, 'Yes Baba, but let it be, we can talk about it in the morning.'

Pareshbabu said, 'Sit down.'

When Sucharita sat down he said, 'I know that your Masi has been facing great trouble here and I am thinking about it. I had never guessed earlier that her religious beliefs and her conduct could hurt your mother's belief so much. I see that in this situation if your Masi has to stay in this house any longer she will feel very uncomfortable.'

Sucharita said, 'Masi is already set for leaving.'

Pareshbabu replied, 'I knew she would leave. You two are her only relatives—you cannot let her depart like an abandoned person. I know that. So I had been thinking about it for the last few days.'

Sucharita had never guessed that Pareshbabu knew about her Masi's trouble and was thinking about it. Lest he comes to know and feels pained, she was proceeding with the utmost caution; today after hearing from Pareshbabu she felt astonished and her eyes were filled with tears.

Pareshbabu said, 'I have got a house for your Masi.'

Sucharita said, 'But she—'

Pareshbabu. Cannot give the rent. Why will she give the rent? You will pay it.

Sucharita was stunned and looked at Pareshbabu's face. Pareshbabu smiled and said, 'Let her live in your house—no need of giving rent.'

Sucharita was more astonished. Pareshbabu said, 'In Calcutta you have two houses, you don't know! One is yours, and the other is for Satish. Your father gave me some money when he died. I invested it in business and bought two houses in Calcutta. Till now I was getting rent, and was also accumulating it. A few days ago your tenants have vacated the house; your Masi will face no trouble living there.'

Sucharita said, 'But, can she live there all alone?'

Pareshbabu replied, 'Why will she have to live alone when she has near and dear ones like you all?'

Sucharita said, 'I had come to talk about it with you today. Masi has got ready to leave; I was thinking how I could let her go all by herself. So I came to seek your advice. I will do whatever you say.'

Pareshbabu said, 'Your house is located just after two or three houses in the lane next to this house—you can see it if you stand on that verandah. If you live there you will not feel insecure. I can look after you.'

Sucharita felt a load gone off her heart and she remained sitting near Pareshbabu quietly. Pareshbabu too sat silently, deeply withdrawn into himself. Sucharita was his pupil, his daughter, his companion. She had become involved not only with his life, but also with his meditation that he offered to his God. The days when she came calmly and joined with him in prayer, his prayer attended a special completeness in itself. He had begun moulding Sucharita's life with goodwill and affection and his own life was attaining a fulfillment through it. Sucharita had come and stood near him with devotion and gentleness as no one before had come; just as a flower looks towards the sky similarly she looked up and revealed her entire nature to him. When someone comes with such a dedication then a person's power to give also increases. Like a cloud heavy with droplets of rain, the entire interior self bows down attaining a completeness in itself. Nothing can be more fortunate for one who gets the rare opportunity to give what is truth to oneself, what is best, to a like-minded person. This rare opportunity was given by Sucharita to Pareshbabu. So he shared a deep relationship with Sucharita. Today the time has come to break the exterior shell of that relationship with her—he has to make the fruit juicy with the juice of his life and then free it. So the pain that he was suffering today was his offering to his God. Sucharita was not weak or afraid to travel the path; she was ready to respond to this call for new expression of joy and sorrow. He was reflecting in his own mind, 'Child, start your journey—that I will through my intellect and shelter protect your whole life can never be the case—let God free you from me by taking you through stranger things in life, attracting you to the ultimate goal—let your life attain success through it.' Saying so he had been in his vision holding up the child, nurtured with years of care and affection, as a holy offering to his God. Pareshbabu was not angry with Baradasundari, he had never encouraged himself to feel opposed to his family. He knew that when a sudden heavy rain flooded a narrow riverbed the only way out was to release it in some open field. He knew that an unexpected situation had arisen in his small family since the last few days and it would be better to let it run its course; eventually it will calm down. Therefore, he was silently taking preparation so that peace and harmony could be restored without much fanfare.

After the two sat silently for sometime the clock struck eleven. Then Pareshbabu stood up, and taking Sucharita's hand took her to the roof of the portico. The mist of the evening had cleared away and the stars shone in the splendid darkness. With Sucharita by his side Pareshbabu prayed in the peaceful evening—let all the untruth of life be cleansed to yield place to complete truth enlightening our lives.

42

The next day at dawn Harimohini came to kneel on the floor before Pareshbabu. Pareshbabu hurriedly stepped aside saying, "What are you doing?"

Harimohini said with tear-filled eyes, 'I will never be able to repay the debt that I owe you even if I live countless lives. You have solved the problem of a helpless person like me; none else could have done it. I have seen that one cannot do any good to others even if one is willing enough—God has showered his grace on people like you, so you are able to bestow grace upon me.'

Pareshbabu was feeling greatly embarrassed; and said, 'I have done nothing as such—all this is Radharani's—.'

Harimohini interrupted and said, 'I know, I know—but Radharani is yours—whatever she does is actually your doing. When her mother died, and then her father died too, I thought that the girl was very unfortunate—but how could I know that God would change her sad fortune to something so fortunate. See; when I have met you at last after roaming everywhere I feel that God has been kind to me.'

Binoy entered to announce, 'Masi, *Mā* has come to take you.' Sucharita stood up and eagerly asked, 'Where is she?'

Binoy replied, 'She is sitting downstairs with your mother.'

Sucharita hastened downstairs.

Pareshbabu said to Harimohini, 'Let me arrange the things in your house.'

After Pareshbabu had left Binoy, quite surprised, said, 'Masi, your house—I never knew about it.'

Harimohini replied, 'Even I didn't know it Baba! Only Pareshbabu knew about it. It is the house of our Radharani.'

After Binoy heard the full details he said, 'I thought that at lest Binoy would be of some help to someone in this world. But that chance too is lost. So far I could never do anything for my *Mā*, she does everything for me—I cannot do anything even for Masi. My destiny is to take help, and never to give.'

After some time Anandamoyee appeared with Lalita and Sucharita. Harimohini went up to her and said, 'When God shows his grace he is bounteous—Didi, I have got you too today.'

Saying so she took her hands and made her sit down on the straw mat.

Harimohini said, 'Didi, I have heard so much about you from Binoy.'

Anandamoyee smiled and replied, 'He suffers from such a malady since boyhood, whatever he starts speaking about is not easily discarded. Masi's turn will also come very soon.'

Binoy replied, 'I have got Masi when I am already a grown-up, I have secured her myself, I have been deprived of her so long that now I have to compensate for what I had been deprived of.'

Anandamoyee looked at Lalita and smilingly said, 'Our Binoy knows how to get what he has been deprived of and also knows how to take care of it with his heart and soul. I don't know what his views are about you all—but he has got what he had never thought of getting. How can I explain *Mā* the happiness that I feel on his being introduced to you all! His happy assimilation into this family has done him immense good. He understands it very well and he always admits it.'

Lalita tried to say something in reply but failed to find the right words; her face turned red. Sucharita felt Lalita's predicament and said, 'Binoybabu can perceive the inner qualities of every person, so the little good that a person has is apparent to him. That is largely due to his goodness.'

Binoy replied, '*Mā*, you want to make Binoy a great subject of discussion but in the society he does not enjoy so great a position. I often think of explaining this situation to you but I cannot possibly due to my vanity. Anyway, it can continue no longer. *Mā* no more, your "Binoy Charit" is over today.'

All of a sudden Satish came jumping with a little puppy pressed to his bossom.

Harimohini hurriedly said, 'Baba Satish, my good boy, take that dog away!'

Satish replied, 'He will do nothing Masi! He will not enter your room. You love him just a little, he will do nothing to you.'

Harimohini stepped back and said, 'No my boy, no, take him away.'

Then Anandamoyee pulled Satish along with the dog close to her. After taking the dog on her lap she asked Satish, 'You are Satish, aren't you? A friend of our Binoy?'

He never felt uneasy when addressed as Binoy's friend. So he unhesitatingly replied, 'Yes.'

Saying so he stared inquisitively at Anandamoyee's face.

Anandamoyee replied, 'I am Binoy's mother.'

The puppy was happily engaged in chewing Anandamoyee's bracelet. Sucharita said, 'You Chatterton, touch the feet of *Mā*.'

Satish felt ashamed and somehow managed to do it.

Baradasundari came upstairs at this time and without looking at Harimohini for a moment asked Anandamoyee, 'Will you eat something at our place?'

Anandamoyee replied, 'I never bother about edibility or touchability of food. But please excuse me today—let Gora come back, I will have my food here after he returns.'

In the absence of Gora Anandamoyee did not want to do any such thing that he would have disliked.

Baradasundari looked at Binoy and said, 'So Binoybabu, you are here too! I thought you had not come.'

Binoy quickly replied, 'Do you think that I will depart without letting you knew about my arrival?'

Baradasundari said, 'Yesterday you responded to the invitation by not eating, today you will take the food without invitation.'

Binoy said, 'I will profit much from it. The bonus is always more attractive than the regular income.'

Harimohini was surprised. Binoy eats in this house! Also she did not like the idea that Anandamoyee is never particular about where she eats and from whom she takes it.

When Baradasundari left she asked hesitatingly, 'Didi, is your husband—'

Anandamoyee replied, 'My husband is very much a Hindu.'

Harimohini felt even more puzzled. Anandamoyee understood what she felt and said, 'Sister, I obeyed the norms of the society till the day the society was greater for me than all the members of the family, but one day God revealed Himself in my house all of a sudden and in such a way that it was no longer possible for me to obey the rules of society. When He Himself came and snatched away my caste, then whom have I to fear?'

Harimohini could not understand the meaning of this excuse and asked, 'But your husband—.'

Anandamoyee replied, 'My husband gets angry.'

Harimohini. The boys?

Anandamoyee. 'The boys are not happy. But how can I live otherwise? Sister, I can't explain this to anybody—only He will understand who knows everything.'

Saying so Anandamoyee bowed joining her palms.

Harimohini thought maybe some Christian missionary girl had come and indoctrinated her. She felt extremely uneasy.

43

Sucharita felt greatly relieved by the idea that she will be able to live near the house of Pareshbabu under his guardianship. But when the arrangements were completed in her new house and as the time neared to take leave she felt something like an arresting pain within her heart. It was not the question of living or not living near Pareshbabu, but that the world that they shared in every aspect of their life was going to break. For Sucharita this was but a kind of death. The little position that she enjoyed in this family, the minor work that she did, the relation she shared with each servant, all this made her heart ache.

The knowledge that Sucharita had some means of her own and she was trying to become independent on the strength of it made Baradasundari apparently so happy that she repeatedly expressed her joy in being free at last from the responsibility which she had been carefully carrying all these years. But at heart she felt annoyed with Sucharita; as if it was a crime on Sucharita's part to be able to stand on her own means, independently of them. Indeed often she had thought that Sucharita had nowhere to go and had no one to depend on, that she was a liability for the family, and thinking such things she pitied herself. But when she heard the news of a sudden that this burden was ultimately lifted she did not feel the least satisfaction in her mind. She considered Sucharita an offender thinking that she might now be proudly considering their house as unnecessary, and that she could also disregard their authority. For the last few days she was particular about maintaining a studied distance from her. Previously she would call her to help her with the household chores but now she purposely started to show unnatural respect. Sucharita, with her heart filled with sadness, was trying to participate increasingly in the household works before leaving; on many occasions she was hanging around her; but Baradasundari would not allow her to work for her as if that would be beneath the dignity of Sucharita. Sucharita was deeply pained because the person who had nurtured her since her childhood and whom she had called '*Mā*' kept aloof like an adversary even when she was going to depart.

Labanya, Lalita, Leela started hanging around Sucharita. They went to decorate her new home with great excitement, but even within that excitement there was an expression of untold grief.

So long Sucharita used to do little jobs for Pareshbabu on simple pretexts. May be she arranged the flowers in the vase, adjusted the books on the table with her own hands, warmed the bedclothes in the sun, reminded him in time to take his bath. No one pays any importance to these habitual jobs. But when the time comes to leave even these inconsequential works then these little services, which anybody can do easily, and which, even if not done, may not be of great damage, can yet pain the hearts of both the persons involved. Nowadays when Sucharita comes to Paresh's room to do some little job it becomes for him a service of immense importance and a deep sigh fills his heart and Sucharita's eyes also fill with tears when she remembers that in the coming days these works will be executed by some other hand.

When Pareshbabu came to his secluded prayer room at dawn on the day Sucharita was to leave after lunch, he saw that Sucharita had been silently waiting for him at one corner of the room after decorating with flowers the small carpet on which he was to sit. Lavanya and Lila had also planned to come but Lalita had forbidden them. Lalita knew that by participating with Pareshbabu in his silent prayer Sucharita became his object of happiness and secured his blessings in a special way—she felt that today at early morning it was necessary for Sucharita to secure his blessings and so Lalita had not let them encroach.

After the prayer was over as tears rolled down Sucharita's cheeks Pareshbabu said, '*Mā*, don't turn to look back, fare forward—don't hesitate. Let anything happen, let anything cross your path; through your capability extract the best from it. Taking this oath go ahead happily. Offering yourself completely to God take Him as your guide—then you can gain even from your mistakes, shortcomings; but if you divide yourself into two halves, and give one part to God and the other to something else, then things will become difficult for you.

May God bless you, that you do not have to depend on the little shelter that we gave you.'

When both came out after the prayer they saw that Haranbabu was waiting for them in the drawing room. Sucharita had decided that today she would not nurse any grudge against anybody and so she greeted Haranbabu politely. Haranbabu instantly sat up erect on the chair and spoke in a serious tone, 'Sucharita, till today you had taken shelter in truth but today you are falling away from it. Today is a day of mourning for us.'

Sucharita did not reply. But it struck a note of discord in her mind in the melody of mingled peace and pathos.

Pareshbabu replied, 'The Lord dwelling within knows who is moving forward and who is regressing; we only become unnecessarily anxious as we judge from the outside.'

Haranbabu replied, 'Then do you want to say that you don't feel worried? And you didn't even find any cause for repentance?'

Pareshbabu replied, 'Panubabu, I don't bother about imaginary problems and I will come to know whether there is any cause of repentance only when I feel any repentance.'

Haranbabu replied, 'That your daughter Lalita came alone with Binoybabu in a steamer—is it imaginary?'

Sucharita flushed. Pareshbabu replied, 'Panubabu, you are excited for some unknown reasons. So it will be unfair to discuss this matter with you now.'

Haranbabu raised his head and replied, 'I don't speak anything in my excitement—I hold myself responsible for whatever I speak; you don't have to worry about it. What I am telling you I am not telling as an individual but as a representative of Brahmo Samaj—I am speaking because it will be unrighteous not to speak out. If you were not blind, you could have understood from the single incident of Lalita's coming all alone with Binoybabu that your family is about to drift away tearing its anchor from Brahmo Samaj. This will not only be the cause of repentance for you, but will also be a cause of shame for the entire Brahmo Samaj.

Pareshbabu replied, 'One can always condemn from outside, but judgment demands an inside view. Don't blame a person on the basis of one stray incident.'

Haranbabu replied, 'Incidents don't occur of a sudden, you are all contributing to it. You are allowing outsiders in your house as if they were relatives, and they are pulling you family away from their own community. They have dragged you far, can't you see it?'

Pareshbabu felt a bit irritated and said, 'I see things differently.'

Haranbabu replied, 'You may see differently. But I am calling Sucharita as a witness, let her speak the truth, whether the relationship between Lalita and Binoy is confined to the surface level only? Had it not touched their hearts ever? No Sucharita, you cannot leave—you have to reply. This is a serious issue.'

Sucharita hardened herself and said sternly, 'However serious it may be you have no right to talk on the matter.'

Haranbabu replied, 'Had I no right it is not only that I would have kept quiet but I would have also given no thought to it. You may not care for the society, but as long as the society exists it is bound to judge you.'

Lalita stormed into the room and said, 'If the society has put you in the position of the judge then it's better for us to live in seclusion than in your society.'

Haranbabu stood up from the chair and replied, 'Lalita, you have come, I am happy about it. The complaint that is against you should be judged in front of you.'

Sucharita's face and eyes flashed with anger; she replied, 'Haranbabu, go to your home and call a court there. We will never give you the right to stand in our house and insult us. Come Lalita!'

Lalita did not budge an inch. She said, 'No Didi, I will not run away. I want to listen to everything that Panubabu has got to say. Say what you have to say, please!'

Haranbabu was stunned. Pareshbabu said, '*Mā* Lalita, Sucharita will leave today—I cannot let any unpleasant event take place this morning. Haranbabu, whatever may be our mistakes, you have to excuse us today.'

Haranbabu sat in gloomy silence. The more Sucharita was trying to ignore him the more stubbornly he was trying to possess her. He had a strong conviction that he could win her by his extraordinary moral force. It is not that he had abandoned all hope of getting Sucharita, but feared that when Sucharita shifts to another house with Masi, his hold on her will slacken and this made him jittery. So today he had sharpened all the forceful weapons in his armoury and came armed with them. He was determined to thrash out everything that very morning. Today he had come abandoning all his hesitation—but that the other party too can speak unhesitatingly, that Lalita and Sucharita too can give a fight taking out arrows from their own quivers was beyond his imagination. He knew, that when he will start shooting vehemently his fiery moral arrows the other party will just stand hanging their head. But that did not happen and the moment flitted by. But Haranbabu was not one to accept defeat. He reflected in his mind, truth will surely win, that means Haranbabu will surely win. But one does not simply win. One has to fight. So Haranbabu girded his loins and launched into the battlefield.

Sucharita said, 'Masi, today I will take food with everybody—you please don't mind.' Harimohini kept quiet. She had thought that Sucharita had become hers completely—particularly getting her own property she was going to lead her life independently, and that now Harimohini need not hesitate further, she can live wholly as she wished. So, today when Sucharita abandoned the norms of purity and proposed to have her meals with the rest of the family she did not like it; she remained silent.

Sucharita understood and said, 'I can guarantee you that God will be happy about it. My own internal God has asked me to take my meals with others. If I disregard Him He will be angered. I fear His anger more than yours.'

As long as Harimohini was being insulted by Baradasundari Sucharita obeyed her customs in order to palliate the insults and today when the times of insult were over Sucharita did not hesitate a moment to abandon the customs. But Harimohini could not understand it. Harimohini had not understood Sucharita completely; it was also difficult for her.

Harimohini did not stop her directly but felt resentment which she did not express. She reflected, 'My God, how can people do such things I cannot understand. Being born in the house of a Brahmin too!'

After remaining quiet for some time she said, 'Let me tell you something, whatever you do, don't drink the water brought by that waterbearer.'

Sucharita exclaimed, 'Why Masi, Ramdin the waterbearer supplies you the milk by milking his own cow!'

Harimohini dilated her eyes and said, 'You surprise me—are water and milk the same thing!'

Sucharita smiled and replied, 'Okay Masi, I will not drink water touched by Ramdin. But if you forbid Satish then he will do the opposite.'

Harimohini replied, 'It's different for Satish.'

Harimohini knew that for boys violation of rules might be overlooked.

44

Haranbabu stepped into the battlefield.

It is about fifteen days since Lalita had come back with Binoy by steamer. The news had already reached a few and was slowly spreading. But during the last one or two days the news spread quickly like a bundle of dry straw catching fire.

Haranbabu made a lot of people understand that such vulgar practices should be stopped in the interest of the religious life of a Brahmo family. It is also not difficult to make people understand. When we try to express our hatred for the moral lapse of somebody and try to punish him 'for the sake of truth', 'for the sake of duty', then we don't feel any compunction about it. So when Haranbabu began to publicise the 'unpleasant' truth and thereby discharge his stern 'duty' then many people, apprehensive of possible unpleasantness and drastic measures joined him without hesitation. Hiring carriages or palanquins the well-wishers of the Samaj spread the message from door to door that with such incidents taking place, the future of Brahmo Samaj was bleak indeed. The rumour also began to spread that Sucharita had converted to Hinduism, living in the Hindu household of her Masi where she took part in Hindu rituals and idol worship.

Since quite some time Lalita was being tormented by an inner struggle. Every night before dozing off to sleep she used to say 'I will not accept defeat and each morning after awakening she would say 'Under no circumstance I will accept defeat.' The thought of Binoy occupied her entire mind, and her heart would be perturbed if she heard him talking downstairs; if he did not come to their house for a day or two she would feel sulky sometimes; she would find excuses to send Satish to his house and when Satish returned she questioned about what he was doing, what they spoke about, she tried to extract every possible information out of him—the more it was becoming an obsession with her, the more she was grieved about the future. Sometimes she felt angry even with Pareshbabu for not objecting to her being introduced to Gora and Binoy. But she would fight till her last breath, she would die but would not lose,—this was her vow. Thoughts about how she would spend her life shot through her mind. She felt she could emulate the philanthropic lives of the European ladies whose biographies she had read.

One day she approached Pareshbabu and said, 'Baba, can't I take up the job of teaching in some girls' school?'

Looking up at the face of his daughter he saw the pain of a hungry heart in her pitiful eyes. He spoke tenderly, 'Why not? But where is such a girls' school?'

At that time there were few girls' schools; some primary schools for boys were there and ladies from good families had not yet begun teaching in the schools. Lalita felt concerned and said, 'Is there no such school Baba?'

Pareshbabu replied, 'I don't see any around.'

Lalita said, 'Baba, can't a girls' school be founded?'

Pareshbabu replied, 'It involves a lot of money and needs the support of many people.'

Lalita knew that to do something good was difficult, but she had never thought that obstruction might come even in the way of trying it. After sitting silently for some time she slowly got up and went away. Pareshbabu sat thinking where the pain of his dearest daughter actually lay. He was reminded of the comment that Haranbabu had made about Binoy a few days back. Sighing deeply he questioned himself—'Have I done something indiscreet?' It would not have mattered much if it concerned the other daughters—but Lalita was so genuine, she did not know to take things by half.

How will Lalita lead her day-to-day life with the burden of a baseless scandal? She cannot look forward to any good prospect, any happy denouement. To drift away helplessly is not her nature.

On that very day Lalita came to Sucharita's house around noon. The room was practically bare but for a few decorations. A carpet was spread on the floor, on one side of it Sucharita had made her bed and Harimohini on the other. Harimohini did not have the habit of sleeping on a cot. So Sucharita also slept with her on another bed made on the floor. A picture of Pareshbabu hung on the wall. In the other small room a cot was laid for Satish and on one side there was a small table on which inkpot, pen, books, slate lay in a disorganized way. Satish had gone to school. The house was quiet.

Harimohini was about to go for her afternoon siesta following her midday meal and Sucharita with her hair let loose on her back sat on the carpet and with a book on the pillow in her lap and was reading with all attention. A few more books were lying in front of her.

Seeing Lalita entering the room she, feeling ashamed as it were, shut the book but the next moment she overcame her shyness and reopened the book. The book contained Gora's essays.

Harimohini sat up and said, 'Come, come, dear Lalita, come. I know how Sucharita might be feeling after leaving your house. Whenever she feels sad she sits to read those books. It was just now that I was lying and thinking that it would be good if any one among you had come—on that very moment you arrived—you will live for a long time.'

Lalita at once launched her idea. 'Suchididi, suppose we start a girls' school in our locality?'

Harimohini was stunned and said, 'Just listen to her! How dare you start a school!'

Sucharita said, 'How can it be possible? Who will help us? Have you talked with Baba about it?'

Lalita replied, 'Both of us can teach. It is possible that our elder sister will also agree to it.'

Sucharita said, 'It is not just a question of teaching. The rules and regulations have to be framed, administrative details are to be decided, a site is to be selected, girls are to be collected, the expense is to be met up. How can two girls like us manage all these?'

Lalita replied, 'Didi, don't say like that. Should we remain confined within the home because we have been born as girls? Can't we be of any use to the world?'

The pain that was there in Lalita's words touched Sucharita's heart. She began thinking without making an answer.

Lalita said, 'There are many girls in our area. If we teach them free of cost their parents will be happy. The few girls whom we shall gather can be taught in this house. Where is expense involved in it?'

Harimohini felt disconcerted by the plan of teaching unfamiliar girls in the house. She wanted to live in total 'purity' with her rites and practices. She began to protest sensing that it would not be possible.

Sucharita replied, 'Masi, don't fear, if any students come I can manage in the room downstairs, we will not come to disturb you upstairs. So Lalita, if we get the students I am ready to teach.'

Lalita replied, 'Okay, let us see.'

Harimohini began to grumble again, 'How will it be possible if you behave like Christians about each and every matter? Since my father's time I have never heard of respectable ladies teaching in schools.'

From the roof of Pareshbabu's house conversation used to take place between girls of neighbouring houses. But there was a great impediment to real interaction. The girls of the neighbouring houses usually questioned and were astonished about the fact that the girls of Pareshbabu's family were still unmarried though they had considerably grown up. So Lalita never participated in the conversation that took place across the roof tops.

Labanya was the most interested one in making friends through the roof top dialogues. She was always inquisitive about the domestic details of other homes. The matters of primary and secondary interest of her neighbours' every day life used to reach her from far, floating in the air. Most of the evenings she would be deeply engaged in the open air conversations across the roof tops while combing her hair.

Lalita entrusted Labanya with the responsibility of collecting pupils for her proposed school. When Lavanya sent feelers from the roof top many girls felt interested. Lalita started sweeping, washing and decorating the ground floor to make it ready for the school. But the schoolroom remained vacant. The male members of the neighbouring families were enraged that in the name of education their daughters were about to be lured to a Brahmo house. And when they came to know that their daughters held discussions regarding it with the daughters of Pareshbabu they considered it their responsibility to obstruct. They prevented their daughters to go to the roof and they did not in the least support the proposal of the daughters of the neighbouring house. Poor Labanya! When she went up to the roof as usual with a comb in her hand she found that instead of the young girls the elders had assembled on the neighbouring rooves and none greeted her with affection.

Lalita was not discouraged. She said—many poor Brahmo girls cannot afford to go and read in Bethune, if we take the responsibility of teaching them they will feel deeply obliged.

She engaged herself in searching this kind of girls and she also involved Sudhir in the job.

It was known far and wide that Pareshbabu's daughters were well-educated. In fact the fame surpassed the truth. So when the parents heard that they were taking the responsibility of teaching without charging any fees they were gladdened.

With five or six girls Lalita's school started within a few days. Without losing time she discussed about the school with Pareshbabu towards drafting proper rules and regulations. Labanya and Lalita even debated energetically about the kind of prize to be awarded to the girls after the annual examinations. The books suggested by Lalita were disapproved by Labanya and Labanya's taste also varied from Lalita's. There was also discussion regarding the panel of examiners. Though Labanya could not stand Haranbabu, he was well-known for his knowledge. She had no doubt about the fact that it would be a matter of great pride if Haranbabu could be associated with the school in the matter of examination or teaching or any other activity. But Lalita did not pay heed to her suggestion—the school cannot have any connection with Haranbabu.

Within two or three days, however, there was a sharp fall in attendance and before long the classroom became empty. Whenever Lalita heard any footsteps she thought perhaps some student was coming, but nobody came. When two days passed like this she had a hunch that something was wrong somewhere.

Lalita went to the house of the student who lived nearest. The student with tear-filled eyes remonstrated, '*Mā* is not permitting me to go.'

Her mother replied, 'There are some problems.' But the problem was not specified. A sensitive girl as she was Lalita could not pester for reason if she found the other party unwilling to state it. She replied, 'If there is problem then don't come!'

Lalita learnt the actual reason in the house she went next. They replied in a clear-cut manner, 'Sucharita has been converted into a Hindu, she believes in caste, indulges in idol worship, etc. in her house.'

Lalita replied, 'If that be the point of objection the school can be held in our house.'

But things still did not straighten out. Lalita did not visit any more houses. Instead she called Sudhir. She questioned, 'Sudhir, frankly tell me what the matter is.'

Sudhir replied, 'Panubabu has started a powerful campaign against your school.'

Lalita questioned, 'Why? Is it because idol worship is done in Didi's house?'

Sudhir replied, 'Not only that.'

Lalita impatiently said, 'What else? Tell me.'

Sudhir replied, 'That's a long story.'

Lalita replied, 'Have I too given offense?'

Sudhir remained silent. Lalita reddened and said, 'This is my punishment for coming in the steamer! If I have done something indiscreet, is there no way of atonement in our society! Am I forbidden by the society to take part in any good work? Is this the measure you have taken for the spiritual upliftment of me and society?'

In order to lighten the matter Sudhir said, 'Not exactly that. They are afraid that Binoybabu might become associated with the school.'

Lalita flew into a rage and replied, 'Is it a thing to fear, or to welcome as our good luck! How many persons are there among them who can be compared to Binoybabu in the matter of competence!'

Lalita's anger made Sudhir shrink and he muttered, 'That is correct. But Binoybabu is—.'

Lalita replied, 'He is not a member of Brahmo Samaj! So Brahmo Samaj will punish him. I must say I don't feel proud of such a Samaj like this.'

As Sucharita noticed the disappearance of the students she guessed who was behind all this. She did not speak anything about it and took Satish to the upstairs room to prepare him for his approaching examination.

After Lalita had spoken to Sudhir she went straight to Sucharita and said, 'Didi, have you heard?'

Sucharita smiled a little and said, 'I have not heard; but I can guess.'

Lalita asked, 'Must we tolerate all this?'

Sucharita held Lalita's hand and said, 'There is no shame in tolerating. Have you not seen how Baba tolerates everything?'

Lalita replied, 'But Suchididi, many a time I have felt that to tolerate something wrong amounts to approving it. The right reaction is not to tolerate any wrong.'

Sucharita said, 'Tell me what would you like to do.'

Lalita replied, 'I have not thought about it—I am not even aware of what I can do—but something must be done. The people who have troubled girls like us in this manner are cowards though they may be considering themselves brave and courageous. But I will not accept defeat to them—never. Let them do whatever they want.'

Saying so, Lalita stamped her feet. Without saying anything further Sucharita began to stroke Lalita's hand gently. After a while she said, 'Lalita my dear, first speak to Baba about it.'

Lalita stood up and said, 'I am going to him right now.'

On reaching near the door Lalita saw Binoy coming out hanging his head. Seeing Lalita Binoy stopped for a moment. He debated in his mind whether he would speak a few words to Lalita. But he controlled himself and without looking at Lalita's face showed his regards and walked away hanging his head.

It was as if a fiery shell had pierced Lalita. She entered her house with quickened steps and entered her mother's room at once. Her mother had been bending over a big register apparently trying to concentrate on the accounts.

Seeing Lalita's face Baradasundari sensed trouble. She pretended instantly to get lost in the accounts register with such an urgency as if the fate of her whole family hung on it.

Lalita pulled a chair and sat near the table. Still Baradasundari did not lift her face. Lalita said, '*Mā*!'

Baradasundari said, 'Wait dear, I am just—'

Saying so, she completely bent over the register.

Lalita said, 'I won't take much of your time. I want to know something. Did Binoybabu come?'

Without raising her head from the register Baradasundari replied, 'Yes.'

Lalita questioned, 'What did you talk to him about?'

Baradasundari replied, 'About many things.'

Lalita questioned, 'Did you talk about me or not?'

Baradasundari saw that there was no way to escape. So she put down her pen, raised her head and said, 'Yes dear, we did. I saw that things were gradually crossing limits; the people of our samaj are speaking ill about it everywhere, so I had to warn him.'

Lalita's face reddened, the heat seemed to go up into the head. She asked pointblank, 'Did Baba forbid Binoybabu to come to our house?'

Baradasundari replied, 'Does he think about it at all? If he had then such things would not have taken place at all.'

Lalita questioned, 'Can Panubabu come to our house?'

Baradasundari got astonished and said, 'Just listen! Why will Panubabu not come?'

Lalita questioned, 'Then why will Binoybabu not come?'

Baradasundari applied herself to the register once again and said, 'Lalita, don't disturb me now—I have lots to do.'

Every afternoon Lalita used to go to Sucharita's house to conduct the school. Taking advantage of her absence during the period Baradasundari had called Binoy and had said what she felt necessary. She had thought, Lalita would never come to know about it. When she saw that her plot had been found out she sensed danger. She understood, that there would be no peace now and there was also no way to escape. All her anger was directed at her husband who had no practical sense at all. It was indeed a great trouble for a woman to lead a family life with such an inconsiderate person!

Lalita left with all the storm raging within her. In the room downstairs Pareshbabu sat writing a letter; she stormed in and bolted out at once: 'Baba, is Binoybabu not fit to mix with us?'

Hearing the question Pareshbabu at once understood the situation. Pareshbabu was not unaware about the opposition that was rising in the Samaj regarding his family. Even he had also to think a lot about it. He would not have given any attention to what was spoken outside if there was no hunch in his mind about Lalita's attitude to Binoy. He asked himself time and again what was his duty if Lalita had fallen in love with Binoy. After he had publicly embraced the Brahmo religion this was the second time a crisis has developed in his family. So on the one hand some fear and pain were hurting him from inside while on the other hand all the power that was stored in his heart, was telling him, 'while embracing Brahmo religion I passed all the difficult tests because I had my eyes fixed on God. By taking truth above comfort, society and everything else I have been blessed in my life. So, if today a time for test arrives I will fix my eyes on Him and pass the test.'

In answer to Lalita's question Pareshbabu said, 'As far I know Binoy is a very good man. His learning and intelligence are as fine as his character.'

After keeping quiet for some time Lalita said, 'Gaurbabu's mother had come to our house for two days recently. May I go to her place today along with Suchididi?'

For a few moments Pareshbabu could make no reply. He knew in the present situation these visits will add to the vilification. But his conscience said, 'I cannot forbid it till I find something wrong in it.' He said, 'You can go. I have work to do, or else I would have accompanied you.'

45

Binoy had never dreamt that the place in which he had trod confidently for a few days as a guest and friend had an active volcano hidden beneath. He was hesitant at first when he mixed with Pareshbabu's family; he did not know the limits of his rights and so he always moved cautiously. When eventually his fears disappeared he never thought that there might be some danger around. He was thunder-stuck when he heard today that Lalita's reputation in society was at stake because of his behaviour. He was particularly distressed because he was aware of his feelings for Lalita surpassing the bond of mere friendship and he had a sense of guilt. They belonged to different communities. He had thought many a time that in this family he had failed to maintain his correct position as a guest—he had deceived them in a particular spot; it would be a matter of shame if his feelings were revealed to the members of the family.

Meanwhile one afternoon Baradasundari wrote a special letter to Binoy calling him to her place. She asked him—'Binoybabu, you are a Hindu; aren't you? After Binoy admitted it she further asked him—'You cannot abandon your Hindu society, can you?' and Binoy agreed that it was impossible for him. Hearing so Baradasundari blurted out at once 'Then why do you—?' Binoy found no answer to the question 'Why do you—.' He kept sitting there hanging his head. He began to feel that he had been caught; a thing which he had wanted to hide even from the moon, sun and air was revealed to them. He began to feel again and again—what Pareshbabu could be thinking, what Lalita could be thinking, what Sucharita could be thinking about him! Due to some mistake of an angel he had been allowed into this paradise! Today he has to leave it carrying the burden of all the shame of trespassing.

After this when he came out and stood at the door of Pareshbabu and saw Lalita he felt 'Let me bid her my final farewell, accepting all the insults and cutting off all the relations that we shared previously'—but he could not think how it could be made possible; so without looking at Lalita's face he silently showed his regards and went away.

Till the other day Binoy was an outsider to Pareshbabu's family—today too he came out and stood outside his house. But what a difference! Why is that outside so empty today? In the days gone by he had not suffered any loss—his Gora, his Anandamoyee are still there. But still he began to feel that like the fish out of water—he could not find any support for his life anywhere. In this city filled with large mansions and the crowded highways Binoy began to see his life as a faded shadow of nothingness. He himself was surprised at the total dryness and emptiness. Why did it happen, when did it happen, how can it happen,—these were the questions he repeatedly asked the heartless unresponsive emptiness again and again.

'Binoybabu! Binoybabu!'

Binoy turned around and found Satish. Binoy embraced him. He said, 'What is it brother, what is it my friend!' Binoy's voice was choked with tears. He had never felt before how much the boy contributed to the sweetness that he experienced in Pareshbabu's house.

Satish said, 'Why don't you come to our house nowadays? Tomorrow Lavanyadidi and Lalitadidi will have lunch in our house. Masi has sent me to invite you.'

Binoy understood that Masi was not adequately updated. He said, 'Satishbabu, please convey my regards to Masi—but I cannot go.'

Satish caught his hand and asked entreatingly, 'Why can't you? You must come, I won't let you go.'

Satish had a reason for his earnest entreaty. In his school he was asked to write an essay on 'Treatment of Animals'; in that essay he had scored forty-two out of fifty—he longed to show that essay to Binoy. He knew Binoy to be a learned and appreciative man; he had felt that a sympathetic reader like Binoy could make a proper estimate of his writing. If Binoy accepts it as a fine piece of writing then Leela's contempt for Satish's talent could be disregarded. It was he who had asked Masi to invite Binoy—he wished all his sisters to be present when Binoy would articulate his opinion about his writing.

Satish was disheartened when he heard that Binoy under no circumstance could accept the invitation.

Binoy embraced him and said, 'Satishbabu, you come to our house.'

Satish had the essay in his pocket, so he could not disregard Binoy's proposal. This boy who was aspiring after literary fame went to his house knowing fully well that that it was wrong to waste his time before examination.

Binoy apparently did not want to let him go. He heard the essay—and the praise which was showered did not express the sober impartiality of the critic. In addition to it he bought refreshments from the market and made him have it.

After that he escorted Satish to the vicinity of his house and said with unnecessary trepidation, 'Satishbabu, let me leave today!'

Satish began to pull his hand, 'No, you have to come to our home.'

But today this request yielded no result.

Walking in a dream as it were he reached Anandamoyee's house, but could not meet her. He went to the secluded room upstairs in which Gora used to sleep; in this room they had spent many days and nights of happiness in their childhood; so many talks about their joys, so many resolutions, so many discussions regarding serious matters; so many friendly quarrels which ended in friendly reconciliation. Binoy tried to forget himself into this past life—but the new identity which he had acquired during the last few days stood in the way and did not let him relive the past memories. Binoy had never realised when the center of his life has deviated and the path has also changed—today when it became clear to him he became afraid.

Anandamoyee had put her clothes on the terrace for drying; in late afternoon with the air getting cold she came to the roof to collect the clothes. Seeing Binoy in Gora's room she was surprised. She quickly came to his side and keeping her hand on his shoulder anxiously queried, 'Binoy, what's the matter? Why do you look so pale?'

Binoy sat up and replied, '*Mā*, when I first started visiting Pareshbabu's family, Gora used to get furious. I then thought his anger was unjust—but he was not wrong; I was a blockhead.'

Anandamoyee smiled a little and said, 'I won't say that you are our most intelligent boy, but in this case how did you find confirmation about your lack of intelligence?'

Binoy replied, '*Mā*, for once I had never thought that our society was completely different. Meeting their friendly behaviour and views I felt gladdened and gratified; I was attracted by it, and for once I did not think that there could be other aspects to be considered.'

Anandamoyee said, 'I cannot think about any such aspect even after hearing you.'

Binoy replied, '*Mā* you don't know, what a trouble I have landed them in—people have begun to vilify them in such a way that I can no more—'

Anandamoyee replied, 'Gora often says a thing, and I think this right. He says, where there is an injustice taking place within, maintaining the posture of external calm is most harmful. If there is turmoil in the society for them I don't think there is any reason for you to be repentant, it will be ultimately beneficial, you shall see. Only you should remain true to yourself in your action.'

This is where Binoy was facing a great trouble. He could not understand whether his behaviour was above blame or not. When Lalita belonged to a different society, marriage between them being impossible, his affection for Lalita was like a secret sin which pricked him and again he was pained to think the time had come when he was to repent for his sin.

Binoy of a sudden said, '*Mā*, it would have been better if my marriage with Shashimukhi had been settled. Then I would have remained confined within the specified limits—it would have been such that I could never deviate from it.'

Anandamoyee smiled and replied, 'That means, instead of making Shashimukhi your wife, you want her to be your shackle —what luck for Shashi indeed!'

Of a sudden the bearer came and gave the news that two girls had arrived from Pareshbabu's house. Binoy's heart missed a beat. He thought, then they have come to complain to Anandamoyee in order to warn Binoy. He at once stood up and said, 'I will take leave *Mā*!'

Anandamoyee stood up and holding his hand said, 'Don't leave the house Binoy! Please wait downstairs for a while.'

While going downstairs he repeatedly muttered to himself, 'This was unnecessary. What I had done is past, but I would not have stepped there even if I died. When the flame of punishment begins to burn a person, it keeps on smouldering even after the culprit is burnt to death.'

When Binoy entered the ground floor room of Gora by the roadside he saw Mahim returning home from his office while unbuttoning his coat to bring relief to his swollen belly. Holding Binoy's hand he said, 'Binoy, you are here! Good! I was looking for you.'

Saying so he took Binoy to Gora's room and made Binoy sit down on a bench and himself too sat down. He took out a box from his pocket and offered Binoy a betel leaf.

He loudly ordered, 'Heigh, someone bring the hookah' and at once came to the point. He asked, 'What did you decide about the matter? Now there is—.'

He saw that Binoy's expression was not as stern as it was previously. Not that he was very much interested, but he did not try to avoid the matter all the same. Mahim wanted to finalize the day and time; Binoy replied, 'Let Gora return.'

Mahim felt assured and replied, 'There are only few days left. Binoy, let me order for some snacks—what do you say? Your face is looking quite pale! Hope you are not ill?'

When Binoy assured him that he did not want to eat Mahim entered the inner house in order to satisfy his own hunger. Binoy casually pulled out one of Gora's books from his table and began to flip through the pages, then he left the book and began to walk from one end of the room to another.

The bearer camc and said, '*Mā* is calling.'

Binoy asked, 'Calling whom?'

The bearer replied, 'You.'

Binoy asked, 'Are all the others present?'

The bearer replied, 'Yes.'

Binoy went upstairs just like a student nervously entering an examination hall. He stood near the door hesitating and then Sucharita called him in her tender friendly tone. 'Binoybabu, come in please.' Hearing her tone Binoy felt he had suddenly come upon an unexpected treasure.

When Binoy entered the room both Sucharita and Lalita were surprised to see him; his face showed the signs of a deep wound that he had received of a sudden. His face looked like a field of lush crop that had been ravaged by a sudden attack of locusts. Lalita felt pained and pity in her heart, but she also experienced a touch of happiness about it.

If it were some other day she would not have spoken to Binoy—today as Binoy entered she said, 'Binoybabu, we seek your advice regarding an important matter.'

It seemed that somebody had suddenly shot an arrow of happiness which pierced his heart by its sound. He was beside himself with joy. His pale lustreless face became radiant in an instant.

Lalita said, 'We the sisters together are trying to run a girls' school.'

Binoy became interested at once and said, 'Even I for long had thought of starting a girls' school.'

Lalita said, 'You have to help us about it.'

Binoy replied, 'I will try my best and there will be no lapse from my side. You instruct me what I should do.'

Lalita replied, 'As we are Brahmo the Hindus do not believe us. You have to do something in this regard.'

Binoy felt inspired and replied, 'have no worry—I can do it.'

Anandamoyee said, 'That he can do indeed. He has no match in his power to charm people by words.'

Lalita said, 'You have to help us in planning regarding management of time, planning of class, selection of books, and all such things.'

This task too was not difficult for Binoy, but it perplexed him. Baradasundari had forbidden him to mix with his daughters and there was a movement going on in the society against them. Was this unknown to Lalita? In this case if he keeps her request that will be wrong and it may bring trouble for Lalita—he began to worry about this question. On the other hand if Lalita requests him for help in some philanthropic work has he the capacity not to comply with her request to the best of his ability? Sucharita too became astonished. She had never dreamt that Lalita of a sudden would request Binoy about the girls' school. Already there were complications involving Binoy and she had now created further troubles. Sucharita was nervous because Lalita was purposefully creating the adverse situation. She understood that Lalita was rebelling in her mind, but was it proper to involve poor Binoy in all these troubles? Sucharita became anxious and said, 'We should consult Baba regarding the matter. Binoybabu should not become too optimistic about getting the post of a school inspector in the girls' school.'

Binoy understood that Sucharita slyly objected to the proposal, so he became more suspicious. It was clearly understood, that Sucharita was aware of the trouble that was imminent, so it was not hidden to Lalita, then why Lalita—.

Nothing was clear.

Lalita replied, 'Baba is to be consulted. I will tell him as soon as I come to know that Binoybabu is agreeable. He will never object to it—he too has to be associated with our school.'

Turning towards Anandamoyee she said, 'We will not leave you too.'

Anandamoyee smiled and said, 'I can sweep the classroom. Can I do anything more than it?'

Binoy replied, 'It will be enough *Mā*! The school will become sanctified.'

As soon as Sucharita and Lalita departed Binoy with a quickened gait made straight for the Eden Gardens. Mahim came to Anandamoyee and said, 'I see that Binoy is almost agreeable to the proposal—it's best to have it over as soon as possible—God knows when he will again change his mind.'

Anandamoyee was surprised and said, 'What are you saying! When did Binoy agree? He did not tell me anything.'

Mahim replied, 'Today we spoke about the matter. He said that as soon as Gora returns a day can be fixed.'

Anandamoyee shook her head and said, 'Mahim you have misunderstood, I think.'

Mahim replied, 'I may be thick headed, but I think I've grown up sufficiently to understand plain talk.'

Anandamoyee replied, 'I knew you will get angry my son, but I can see there will be problem regarding this.'

Mahim became grave and said, 'If problems are created there will be problems.'

Anandamoyee replied, 'Mahim, I will bear with everything you all may say to me but I will never support anything that may lead to troubles—it's for your own good.'

Mahim curtly replied, 'If you let us think about our own good then you will not have to listen to anything, and perhaps we too will be benefited. It'll be better if you think about our good after the marriage of Shashimukhi. What do you say?'

Anandamoyee did not reply and sighed deeply as Mahim departed chewing a betel leaf that he took out of the box in his pocket.

46

Lalita said to Pareshbabu, 'As we are Brahmo no girls from Hindu families want to come to learn from us—so I think it would be better if we could include someone who is Hindu, in our project. What do you say Baba?'

Pareshbabu asked, 'How to get someone from the Hindu society?'

Lalita had come fully prepared, but still she had hesitation to mention directly about Binoy; she forcefully overcame her hesitation and said, 'Why can't one be found? There is Binoybabu—or—.'

This 'or' was a sheer waste of a conjunction; the sentence remained incomplete.

Paresh replied, 'Binoy! Why should Binoy agree?'

Lalita's ego was hurt. Binoybabu won't agree! Lalita had clearly understood that it was not impossible for her to make Binoy agree.

Lalita replied, 'He may agree.'

Paresh was silent for a while; then he said, 'If he considers all the aspects he will not agree.'

Lalita's ear lobes turned red. She started to play with the key hanging from the end of her sari.

Looking at the face of his suffering child Paresh felt sad. But he could not find any word of consolation. After some time she slowly raised her face and said, 'Baba, so this school cannot be started any way.'

Paresh replied, 'I can see opposition coming up. Any effort on our part will lead to unpleasant confrontation.'

Nothing could be more depressing for Lalita than to see the final triumph of Panubabu and her own silent surrender to injustice. In this matter she could never accept the orders of anyone other than her father. She was not afraid of any kind of unpleasantness, but how can she support injustice! She slowly went away from Paresh.

Coming to her room she found a letter addressed to her which had come by post. Seeing the handwriting she knew it to be from her childhood friend Shailabala. She was married and lived with her husband in Bankipur.

The letter ran as follows:

'I was grieved to hear many things about you all. For quite some time I had been thinking to write a letter to ascertain the facts—but I did not have time enough. But the day before yesterday I heard a news from someone (I will not name him) and was thunderstruck. I had never thought this could be possible. But the person who wrote it cannot be disbelieved. It is rumoured that you are going to marry a Hindu boy. If this is true'—etc., etc.

A fierce anger seemed to consume Lalita. She could not wait even for a second. Immediately she replied:

'I am astonished that you have enquired of me about the truth of the news. Do you have any need to verify the authenticity of a rumour when the source happens to be a member of Brahmo Samaj! Such distrust! And then, you were thunderstruck hearing the news that I am going to marry a Hindu boy, but I can fully assure you—that the prospect of marriage with certain eminent honest men in the Brahmo Samaj can be considered as horrifying as death by lightning; and I also know one or two Hindu boys marrying whom can be a matter of pride for any Brahmo girl. I don't want to waste a single word on the subject.'

In the meantime Pareshbabu could not apply his mind any more to his routine work. He sat silently, thinking a long time. After this he went to Sucharita's room still preoccupied with his thought. Sucharita felt pained seeing the tense face of Pareshbabu. She guessed what worried him so and Sucharita herself was deeply anxious about it since some time.

Pareshbabu sat down with Sucharita in a secluded room and said, 'The time has come to worry about Lalita.'

Sucharita turned her pitiful gaze on Pareshbabu's face and replied, 'I know Baba!'

Pareshbabu continued, 'I am not thinking about the social scandal. I am thinking—if Lalita—.'

Seeing Pareshbabu hesitating she herself tried to make the matter clear. She said, 'Lalita always used to speak her mind to me. But recently she no longer confides in me as she used to. I can very well guess—.'

Pareshbabu resumed, 'A certain feeling has stirred in her mind that she does not want to admit to herself. I cannot understand what will be the best course for her—do you think that by allowing Binoy to be associated with our family any harm has been done to Lalita?'

Sucharita replied, 'Baba, you know that Binoybabu cannot do anything wrong—he has a pure nature—very few people can be found with such a nature as his.'

Pareshbabu seemed to see a new light, and exclaimed, 'You're right Radhe, you're right. We have to see whether he is a good man; God also sees only that. I feel grateful to God that I have not made any mistake about the fact that Binoy is a good man.'

A web seemed to break—Pareshbabu felt relieved. Pareshbabu had committed no offence to his God. He had measured people in the same scales that God approves—he had not used any mechanical balance constructed by his society. He had no regret in his mind when he realized this. He was surprised that he had failed to understand this simple truth and had been unnecessarily suffering in his mind. He touched Sucharita's head and said, 'Today I learnt a lesson from you *Mā*!'

Sucharita immediately bent to touch his feet and replied, 'No no, what are you saying Baba!'

Pareshbabu said, 'Community is such a thing that it makes one forget this simplest truth that a man is first of all a human being. It makes things complicated by upholding the societal identity—whether a person is a Brahmo or a Hindu and holds it to be more important than universal truth—so long I had been wandering in a labyrinth of untruth.'

After remaining quiet for some time Pareshbabu said, 'Lalita cannot give up her dreams about the girls' school. She wants my permission to take help from Binoy regarding this.'

Sucharita replied, 'No Baba, let us wait for some time.'

The image of Lalita—quietly withdrawing from his room, restraining the surge of her grieving heart on being forbidden—continued to haunt and sadden his affectionate heart like anything. He knew, that this daughter of his was more hurt by the restraint that he put upon her revolt against the society than all the troubles and injustice that the society had inflicted on her. She was all the more hurt because it was her father who restrained her. So he was eager to get that weight off her chest. He asked, 'Why Radhe, why should we wait?'

Sucharita replied, '*Mā* will be very irritated.'

Pareshbabu thought a little and saw it was true.

Satish came in and whispered something in Sucharita's ear. She implored, 'No brother, my dear Chatterton, not now. Tomorrow.'

Satish became disheartened and said, 'Tomorrow I'll be at school.'

Pareshbabu smiled affectionately and said, 'What is it Satish? What do you want?'

Sucharita replied, 'He wants a—'

Satish quickly put his palm on Sucharita's mouth and said, 'No, no, don't tell, don't tell.'

Pareshbabu said, 'If it is a secret why should Sucharita say?'

Sucharita replied, 'No Baba, I am sure it is his sincere desire that this secret be revealed to you.'

Satish said loudly, 'No, never. Not at all.'

Saying so he ran away.

He was to show Sucharita the essay that Binoy had praised so high. It is needless to say that Sucharita knew exactly the purpose of reminding her in whisper in the presence of Pareshbabu. Poor Satish never knew that the secret wishes that lurked deep within could be detected so easily!

47

Four days later Haranbabu came to Baradasundari holding a letter. He had completely given up hope about gaining Pareshbabu's support.

Haranbabu handed the letter to Baradasundari and said, 'I have been trying to warn you from the very beginning, and, consequently I incurred your displeasure. Now you can understand from the letter itself how far the matter has developed without your knowledge.'

Baradasundari read the letter that Lalita had written to Shailabala. She said, 'How can I know, you only tell me. Things which I could never think of have been occurring. You don't blame me about it. You all used to shower so much praise on Sucharita,—a girl who has no match in the Brahmo society, etc., etc.,—enough to turn her head. Now it is your responsibility to control the damage done by your ideal Brahmo girl. It was she who brought Binoy and Gaur to this house. I still managed to draw Binoy gradually towards our religion when she brought over this Masi and started idol worship within our very premise. She also cast her evil spell on Binoy in such a way, that nowadays he avoids me like plague. I tell you it is Sucharita who is at the root of all this. I knew from the very beginning what kind of girl she was—but I never uttered a word. I have brought her up from the beginning in such a way that nobody could even guess that she was not my own child—today I get a fine return indeed. Now it is useless to show me this letter—you may do as you please.'

Haranbabu admitted the fact that he had misunderstood Baradasundari and now he generously expressed his regrets about it. At last Pareshbabu was called in.

'See this', saying so Baradasundari threw the letter on the table before him. Pareshbabu read the letter two to three times and asked, 'So, what's the problem?'

Baradasundari became excited, 'What's the problem? What else can happen? What also remains to happen! Idol worship, belief in caste, everything has started, now the only thing that remains is to marry your daughter in a Hindu family. Then you may enter the Hindu society through penance—But I tell you—.'

Paresh smiled calmly and replied, 'You have to say nothing. The time has not yet come for that. But the point is, why do you all take it as settled that Lalita is to going be married to a Hindu. I don't see anything of that kind mentioned in this letter.'

Baradasundari said, 'I never understand what could make you see. If you could see when there was time enough these things would not have happened. Tell me how can a person be more explicit in a letter?'

Haranbabu said, 'I think we ought to show this letter to Lalita and ask her to confess her real intention. If you all permit me I may ask her about it.'

Of a sudden Lalita stormed into the scene and said, 'Baba, see here, the sort of anonymous letters that are coming from the Brahmo samaj these days!'

Pareshbabu read the letter. The writer was apparently certain that Binoy and Lalita had secretly planned their marriage and hence he shot endless strictures and abuses. The writer also warned that Binoy's intention was not good, and before long he would divorce his Brahmo wife to marry some Hindu girl.

After Paresh completed reading the letter Haranbabu took the letter and read it and said, 'Lalita, are you angry over this letter? But are you not yourself responsible for inviting it? How could you write a letter like this, do tell us.'

Lalita was stunned for a moment and then said, 'So you have been exchanging letters with Shaila on the subject!'

Haranbabu made an evasive reply: 'Remembering her duty to the Brahmo society Shaila felt bound to send me this letter of yours.'

Lalita went stiff, and said sternly, 'Now Mr Brahmo samaj, say what you have to say.'

Haranbabu replied, 'I can never believe under any circumstances what is rumoured in the society regarding Binoybabu and you, but still I want to hear a clear denial of it from your lips.'

Lalita's eyes glowed like fire—she held the back of a chair with her shaking hands and asked, 'Why can't you believe it under any circumstances, may I know?'

Paresh patted Lalita's back and said, 'Lalita your mind is disturbed now, we can speak about it later—now let it be!'

Haranbabu replied, 'Pareshbabu, please don't try to evade the issue.'

Lalita flared up again, 'You accuse Baba of evasion!! Baba is not afraid to face the truth like the pack of you all—Baba holds truth above everything, even the Brahmo Samaj. I tell you I don't consider the prospect of marriage with Binoybabu to be anything impossible or inglorious.'

Haranbabu said, 'But has he agreed to convert to Brahmoism?'

Lalita replied, 'Nothing has been decided—and what's the great compulsion that he must convert?'

Baradasundari had not spoken so far—she had earnestly wanted Haranbabu to win in today's argument and Pareshbabu to repent by admitting his fault. She could no longer remain quiet; she said, 'Have you gone mad Lalita! What are you saying!'

Lalita said, 'No *Mā*, I am not talking insane—whatever I am saying it is after great consideration. I cannot surrender to them raising barriers for me circling in from all sides—I want to have my freedom from this samaj of Haranbabu.'

Haran said, 'So your freedom is this lawlessness!'

Lalita replied, 'No, my freedom is the liberation from the aggression of meanness, from the slavery of untruth. Why will Brahmo samaj interfere or fetter me where I see no injustice or untruth?'

Haranbabu spoke with a tinge of challenging arrogance, 'Pareshbabu, just see. I knew this kind of thing was bound to happen eventually. I had tried to warn you as much as I could—but with no result.'

Lalita interrupted, 'Look here Panubabu, it's time you too got a warning—please get over the haughtiness to warn those who are far above you in every respect.'

Saying so Lalita stormed out of the room.

Baradasundari said, 'What is all this? Let's discuss what is to be done now, let us discuss.'

Pareshbabu said, 'We have to do our duty, but you cannot decide on the right course in the midst of such sound and fury. You must excuse me. Please don't pester me now. I want to be alone for some time.'

48

Sucharita was worried; what a crisis Lalita had generated! After remaining quiet for some time she hugged Lalita and said, 'My dear, I have fears.'

Lalita asked, 'Fear about what?'

Sucharita said, 'The Brahmo Samaj has already raised a hue and cry—but in case Binoybabu doesn't agree after all this?'

Lalita lowered her head but replied adamantly, 'He will certainly agree.'

Sucharita said, 'You know quite well that Panubabu has assured *Mā* that Binoy will never give up his Hindu society and become a Brahmo. Lalita, why did you say the thing to Panubabu so unthinkingly?'

Lalita replied, 'I am still not repentant for what I have said. Panubabu and his society had assumed that they had hounded me down like a hunted animal to the brink of some bottomless abyss, where I had no choice but to surrender. He is not aware that I won't think twice before taking my plunge into the sea—rather than being forced by his hounds into his cage.

Sucharita said, 'Let me consult Baba about it.'

Lalita replied, 'Baba will never be one with the hunters,—that I can tell you definitely. He had never tried to put us in fetters. Has he ever expressed the least annoyance when we differed from him on some point? Has he ever tried to stifle our voice in the name of Brahmo samaj? Rather *Mā* was annoyed on so many occasions, but Baba had only one fear, lest we lost the courage to think independently. Did he bring us up this way only to hand over at the end to Panubabu, the self-appointed jailor of the samaj?'

Sucharita said, 'Okay, suppose Baba does not oppose in any way, then what should be our next step?'

Lalita said, 'If none of you can take any step then of course I myself—.'

Sucharita was nervous, 'No, no dear, please, you don't have to do anything! I am devising some way.'

In the evening Sucharita was getting ready to go to Pareshbabu, when Pareshbabu himself appeared. At this time of the day Pareshbabu usually takes a walk in the garden while thinking alone—thereby absorbing the soothing pure balm of the darkness to erase all the taints the mind accumulated during the day and attaining a state of unruffled peace prior to the night's sleep. Today when Pareshbabu sacrificed this pleasure of his exclusive evening meditation and entered Sucharita's room with a disturbed look, Sucharita was deeply pained—like a mother who sees her sick child lying quietly under the spell of sickness when normally it should have played around.

Pareshbabu asked in a low voice, 'Radhe, have you heard everything?'

Sucharita replied, 'Yes Baba, I have heard everything. But why are you getting so upset about it?'

Pareshbabu replied, 'I am not upset. But my main worry is: will Lalita be able to absorb all the lashes of the storm she has raised? In the face of excitement often we are carried away by a blind impulse of challenge, but when the time comes to face the chain of consequences, we may not have the strength to bear it. Has Lalita taken her decision after considering all the possible consequences?'

Sucharita said, 'I can emphatically say this much that no persecution from the society can defeat Lalita.'

Pareshbabu said, 'What I want to feel with absolute conviction is that Lalita has not been rebelliously asserting her point just out of angry exasperation.'

Lowering her face Sucharita replied, 'No Baba, had that been the case I would have never paid any heed to it. The secret that was lying deep within her mind came out when she was suddenly struck. Now if we try to cover it up somehow it may prove disastrous for a girl like Lalita. Baba, Binoybabu is in any case a very nice person; isn't he?'

Pareshbabu asked, 'Well, do you think Binoy will agree to join the Brahmo samaj?'

Sucharita said, 'I am not sure. Well Baba, shall I go to Gaurbabu's *Mā* for once?'

Pareshbabu said, 'I was also thinking that way. It would be good if you could go.'

49

Binoy used to come from Anandamoyee's place to his house once a day. Today he found a letter waiting for him there. The name of the sender was not mentioned. The letter contained the admonition that if Binoy marries it cannot be a happy marriage; for Lalita it will be disastrous. The letter further contained a long sermon on the issue which was clinched off with the warning that if after all such knowledge Binoy was still bent on marrying the girl he should first that Lalita's lungs were weak and the doctors apprehended tuberculosis.

Binoy was dumbstruck. Binoy had never imagined such lies could be concocted. Wasn't everybody aware of the fact that marriage between Binoy and Lalita was impossible due to the various hurdles from the society! Was it not precisely for this reason that he had all along felt guilty about his feelings for Lalita! But as he had received the letter he knew already a thorough churning had started in the society around the issue. He was deeply distressed at imagining Lalita's public humiliation. He also felt like shrinking in shame when he thought how people were publicly linking Lalita's name with his own. He began to feel that perhaps Lalita was cursing their relationship and repenting that they had ever met; perhaps Lalita will never be able to stand his very sight any more.

Yet, O you poor heart of man! Even in spite of all this self-reproach he felt a new stirring of a deep fine exquisite joy that radiated his mind from end to end; it could not be subdued—it paid no heed to any thought of insult or shame. It was precisely to keep this feeling at bay somehow he began to walk up and down in the verandah with a brisk pace—yet the morning light thrilled through him like some inebriating wine; the hawkers were shouting loudly in the streets, even that shout seemed to send an uncontainable ripple in his soul. The very public condemnation seemed to sweep Lalita away on its crest like some strong flood and land her on the shore of his heart—he could not resist the image. His mind began to clamour again and again, 'Lalita is mine, only mine!' Previously he had not dared to allow his mind proclaim so far; today when the outside world was of a sudden resonant with the message then Binoy could no longer restrain his heart saying to it 'quiet quiet'.

When Binoy was walking in the verandah so restlessly he saw Haranbabu approaching along the road. He understood then and there that he was coming to him and he also became sure of the fact that there was a great mobilization operative behind that anonymous letter.

Binoy did not display his natural warmth to Haranbabu as he would on some other day; he asked him to sit on a bench and waited silently for him to speak.

Haranbabu asked, 'Binoybabu, you are a Hindu, I think?'

Binoy replied, 'Yes, certainly.'

Haranbabu said, 'Don't get angry at this question of mine. Many times we walk blindly without considering the circumstances that surround us—that leads to debacles in the world. In a situation like this if one asks what we are, what are our limitations, what may be the result of our behaviour, he is to be considered your friend.'

Binoy tried to smile and said, 'Such a long introduction is unnecessary. It's not my nature to be provoked into violence by unpleasant questions. You can safely ask me all kinds of questions.'

Haranbabu said, 'I don't want to accuse you of any deliberate misdeed. But it is needless to tell you that an act of indiscretion too can lead to disastrous consequences.'

Binoy felt irritated and said, 'Then don't beat about the bush; come straight to the point.'

Haranbabu replied, 'When you belong to your Hindu society and it is impossible for you to abandon it either, then should you mix with Pareshbabu's family in such a way that his daughters are talked about in the society?'

Binoy sat gloomily for a while and then said, 'See, Panubabu, how the people will react to a particular issue depends largely on their nature, and I cannot take the entire responsibility. If the daughter of Pareshbabu becomes the object of criticism in your society, then it is your society that should feel more ashamed than the ladies.

Haranbabu said, 'If a young lady is allowed to abandon her mother's company and return with a young man in a ship, which society is there that has no right to criticize it, I ask.'

Binoy said, 'If you give as much importance to an external event as to the internal aberration then why did you abandon Hindu society and join the Bramho samaj at all? However, Panubabu, I don't see any point in debating the issue. I myself will think and decide what is my duty; I don't think you can be any help in this matter.'

Haranbabu said, 'I do not have much to say either; but my last command to you is that you must have your hands off from all this. Otherwise it'll be a great wrong. You all encroached into Pareshbabu's family only to create a total dislocation; you have no idea of the harm you have done to them.'

When Haranbabu left a sharp pain seemed to pierce his heart. Pareshbabu was simple hearted and broad minded and had received the two of them with such affection into his family. May be Binoy was all the time unknowingly crossing his limits at every step, but still he was not deprived of the affectionate regard of Pareshbabu even for a day; his personality had found such a congenial shelter in this family that he had never found previously. After getting introduced to them he realized the existence of a special dimension of himself. So much love, so much happiness, such a shelter that he had got here, and yet the family would always remember him like a thorn in the flesh! He became a cause for the calumny of Pareshbabu's daughters! He had only brought humiliation for Lalita's entire future. What can be the remedy! Alas, what a great impediment to truth is the thing they called society! There is no real obstacle in the union of Binoy and Lalita; the omniscient God who can look into the hearts of both of them only knows how Binoy can sacrifice everything for the benefit and happiness of Lalita—it was God who had brought Binoy closer to Lalita through the attraction of love—it did not violate the universal laws of religion. Then the god whom persons of Brahmo Samaj like Panubabu pray to—is he someone different? Is he not the god who dwells deep within the human heart? If some injunction stands barring its terrible truth, between the union of him and Lalita, and if he follows that social injunction and not the dictates of one who is the Lord of all men, then is it not a sin? But alas, this forbidding is possibly a barrier for Lalita also. Moreover, what about Lalita's attitude to Binoy! There are so many doubts. Where can he find a solution to all this?

50

When Haranbabu had come to Binoy's house Abhinash came to Anandamoyee and gave her the information that Binoy's marriage with Lalita was settled.

Anandamoyee said, 'This can never be true.'

Abhinash replied, 'Why can't it be true? Is it impossible for Binoy?'

Anandamoyee said, 'I don't know, but Binoy would not have hidden such a vital information from me.'

Abhinash insisted that he had heard the news from the people of Brahmo Samaj and his source was absolutely reliable. Abhinash knew from the beginning that such a lamentable situation would arise sooner or later; not only that, he had also warned Gora about it. Declaring so to Anandomayee he went downstairs and left after giving the news to Mahim.

Today when Binoy came Anandamoyee understood from his look that he was disturbed. She made him take his meal and then called him in her room, 'Binoy, tell me what is the matter with you?'

Binoy said, '*Mā*, please read this letter.'

When Anandamoyee had finished reading the letter Binoy said, 'This morning Panubabu came to my place and gave me a good thrashing.'

Anandamoyee asked, 'But why?'

Binoy said, 'He said that my behaviour has become a cause of calumny for Pareshbabu's daughters.'

Anandamoyee said, 'People are saying that your marriage with Lalita is fixed. I don't find any cause of calumny in it.'

Binay said, 'If the marriage was possible then there would not be any cause of calumny. But where there is no such possibility it is damaging to spread such rumours! It is particularly unfair to spread such scandal about Lalita.'

Anandamoyee said, 'If you have the least manliness in you Binu, you can easily rescue Lalita from such assaults.'

Binoy was surprised and asked, 'But how *Mā*?'

Anandamoyee said, 'How! By marrying Lalita, of course.'

Binoy said, 'What are you saying *Mā*! I don't understand what you think your Binoy to be. You think if for once Binoy says, "I shall marry" then no further questions can arise in this world—all are only waiting for a hint from me.'

Anandamoyee said, 'I don't find any cause for you to worry so much. If you do what is possible from your side that will be enough. You can say I am ready to marry.'

Binoy said, 'If I say such an absurd thing won't it be insulting to Lalita?'

Anandamoyee said, 'Why should you call it absurd? It is evident from rumours about your marriage that people consider it possible and so they talk about it. I tell you, you needn't have any hesitation about it.'

Binoy said, 'But *Mā*, we have to think of Gora also.'

Anandamoyee firmly replied, 'No my son, Gora does not come in this matter by any means. I know he will feel angry—but I don't want him to be angry with you. But what you can do, if you have any regard for Lalita, is removing the stigma that may be permanently clamped by society on the girl.'

But this was such a hard task. Binoy's love for Gora had doubled since he had been condemned to prison and how could he keep such a great shock in store for Gora? Besides, what about the conventions? Society may easily be defied intellectually—but to carry it into effect throws up so many problems, big and small. The fear of the unknown, the inhibition of long habits, all this together tend to pull one backwards.

Binoy said, '*Mā*, the more I see you the more surprised I become. How can your mind be so sharp! Don't you walk with your feet—has God given you wings? Don't you feel any obstruction anywhere?'

Anandamoyee smiled and said, 'God has left no obstacles for me. He has made everything absolutely clear.'

Binoy replied, 'But *Mā*, whatever I may argue with spoken words the mind remains inhibited. I understand so many things, read, hear, argue, yet of a sudden I find that the mind has remained as foolish as ever.'

At this point Mahim entered the room and at once crossed Binoy so rudely about Lalita that his heart shrank in shame. He controlled himself and remained quiet hanging his head. Then, after shooting off some pointed remarks and hurling some nasty insulting comments for all concerned Mahim left. He made them understand, that in order to entrap Binoy and ruin him, a shameless preparation was going on within Pareshbabu's family, Binoy being stupid was entrapped,—but let them try to misguide Gora, then they will know a tough job.

Thus being encircled by humiliation from all corners Binoy sat dumbfounded. Anandamoyee said, 'Do you know Binoy, what your duty is?'

Binoy raised his face to look at her. Anandamoyee replied, 'It is your duty to go to Pareshbabu. Everything will become clear once you have a talk with him.'

51

Sucharita was surprised at the unexpected visit of Anandamoyee. She said, 'I was just getting ready to start for your place.'

Anandamoyee smiled, 'I didn't know that you were getting ready, but on learning the cause for which you were getting ready I could not wait, and so I am here.'

Sucharita was again surprised to learn that Anandamoyee was in the know. Anandamoye said, '*Mā*, I look upon Binoy as my own son. It is through Binoy that I knew about you even before I saw you and had blessed you so from the very beginning. How can I rest in peace if I come to hear that some injustice is being perpetrated upon you? I don't know if I can be of any help to you, but somehow I felt so disturbed; that's why I thus came rushing to you. *Mā*, has there been anything wrong from Binoy's side?'

Sucharita said, 'Nothing at all. Rather it is Lalita who is responsible for the event which has been causing such a furore. Binoybabu had never imagined that Lalita would suddenly come to board the steamer without informing anybody about her decision. But people are enjoying it as a gossip as if it was all done by prior secret complicity between the two. On the other hand Lalita is such a spirited girl that she won't even protest or try to explain what it actually was.'

Anandamoyee said, 'Then we must find a way out. Since Binoy came to know these things he has no peace. He holds himself guilty in fact.'

Sucharita blushed a little and lowering her face asked, 'Do you think Binoybabu—.'

Before she could finish Anandamoyee saved her from the embarrassment by interrupting, 'Listen to me, dear, I tell you Binoy will do whatever you tell him to for Lalita's sake. I have known him since he was a small boy. Once he surrenders to someone he does it with his whole heart; he holds back nothing. That's why I am always in trepidation lest he gives himself away to someone from whom there is no hope of getting anything back in return.'

A weight was lifted off Sucharita's mind. She said, 'Please have no worry about Lalita's consent. I know her mind. But will Binoybabu agree to defect from his society?'

Anandamoyee said, 'The society may eventually expel him, but why should he, on his own, desert the society at the very start? Is it necessary at all?'

Sucharita was surprised, 'What do you say, *Mā*! Will Binoybabu marry a girl from a Brahmo family, while himself still remaining in the Hindu society?'

Anandamoyee said, 'If he agrees to do it, do you have any objection?'

Sucharita was puzzled altogether; she said, 'I cannot see how it is going to materialize.'

Anandamoyee said, 'But *Mā*, to me it seems quite easy! Look at me; I cannot adhere to the customs which are followed in our household. So many people call me a Christian for that. I willingly keep a distance when there is some social ceremomy or feast. You will perhaps laugh dear if I tell you that Gora does not drink water in my room. But, be it as it may, why should I say, "This room is not my room, this society is not my society?" I cannot say that; and that I am still within this room, and this society in spite of this slander and abuse, does not put me into any great difficulty as such. In case a time comes when it becomes too difficult to carry on, then I shall take the road as directed by God. But till the end I shall call my own my own; whether others should accept me or reject me will be up to them.'

Still it was not clear to Sucharita; she said, 'But suppose there is a clash between the opinions of the Brahmo samaj and those of Binoybabu—.'

Anandamoyee said, 'But he too holds more or less similar opinions. The ideas of the Brahmo samaj are not something absurd. He often reads out to me the instructions and sermons issued in your papers; I don't see any radical difference.'

At this point Lalita entered, calling 'Suchididi', and seeing Anandamoyee blushed. From Sucharita's expression she guessed she was the topic of their conversation so long. She would have been happy to escape from the room but there was no chance for the escape any more.

Anandamoyee warmly greeted her, 'Come in, Lalita darling, come in.' Saying this she held her by the hand and drew her close with a special warmth as if Lalita had become a very special precious one to her.

Then in continuation of her previous talk she told Sucharita, 'See dear, the most difficult thing is to reconcile good with bad; but even that happens in the world, and somehow it works as well—indeed this does not necessarily lead to evil, sometimes good too cometh out of it. If this is possible then why should not two persons be able to carry on together with just a wee bit of difference in their opinions; I don't understand the point. Is it on the basis of opinions that the real understanding between human hearts takes place?'

Sucharita sat with her face lowered. Anandamoyee went on, 'Will your Brahmo samaj too put its foot down on the union of a human with a human? Will your society keep them apart whom God has united? My girl, is there nowhere such a society which can ignore small differences, and bring people together within some greater vision of unity? Will man quarrel thus with God for ever? Is it the sole purpose of a society?'

Was it just to remove the obstacles to Binoy's marriage with Lalita that Anandamoyee had plunged into the subject so enthusiastically and with such earnestness? On getting a hunch of the slightest hesitation in Sucharita's mind regarding the issue she was at once eager to squash it; didn't she have some other purpose as well at the back of her mind? If Sucharita continued to be thus enmeshed in her own inhibitions it won't do. If this be the verdict that unless Binoy converted to Brahmoism the marriage could not take place, then the hope she had been nurturing through this trying time will also collapse. This very day Binoy had asked her, '*Mā*, must I register myself with the Brahmo society? Must I accept that too?' Anandamoyee had said, 'I don't think it is necessary.' Binoy asked, 'If they insist?' Anandamoyee was silent for a long time, and then replied, 'No, insistence won't work in the present case.'

Sucharita did not join the conversation with Anandamoyee. She remained silent. Anandamoyee guessed, Sucharita could not still accept the idea.

Anandamoyee mused, 'It was only out of my affection for Gora that I could ignore all the customs and inhibitions of the society. Then is it possible that Sucharita has not been drawn towards Gora? If she were, that trivial detail would not have appeared so big in her perception.

Anandamoyee felt a little depressed. Only two days remained for Gora's release from prison. She had imagined that an area of happiness was waiting ready for him. It was time Gora must be bound up in some tie; otherwise what dangers he will land in and where and when, was nobody's guess. But who could bind Gora? It was beyond an average girl. Again, it would be wrong to negotiate for Gora's marriage with some girl of the Hindu society—that's why she has outright rejected the proposals from so many parents of so many prospective brides. Gora has announced, 'I won't marry'. It was a matter of general amazement that in spite of being his mother she had never once protested to this. Recently she felt elated at noticing one or two symptoms in Gora. It was precisely due to this that she was deeply hurt by Sucharita's silent resistance. But she was not a person to concede defeat easily; she told to herself, 'Well, let's wait and see.'

52

Pareshbabu said, 'Binoy, it is not my wish that you should enter into such a daring course just in order to rescue Lalita from a crisis. Public criticism is not too important; the matter which has been stirring so much controversy today may not be even remembered after some time.'

Binoy did not have the least doubt that he had geared himself up precisely out of his sense of duty to Lalita. He knew very well the social troubles that such a marriage would involve, and far more importantly, Gora would be angered to any extent. But he had warded off the thought of such unpleasant prospects by means of the excuse of 'duty'. When Pareshbabu suddenly laid his finger on that very sense of duty and sought to dismiss its claim, Binoy was not ready to give in.

He said, 'I shall never be able to return what I owe to your affection. If I be the cause of even a brief disturbance to your family, I should consider it unbearable for me.'

Pareshbabu said, 'Binoy, perhaps you do not get my point. I am very happy at your respectful consideration for us. But if you prepare to marry my daughter just out of your sense of commitment to that respect, that is not honourable for my daughter. That's why I had been telling you, the crisis in the present case is not so serious that it necessitates any sacrifice on your part.'

So Binoy was released from the obligation to act on the call of duty. But how come that his mind did not immediately rush out through the opened doors of release like some bird quickly taking flight the moment it finds the cage-door loose? Even now it did not want to budge. Under the excuse of duty he had already allowed the barricade of restraint—so carefully built up day by day—to collapse. The zones where, in the earlier days, imagination only tentatively reached with hesitant steps and at once retreated in guilty diffidence, had in the meantime possessed his mind entirely—and it was difficult to evict the usurper. The sense of duty which had led him to this, might now say, 'It has been enough, let's beat retreat, brother'; but the mind dismissed the suggestion and would say instead, 'You can go back if you want,—I pitch my camp here.'

When Paresh did not allow him to retain any façade of an excuse Binoy came out desperately, 'Please don't think for once that I am going to make some sacrifice at the call of duty. If you give your consent, there can't be any greater blessing for me. My only apprehension is in case—.'

The honest truth-loving man assured without the least hesitation, 'There is no ground for your apprehension. I have learnt from Sucharita, Lalita is not unfavourably disposed towards you.'

Binoy felt a thrill of joy passing through his mind like lightning. A tender secret of Lalita's mind has been disclosed to Sucharita. When was it disclosed, how was it expressed? The thought of this intimate exchange between the two friends, through hints and guesses, seemed to pierce Binoy with the sharp delight of its intense mysterious pleasure.

Binoy said automatically, 'If you consider me acceptable then nothing can make me happier.'

Pareshbabu said, 'You just wait a bit. Let me come back from upstairs.'

He went to seek Baradasundari's consent. Baradasundari said, 'But Binoy must have his initiation first.'

Pareshbabu said, 'That's right.'

Baradasundari said, 'First settle about that. Why don't you call him upstairs?'

As Binoy came up Baradasundari said, 'Then let us fix a date for the initiation.'

Binoy asked, 'Is it a must?'

Baradasundari reacted sharply, 'Isn't it a must? What do you say! How can you marry into the Brahmo society without it?'

Binoy sat silently with bent head. Just on hearing Binoy agreeing to marry into his family Pareshbabu had assumed Binoy would enter the Brahmo society through the initiation ritual.

Binoy said, 'You know of my respect for the religious ideology of the Brahmo samaj. Nor did I ever show any sign of irreverence towards the Samaj. Then is there any special need for going through this ritual of initiation?'

Baradasundari argued, 'If you accept the ideology then what's wrong in undergoing initiation?'

Binoy said, 'It is impossible for me to declare that I do not belong to the Hindu society.'

Baradasundari did not hide her vexation, 'In that case you should not have broached the issue at all. Have you agreed to marry our daughter just out of sheer charity, merely in order to do us a good turn?'

Binoy was deeply hurt. He perceived that his proposal had ironically caused real offence to these people.

When the law of Civil Marriage was introduced in recent past Gora and Binoy had strongly criticized the law in the news media. It was not very easy for Binoy to accept that very civil marriage today and declare himself 'non-Hindu'.

Paresh could not get reconciled to the idea that Binoy should marry Lalita while continuing within the fold of the Hindu society. Binoy sighed and stood up. Greeting both with a *namaskār* he said, 'Excuse me then. Let me not add up to my offences any more.'

Saying this he left the room. While heading for the staircase he saw Lalita sitting alone at a small desk at one corner of the front balcony, writing letter. At the sound of his footstep Lalita turned her eyes and looked up at Binoy's face. That look for the fraction of a moment seemed to flood his entire heart in an instant. It was not the first time they were meeting; on so many occasions indeed she had turned her eyes to look at him. But what immense mystery was evoked by her glance today! Sucharita had come to know one secret of Lalita's mind—that intimate secret manifested itself today before Binoy's glance, like some soothing monsoon cloud, under the long lashes of her dark eyes, filled to the brim with love and compassion. Binoy's aching heart too flashed up in his quick glance like some piercing lightning flashing past the sky. Bidding a *namaskār* at her direction he went down the steps without a word.

53

As soon as he stepped out of the prison Gora found Pareshbabu and Binoy waiting for him by the gate.

One month is by no means a very long time. During his tours Gora used to remain cut off from friends and relatives for longer spells than a month. But when he came out from the month-long isolation of the prison to be immediately received by Paresh and Binoy he felt as if he were born afresh to the old world of dear kins. Seeing Paresh, with his calm, affectionate, naturally benign expression, on that wide road, under the open sky, in the morning light, Gora touched his feet with such joyous obeisance as he had never done before. Paresh embraced him affectionately.

Taking Binoy's hand Gora smiled, 'Binoy, since our schooldays we took all the exams together. But this time I have stolen a march on you in this particular school.'

Binoy could neither smile, nor speak. Through the alchemy of the prison ordeal his friend seemed to have emerged much taller than his own dear pal of the past. A deep sense of respect held him mum. Gora asked, 'How is *Mā*?'

Binoy said, '*Mā* is fine.'

Pareshbabu said, 'Come on son, the carriage is waiting for you.'

Just as the three were about to board the carriage Abinash rushed up in breathless speed, while a crowd of boys trailed behind him.

Spotting Abinash Gora hastened for the carriage; but before he could get in Abinash strode up and intercepted, crying, 'Gaurmohanbabu, please, just a moment, please!'

Before he had finished the boys started blaring at their shrillest possible pitch—.

The sad night is over at last.
Snapped are the ropes that tied you fast.

Gora's face reddened. He roared in his thunderous voice, 'Stop it.'

The boys stopped in surprise. Gora charged, 'Abinash, what's this nonsense?'

Abinash brought out from under his shawl a thick garland of white flowers rolled in a banana leaf, and a small boy following him started reading aloud in thin voice and great speed—like some fine spring organ—from a sheet printed in gold coloured letters, a sort of felicitation speech on the event of his release from prison.

Resisting the garland energetically Gora cried in a voice of suppressed anger, 'So it is now time for starting your drama! Was it for thus clowning me on the roadside that you had been rehearsing this last one month?'

Abinash had planned for this event for quite some time; he had assumed that he would take all by a superb feat of surprise.

This kind of nuisance had not yet come into vogue at the time we are referring to. Abinash had not even taken Binoy in confidence; he was keen to grab the entire credit for this excellent feat. Indeed, he had already kept a written report on the event nearly ready for the press; as soon as he would go home he would fill up the one or two gaps and send it for the press. This was the idea.

Abinash was resentful at Gora's scolding, 'You are being unfair. You have suffered inside the prison, but our suffering has been no less than yours. Every moment of this one month the ribs of our chest have been consumed by the slow fire of husks.'

Gora said, 'You are making a mistake Abinash. Examine just a bit closely; you shall find all the husks fine and intact still, whereas the ribs too have not been much damaged either.'

Abinash was unquenchable; he said, 'The government's police have insulted you. But we today on behalf of the entire motherland bring this garland of honour—.'

Gora exclaimed, 'Oh, can't stand it any longer.'

Pushing aside Abinash and his team Gora called out, 'Pareshbabu, please get into the carriage.'

On boarding the carriage Pareshbabu heaved a sigh of relief. Gora and Binoy followed him.

Gora took the steamer and reached home the following morning. A lot of people of his party had already gathered outside the house. Somehow wriggling himself free from encroachment he made for the inner house to see Anandamoyee. She had finished her bath early in the morning and was waiting for him. As soon as Gora came up to her and touched her feet tears started rolling down from her eyes. The tears she had kept in check all these days could not be controlled any more by any means today.

When Krishnadayal returned after having his dip in the Ganga Gora met him. He bowed from a distance without touching his feet. Krishnadayal too maintained distance and took a separate seat away from him. Gora said, 'Baba, I want to perform a purification rite.'

Krishnadayal said, 'I don't see the point.'

Gora said, 'Inside the prison I did not consider any hardship too hard; but the only thing that troubled me was the feeling of impurity; I felt myself so contaminated; I am yet to get over that feeling of ignominy. So I must undergo the ceremonial purification.'

Krishnamohan anxiously exclaimed, 'No, no, you should not make such a fuss of it. No, indeed. I, on my part, can't give consent to such a plan.'

Gora said, 'Okay, I shall seek the opinion of pundits on the matter if that makes you happy.'

Krishnadayal said, 'No pundit's opinion is necessary. I give you the verdict,—you do not require any purification.'

Gora had never been able to understand why a man like Krishnadayal, who was himself so obsessed with rites and notions of purity, used to be so averse to any suggestion of applying the same in Gora's case; not only did he refuse to accept the idea, but would go to the end of stubbornly opposing it.

During midday meal Anandamoyee had placed Binoy's plate immediately next to Gora's. Gora said, '*Mā*, move Binoy's mat a little away from mine.'

Anandamoyee was surprised, 'Why son, what's his offence?'

Gora said, 'Binoy has done nothing, but it is my fault. I am in an impure state.'

Anandamoyee said, 'Let it be. Binoy is not so fussy about purity or impurity.'

Gora said, 'Binoy may not care, but I do.'

After meal when the two friends retired into the privacy of their upper floor room, both seemed to be at a loss for words. Binoy could not think out a way how to broach to Gora the subject which has become all too important for him during the last one month. Gora too had a kind of curiosity stirring within him regarding the members of Pareshbabu's family, but he did not say anything. He had been in fact, waiting for Binoy to broach the subject. Of course Gora had inquired Pareshbabu about the well-being of the ladies in the family, but was it not just formal talk! There was a longing in his mind to know more than just this news that they were all doing fine.

At this point Mahim entered the room, and taking his seat took a little time to recover from the strain of climbing up the stairs. Then he said, 'Well, Binoy, so long we waited for Gora. Now there is no problem. Let us then fix the dates and time. What do you say to this, Gora? Do you follow my point?'

Without saying anything Gora smiled a little.

Mahim said, 'You smile at this! I guess you are wondering that your Dada has not forgotten the matter! But dear, the daughter is no dream—I can clearly see how very real a thing she is—so what chance is there to forget? No Gora, it's no joke, please come to a decision.'

Gora said, 'But the one who is to take the decision is present here in person.'

Mahim said, 'Indeed! Then I give up all hope! He does not know his own mind, how can he take the decision! Now that you have come home, I leave everything to your responsibility.'

Binoy remained silent and looked serious. He did not venture to make the least conversation even in the way of his natural humour.

Gora guessed there was some problem. He said, 'I can take the responsibility of inviting people going from door to door; it is also possible to take charge for ordering sweets; I do even agree to serve at the feast; but I cannot take the responsibility to ensure that Binoy will certainly marry your daughter. I do not have much contact with the particular deity under whose plans these occasions take place in this world; all along I have kept him at bay with a *namaskār* from a distance.'

Mahim said, 'Don't take it for granted that just because you keep distance he too will hold aloof. None can predict when he will spring some sudden surprise. I can't define at this moment what plans he has about you up his sleeves, but regarding this other gentleman it seems quite intriguing. I can foretell this much that unless you take some initiative yourself instead of leaving all to the mercy of the marriage god, then there may be occasion for repentance in near future.'

Gora said, 'I agree to repent by not undertaking the task for which I am not fit; but if I attempt it and then repent in consequence that should be worse. I want to be spared that possibility.'

Mahim said, 'The son of a Brahmin is going to ruin the prestige and heritage of his caste and family; and will you just watch as an idle spectator? You have been dedicating your day and night forgetting your food and sleep for saving Hinduism; now if your own best friend throws all considerations of caste and creed to the wind in order to marry in a Brahmo family, how will you show your face to the public? Binoy, perhaps you are angry with me, but there are many people who would have told all this to Gora in your absence—in fact they are too eager to—and I spoke in your presence—I think it should be for the good of all concerned. If the rumour is false then just say it and have it over; if it is true that too should be thrashed out.'

Mahim got up and left. Binoy did not utter a single word even afterwards. Gora asked, 'Well Binoy, what's the matter?'

Binoy said, 'It is very difficult to explain the situation just by means of a few shreds of information. So, I had intended to discuss the entire matter at length with you at leisure. But nothing in this world happens in that slow rhythm according to our own convenience. Initially the events proceed with small sneaking leaps like some predatory tiger, then it suddenly takes a spring at one point on your neck. Again the news of the happening also remains unnoticed initially like some suppressed fire, and then suddenly it explodes into tall flames which cannot be controlled by any means. That's why I feel sometimes that man can be free only if he abandons all work and remains inert.'

Gora smiled, 'Even if you alone sit inert what is the guarantee of freedom? If the world too does not go inert along with you, how can it allow you to remain quiet? It will be even more dangerous. If you do not work when the rest of the world is working then you will be the one to lose repeatedly.

Therefore, you have to take care that the events do not overtake your cautiousness. Don't let this happen that everything else is on the move while you alone are not ready.'

Binoy said, 'That's right. I myself fail to remain prepared. This time too I was not prepared. I did not even guess what was coming from which direction. But when it has happened I have to accept the responsibility. Perhaps it would have been better if this had not started at all; but now I cannot disown it, however unpleasant that may be.'

Gora said, 'It is tough for me to enter into theoretical discussion without knowing the actual event.'

Binoy sat up straight and blurted out, 'In course of unavoidable circumstances my relationship with Lalita has taken such a turn that if I do not marry her she will have to undergo unfair and undeserved humiliation for the rest of her life.'

Gora said, 'May I know what kind of turn it is exactly?'

Binoy said, 'That's a long story. That I shall tell you eventually. For the time being you accept this part.'

Gora said, 'Okay. Accepting. Now about that my opinion is this—if the events are unavoidable then the consequent suffering is also unavoidable. If Lalita must undergo social humiliation then she must.'

Binoy said, 'But it is within my power to prevent that.'

Gora said, 'If you really have that power that's good. But just saying it loud is not enough. It is within man's power to steal or murder in case of dire adversity. But does he really have that power? You want to do your duty towards Lalita by marrying Lalita. But is that your supreme duty? Don't you have any duty to the society?'

Binoy did not mention that it was because he remembered his duty to the society that he did not agree to marry according to the Brahmo way. The debater within him sprang up. He said, 'I don't think we shall see eye to eye on this point. It is not that I am upholding the individual above and against the society. What I say is—we have to follow a religion which is above both individual and community. Just as saving the individual is not my supreme concern, similarly saving the society too cannot be my supreme duty; my supreme commitment is to save my own religion.'

Gora said, 'You claim for a religion which exists irrespective of both individual and society. I don't accept such a religion.'

Binoy was provoked. He said, 'I accept. Religion should not be founded on individual and society; rather it is religion which should provide the basis for individual and society. If we have to accept the demand of the society as religion, then it is ruinous pampering of the society. If society intercepts my justified freedom then defiance of that unfair obstacle should be the right duty to society. If marrying Lalita is not wrong on my part, or if I ought to marry her, then if I abstain from doing so just because society is against it, I think that is irreligion for me.'

Gora said, 'Do you think this question of right or wrong concerns you alone? Won't you consider where you are leading the prospective children of your marriage?'

Binoy said, 'If you take that line then it would lead to accepting all social wrong as some permanent settlement. Why do you then blame the clerk who is kicked around by the foreign boss and yet refrains from protesting just because of consideration of his children.'

Through this argument with Gora Binoy reached a clarity which he had not attained before. Till the other day he was anxious about the impending separation from society. He did not sort it out with himself, and in case no such debate broke out between them he would have, as was his usual nature, mentally drifted along the opposite direction of his desire. But in course of arguing his desire, supported by his sense of duty, stood up strong and adamant.

Soon the debate with Gora turned hot. Usually in such cases Gora does not care about fine logic or reason; instead he asserts his own opinions with great force. Such force is rare to find among average men. It was by using this force that he tried to push back and shatter all the points of Binoy, but today he seemed to meet some serious obstacle. So long as it was just two sets of opinions on two sides, Gora's ideas and Binoy's ideas, then Binoy used to readily accept defeat. But today on both sides there appeared real human personalities. It was no more aerial shafts meeting aerial shafts, abstract points cutting abstract points. Today the arrow was directly piercing the spot which belonged to the zone of human heart.

Finally Gora said, 'I don't want to argue with you. There is not much to argue either. Rather there is a point which is to be grasped with your heart. You want to dissociate yourself from the common public of the country by marrying a Brahmo girl; this is what causes me great pain. You can do this, but I cannot by any means. This is the difference between you and me. We are not different in knowledge or intelligence. Your love does not reside where my love dwells. Since you are ready to free yourself by cutting the bond with a knife, it only goes to prove you are not attached to that bond. But for me it is my umbilical cord. I belong to my India—however much you may blame her, accuse her, I want precisely her. I want none else, not even myself, above her. I don't want to cause the least occasion that might lead to the slightest fissure between me and my India.'

As Binoy was about to answer Gora stopped him, 'No, Binoy. You are arguing with me in vain. It's no use. The Bharatbarsha which has been discarded, humiliated by the entire world,—I want to share my lot with that Bharat, with all the infamy. This is my India, the India of caste divisions, of superstitions, of idolatry. If you want to dissociate from this India you must also dissociate from me.'

Saying this Gora got up and going out of the room started strolling on the roof top. Binoy sat inside in silence. The bearer came to announce that quite a number of babus were waiting outside to meet Gora. Gora too felt relieved at getting this ruse for escaping. He went down.

Coming out he found Abinash too had been there among a number of other people. Gora had presumed Abinash was angry. But no sign of anger was visible. Rather he was describing with even more enthusiastic appreciation the event of Gora's refusal yesterday. He was saying, 'My admiration for Gaurmohanbabu has increased many times; so long I knew he is extraordinary. But since yesterday I have come to know he is a great man. Yesterday we had gone to pay him our respect. But the way he publicly refused that show of respect! How many these days can act like that! Is it a simple matter?'

Gora was already depressed and despondent; now this exuberance of Abinash, added to his own bleak mood, seemed to irritate him to any extent. Impatiently he said, 'Look here Abinash. It is your very devotion that can be humiliating for one. You can make a fool of me on the public road and you do not expect this much decency from me that I should protest! This you call the signs of a great man! Have you come to the conclusion that this our country is but an opera troupe, where everybody is just dancing for profit? And nobody is working from genuine motive? If you want to follow, okay; if you want to quarrel that too is welcome. But for God's sake don't eulogize me.'

Abinash's admiration only rose by leaps and bounds at this expression of exasperation. He turned his happy face to all the gentlemen around, and gesticulated as if he were drawing their attention to the amazing uniqueness of Gora's comments. He said, 'Bless us, so that we too may be able to dedicate our lives towards saving the traditional glory of India in a similar spirit of detachment.'

Saying this Abinash stretched out his hand to touch his feet. Gora quickly stepped back.

Abinash said, 'Gaurmohanbabu, it seems you have resolved not to accept any gesture of reverence from us. But it won't do if you remain averse to allow us a chance of happiness. We have planned a feast where you will join us. You must give your consent to this.'

Gora said, 'I cannot share a meal with you unless and until I have my purification.'

Purification! Abinash's eyes glistened at the very idea. He said, 'This did not even occur to any of us. But no stricture of Hindu religion can escape Gaurmohanbabu's notice.'

All agreed that it was a fine idea. Indeed, on the very occasion of purification they could have the feast as well. The eminent scholars of the country should be invited on the occasion. This very invitation, to be sent out on the occasion of Gaurmohanbabu's purification, will go a long way to demonstrate the continuing vitality of the Hindu religion.

The question of the date and venue too arose. Gora said this house won't be convenient for the purpose. One of his admirers suggested that the ritual be performed in his garden by the Ganga. It was also decided that the expenses to be incurred on the occasion would be borne jointly by all the members of the group.

On the eve of dispersing Abinash stood up, and waving his hands in an oratorical posture addressed the gathering, 'Gaurmohanbabu may be displeased, but since my heart is too full today I cannot but say this—God had taken incarnations on this our holy land to reify our scriptures, and similarly we have got among ourselves this incarnation today in order to revive Hindu religion. It is only in our country in the whole world that there are six distinct seasons, and it is only in this country that incarnations have been born at various turns of history in the past, and will continue to be born in future. We are fortunate that such a truth was made manifest to our eyes. Say brothers, 'Long live Gaurmohan!'

Being moved by Abinash's oratory all began to shout slogans plauding Gaurmohan. Distressed beyond measure Gora strode off from the spot.

A deep depression overpowered Gora's mind on this day of his release from the prison. He had imagined long during his confinement in jail about his plans regarding work for the country with new zeal on the event of his release. Today he had been continually asking himself, 'Alas, where is my country! Does it exist only to *my* perception! My friend since childhood, with whom I shared all the dreams and plans of my life, is now, after so many years, ready to snap all his ties with the past and future of the country so ruthlessly just in order to marry a woman! And those who are supposed to be my followers,—they too, after so much coaching and for so long, now come to conclude that I have been born an incarnation just in order to restore Hinduism? Am I then just an embodiment of the scripture! And, Bharatbarsha figures nowhere! Six seasons indeed! There are six seasons in India. If the conspiracy of the six seasons produced such fruits as Abinash one or two seasons less would have been no loss.'

The bearer came with the message that *Mā* was calling Gora. Gora seemed to have been startled. He murmured to himself, '*Mā* is calling!' He seemed to read a new meaning in the message. He said, 'Whatever may happen, I have my mother. And it is she who is calling me. It is she who will unite me with all; she will bridge up gaps with all. When I go to her I shall find my dearest ones waiting inside her room. Even inside the jail I had felt this call of mother, I had seen her in my vision; now outside the jail too *Mā* is calling me, and so I set out to meet her.' Saying this Gora looked outside towards the sky in this wintry noon. The note of disharmony that had been stirred by Binoy on one hand, and Abinash on the other, seemed to clear up a little. Under the light of this midday sun India seemed to open her arms. Her vast sea-lapped expanse along with the rivers, mountains, human habitations, stretched out before Gora's vision. An open clear light from the direction of some infinite source flooded in and bestowed a lustrous halo over the entire expanse. Gora's heart became full, his eyes glowed, and the last trace of depression disappeared from his mind. His spirit took a joyous plunge towards the endless work for Bharatbarsha, whose results would show only in distant future. That he would not be able to see in his own life the material manifestation of the glorious and noble image of Bharatbarsha which he has envisioned in his meditation did not cause the least resentment in him. He said to himself again and again, '*Mā* is calling me—I set out for the destination where *Mā* the *Annapūrṇā,* the *Jagatdhātrī* is waiting; it is in distant future and yet it is contained in this very moment; it is beyond death and yet it is within this very life; I am headed for that superb noble future which lends complete fulfillment and lustre to this my humble lowly present. I am set for that *Mā* who is so far yet so near.' In this moment of joy Gora felt even Binoy and Abinash too were with him, and not alienated from him any more; all the petty acrimonies of the day seemed to evaporate within a vast fulfillment.

When Gora entered Anandamoyee's room his face was radiant with the glow of joy, while his eyes seemed to have been beholding some exquisite vision through and beyond all the material objects before them. On entering the room at first he did not seem to recognize who was sitting by his mother.

Sucharita stood up and greeted Gora with *namaskār*. Gora said, 'Oh! You have come, please take your seat.'

The way Gora said, 'Oh! You have come', suggested that Sucharita's coming was no mundane event, but some special boon or revelation.

There was a time when Gora avoided Sucharita's company. So long as he was occupied with his travel, various troubles, and works, he could keep her thought at bay. But during his confinement within the jail, he could not resist her. There was a time when it did not even occur to Gora that there were women in India. After such a long time he discovered the truth through Sucharita. This sudden instantaneous discovery of such an ancient and immense reality had struck his whole strong nature so powerfully that it was shaken and sent quivering. Inside the prison when yearning for the outside world of sunlight and open air pained him he did not imagine that world just as his work-field or an exclusive male domain. Whichever way he tried to envision that beautiful outside world he saw the faces of only two ruling deities; all the light of the sun, moon and planets fell specially on these two faces; the cool azure sky encircled only these two faces. One of these was the face he knew since birth,—his mother's face; the other face—radiant with intelligence, yet modest and beautiful—he had come to know recently.

In the bleak constricted prison Gora could not resist the memory of this face. The joy of this meditation brought him a deeper release inside his prison. The stern, crude shackles of prison seemed to fade out like some unreal shadowy nightmare.

The hypersensuous waves of his throbbing heart would at ease pierce through all the prison walls, and get merged into the sky, blossomed with the flowers and leaves, and spread playfully in all walks of life.

Gora had assumed that there was no cause for concern from an imaginary vision. That is why he had allowed it free reign for this one full month. Gora thought that only tangible reality was to be feared.

When Gora saw Pareshbabu immediately on coming out of the jail his heart bounced in joy. Initially Gora was not conscious that it was not just the joy of seeing Pareshbabu; it was also mixed up with the spell of his own imagination, his constant partner during these few days. But eventually it dawned on him. While coming by steamer he clearly felt that Pareshbabu was drawing him not just by virtue of being what he was.

After so many days Gora again geared himself up. He said, 'No, I won't accept defeat.' While sitting on board the steamer he took the silent resolve to set out again for some distant place, and not to allow himself to be bound even by any subtle tie.

It was at this time that the argument with Binoy flared up. The debate would not have been so acrimonious on this first occasion of union with the friend after the spell of separation. But today this debate was also a debate with himself. Using the ruse of this debate Gora was trying to clarify his own premise to himself. That is why Gora had been speaking today with such special emphasis; the force was necessary for himself. When his own force today was but provoking the opposition in Binoy's mind—when he was countering Gora's points and feeling revolted by Gora's attitude which he felt to be unfair orthodoxy—Binoy had not imagined that Gora's attack would not have been so forceful today had he not been striking himself all the time.

After his debate with Binoy Gora resolved, 'It is no use abandoning the war front. If I abandon Binoy out of fear for myself, Binoy will not survive.'

54

Gora was then absorbed with idea. He had not been considering Sucharita as a particular person, but rather as an idea. The essence of womanhood in India became revealed to him in the form of Sucharita. It was as if she was born to bring sweetness and sanctity to the homes of India, by means of her purity and beauty. The goddess of benediction who nurtured the children of India, nursed the sick, consoled the miserable, glorified the humblest with love—who had not abandoned or despised our lowliest in spite of misery and destitution—who deserved all our worship and yet sincerely worshipped the most undeserving among us, whose pair of beautiful efficient hands have been dedicated to serve us, and whose perpetually forbearing forgiving love has been bestowed upon us as God's gift—Gora saw a manifestation of that goddess *Lakshmi* seated by his mother, and his heart filled with joy. He continued to think, we have not noticed this *Lakshmi*, indeed we had pushed her behind all—and what could be a better indication of our degradation. Gora then felt—it was she who was the land; she was sitting on the centripetal lotus at the heart centre of the whole India, and we are her devotees. The degradation of the country means humiliation of her—and since we have remained indifferent to her degradation our virility is put under shame today.

Gora was surprised by his own thoughts. Previously he did not know how incomplete his perception of India was so long as the women of India were outside his purview. When a woman was a very vague shadow to Gora something was lacking in his commitment to the country. As if he had strength but no vitality, muscles but no nerves. Gora now realized at once that as we have pushed the woman backwards, considered her insignificant, proportionately our manliness has been reduced.

So, when Gora said to Sucharita, 'Oh! You have come', it was not just a customary formal address on his part; the greeting was informed by a newly gained joy and wonder of his life.

Gora's physical appearance bore certain signs of his prison-ordeal. He had become considerably reduced. Owing to his abhorrence of the jail food he had nearly starved during this period of one month. His bright white complexion too had lost its usual glaze to some extent. His hair being very closely cropped the thinness of his face was all the more apparent.

This very thinness of Gora stirred in Sucharita's mind a special respect tinged with sadness. She longed to touch Gora's feet and wipe the dust off them. Gora appeared before her eyes like some pure dazzling flame in which the smoke or the firewood was not visible. Her heart seemed to quiver under the mixed emotion of compassion and admiration. She could not speak a word.

Anandamoyee said, 'Gora, this time I have guessed the kind of happiness I could enjoy if I had a daughter of my own. The few days you were away, Sucharita has been such a consolation to me, that I can barely tell. I did not know them before. But sorrow brings you closer to many good and great things in this world. Now I have realized this positive side of sorrow. It is because we do not always realize how and where God bestows his solace for suffering that we suffer.—*Mā*, you feel shy, but you have brought me such happiness during my days of misery—how can I be at peace without expressing that before you!'

Gora glanced once at Sucharita's blushing face with deep gratitude and then told Anandamoyee, '*Mā*, she had come to you in your days of misery to share your sorrow; again she has come today when you are happy, to add to your happiness. This kind of generous warmth is the mark of those who are large-hearted.'

Noticing Sucharita's shyness Binoy said, 'Didi, when the thief is caught red-handed everybody deals one or two punitary blows. Today you have been found out by all of them. Therefore, you have to endure the consequences. Where shall you escape now! I know you since a long time. But I have not disclosed to anybody, and have kept tight-lipped—I know for certain that nothing will remain hidden for long.'

Anandamoyee laughed and said, 'You have been tight-lipped indeed! Are you the fellow to remain tight-lipped!—Since the day he has come to know you, he has been all praise for you, and he is never tired of singing your praise.'

Binoy said, 'Remember Didi! So here is unmistakable evidence that I can appreciate quality and that I am not an ungrateful person at all.'

Sucharita said, 'That only proves your goodness.'

Binoy said, 'You won't get any evidence of my qualities from me. If you want to have some idea please come to *Mā*, you'll be stunned—when I hear about myself from her lips I myself get fascinated. If *Mā* agrees to write my biography I am ready to die at an early date.'

Anandamoyee said, 'Just hear what the boy says!'

Gora said, 'Binoy, your parents had chosen the most appropriate name for you.'

Binoy said, 'Perhaps they did not expect any other quality in me, and therefore used the pretext of '*binoy*' or modesty, lest I appeared ridiculous to all and sundry.'

Thus the initial uneasiness was got over.

On the eve of taking leave Sucharita asked Binoy, 'Won't you come sometime to our place?'

Sucharita asked Binoy to visit, but could not invite Gora. Gora did not get at the right meaning and felt a little hurt. Binoy could secure his way into any company, whereas Gora did not have the ability; for this Gora had never felt any sorrow. But today he felt this lack in his temperament as a real deficiency.

55

Binoy guessed that Sucharita invited him specifically to discuss the issue of his marriage with Lalita. Though on his part he had clinched the issue the trouble was not yet over. So long as it was kept alive no side could expect any respite.

So long Binoy's main worry was, 'How can I hurt Gora!' Because Gora did not mean just Gora the person; Gora also meant the idea, the conviction, the kind of life he was committed to. All along Binoy's habit and pleasure were to tune himself up to this. Any clash with this was, as it were, clash with his own self.

But the initial inhibition about hurting Gora was got over. Following his open exchange with Gora about Lalita Binoy reached a kind of self-assurance. Till the abscess was operated upon the patient had no end of tension and anxiety; but when at last the surgeon's knife came down the patient found it brought pain as well as relief, and the whole thing was not as terrible as it had appeared to his imagination.

So long Binoy could not argue with himself too. Now that door opened. Now he continued his debate with Gora in silence. He raised all the possible arguments that could be assorted on Gora's side, and then continued to counter them from various angles. If this could be a real direct encounter with Gora, then excitement would have been stirred no doubt; but it would also have spent itself out eventually. But now Binoy found Gora unwilling to carry the debate to its end. That too stirred a sort of resentment in Binoy. He thought, 'Gora will not try to understand; nor will he try to make you understand; but he will only try to force you. Force! I cannot submit to force.' Binoy said, 'Whatever may happen, I will take the side of truth.' Saying this he grasped the word 'truth' with both hands and held it close to his bosom. It was necessary to pit a very strong opponent against Gora. Therefore, Binoy repeated to himself that it was truth to which he held on as his final support. He did even feel a considerable respect for himself by thinking that he has chosen to hold on to the truth alone. So, when he set out for Sucharita's place in the afternoon he walked very straight with his head held high. Binoy was not in the condition to perceive whether his posture of assurance derived from his inclination towards the truth, or from some other inclination.

Harimohini was then making preparation for cooking. Binoy stopped at the kitchen door, got his demand for Brahmin-lunch sanctioned and then went upstairs.

Sucharita picked up a piece of embroidery and with her eyes bent over it, and fingers engaged in the sewing, she opened the subject. She said, 'Look here Binoybabu, if there is no mental inhibition then must you submit to the external opposition?'

When arguing with Gora Binoy used his logic against this very practice. But now, while discussing with Sucharita, he stressed the counter logic. Listening to him now none could have guessed he had the least difference with Gora on the issue.

Binoy said, 'Didi, neither are you extenuating the external obstacles on your part.'

Sucharita said, 'But we have a reason for doing so Binoybabu! Our obstacle is not external. Our society is founded on religious faith. But the society to which you belong binds you with only a social tie. That's why if Lalita has to leave the folds of Brahmo samaj it will affect her much more adversely than your desertion of the society may affect you.'

Binoy tried to emphasise the view that religion was a matter of one's personal pursuit, and that it should not be confused with society.

At this time Satish entered with a letter and an English newspaper. Seeing Binoy he was excited at once. He grew busy to sort out some device by which Friday could be transformed into Sunday. Before long Binoy and Satish were absorbed in their plans. In the meantime Sucharita turned to Lalita's letter and the paper sent along with it.

The paper, which was a mouthpiece for the Brahmo samaj, carried a report that the recently rumoured prospect of the marital relation between a famous Brahmo family and the Hindu society has been fortunately eliminated owing to the retraction of the Hindu youth. On this occasion the column writer compared the sincerity of the Hindu youth with the miserable frailty of the Brahmo family and deplored the latter.

Sucharita told herself, the marriage between Binoy and Lalita must be made to take place by any means. But that can't be done just by debating with this youth. She sent a note to Lalita asking her to come to her place; she did not mention in the note that Binoy was here.

As there was no scope sanctioned by any almanac by which, through any favourable assortment of the planets Friday could be considered Sunday for once, Satish had to leave for getting ready for school. Sucharita also took leave for a little while in order to take her bath.

When the excitement of argument abated, sitting alone in that private room of Sucharita the young man within Binoy surfaced. It was around nine/nine thirty in the morning. There was no din and bustle in the lane outside. A small watch was ticking on Sucharita's writing table. The room made an impact on Binoy which twined round him like a spell. The small decoration pieces all around seemed to engage Binoy in a conversation. The neatness of the table, the embroidered cover on the chair, the deerskin spread near the footstool under the chair, the few pictures hanging on the wall, the small book-shelf with neatly arranged books and covered by a thick piece of red cloth, all together played a profound symphony to him. What a beautiful charm the room seemed to contain. In this room during some lonely noontide one friend had disclosed the secret of her heart to another; their beautiful coyness seemed to pervade the room still. Binoy envisioned in imagination who sat where during that talk, how they sat. The other day Pareshbabu told him 'I have learnt from Sucharita Lalita's mind is not disinclined towards you'; he imagined this moment of confiding in various forms, from various angles, like varied sets of pictures. An exquisite emotion played within Binoy like some very sad remote entrancing music. Because Binoy did not have the capability to express in some manifest form these subtle nuances which could be felt so deeply and intensely like some inarticulate hints in the intimate privacy of the mind—because Binoy was no poet or painter—his entire consciousness became restive. He felt he longed to do something and he had no way of doing it. A curtain was hanging before him, which had removed the nearest one to the furthest distance; didn't Binoy have the strength to forcibly tear apart that curtain!

Harimohini enetered the room to ask if Binoy wanted some snacks now. Binoy said, 'No.'

Then Harimohini sat down.

So long as Harimohini was in Pareshbabu's residence she was considerably drawn towards Binoy. But since the day she started her own separate establishment with Sucharita she found their visits quite unpalatable. She had decided that it was because of the company of such people that Sucharita did not quite obey her these days in her decisions and ways. Although she knew Binoy was not a Brahma, still she also distinctly felt his lack of any firm faith in Hindu ways. Therefore, she did not invite him with the warmth of the earlier days and thus saved wastage of her god's *prasād*.

Today Harimohini asked Binoy in course of the talk, 'Well son, how come that in spite of your being the son of a Brahmin, you do not care about the daily rituals of the Brahmin?'

Binoy said, 'Masi, while spending all the days and nights in learning my lessons by heart I have forgotten those mantras.'

Harimohini said, 'But Pareshbabu is also a learned man. Still he performs certain daily rites according to the custom of his own religion.'

Binoy said, 'Masi, what he does is not possible just by memorizing certain mantras. If I can ever be like him then I shall follow his ways.'

Harimohini said a bit sharply, 'So why don't follow your own ancestors until then? You are neither here nor there; is this desirable? A man should have some religious identity. This is neither Rama, nor Ganga,—O God, how strange this is indeed!'

At this time Lalita entered and at once started seeing Binoy there. She asked Harimohini, 'Where is Didi?'

Harimohini said, 'Gone for her bath.'

Lalita said in the way of some unnecessary excuse, 'Didi sent for me.'

Harimohini said, 'Wait a bit, she will come any moment.'

Harimohini was not favourably disposed towards Lalita either. Harimohini now wanted to have Sucharita cut off from all her earlier circles and have her completely under her own control. The other daughters of Pareshbabu did not frequent this house. It was only Lalita who dropped in every now and then and drew Sucharita aside into intimate talks. This was not to Harimohini's liking. Often she would interrupt their talk and try to call Sucharita away under the pretext of this or that work. Alternatively, she would complain that Sucharita's studies were not carried on uninterrupted these days unlike earlier times. Yet, when Sucharita concentrates on her studies she does not forget to remind her that excessive studies were unnecessary and harmful for women. The real problem was that she was not being able to possess Sucharita as completely as she wanted and as a result she was all the time blaming either Sucharita's associates or her education.

Not that it was pleasant for Harimohini to sit there with Lalita and Binoy. Yet, because of her very resentment against both she stayed on. She had guessed a mysterious relationship between Binoy and Lalita. Therefore, she said to herself, 'Whatever be the custom of your society, I won't allow this sort of shameless mixing in my house.'

On the other side in Lalita's mind too a thorny feeling of acrimony was raising its head. Yesterday she too had decided to accompany Sucharita to Anandamoyee's house, but finally she could not make it. Lalita had great respect for Gora, but at the same time her reservations against him too were very strong. Not only that; since the day Gora had been released from prison her own attitude to Binoy too seemed to have undergone a change. A few days ago she had quite boastfully assumed that she had a hold on Binoy. But now the very thought that Binoy would never be able to get over Gora's influence made her turn aggressive toward Binoy.

As soon as Binoy saw Lalita entering the room he was greatly agitated. These days Binoy could never be at ease with Lalita. Since the time the rumour spread about their prospective marriage, Binoy's mind gets quivering like some electrified magnetic splinter as soon as he sets his eyes on Lalita.

Lalita felt angry at Sucharita on seeing Binoy waiting there in Sucharita's room. She guessed Sucharita has set herself to the task of persuading Binoy's unwilling mind towards some congenial direction and Lalita has been summoned precisely to help this job of moulding the intractable into a manageable one.

Turning towards Harimohini she said, 'Tell Didi I cannot wait now. I shall come some other time.'

Saying this she did not even cast a glance at Binoy and quickly went out. Since it was not necessary to guard Binoy any more Harimohini too got up under the pretext of some domestic chore.

Binoy was not unfamiliar with this fiery expression of Lalita. But he had not seen it for quite some time. Binoy had assumed that those miserable times were gone forever, when Lalita used to be always ready with her fiery shafts for targeting Binoy. He saw today that old shaft had again been brought down from the quiver. There was no trace of rust on it. One can bear with anger, but bearing with hatred was too painful for a man like Binoy. Binoy remembered how fiercely contemptuous Lalita was towards him once on the assumption that he was just a satellite to Gora. Binoy felt restless at the imagination that he was appearing a coward to Lalita's perception again today. His hesitation caused by his sense of duty should be considered cowardice by Lalita, and yet he won't get a chance to throw in a word or two in self-defence—this seemed unbearable to Binoy. It was great punishment for Binoy if he was denied the right to argument; because Binoy knew he could argue a point, and had unusual command of the art of speech and of presenting a case convincingly. But whenever Lalita fought with him she gave him no chance to apply his logic; today too he did not get that chance.

That newspaper lay open before him. On an impulse of restiveness Binoy picked it up and suddenly noticed a portion was marked by pencil. He read it and realized the targets of this exposition and stricture were but the two of them. Binoy clearly understood the kind of humiliations Lalita had been undergoing at the hands of members of her society. Yet Binoy was taking no measure to protect her from this ignominy; instead he was bent on delivering a fine discourse about sociology. Considering this Binoy found it perfectly justified that he should be held in contempt by a spirited girl like Lalita. Remembering Lalita's courage that could completely ignore society's sneers, and comparing himself with this flamboyant woman Binoy felt ashamed.

After taking her bath, serving meal to Satish and sending him off for school, when Sucharita came back to Binoy he was sitting completely silent. Sucharita did not resume the previous subject. Binoy sat down at his meal, but forgot to do the rite of washing prior to that.

Harimohini said saucily, 'Well son, you do not observe the smallest of the Hindu customs—then what is the harm in your becoming a Brahmo?'

Binoy was a bit hurt and said, 'The day I shall come to consider Hinduism as just a set of meaningless rules concerning touch and food, I shall become a Brahmo, or a Christian or a Muslim, or whatever it may be. I have not yet felt that extent of disrespect towards Hinduism.'

When Binoy came out of Sucharita's house he was in a deeply despondent mood. He felt as if he were being pushed back from all corners and heading for an empty shelterless vacuity. He could not take his old position by Gora's side, Lalita too was holding him at a distance—even his rapport with Harimohini too was about to snap within a short time. There was a time when Baradasundari held him in genuine affection. Pareshbabu still holds him in affection. But in return to that affection he has caused such a disturbance in their family that there too he has no place today. Binoy has all along been keen to secure the respect and love of those whom he loved; the ability to attract their affection by different means was well within his command. Why was he, this Binoy, then suddenly thrown out of the old accustomed orbit of their love and affection! He brooded over the matter as he walked. For instance, now that he came out of Sucharita's house he could not think of a place where he could go. There was a time when he did not need to think for a moment before he automatically took the path leading to Gora's house. But it is not that easy today; if he goes then he will have to keep mum in front of Gora. That silence should be too unbearable. On the other hand the road to Pareshbabu's residence too was not smooth any more.

'Why did I arrive at such an unnatural situation!' Brooding on the question he slowly walked along the road with his head bent. Coming near the Hedua tank he sat down under a tree. So far whenever any big or small problem arose in his life he had thrashed it out by discussing or debating with his friend. Today that avenue was closed. Today he will have to think out his own thoughts alone.

Binoy had no dearth of the ability for self-analysis. It was not easy for him to attribute all the blame upon external factors and thus extricate himself from the responsibility. Therefore, sitting alone he held himself responsible. He told himself, 'To eat the cake and have it too, such cunning does not work in the real world. If you have to opt for one thing you must do away with its alternative. One who cannot decide which course to forego, eventually comes to my situation; he is rejected by all. It is only those who have selected their own course of life and unhesitantly followed that course, have found peace. The luckless fellow who wants to follow both this and that road, and cannot abandon either, ultimately fails to reach his very goal—he would only wander aimlessly like the stray dog in the street.'

It is difficult to diagnose a disease, but the diagnosis does not necessarily make the remedy easier. Binoy had a sharp analytical mind, but he lacked the strength for taking decisive action. That's why he has so far depended more on his friend who possessed a stronger will force than upon himself. Finally, on arriving at this very crucial juncture, he has suddenly discovered that if you had no will power of your own you can at best steer through the smaller problems by means of borrowing the same from others, but in times of real need you cannot tide over by borrowing from another's treasury.

With the sun tilting westward the shadow was withdrawn, and Binoy had to get up from his shelter under the tree. While going a few steps he heard someone shouting, 'Binoybabu! Binoybabu!' The next moment Satish appeared and held his hands. After finishing school for the day Satish was then returning home.

Satish pleaded, 'Binoybabu, come on, please, come to our house with me.'

Binoy remonstrated, 'How can that be Satishbabu!'

Satish asked, 'Why not?'

Binoy said, 'If I visit your house so frequently how can the people there stand me?'

Considering this logic of Binoy as not even deserving an answer Satish only implored, 'No, you please come.'

Binoy felt deeply moved at thinking that this little boy knew nothing about the radical shift that had taken place in Binoy's relation with their family. He just loved Binoy. The joy of the charming wonderland to which Pareshbabu's family had introduced him remained intact only in this child. Even during these days of catastrophic upheaval no doubt had cast its cloudy shadow on his mind, no social assault had undermined it. Putting his arm around Satish's shoulder Binoy said, 'Come dear, let me see you to the gate of your house.'

Satish had been the repository of the love and affection of Sucharita and Lalita since his childhood; encircling him with his arm Binoy seemed to feel the touch of that accumulated sweetness.

For the rest of the entire road Satish continued to babble all sorts of odd irrelevant things which seemed like showering of nectar to Binoy's ears. Coming in touch with the child's innocent mind he could altogether forget the complex problems of his own life for a little while.

In order to reach Sucharita's house one had to go by Pareshbabu's residence on the way. The ground floor drawing room of Pareshbabu's house could be seen from the road outside. While passing by that room Binoy could not but raise his eyes for once. He saw Pareshbabu was sitting in front of the table; and Lalita was sitting on a small cane stool beside him, motionless like some obedient disciple with her back towards the road.

Lalita did not know how to put down the restiveness that churned up her mind uncontrollably on returning from

Sucharita's house. So she had slowly come to Paresh and sat down near him. There was such a peace in Paresh that whenever the excitable girl failed to control her restiveness she would come and sit silently near him. Pareshbabu used to ask, 'What's it, Lalita?' She used to answer, 'Nothing, Baba. This room of yours is so nice and cool.'

Pareshbabu had clearly understood that Lalita had come to him today with a heavy heart. An unarticulated sadness was weighing down on his mind too. So he had slowly started talking on a subject which could help to lighten the weight of the trivia of personal joys and sorrows.

Looking at this scene of quiet high-toned discussion between father and daughter Binoy's pace came to a halt for a moment. He did not get what Satish was asking. Satish had asked a very difficult question indeed regarding military strategy. His question concerned the prospect of victory in a war if a horde of tigers, after being trained for a long time, were placed on the front rank of one's army. So long their question-answer session was going on uninterrupted; receiving the sudden jolt at this point Satish scrutinized Binoy's face, and following his glance looked inside. Instantly he shouted at the top of his voice, 'Lalitadidi, Lalitadidi, just see whom I have captured from the streets.'

Binoy sweated in embarrassment. Inside the room Lalita immediately sprang up from her seat. Pareshbabu turned his face towards the road. On the whole it was quite a scene.

Then Binoy bade good-bye to Satish and came up to Pareshbabu's house. Entering the room he saw Lalita had already left. Thinking that everybody was looking at him like some intrusive ruffian who disturbs others' peace he cringed and shyly sat down on the chair.

As soon as the customary talks about physical well-being, etc. were over Binoy came right to the point, 'Since I do not follow or seriously accept the rites and rituals of Hindu society and indeed everyday overstep it, I think it is my duty to join the Brahmo samaj. My earnest wish is to take my initiation at your hand.'

Even before fifteen minutes this wish or resolve had not even taken its embryonic form in Binoy's mind. After a silence Pareshbabu asked, 'Have you thoroughly considered all the aspects?'

Binoy said, 'Is there much to think about in this case, excepting the question of right and wrong? And that is a very simple thing. The kind of education that we have received does not allow me to honestly accept sheer rites and rituals as inviolable religion by any means. That is why many oddities get manifest in my ways at every step; my daily involvement with those who have been clinging to Hindu ways with all reverence does only serve to hurt them. I do not have the least doubt that this amounts to doing great wrong on my part. Given this situation I must not take time and must immediately get ready to be free from this wrong. Otherwise I won't be able to retain my own self-respect.'

So much explanation was not necessary in order to make Pareshbabu see the point, but this was required for himself, to draw strength in support of his decision. As he claimed that he had somehow become involved in a war between right and wrong, and that in this war he must forego everything else in order to emerge triumphant on the side of the right, filled him with a sense of self-satisfaction. Wasn't this his minimum commitment to human dignity!

Pareshbabu asked, 'Are you sure that you really agree with the Brahmo samaj regarding religious faith?'

Binoy fell silent for a while. Then he said, 'To tell you the truth, in the past I used to think I had some particular religious faith—indeed I have quarreled too with many people on many occasions on that account. But today I have known for sure that no such religious faith has actually struck roots within me. It was after seeing you that I came to realize this. Since the need of religion had never really occurred in my life, and neither did I develop any real faith in it, I had all along used the conventional religion prevailing in our society as a butt of debating skill by amassing imagination, logical skill and subtle analyses. I have apparently tried to prove the validity of the religion while my real aim was to prove the edge of my debating skill. The more difficult it was to prove, the greater pride I have felt at proving it. I cannot tell even today if in future religious faith will grow in me fully truly and naturally, but there is a good possibility if I am granted congenial situation and good examples. At least I shall be saved from the ignominy of eternally carrying the flag of the very thing that constrains my intelligence from within.'

Even as he spoke with Pareshbabu, Binoy was actually giving shape to the logic that went in favour of his present decision. He did it with such zeal as if he, after considering all the aspects over a long time, had arrived at this firm conviction.

Still Pareshbabu earnestly insisted that he should take a little more time. At this Binoy thought perhaps Pareshbabu was not sure about his firmness. Therefore, he became more stubborn. He repeatedly asserted that he had arrived at a conviction which was incontrovertible, and from which there was no possibility of his budging at any event. Neither side mentioned the subject of his marriage with Lalita.

At this time Baradasundari entered in connection with some domestic work. Binoy expected that Pareshbabu would call out to Baradasundari to break this new information about Binoy. But Pareshbabu said nothing. He preferred to keep this confidential. But as Baradasundari was about to leave after showing unmistakable indications of contempt and anger towards Binoy, he could not restrain himself any more. He went up to Baradasundari and bending low to touch her feet said, 'I have come to you today with the proposal to have my initiation in the Brahmo samaj. I am not worthy, but my hope is that you shall make me worthy of it.'

Baradasundari turned back in surprise and slowly came back inside the room. She looked askance at Pareshbabu's face.

Paresh said, 'Binoy is seeking initiation!'

On hearing this Baradasundari felt a triumphant pride of course; but why didn't she feel total elation! She had a great longing that Pareshbabu should get some good lesson this time. She had repeatedly and forcefully announced the prediction that her husband will have to repent a lot; so she was getting quite impatient these days as Paresh showed no sign of disturbance at the mounting social castigation. That all the crises should be so finely solved at this juncture was not thus quite pleasing for Baradasundari. Pulling a long face she said, 'If this proposal for initiation came a few days earlier we would not have to go through so much humiliation and suffering.'

Pareshbabu. 'We are not talking about our trials or humiliation. It is just this that Binoy wants to have initiation.'

Baradasundari could not stop herself, 'Only initiation!'

Binoy said, 'Only omniscient God knows how I accept all your suffering and humiliation as my own.'

Paresh said, 'Look here Binoy, do not trivialize your decision of taking a religious initiation. I have told you also on an earlier occasion—Don't take a drastic action for our sake,—on imagining that we have been landed into some social crisis.'

Baradasundari said, 'That's alright. But at the same time I would also add, neither is it his duty to enmesh us in trouble and then idly sit back.'

Pareshbabu said, 'If you are restive instead of sitting quietly the mesh becomes only more enmeshing. Just rushing into any action is not called duty; sometimes doing nothing could be doing the best duty.'

Baradasundari said, 'May be. I am an ignorant fool. I cannot get all this. Now what I want to know is what is the final decision—I have many chores to attend.'

Binoy said, 'I shall receive my initiation on the day after tomorrow, that is Sunday. I wish if Pareshbabu—.'

Pareshbabu said, 'An initiation, the result of which can directly affect my family cannot be performed by me. You'll have to apply to the Brahmo samaj.'

Binoy's mind instantly shrank from the idea. Mentally he was not in the right condition for making the formal, protocol-approved application for conversion into Brahmoism—especially in view of the scandal regarding his connection with Lalita which had been so much slandered by the very same samaj. How can he get over all inhibition and by what kind of language should he frame his letter of application? How can he keep his head high after that letter is circulated in the papers run by the Brahmo samaj! Gora will read the letter, Anandamoyee will read. The letter will tell nothing about the history behind it; it will only indicate this much that Binoy had suddenly felt too eager to seek initiation in the Brahmo religion. But it was not so true as it will be made to appear; and if one did not see its connection with other matters then he will be put to great shame.

Noticing Binoy's silence Baradasundari felt anxious. She said, 'He does not know who is who in the Brahmo samaj; but no problem; we shall look after all the arrangement. I am sending for Panubabu right now. There is no time either. Sunday follows just the day after tomorrow.'

At this time Sudhir was seen passing by the room, heading for upstairs. Baradasundari called out to him, 'Sudhir, Binoy will take his initiation in our samaj the day after tomorrow.'

Sudhir was excited. Sudhir, in fact admired Binoy from the core of his heart. Now learning that Binoy should be available in the Brahmo samaj he was greatly enthused. Indeed it seemed inexplicable to Sudhir how a man like Binoy, who wrote such superb English, and was so educated and intelligent, could remain outside the pale of Brahmo samaj. Now the evidence in favour of his conviction that a man like Binoy could not remain outside the fold of the samaj by any means, made him swell in pride. He said, 'But can it be arranged so quickly by this very Sunday? Many won't even get the news.'

Sudhir wished that this initiation rite of Binoy be publicized widely as an example.

Baradasundari intercepted, 'No, no, it will be managed by this very Sunday. Sudhir, you please hasten to Panubabu and bring him here immediately.'

The poor fellow by whose example Sudhir was excitedly envisioning to propagate the invincibility of Brahmo samaj, was by then mentally shrinking smaller and smaller into the smallest dot. So long as the whole thing was in the domain of debate or reasoning it seemed not serious at all. But the moment Binoy saw its concrete manifested form he felt shaken.

As soon as Panubabu was sent for, Binoy stood up. Baradasundari said, 'Please wait a little. Panubabu will come right now. He won't be late.'

Binoy said, 'No. Excuse me.'

He now longed to move away from this confine and seek some respite for thinking everything alone in the privacy of his own room.

Pareshbabu too got up after him and placing a hand on his shoulder said, 'Binoy, do nothing in haste—think everything quietly, with calm mind. Don't take your plunge in such a serious matter without completely understanding your own mind.'

Getting extremely displeased with her husband Baradasundari said, 'First one creates a pandemonium without the least forethought, and then when the noose closes tight on the neck one would say, "sit cool and think". You people may sit quietly and think calmly, but we are being brought to our tether's end.'

Following Binoy Sudhir too came out on the road. Like the wish to taste a dish before starting the meal proper in earnest, Sudhir felt impatient at once. He wished to take Binoy at this very moment to his friends, and sharing the good news with them start celebrations immediately. But this exuberance of Sudhir only served to make Binoy sink deeper into depression. When Sudhir suggested, 'Binoybabu, let us both go to Panubabu together,' Binoy did not pay any heed and forcibly withdrawing his hand from Sudhir's grasp he went away.

After going a part of the road, Binoy saw Abinash along with a few people of his team rushing by. As soon as he spotted Binoy Abinash cried, 'Oh, here is Binoybabu. Fine. Come along with us.'

Binoy asked, 'Where are you going?'

Abinash said, 'To finalise about the garden at Kashipore. That is to be the venue for Gaurmohanbabu's purification ceremony.'

Binoy said, 'No, I can't go now.'

Abinash was surprised, 'What do you say! Do you understand what a grand thing it is going to be! Otherwise would Gaurmohanbabu have made such an unnecessary proposal! These days the Hindu society has to assert its strength. This purification of Gaurmohanbabu,—what a great impact it will produce on the public mind! We'll invite eminent scholars from far and near. This will have great impact on the entire Hindu society. People will be given to understand that we are still alive. They will realize that Hindu samaj is immortal.'

Binoy excused himself and went his way.

56

When Baradasundari summoned Haranbabu and reported everything he sat in solemn silence for a while and said, 'It is our duty to talk once with Lalita about this.'

As Lalita came Haranbabu raised the degree of his solemnity to the C-sharp scale and said with appropriate gravity, 'Listen Lalita, a moment of very great responsibility has arrived in your life. On the one side is your religion, on the other side is your desire; you have to choose your course between them.'

Saying this Haranbabu took a pause and fixed his eyes on Lalita's face. Haranbabu knew that before this glance of his,—made glowing by the fire of righteousness—cowardice cowered, pretensions were burnt to ashes. This fiery spiritual glance of Haranbabu happened to be a precious treasure of the Brahmo samaj.

Lalita said nothing.

Haranbabu said, 'Perhaps you have heard, that considering your situation, or for whatever reason, Binoybabu has at last agreed to have initiation in our samaj.'

Lalita had not heard the news before this moment. But she did not express her reaction at hearing it either. Only her eyes glared while she sat still like some stone statue.

Haranbabu said, 'Surely Pareshbabu has been very happy at this flexibility of Binoy. But it is you who have to decide if there is any real cause for jubilation in this. Therefore, I am requesting you in the name of the Brahmo samaj—forget your own lustful desire and just keeping your focus on religion ask your own heart,—is there any real cause for jubilation here?'

Lalita was still silent. Haranbabu thought he had created a great impact. He continued with redoubled zeal, 'Initiation! Must I say in so many words what a great holy moment it is in one's life! Would you allow that initiation to be polluted! Should we make way for falsehood in Brahmo samaj, should we invite and felicitate hypocrisy for the sake of happiness, comfort or lust! Tell me Lalita, do you want this history of the abomination of Brahmo samaj clinging to your life forever?'

Still Lalita did not utter a word, and sat motionless while tightly gripping the arms of the chair. Haranbabu went on, 'Many a time have I seen how weakness assaults on man through the chinks forged by lust. I also know how to forgive man's weakness. But the weakness that ruins not only one's own life but also the very foundation of the shelter for hundreds and thousands of lives—you tell me Lalita, can it be forgiven even for a moment? Has God given us the right to forgive it?'

Lalita left her chair and stood up, 'Oh no Panubabu, no. You please don't forgive. All the world have become accustomed to your attacks—but your forgiveness will be perhaps altogether unbearable for everybody.'

Saying this Lalita walked out of the room.

Baradasundari got anxious at Haranbabu's speech. She could not now afford to let Binoy escape by any means. She appealed a lot to Haranbabu but in vain. At last she angrily told him to leave. For Baradasundari the problem now took shape like this,—she did neither get Pareshbabu on her side nor did she receive the support of Haranbabu on the other. Nobody could ever imagine such an unenviable situation. Once again it seemed time that Baradasundari changed her opinion regarding Haranbabu.

So long as Binoy had been vaguely envisioning the initiation issue he had been voicing his resolution quite decisively. But now as he found he would have to formally apply to the

Brahmo samaj for this and the subsequent plannings will have to be taken up with Haranbabu, the horror of this crude exposure made him feel altogether shrunk and withdrawn. He could not think out where to go or whom to consult; he could not even go to Anandamoyee. So he came back to his lonely apartment and going upstairs lay down on the plank.

It was nearly evening. As the servant brought a lamp in the darkening room he was going to stop him when the call came up from downstairs, 'Binoybabu! Binoybabu!'

It was a great relief for Binoy. The call seemed to him like suddenly discovering drinking water in the midst of a desert. At this moment none else than Satish could bring him comfort. The insipidness disappeared at once. Responding, 'What's it Satish *bhai*?', Binoy jumped out of the bed and without getting into his shoes rushed downstairs.

There he saw just in front of the staircase Baradasundari waiting with Satish by her side inside the small inner courtyard. Flustered, Binoy took them to the upper floor.

Baradasundari told Satish, 'Satish, you go to that far corner of the balcony and keep there for a while.'

Being pained at this verdict of joyless exile being slumped on Satish, Binoy brought out a few picture books and took him to the adjoining room, lighted the lamp and made the boy sit there comfortably.

Baradasundari told him, 'Binoy, you don't know the members of the Brahmo samaj; you write a letter and give it to me. I shall personally go tomorrow morning, meet the secretary and make all the arrangements so that the day after tomorrow, on this Sunday itself, your initiation is over, you need have no worry at all.' Binoy could not utter a single word in protest. He wrote a letter as demanded by her and handed it over to Baradasundari. It had been necessary for him to seek out any course anyhow so that he was left with no chance of hesitation or withdrawal.

Baradasundari also made a brief mention of the subject of marriage with Lalita.

After Baradasundari's departure Binoy felt a strange revulsion. Even the thought of Lalita seemed slightly repugnant.

He had the feeling that perhaps Lalita too may have some connection with this unseemly haste on Baradasundari's part. The moment he lost self-respect, respect for all others too dwindled proportionately.

Coming home Baradasundari thought today she would make Lalita happy. She had been sure that Lalita loved Binoy. It was precisely because of this that so much trouble shot up regarding their marriage. At that time she had held everybody responsible for this excepting herself. For some days she had not spoken a single word to Lalita. Therefore, when a solution was within the ken, she was eager to make it up with Lalita by claiming the credit of this development to her own contrivance. Lalita's father had ruined everything. Lalita herself too could not bring Binoy round. Panubabu too was no good. Yes, oh dear, yes! Five men together cannot achieve what a woman can do singlehanded.

On returning home she learnt Lalita had retired to bed rather early that day; she was not very well. She laughed to herself, 'I am going to cure your illness.'

Taking a candle she entered her dark bedroom and saw Lalita had not yet gone to bed; she lay stretched on an arm-chair.

Lalita instantly sat up and charged, '*Mā*, where did you go?'

There was a certain sharpness in her tone. She had got the news that she had taken Satish and been to Binoy's apartment.

Baradasundari said, 'I had been to Binoy's house.'

'Why!'

Why! Baradasundari felt a little angry. 'Lalita thinks all the time I have been acting against her! Ungrateful!'

Baradasundari said, 'Then see why.' Saying this she held that letter of Binoy before Lalita's eyes. Glancing through the letter her face reddened. In order to claim her own credit in the matter Baradasundari informed her with a degree of exaggeration,—was it easy to get that letter written by Binoy; she could say with justified pride that no other person did have the ability to get this done.

Lalita lay back on her arm-chair covering her face with both palms. Baradasundari presumed Lalita was feeling shy to express strong emotion in her presence. She left the room.

The following morning as she was ready to start for Brahmo samaj with the letter she found somebody had torn the letter into the finest shreds.

57

In the afternoon Sucharita was getting ready for going to Pareshbabu when the bearer came to announce that a babu had come.

'Which babu? Binoybabu?'

The bearer said, 'No, here is a very fair, very tall babu.'

Sucharita started and said, 'Bring the babu upstairs to the drawing room.'

So long Sucharita had given no attention to what *sari* she was wearing today or how she had draped it. Now standing before the mirror she could by no means approve the *sari*. But there was no time to change. With trembling hands she touched up here and there—the end of the *sari*, the hair—and then entered the room with a throbbing heart. She did not remember that the writings of Gora lay right on the near end of her table. The books were shamelessly lying right under Gora's eyes—there was no way to cover or remove them.

'Masima has been waiting eagerly for quite some time to see you, let me send the news.' Saying this Sucharita went out immediately after entering the room. She did not find enough strength to talk with Gora sitting there alone.

After some time Sucharita returned with Harimohini. For some time Harimohini has been hearing from Binoy about Gora's opinions, faith, sincerity and dedicated life. Often at her request Sucharita had to read out to her from Gora's writings during her noontide siesta. Although she did not exactly understand all these writings and these would rather help to send her to sleep, still she more or less gathered the idea that Gora had been fighting on behalf of scripture and social customs against the lack of rituality in the present times. What could be stranger and more commendable in a modern English-knowing youth! When she saw Binoy first among the Brahmo family Binoy had given her enough cause for satisfaction. But eventually when she got accustomed to it, and saw Binoy in her own house then the very lapses of Binoy regarding rites and rituals displeased her more and more. Precisely because she had come to trust Binoy so much her condemnation of Binoy grew stronger by each passing day. That is why she had been waiting for Gora with great eagerness.

Just once looking at Gora Harimohini was taken by complete surprise. Here was a Brahmin indeed! He was as it were a flame from the altar. As if the bright white Mahadeva! Such an admiration was stirred within her that she shrank when Gora touched her feet.

Harimohini said, 'I have heard a lot about you, my son! You are Gaur then? Indeed you are Gaur. That *Kirtan* song we used to hear—

> Who scrubbed Gora's beautiful body
> By mixing the moon's lustre with sandal paste—

Today I see that with my own eyes. I wonder how heartless was the magistrate to throw you into the prison!'

Gora laughed, 'If people like you were magistrates then the jails would have been turned into habitats of rats and bats.'

Harimohini said, 'No my son, where's the dearth of thieves and frauds in this world? Didn't the magistrate have eyes to see! That you are not just another rascal, that you are God's chosen one, can be guessed by anybody by once looking at your face. Must you imprison people just because you have a prison! O God! What sort of justice is this!'

Gora said, 'Lest by looking at men's faces they by mistake chance to have glimpse of God, the magistrates prefer to work with their eyes glued to the pages of lawbooks. Otherwise could they enjoy sleep or relish food after issuing the verdict of lashing, imprisonment, deportment, or death by hanging?'

Harimohini said, 'Whenever I get the time I make Radharani read out to me from your writings. All these days I have been waiting with the hope to hear the good things from your own lips. I am an ignorant woman, very unfortunate too; neither do I understand everything, nor can I concentrate always. But my son, I have come to the conviction that I shall receive some real wisdom from you.'

Gora modestly maintained silence without protesting.

Harimohini said, 'Son, you must take some food here before you leave. It has not been my good luck for a long time to serve a meal to a Brahmin like you. Today have some sweets which are ready at home, but I invite you to come another day and have your meal here.'

Saying this Harimohini went inside to make arrangement for sweets and Sucharita could hardly control the turbulence within her heart.

But Gora started without any preliminaries, 'Did Binoy come to you here today?'

Sucharita said, 'Yes.'

Gora said, 'I have not met Binoy since. But I know why he came.'

Gora paused a little. Sucharita also kept silent.

Gora said, 'You are trying to arrange Binoy's marriage according to the Brahmo custom. But is it right?'

At this attack Sucharita's shyness was completely overthrown. She looked straight at Gora's face and said, 'Do you expect me to consider a marriage according to the Brahma custom as not the right thing?'

Gora said, 'You can know it for certain that I do not expect any small thing from you. I expect from you much more than the kind of expectation one normally has from a member of a community. I can say emphatically that you are not of the class of gangmen whose job is to increase the number of his gang. What I wish is that you too should assess yourself properly. Don't consider yourself inferior at the instigation of others. You are not just a member of a particular community, you must understand this clearly and get the feeling within yourself.'

Sucharita gathered all her strength, sat up stiffly and said, 'But aren't you too a member of a particular community?'

Gora said, 'I am Hindu. Hindus are no community. Hindu is a race. This race is so huge that it is impossible to define what constitutes its uniqueness. Just as the sea is not mere waves, so Hindus are not community.'

Sucharita said, 'If Hindus are no community then why do they get into petty squabbles?'

Gora replied, 'Why does one try to resist an attack upon oneself? It is because one is alive. It is the rock which remains unresponsive to all sorts of attack.'

Sucharita said, 'Suppose what I consider religion is considered as assault by the Hindu then what do you advise me to do in such a case?'

Gora said, 'Then I shall tell you—since what you consider your commitment amounts to be a painful attack for such a great and immense entity as the Hindu race, you must think very deeply if there is any confusion or blindness on your part, if you have carefully considered all the aspects of the situation. It is not right to subscribe to such a nuisance just because of one's acceptance of the bias of one's own community through sheer habit or lethargy. When a mouse applies its teeth to the bottom of a ship, it acts in accordance with its rodent instinct and convenience; it does not see the possibility of the enormous damage to all, which is immensely more huge by any comparison to its own small advantage. You too have to think whether you are thinking only of your community or of all mankind. Do you know what I mean when I say all mankind—what great variety of nature, temperament, need it implies? All men are not standing at the same point or following the same path; some have the sea facing them, some others a wild stretch of land. Yet none can stop, everyone has got to go ahead. Do you want to impose the ruling of your own party over all the others? Do you want to shut your eyes tight and then think there is no variety in mankind, that everybody in this world has been born just to get himself or herself enrolled on the Brahmo samaj register? What is then your difference from the barbaric races which imagine that the only beneficial course for the world lies in conquering all the other races and establishing its own monolithic empire, who—in the pride of power—refuse to accept that in the recognition of the uniqueness of every race lies the most precious course to the good of the world!'

For some time Sucharita forgot all her logic and opposition. The thunderous voice of Gora churned up her entire consciousness to a strange intensity. Sucharita forgot that Gora was arguing on some particular subject; she was conscious of only this much that Gora was speaking.

Gora said, 'It is not your community that has produced the twenty crores of people of India. Which course should be suitable for this twenty crores, which faith or rite will bring food to them or provide shelter? How can you wish to assume by force the responsibility to decide all this and thereby reduce Bharatbarsha into a regimented monolith! The more obstacles you find to this end, the angrier you get, and irreverent towards the country, and the more you alienate by your hatred those very people whose benefit you seek! Yet you imagine that you are worshipping that very God who has created this variegated mankind and desires to keep them variegated. If you genuinely accept him then why don't you see his decree clearly, why don't you accept its significance under the pride of your own intellect and community?'

Sucharita made no attempt to answer and silently listened to Gora. Noticing this Gora had a feeling of compassion. He paused a little and lowering his voice added, 'Perhaps I sound harsh to you—but please nurse no resentment against me as an antagonist. If I considered you an enemy I would not have talked with you at all. You have a natural generous spirit and I feel sad to see it constrained on account of community considerations.'

Sucharita blushed; she said, 'No, no, please don't bother about me. You go on, I am trying to follow.'

Gora said, 'I have nothing more to say—you look at Bharatbarsha with your natural intelligence, genuine heart, you bestow your love upon her. If you look down upon the people of Bharatbarsha as non-Brahmos, that will be a distorted and contemptuous view; then you will only continue to misunderstand them. They won't be seen from the vantage point from which they could be seen completely. God has created them as human, they think and live in various ways, they have varied forms of faith and belief—but there is a basic humanism at the root of all. Within everything there is a special element which is my own, which is of my Bharatbarsha. If you can look at it the right way a wonderful noble aspect will appear before your eyes, piercing through the veil of all its pettiness, incompleteness. Many a pursuit of many ages can be seen lying hidden within it; you can perceive the fire of ancient *yagnas* still smouldering in it; and you won't have the least doubt that one day that fire will surmount its own limited time and space to blaze up into a brilliant flame at the heart centre of the world. In this Bharatbarsha men have announced great truths for ages, have performed great deeds; if we even imagine that all this have been nullified it could mean irreverence to truth, and that is what may be called atheism.'

Sucharita was listening with her face bent low. Now raising her face she asked, 'What do you want me to do?'

Gora said, 'I say nothing more than this—you have to understand that Hindu religion has tried to accommodate like a mother people of various ideas and opinions; that is, Hindu religion has accepted man as man, not as member of some community. Hindu religion accepts the ignorant as well as the wise; and it recognizes not just one single form of wisdom, but the multifarious manifestations of that wisdom. The Christians refuse to accept this multifariousness; they claim that on the one hand there is Christianity and on the other hand there is eternal damnation, and there is no midway inbetween. We have taken our lesson from the Christians; so we are ashamed with the variegatedness of Hindu religion. We fail to perceive it is through this very multifacetedness that Hindu religion has been pursuing the vision of the One. Until we release ourselves from this Christian education coiling round our mind we won't be able to attain the glory of getting a true glimpse of the Hindu religion.'

Sucharita was not only listening to Gora's speech, she was, as it were, seeing his speech manifested before her eyes. Gora's eyes expressed an absorbed meditative vision fixed at some point in a remote future; that look and the speech became merged in Sucharita's perception. Forgetting coyness, forgetting herself Sucharita fixed her absorbed gaze on Gora's face. Sucharita saw such a strength in this face which could perhaps be instrumental in materializing, by sheer spiritual force, great resolves in this world. Sucharita had listened to the theoretical discourse of many intelligent and scholarly speakers in her community. But in the case of Gora it was not discussion, it was instead a creative act. It was such a living thing that instantaneously took over one's body and mind. Sucharita was observing today the image of Lord Indra, the god holding thunder in his hand. When speech was sonorously hitting her ears and shaking the door of her heart, intense flashes of lightning danced through her blood simultaneously at every beat. Sucharita did not have the strength any more to see distinctly how far and on what points did she agree or disagree with Gora.

At this time Satish came in. He was afraid of Gora; so avoiding him he crept close to his didi and said in a low voice, 'Panubabu has come'.

Sucharita startled—as if somebody had given her a lashing. She felt she would be happy if she could by any means erase this arrival of Panubabu, by somehow pushing, removing, burying the event. Assuming that Satish's low voice had not reached Gora's ears Sucharita got up quickly. She went straight downstairs and intercepting Haranbabu said, 'Excuse me, today I cannot talk to you.'

Haranbabu asked, 'Why not?'

Without answering this question she said, 'If you come to Baba's place tomorrow morning then you can meet me.'

Haranbabu asked, 'Do you have any visitor today?'

Sucharita evaded this question too and said, 'I don't have the time today. Kindly excuse me.'

Haranbabu said, 'But I heard Gaurmohanbabu's voice from the road. Is it he sitting inside?'

Sucharita could not avoid this question. Her face reddened and she said, 'Yes, he is.'

Haranbabu said, 'Then it is even better. I too had something to discuss with him. If you are preoccupied with some special chore I can talk with Gaurmohanbabu till then.'

Saying this he did not wait for Sucharita's consent and started climbing the stairs. Sucharita entered the room and completely ignoring Haranbabu standing alongside told Gora, 'Masi has been preparing some dish for you. Let me see her about it.'

Saying this she quickly went out and Haranbabu, with a sullen expression, settled himself on a chair.

Haranbabu said, 'I think you look a bit reduced?'

Gora said, 'Oh yes, it was actually the treatment towards reducing that had been carried on for some time.'

Softening his voice Haranbabu said, 'Indeed, you had to suffer a lot.'

Gora said, 'It was not more than can be expected.'

Haranbabu said, 'I wanted to discuss a matter with you regarding Binoybabu. Perhaps you have heard he is preparing for initiation into the Brahmo samaj on the coming Sunday.'

Gora said, 'No I have not heard.'

Haranbabu asked, 'Do you approve this?'

Gora said, 'But Binoy did not seek my approval.'

Haranbabu said, 'Do you think Binoybabu proceeds for this initiation ceremony with appropriate faith?'

Gora said, 'Since he has agreed to go for this your question becomes redundant.'

Haranbabu said, 'When lust becomes strong we do not get the opportunity to probe what we believe or what we don't believe. You know human psychology.'

Gora said, 'No. I do not make unnecessary discussion about human psychology.'

Haranbabu said, 'My opinions and my community are different from yours. But I respect you. I know for certain that no temptation can make you budge from your faith, be it right or wrong. But—.'

Gora intercepted him, 'What is the value of that minimal respect you have saved for me that its denial should count so great a loss for Binoy! There are of course good and bad things in the world; you may also decide about their respective values in proportion to your respect or disrespect; anyway, don't insist upon the world population to accept your evaluation.'

Haranbabu said, 'Okay. That issue may be left unclinched at the moment. But I ask you—won't you oppose this attempt of Binoy to marry into Pareshbabu's family?'

Gora reddened and said, 'Haranbabu, how can I discuss these matters concerning Binoy with you of all persons? Since you are ever so preoccupied with human psychology you ought to have understood as well that Binoy is my friend and that he is not your friend.'

Haranbabu said, 'Because this matter is related to Brahmo samaj I have raised the issue, otherwise—'

Gora said, 'But I do not belong to the Brahmo samaj. How does your worry in this respect concern me?'

At this point Sucharita entered the room. Addressing her Haranbabu said, 'Sucharita, I have some special discussion with you.'

Not that there was any special need to say this. Haranbabu said this precisely with the purpose to show off to Gora his special intimacy with Sucharita. Sucharita made no response. Gora sat unperturbed in his own chair. He showed no sign of leaving and did not give any opportunity to Haranbabu for a private talk.

Haranbabu said, 'Sucharita, come to the other room for once, and let me tell you something.'

Without responding to him Sucharita turned to Gora and asked, 'Is your mother alright?'

Gora said, 'I do not remember any occasion when *Mā* was not alright.'

Sucharita said, 'I have seen how natural is her ability to keep fine.'

Sucharita remembered her meeting Anandamoyee during the period of Gora's imprisonment.

At this point Haranbabu suddenly picked up a book from the table and opening it first noted the writer's name, then started browsing through it here and there.

Sucharita reddened. Gora knew what the book was, so he smiled a little to himself.

Haranbabu asked, 'Gaurmohanbabu, is this a work of your juvenile period?'

Gora replied with a smile, 'That childhood is still continuing. Some creatures have a very brief calfing, whereas for some others childhood is rather prolonged.'

Getting up from her chair Sucharita said, 'Gaurmohanbabu, I think your food is ready by now. So you please come to the inner room. Masi, you know, won't appear before Panubabu, perhaps she is waiting for you.'

This last sentence Sucharita added precisely for hitting Panubabu. She has been made to take too much today; and she had to return a little.

Gora got up. Haranbabu, the undefeatable, said, 'I am waiting then.'

Sucharita said, 'Why should you wait in vain? There will be no time today.'

But Haranbabu did not leave. Sucharita and Gora went out of the room.

Seeing Gora in this house and noticing Sucharita's disposition towards him Haranbabu felt alarmed. Will she in due course drop off from the Brahmo samaj! Was there no one to protect her! This must be stopped by any means.

Haranbabu drew a piece of paper and started writing a letter to Sucharita. Haranbabu had a set of fixed beliefs. One of these was, when he rebuked someone in the name of truth his spirited words could never be lost upon the addressee. That words were not the only thing, and that there was also another thing called human mind was beyond his ken.

After finishing his meal and talking long with Harimohini when Gora came to Sucharita's room to take his walking stick it was already evening. A letter with Sucharita's name on the envelope was lying on the table; it would meet the eye of anybody instantly on entering the room.

Seeing the letter something went stiff inside Gora's bosom. The letter was no doubt written by Haranbabu. Gora knew Haranbabu had some special right over Sucharita. He did not know of any change having taken place in that respect. Today when Satish whispered to Sucharita about Haranbabu's arrival and Sucharita quickly made for the ground floor and very soon came up along with him, it seemed to touch a discordant note for Gora. When Sucharita left Haranbabu alone to accompany him to his meal that treatment appeared rather rude no doubt, but Gora had assumed it to be a sign of special informal relationship since in the case of really intimate relationship such rudeness was permissible. Finally seeing this letter on the table Gora received a good jolt. A letter can be a very mysterious thing; since it shows only the name on the outside while the rest is sealed inside it can distress a person for no apparent reason.

Looking at Sucharita's face Gora said, 'I shall come tomorrow.'

Sucharita said with lowered eyes, 'Okay.'

While on the point of leaving Gora suddenly stopped and exclaimed, [using '*tumi*', the intimate form of address]: 'Your place is within the solar system of India. You are of my own country. Some meteor cannot be allowed to sweep you away with its tail into the void. I won't rest until I establish you firmly where you should be established. They have given you to understand that your truth, your religion will abandon you there. I shall clearly show you that your truth, your religion are not just the abstract words of yours or a few others. It is connected with the world all around you through countless threads of life. One cannot just pull it up from the forest and transplant it in a flower pot at one's whim. If you want to keep it bright and fresh, if you want to make it attain all-round fulfillment, you must occupy your seat within the heart of the big society which has been predestined long before your birth. You will not be able to say by any means, "I do not belong there; they are not my own." If you say this all your truth, your religion, your strength will fade out like a shadow. God has marked out a place for you; whatever kind of place that may be, if your ideology pulls you away from that place, that will never bring triumph to that ideology either. I will certainly convince you of this. I shall come again tomorrow.'

Saying this Gora left. The air inside the room seemed to quiver for a long time. Sucharita sat motionless like some statue.

58

Binoy said to Anandamoyee, 'Listen to me *Mā*, to tell you the truth, whenever I bowed before the idol, I felt a kind of uneasiness within, though I have suppressed that uneasiness and instead wrote fine articles in support of idol worship. But I am telling you the truth *Mā*, when I knelt before the idol I did not get the approval of my own mind.'

Anandamoyee said, 'Thy mind! Is it a simple thing! You can't see anything in the casual way. You always think of some finer aspects in every matter. That is why you can never get over your fastidiousness.'

Binoy said, 'That's the thing. Because I have a superfine intelligence I can prove the validity of a thing with fine logic even when I don't believe in it at all. According to the dictates of convenience I delude myself and others. So long the debates I have fought in support of religion were not for the sake of my religious faith as for the sake of my group.'

Anandamoyee said, 'When you do not have a true inclination towards religion such things happen. Then religion too become a matter for boasting like money, family, or prestige.'

Binoy. Yes. Then we forget that it is a matter of religion; then we fight with the assumption that this is our religion. I myself too have done precisely the same thing so long. But even so I could not completely delude myself. I have all along felt ashamed of pretending piety where actually my faith failed to reach.

Anandamoyee said, 'Don't I understand that! That you overdo it much more than the average people is itself a clear evidence that you have to apply a lot of material to fill up the gap within your mind. If it is simple devotion not much else is required.

Binoy said, 'That's why I have come to ask you is it good to pretend faith where I do not have genuine faith?'

Anandamoyee said, 'Just hear the boy! Is it a question worth asking?'

Binoy said, '*Mā*, I shall receive initiation at the Brahmo samaj the day after tomorrow.'

Anandamoyee was taken aback, 'What do you say Binoy! What is the great necessity for seeking conversion!'

Binoy said, 'It is precisely this necessity that I have been trying to explain to you so long *Mā*!'

Anandamoyee asked, 'Can't thou continue in our society with whatever be your faith?'

Binoy said, 'To continue I have to practise hypocrisy.'

Anandamoyee asked, 'Don't you have the courage to stay on without practicing hypocrisy? Well, the people in the society will make you miserable—but can't you endure the misery and continue?'

Binoy said, '*Mā*, if I do not obey the strictures of the Hindu society then—'

Anandamoyee said, 'If Hindu samaj can accommodate three hundred thirty-three billion shades of ideologies, then why shouldn't your idea too hold as good as others'?'

Binoy said, 'But *Mā*, suppose the people of our society declare, 'You are not Hindu'—then is it sufficient to cry myself hoarse, 'I am Hindu?'

Anandamoyee said, 'You know people of our community brand me a Christian—I don't even join them in feasts on social and religious occasions. But even then, I don't see the point in accepting that I am a Christian just because they happen to call me Christian. I think it wrong to escape and hide for the sake of a cause which I know to be just.'

Binoy was going to answer. But Anandamoyee stopped him and said, 'Binu, I won't allow you to start a debate. This is not a matter for debating. Can you really conceal a thing from me? I can see very well that under the pretext of debating with me you are trying to delude yourself. But don't play clever in such a tremendously serious matter.'

Binoy bent his head and said, 'But *Mā*, I have already given my promise in writing that I will receive my initiation tomorrow.'

Anandamoyee said, 'That cannot be. If you clearly tell everything to Pareshbabu he will never insist.'

Binoy said, 'Pareshbabu takes no interest in this initiation; he is not going to join the ritual.'

Anandamoyee said, 'Then you needn't give a single thought to this.'

Binoy said, 'No *Mā*, it has been decided, now there cannot be any turning back. By no means.'

Anandamoyee said, 'Have you told Gora?'

Binoy said, 'I could not meet Gora.'

Anandamoyee asked, 'Why? Is he not at home?'

Binoy said, 'No, I learnt that he has been to Sucharita's house.'

Anandamoyee was surprised, 'But he had gone there yesterday.'

Binoy said, 'Gone today too.'

At this time the bustle of the bearers of an incoming palanquin could be heard outside. Assuming the arrival of some female relative of Anandamoyee, Binoy went out.

Lalita came in and touched Anandamoyee's feet. Anandamoyee had not at all expected Lalita's visit today. In her surprise she scrutinized Lalita's face and at once guessed Lalita had reached a crisis in connection with matters relating to

Binoy's initiation ceremony, and thereby had come to seek her counsel.

To help her broach her problem Anandamoyee said, '*Mā*, I am very glad that you came. Just now Binoy was here; he will receive his initiation in your samaj tomorrow; that was what we were talking about.'

Lalita said, 'Why is he going in for this ceremony? Is it at all necessary?'

Anandamoyee was surprised, 'Is it not necessary, *Mā*?'

Lalita said, 'For myself I don't see any point.'

Failing to get at Lalita's thrust Anandamoyee stared askance at her face without saying anything.

Lowering her face Lalita said, 'This sudden decision for receiving initiation is insulting for him. Why is he going to accept this humiliation?'

'Why!' Does not Lalita know why? Does not she have any cause for rejoicing in this?

Anandamoyee said, 'Tomorrow is fixed for the ceremony; he has given his promise—and now there is no scope for withdrawal; at least this is what he had been telling me.'

Lalita looked at Anandamoyee with her bright glance and said, 'There is nothing sacrosanct about a promise in this kind of things; if change is necessary then change we must.'

Anandamoyee said, '*Mā*, don't be shy with me; let me frankly tell you all. Till this moment I had been telling Binoy he should not and need not desert society whatever be his religious faith. Whatever he may say I don't think he does not understand it deep within his mind. But *Mā*, his mind is not unknown to you. He knows with certainty that without deserting his society he cannot be united with you. Don't be embarrassed, *Mā*, tell me frankly if this is not true!'

Lalita turned up her face and looking directly at Anandamoyee said, '*Mā*, I won't be shy with you—I tell you I don't care about these things. I have thought very deeply and realized that it is an impossible proposition that ironing out all individual religion—faith—must be the precondition for union between one human and another. If it be so then there cannot be any friendship between a Hindu and a Christian either. In that case it is better to erect huge walls to keep each community segregated within its own boundaries.'

Anandamoyee's face brightened up, 'Aha, how glad I feel at hearing you. I too say the same thing. Nothing is identical between two humans—be it beauty, qualities, or temperament. But that does not prevent two persons to unite. Then why should opinions or ideas be able to prevent it? *Mā*, you bring such relief to me. I had been very worried about Binoy. I know he has given himself away to you without the least reservation. If he receives any shock there he won't be able to stand it by any means. So when I tried to dissuade him only God knows how I suffered. But how fortunate he is indeed! Is it a small matter the way you saved him so easily from such a great crisis! Let me ask one thing—did you have any discussion with Pareshbabu in this regard?'

Lalita suppressed her coyness and said, 'No, not yet. But I know, he will certainly understand everything.'

Anandamoyee said, 'Of course he will. Otherwise where did you get such intelligence, such strength of mind! *Mā*, I am calling Binoy, you two should come to a direct understanding. In the meantime let me confide to you *Mā*—I know Binoy since he was a small boy; he is such a person that whatever suffering you undergo for his sake will be fully recompensed by his subsequent conduct. This I can claim emphatically. So many times have I wondered where is that lucky girl who will get Binoy! Now and then there had been offers, but I could not approve. Today I can see he too is no less lucky.'

Saying this Anandamoyee touched Lalita's chin by her fingers and then kissed them. Then she sent for Binoy. Tactfully leaving Lachmya inside the room she went to another part of the house on the pretext of ordering some snacks for Lalita.

Today there was no room for any shyness between Lalita and Binoy. They had reached a serious crucial turn. It was at the call of this very crisis that they saw their mutual relationship clearly and from a broad perspective; no vapour of charming emotion rose to cast a chameleon veil between them. Their two hearts had converged and, like the Ganga and the Yamuna, the two streams of their two lives were about to merge at some auspicious holy point; without even mentioning a single word about this they accepted this humbly, solemnly, silently and without inhibition. The society had not sent out its invitations to them. No common ideology had brought them together. Their bond was no artificial bond. Remembering this they felt their union to be sanctioned by such a religion which is simple in an immensely superb way, which does not squabble over petty issues, which is not confirmed by a community-approved priest. Lalita's face was radiant and her eyes were shining when she said, 'You would kneel and lower yourself in order to accept me—I cannot bear this humiliation. I want you to stand unmoved exactly where you are.'

Binoy said, 'You too stand unmoved where you belong. You need not budge the fraction of a point. If love cannot accept difference then why should there be any variety in the world?'

The essence of the talk the two had for nearly twenty minutes is this. They did not remember whether they were Hindu or Brahmo; the consciousness that they were two human souls continued to shine within their minds like some still unflickering flame from an earthen lamp.

59

After his prayer Pareshbabu was sitting motionless on the balcony in front of his room. The sun had just gone down.

At such an hour Binoy came along with Lalita and prostrated on the floor to touch his feet.

Paresh was a bit surprised to see the two enter thus. There was no chair around; so he said, 'Come along; let's go inside.'

Binoy said, 'No, you please don't get up.'

Saying this he sat down there on the floor itself. Lalita too, moving a little away, sat down near Paresh's feet.

Binoy said, 'We have come together to seek your blessing. That will be the true initiation ceremony of our lives.'

Paresh was surprised and looked askance at their face.

Binoy said, 'I won't announce my resolve in the conventional language according to the conventional custom amidst formal publicity. It is your blessing which will initiate our two lives to be bound by truth everafter. Our two hearts bend down in devotion at your feet; whatever is good for us will be given us by God through your hands.'

For a while Pareshbabu did not speak and sat still. Then he asked, 'Binoy, aren't you going to be a Brahmo then?'

Binoy said, 'No.'

Pareshbabu asked, 'Do you want to continue within the folds of the Hindu samaj?'

Binoy said, 'Yes.'

Pareshbabu turned to Lalita. Lalita understood his mind and said, 'Baba, what is my religion will be mine and will continue to be so till the end. This may cause me trouble, even pain. But I don't believe that any religion will suffer if I do not cast away those from whom I differ in my opinion and conduct.'

Pareshbabu remained silent.

Lalita said, 'Previously I used to think that the Brahmo samaj was the only real world, the rest being just shadows. Alienation from the Brahmo samaj was, as it were, alienation from all truth. But during these last few days I have got over that illusion.'

Pareshbabu smiled faintly.

Lalita said, 'Baba, I could not tell you what a great change has taken place within me. I feel I have nothing in common with the people whom I saw inside the Brahmo samaj—even though my religion was the same as theirs—. Yet under the excuse of a name—Brahmo samaj—I have to claim them as my own and keep at bay all else in this world—I fail to see the validity of such an approach these days.'

While slowly patting his rebellious daughter on the back Pareshbabu said, 'Can we judge correctly when the mind is in a state of agitation owing to personal reasons? For the good of the human life that has a continuity stretching from the ancestors down to the progeny society is required—this is no artificial requirement. The society on which depends the far-reaching future—won't you pay a thought to it?'

Binoy said, 'But the Hindu samaj is there!'

Pareshbabu said, 'If the Hindu samaj does not accept your responsibility, does not recognize you?'

Binoy remembered Anandamoyee's observations and said, 'We have to take the responsibility of making it recognize us. Has not Hindu samaj extended its shelter to newer and newer communities all along? Hindu samaj can be the meeting place for all religious communities.'

Pareshbabu said, 'You can show a thing in one way by sheer reasoning. But in actuality it may not be found exactly like that. Otherwise does anyone willingly desert his inherited society? If you have to obey the society that confines and stagnates man by shackling his religious sensibility with external rituals, you have to reduce yourself perpetually to the predicament of a wooden doll.'

Binoy said, 'If Hindu samaj has reached such a constricting stage then it should be our responsibility to rescue it from that stagnation. If enlarging the doors and windows can ensure an inflow of light and air to the room who would want to demolish a fine structure in a fit of anger!'

Lalita suddenly spoke out, 'Baba, I cannot understand all this talk. I have no commitment to uplift any society. But, I am being pushed around from all sides by such a huge injustice, unfairness, that I feel suffocated. I feel I should not endure this with bowed head for any reason. I don't understand much about right or wrong. But Baba, I can't take any more.'

Pareshbabu said soothingly, 'Wouldn't it have been better if you took a little more time? Your mind is ruffled at the moment.'

Lalita said, 'I have no objection to waiting. But I am sure that false statements and unfair oppression will only be on the mount. So I am really afraid—in case being driven to desperation I drift into doing something which hurts you. Don't think Baba that I have given no consideration to the question. I have thought very carefully and guessed that, in view of my education and upbringing, I may have to undergo considerable uneasiness and inconvenience once outside the periphery of the Brahmo samaj. But my mind does not shrink from the prospect, not in the least; rather I feel the stirring of a new strength in my mind. I have only one worry Baba, lest any of my deeds hurts your feelings.'

Saying this Lalita touched Pareshbabu's feet lightly with her palm. Smiling a little Pareshbabu said, '*Mā*, if I depended solely on my intelligence then I would have been unhappy at any opposition to my wish and opinion. I cannot emphatically say that the emotion flooding your mind today is completely negative. I too had once rebelled and left my home. I did pay no thought to any consideration of advantage or otherwise. This continuous action and counteraction that is striking the society today indicates that it is the divine will that is working. What do I know of His planning,—how will He demolish on various fronts in order to mend, rectify and reconstruct, what particular item will He retain and in which shape—who am I to tell? Be it Brahmo samaj or Hindu samaj—he has been watching the human factor.'

Saying this Pareshbabu shut his eyes for a moment to collect himself in the privacy of his heart and thus get restored to himself.

After a silence Pareshbabu said, 'Look here Binoy, in our country all social rituals are connected with religious rites. It is because people of other religions would not be included within the social ambit. So how are you to avoid this problem? At least I cannot think out a solution.'

Lalita could not understand the point; because she had no first-hand experience of the difference between their social customs and those of the others. She had the notion that on the whole there was no great difference between their own rites and rituals and those of the others. Just as the difference of Binoy from them was not perceptible the same was perhaps applicable in the case of the two communities. Indeed she had no idea that there was any real obstacle for her in the Hindu marriage rituals.

Binoy said, 'Our marriage is performed in the presence of an icon; do you refer to that?'

Pareshbabu stole a glance at Lalita and said, 'Yes. Can Lalita accept that?'

Binoy looked at Lalita's face. He understood her entire mind was shrinking from the idea.

Under the impulse of emotion Lalita had drifted to such a juncture which was completely unfamiliar and crucial for her. At this Binoy felt a deep compassion. He felt he should take all the assault upon himself in order to protect her. Letting such a spirit to recede in defeat! It was intolerable. No less terrible was the prospect that in order to snatch victory it should receive the death-blow on its bosom. It must be allowed victory, and at the same time it must be protected as well.

Lalita sat silent for a while with her head bent. Then turning pitifully to Binoy she asked, 'Do you really accept the idol from the depth of your heart?'

Binoy instantly replied, 'Oh no, not at all, The idol is not god for me, it is just a social sign.'

Lalita said, 'But won't you have to formally accept as God what you know within your mind to be just another sign?'

Turning to Paresh Binoy said, 'I'll do without the idol.'

Paresh said while getting up, 'Binoy, you are not clearly thinking on all sides of the matter. It is not a matter concerning your exclusive opinion or that of somebody else. Marriage is not just a personal affair, it is a social ritual—how can you forget that? You take a little more time and think it over. Don't decide everything in the heat of the moment.'

Saying this Paresh left the room, went out to the garden and began to stroll there.

Lalita too was about to go out. Then she paused a little and turning her back to Binoy said, 'If our wish is not a wrong one, then must we admit defeat and go back with our head hung just because that wish happens to be out of tune with some social custom? I cannot understand the point at all. If there is scope for false conduct in society why is there no scope for reasonable conduct?'

Binoy slowly came up to stand by her side and said, 'I am not afraid of any society. If we two cling to truth together where can one get a better society than that of ours!'

At this point Baradasundari suddenly stormed in and challenged, 'Binoy, I hear you are not taking the initiation?'

Binoy said, 'I shall take my initiation with the right *guru*, not from any samaj.'

Baradasundari flew into a rage and screamed, 'What is the meaning of all this conspiracy and deceit of yours! What drama did you make with your posture of initiation these two days, what fools did you make of me and the entire Brahmo samaj! Didn't it occur to you once how you are ruining Lalita's life!'

Lalita said, 'Don't you know that your Brahmo samaj is not unanimous in welcoming Binoybabu's initiation? Haven't you read the paper? What was the point of seeking such initiation!'

Baradasundari said, 'How can the marriage be held without the initiation?'

Lalita said, 'Why not?'

Baradasundari said, 'Then will it be held the Hindu way?'

Binoy said, 'It can be. I will remove the possible small obstacles that may come up.'

Baradasundari remained dumbfounded for quite some time. Then she said in a choked voice, 'Binoy, go away, you go away please! Please you never come to this house again!'

60

Sucharita was sure that Gora would come today. Since daybreak there was a tremor within her heart. The joy of waiting for his arrival was mingled up with a kind of fear; because Gora had been drawing her towards a particular direction which clashed at every step with the direction that her life had taken since childhood, the roots her life had struck and the twigs and blossoms it had sprouted so far; the conflict made her restless.

Therefore, when Gora bowed before the idol in Masi's room yesterday Sucharita felt as if a knife pierced through her. She could not pacify herself by reasoning thus—well, let Gora bow thus, well let it him follow his belief.

Sucharita feels tremulous in fear when she sees any such thing in Gora's ways which vitally clashed with her religious belief. What a strange ordeal it was into which God had led her!

To set a good example before Sucharita, supposedly proud of her modern approaches, Harimohini took Gora to her room of idols again today, and Gora too again bowed before her idols.

As soon as Gora came down to the drawing room Sucharita asked him, 'Do you respect this idol?'

Gora replied with a bit of forced emphasis, 'Yes, of course, I do.'

At this Sucharita bent down her head and fell silent. Gora was somehow touched by that humble silent sadness. He hastened to add, 'Listen, I shall tell you the truth. I cannot tell you very clearly whether I respect this idol or not; but I must tell you frankly that I admire the devotion of my country. The object which has received the worship of my country for so long becomes necessarily the object of my worship. I cannot denounce that like a Christian missionary by any means.'

Sucharita stared at Gora's face with a preoccupied look. Gora said, 'I know it is very difficult for you to exactly follow what I say. You have been brought up within a small community and as a result the strength to take such things easily has left you. Therefore, you see only a piece of stone in your Masi's room whereas I envision the pathos of your aunt's sad devoted heart. After such knowledge how can I resent, how can I denounce! Do you think that the god dwelling within the heart is but a stone icon!'

Sucharita asked, 'Is it enough to be devoted? Is there no need to consider whom are we offering our devotion?'

Gora got slightly excited, 'That means you think it is a delusion to worship a specific limited object as God! But must we decide about the limits from the perspective of a specific space and time? Suppose you feel devotionally stirred if you remember some particular scriptural quote. Now will you measure the grandeur of that utterance by measuring the length of the page and counting the number of the words? The expanse of emotion is a far greater thing than the expanse of space. That small idol is real infinity to your Masi, much more real than the star-spangled infinite sky. You conceive of the infinite in measurable terms; therefore, you have to close your eyes in order to imagine the infinite; I don't know if you succeed at that. But it is possible to see the infinite who dwells within your own heart as visibly manifested even in a tiny icon. If it was not so, how could your Masi turn thus to her small idol when the last happiness of life was snatched away from her? Is it possible to fill up that terrible chasm in the heart by a mere piece of stone! Without infinite emotion and imagination the void of human heart cannot be filled.'

It was beyond Sucharita to reply to such subtle arguments. But at the same time it was also impossible for her to accept this as the final truth. As a result an inexpressible, irremediable pain continued to wring her mind.

While arguing with an opponent Gora used to have no mercy. Rather, in such matters he indulged in a kind of ruthless ferocity like a preying animal. But today he felt somehow saddened at Sucharita's silent defeat. Softening his voice Gora said, 'I don't want to say a word against your religious belief. I just make this small claim, 'The significance of what you denounce as idol cannot be grasped just by optical perception. Only one whose mind has found an anchorage, whose soul has attained peace, whose character has received a support through this, is in the position to know if that God is just a lump of clay or something living, finite or infinite. I tell you no devotee in our country worships the finite; to touch the infinite through the specific finite icon constitutes the joy of their devotion.'

Sucharita said, 'But everyone is not a devotee.'

Gora said, 'When one is not a devotee what does it matter whom he worships? What does a man without devotion do in Brahmo samaj? All his worship rolls down into a bottomless void. No, it is more dreadful than void; petty squabbles become his God, with his ego performing the priest's role. Haven't you seen this bloodthirsty god's worship in your community?'

Without answering this Sucharita asked Gora pointblank, 'All these things that you are talking about religion—are they attested by your own experience?'

Gora smiled a little, 'I think you are asking if I myself have ever sought God. No, I have never been drawn that way.'

Sucharita was not supposed to be pleased at this admission; still she felt a strange relief. She felt a kind of assurance at the thought that Gora had no right to speak with authority on the subject.

Gora said, 'I make no claim that I can teach religion to anybody. But neither can I stand that you should ridicule the devotion of our countrymen. You are calling the people of your country to tell them, "You are fools, you are idolators." I want to send this message to them all, 'No, you are not fools, not idolators; you are wise, you are the devotees!' There is a nobility in our religion, a profundity in our devotion. Through my reverence I want to awaken the soul of my country to the truth that there is a nobility in our religion, there is a profundity in our devotion. I want to stir my country's pride about that glorious heritage. I won't allow her to bend down her head in shame; I won't let her become blind to her own truth by making her feel ashamed of herself. This is my resolve. Since I saw you a new idea has been haunting me day and night. I did not think of this earlier. I have been thinking, Bharatbarsha will never appear in her full glory if envisioned exclusively by the male. The day she is also manifest before the vision of our women will mark the fullness of her revelation. I long to see my country with you by my side; this longing to see our country together has been consuming me. We the men of India can only labour for her, but without you who will light the lamp to welcome her? Service to the country will remain devoid of beauty so long as you keep away from her.'

Alas, where was this Bharatbarsha! How far away was Sucharita! Then whence came this ascetic votary of Bharatbarsha, this young monk absorbed in his patriotism! Why did he ignore all else and come to take his stand beside her! Why did he particularly call her while remaining oblivious of others! He overthrew all hesitations, ignored all obstacles. He said, 'I can't do without you, I have come to take you out, the noble venture will remain incomplete so long you are kept outside!' Tears rolled down Sucharita's cheeks, she did not know why.

Gora looked straight at her face. Before that gaze Sucharita did not turn away her tearful eyes. Like a dew-drenched unconcerned flower the self-forgetful face blossomed up towards his gaze.

Before those unself-conscious, unhesitant, flooded eyes Gora's entire entity seemed to sway like a stone palace caught in an earthquake. In order to control himself with all his strength Gora turned and looked ouside through the window. It was already evening. At the end of the lane where it met the main road, stars appeared against darkness that was like a black slab of stone covering the sky. The chunk of the sky, the few stars seemed to carry his mind so far adrift—so far from the definitive works and ways of the mundane, familiar, daily world. How far beyond the rise and fall of empires, the aspirations and ambitions of ages, that chunk of sky with its cluster of stars has been waiting in supreme detachment. Yet when a heart—from the depth of its immeasurable mystery—called out to another, then that voiceless longing from that intimate obscure frontier of the world seemed to quiver in that distant sky and pulsate in the scintillation of the remote stars. The traffic and crowd in the busy Calcutta street suddenly became intangible to Gora's perception at this moment. The city noise did not reach his cognition. He looked back at his own heart; that too was like the sky, silent, intimate, dark; and there too two tearful eyes—innocent, sad—seemed to gaze unblinking, since times immemorial towards time infinite.

Gora started at Harimohini's voice and turned back.

'My son, take some sweets before leaving.'

Gora received a jolt, 'Not today, please. I must be excused today. I am leaving right now.'

Saying this he did not wait for a reply and at once shot off in a hurry.

Surprised, Harimohini looked at Sucharita's face. Sucharita went out of the room. Harimohini shook her head, and thought, 'what is this!'

Before long Pareshbabu arrived. Not finding Sucharita in her room he sought out Harimohini, and asked her, 'Where's Radharani?'

Harimohini did not hide her vexation, 'Who knows! So long talk was going on with Gaurbabu in the drawing room. May be strolling alone on the roof top now.'

Paresh was surprised, 'On the roof top? And at such an hour in this cold!'

Harimohini said, 'Let her cool down a little. Cold cannot affect these new age girls.'

As Harimohini was in a nasty mood today she did not call Sucharita for dinner. Sucharita too had lost sense of time today.

Suddenly seeing Pareshbabu himself coming up to the roof top Sucharita felt very much ashamed. She implored, 'Come Baba, let us go down—you may catch cold.'

Coming into the room Sucharita received a jolt as she saw Paresh's worried face in the lamplight. So long he was the father of the fatherless girl, he was the guru; now who was pulling her far away from him snapping all the ties that grew since childhood! Sucharita could not forgive herself by any means. As Paresh sat down tiredly Sucharita stood behind his chair in order to hide the tears that welled up, and slowly ran her fingers through his white hair.

Paresh said, 'Binoy has refused to convert.'

Sucharita did not reply. Paresh said, 'I myself had considerable hesitation regarding his conversion; therefore, I do not quite mind it. But what I gather from Lalita seems to indicate that she does not consider this decision of Binoy against conversion as any bar to their marriage.'

Suddenly Sucharita said with an excessive emphasis, 'Oh no Baba. That cannot be. No, never.'

Normally Sucharita did not express such excessive response about anything. Paresh was, therefore, a little taken aback at this sudden tenor of strong emotion in her voice, and asked, 'What cannot be?'

Sucharita. If Binoybabu refuses to be a Brahmo then what procedure of marriage will be followed?

Paresh replied, 'The Hindu procedure, of course.'

Sucharita shook her head vehemently, 'No, No. What is all this happening! One should not even imagine such things. At last Lalita to be married through idolatrous rituals! This we must not allow.'

Was it because Gora had already taken possession of her mind, that she was expressing such overreaction towards the Hindu form of marriage. The subtext of this remonstration was,—Sucharita was desperately trying to hold on to Paresh, declaring, 'I won't desert you—I still won't allow the snapping of ties with your community, your ideology, your teaching.'

Paresh said, 'Binoy has anyway agreed to do without the idol during the performance of the marriage ritual.'

Sucharita left the backside of his chair and took a seat in front of him. Paresh asked, 'What do you have to say about this?'

After a brief silence Sucharita said, 'Then Lalita will have to leave our society.'

Paresh said, 'I have thought long about this. When there is a clash between an individual and the society, we have to take into account two considerations: on which side lies justice, and who is the stronger? The society is undoubtedly stronger; therefore, the rebel has to suffer. Lalita has repeatedly assured me that she is not only prepared to bear the suffering, but also happy at the prospect. If this is true, and there is no wrong in it, then how can I oppose her?'

Sucharita said, 'But Baba, what'll be the consequences!'

Paresh said, 'I know there will be a crisis. But since there is nothing wrong in the marriage between Binoy and Lalita, and it is even desirable, I think it is my duty not to tow with society in case society objects. It can be never right that individual should curb himself for the society's sake; conversely it is the society which should broaden itself for the sake of the individual. If there are people ready to accept suffering for this, how can I denounce them?'

Sucharita said, 'Baba, I am afraid, you'll have to bear the worst brunt in this matter.'

Paresh said, 'That is not important.'

Sucharita said, 'Baba, have you given your consent?'

Pareshbabu said, 'No, not yet. But I must. Who is there besides me to bless Lalita on the road she has opted for, and who is there besides God to give support?'

After Pareshbabu had left Sucharita sat motionless. She knew how deeply Paresh loved Lalita; now Lalita was about to enter a new domain of uncertainty, abandoning the old familiar track. Sucharita had no difficulty in understanding how worried Paresh was at this; yet he was, at this old age, prepared to go ahead in support of such a radical move, and at the same time there was so little expression of disturbance! He has never made a show of his own strength, yet such an extraordinary courage was residing there, and at such perfect ease.

If it were in the earlier days, this glimpse of Paresh's nature would not have amazed her, as she had seen Paresh since her childhood. But this very day, just a little while ago, Sucharita's mind had borne the onslaught of the powerful impact of Gora's personality. Therefore, she could not but notice the distinct difference of the two personalities. How tremendous Gora's own will was to himself! How could he mesmerize others by applying that indomitable will. Anyone accepting any relationship with Gora had to succumb to his will. Sucharita has succumbed today, has even found joy in that admission, has felt she gained something big by this surrender. Yet when Paresh slowly stepped out of the lamplight of her room into the darkness outside, his head bent in thought, Sucharita could not but compare him specially with the youthful bright Gora. She offered her innermost regards like flowers at Paresh's feet, and sat still for a long time like a picture with her two palms folded on her lap.

61

Since morning there has been a furore in the house. At first Mahim came puffing at his hookah and charged Gora, 'So, Binoy then takes flight at last!'

Failing to understand the meaning Gora looked askance at Mahim. Mahim said, 'What use hiding from us any more? The cat is out of the bag—your friend has now made on the headlines. Don't you hear the drums! Have a look at this.'

Saying this Mahim handed over a copy of a Bengali newspaper to Gora. A pungent abusive essay appeared in the Sunday special on the occasion of Binoy's conversion to Brahmo samaj this morning. The writer has charged in highly derogatory language that when Gora was inside the jail some distinguished member of the Brahmo samaj with a number of marriageable daughters had charmed this weakminded youth by some secret lure and wrenched him off from Hindu society.

When Gora said he did not know this Mahim did not believe him at first, and then he continued to express his amazement again and again at this deep deception of Binoy. He also observed, 'when Binoy began to prevaricate even after agreeing in so many words to marry Shashimukhi, we should have guessed that his ruin was imminent.'

Abinash arrived nearly gasping for breath, 'Gaurmohanbabu, What is this! Who could have imagined this even in dream! Binoybabu at last—'

Abinash could not finish. This harassment of Binoy pleased him so much that he could hardly contain his joy under the pretension of worry.

Within moments most of the major members of Gora's team arrived. Excited discussion and comments continued on the subject. The majority said in one voice,—there was nothing really surprising in the present turn of things, since they had all along noticed symptoms of hesitation and weakness in his behaviour; indeed Binoy had never whole-heartedly surrendered to the team at any point. Many claimed, from the very start Binoy had tried to pass himself off as a peer to Gaurbabu which they ever found unbearable. Whereas the rest of the team maintained the proper distance from Gaurmohanbabu as the diffidence of their devotion demanded, Binoy would unnecessarily make a show of his proximity with Gora as if he were different from others and of the same category as Gora. Furthermore, they claimed, it was because Gora had a fondness for Binoy that they endured his unpardonable audacity, and also such unrestrained audacity was bound to meet such disastrous ends in the long run.

They said, 'We are not educated like Binoybabu; we don't have such an excess of intelligence; however, we have all along followed a principle. We are not hypocrites, saying one thing and holding on to another. It is impossible for us to be one thing today and another tomorrow—you may call us fools or idiots or whatever you like.'

Gora did not add a single word to this noise, and sat still.

As the day advanced and the visitors left one by one, Gora saw Binoy entering the house but without looking into his room he started for upstairs by the adjoining staircase. Gora hastily came out of his room and called, 'Binoy!'

Binoy came down from the stairs and entered Gora's room to hear, 'Binoy, have I wronged you unknowingly that you appear to have abandoned me!'

Binoy had apprehended a showdown with Gora today and toughened his mind accordingly. But when on entering he noticed the sadness of Gora's face, felt an ache of affection in his voice, the resolution that he had forcefully made was shattered.

He said, 'Gora, my brother, please don't misunderstand me. Many changes can take place in one's life, many things may have to be abandoned; but why should I abandon friendship!'

Gora, after remaining silent for a little, said, 'Binoy, have you been led into formally joining the Brahmo samaj?'

Binoy replied, 'No Gora. I have not been a convert and won't be one either. But that is not my point of emphasis.'

Gora asked, 'What's the idea?'

Binoy replied, 'The idea is this; I am no more interested now in making an issue of my conversion or non-conversion to Brahmo religion.'

Gora asked, 'May I ask what were your earlier interests and what are the present ones?'

At this tone of Gora's voice Binoy felt aggressive once again. He said, 'Previously when I used to hear about someone going to embrace Brahmoism I felt particularly angry and wished him some special retribution. But I no more feel like that now. I feel opinion should be countered by opinion, argument should be fought by argument, and it is barbarism to punish a matter of reasoning by anger.'

Gora said, 'So now you don't feel angry at seeing a Hindu converting to Brahmoism; but when you see a Brahmo doing penance and seeking restoration to Hinduism you feel a consuming anger; so this is the difference between your past approach and the present one.'

Binoy said, 'You are speaking this out of anger, not out of reason.'

Gora said, 'With full respect to you I say this is as it should be. I too would have been like that. If embracing or abandoning a religion was just skin-deep like the chameleon changing colours, then it would not matter. But since it is something deeper, a matter of the heart, I cannot take it lightly. If there is no obstacle, if you do not have to pay any punitary tax, why should a man exert all his intelligence on the issue of accepting or converting into a new creed! One must face the test if his acceptance of what he thinks truth is genuine. One must accept the punishment. Matters of truth are not such a dilettante affair that you can buy the jewel without paying the price.

As the debate generated heat restraints disappeared. Comments clashed against comments, arguments attacked arguments and the friction sent flickering splinters all around.

At last after a long debate Binoy stood up and said, 'Gora, there is a basic difference between your nature and mine. So long it was suppressed, whenever it sought to raise head I snubbed it down, because I knew you lacked the aptitude for truce with difference and would run with open sword at the least sign of dissent. Therefore, in order to preserve your friendship I have always curbed my own nature. Today I come to understand that this has not been good and cannot do any good.

Gora said, 'Come out. Tell me what you want to do now.'

Binoy said, 'I have stood alone today. I won't admit by any means that I must appease the demon called society, by human sacrifice daily and move about with its collar round my neck regardless of its being live or dead; I am ready to stake my life for this.'

Gora said, 'Do you plan to take on Bakasur with a toothpick like that Brahmin child in the *Mahābhārata*!'

Binoy said, 'I don't know if the demon will die by my toothpick, but I must refuse to admit his right to gulp me down—not even when he is chewing me up.'

Gora protested, 'You are speaking in allegoric terms; it gets difficult for me to follow.'

Binoy replied, 'It is not difficult for you to follow, but difficult to admit. Although man is born free to live his life, choose his religion, our society has put him in absurd chains at every step. Don't tell me that you don't know this. But you force yourself to submit to this force. I tell you clearly today, I won't submit to any force here. I shall respect the demands of society only so long as society will protect my just demand. If it refuses to respect me as human, and seeks to make a robot of me, I also on my part won't worship it with flowers and sandalwood, and would consider it an iron machine instead.'

Gora said, 'That means, to be precise, you are going to convert into a Brahmo.'

Binoy said, 'No.'

Gora shot pointblank, 'Will you marry Lalita?'

Binoy said, 'Yes.'

Gora asked, 'A Hindu marriage?'

Binoy said, 'Yes.'

Gora. Does Pareshbabu agree to it?

Binoy. Here is his letter.

Gora read the letter twice over. The concluding part of the letter was like this:

'I won't raise the issue of my liking or disliking; nor the question of your advantage or disadvantage in the matter. You know my belief and my society. I think you also know the kind of training that Lalita has received since childhood and the atmosphere in which she has grown up. Knowing all this you have chosen your ways and taken your decision. I have nothing more to say. Don't think I have just given up without a thought or being unable to sort it out. I have tried my best to think over it. So I have come to realize there is no justified ground in the eye of God to oppose your union, because I have complete trust and regard for you. Now if the society opposes it is not compulsive for you to submit to that opposition. I just want to tell you this much—if you want to transgress the society then you must be greater than the society. Let your love, your united life herald not only destructive rebelliousness, but also contain the seeds of creation and stability. It is not enough to prove your daring through just this one act. After this you have to be consistently heroic in all your acts; otherwise it will boomerang on you. Since the society will not give you support from outside like the average people, you have to be taller than this average by means of your own strength; if you fail you'll be pushed down below the average. I have deep anxiety regarding your future and well-being. But I have no right to stop you with this anxiety; because it is those who dare to take on new challenges by experimenting with their own life, that contribute to the ennobling of the society. Those who just obey rules, can merely carry on the system, they do not help it to forge ahead. Therefore, I won't obstruct your path with my apprehensions or anxieties. You carry on against all odds what you have found to be right; may God help you. God does not keep his creation enchained at one particular point; he keeps them everawake, ever-renewing through perpetual changes and evolution. As harbingers of that message of God, you are about to embark on a hazardous journey using your own life as a torch aflame; let the guide of the world show you the way. I won't issue stricture that you must follow my way ever and anon. At your age we too had cut off anchor and sailed out in the face of imminent storm, without listening to any warning. I have no remorse for that either. Even if there was reason for repentance, how does it matter! Man can make mistakes, may fail, may even suffer, but shouldn't sit idle; let him commit himself to what he thinks right; it is thus that the stream of society will continue to flow on and thereby remain pure. Occasionally the current can assault the bank, break a chunk off it, but stopping the current altogether for that fear will amount to inviting pestilence; I have no doubt about this. Therefore, I respectfully bow to the deity who has been irresistibly drawing you beyond the happiness and comfort of approved social custom, and I hand over the two of you in his hands; let him lead your life to fulfillment through all abuses, blames, and separation from near ones. It is He who has invited you to a difficult journey; and it is He who will lead you to the right destination.'

After reading the letter Gora fell silent for a while. Then Binoy said, 'As Pareshbabu has given consent from his end, you too must give consent from your side.'

Gora replied, 'Pareshbabu may give his approval, because the current that has been eating the banks, comes from their direction. I cannot approve, since our current is meant to preserve the shoreline. There are so many monuments of achievement on this side of the river,—standing through centuries and millennia; I cannot say let nature do her work here as a matter of course. We shall instead try to protect the banks with rocks—blame or praise as you like. This is our holy ancient mansion. It is not our desire that layer upon layer of sediment from the riverbed should accumulate on it with every passing year, and peasants will plough it for crop. Let us lose the harvest. This is for our inhabiting, not for cultivating. Therefore, when from your agriculture department you denounce our rocks as tough, we don't really feel greatly ashamed.'

Binoy said, 'That means, to be precise, you won't accept our marriage.'

Gora said, 'Certainly not.'

Binoy said, 'And—.'

Gora said, 'And I shall boycott you.'

Binoy said, 'Suppose I had been a Muslim friend of yours!'

Gora said, 'That's another thing. If a branch of the tree breaks down and becomes separate, then the tree can never restore it back to its earlier position; but the creeper that approaches it from the outside may be sheltered by the tree; even if it is snapped by storm it can be again embraced by the tree. But when your own kin becomes an outsider there remains no other choice but complete desertion. That's the reason behind so many strictures, such desperate tension and strain.'

Binoy said, 'But that's the reason why the cause of desertion should not have been so trifling, nor the rules of desertion so easily applicable. It is true that a snapped arm cannot be restored; but for that very reason an arm is not easily snapped. Its bones are quite strong. When in a society the slightest blow leads to separation, and that separation is perennial, how uncongenial that society must be for man's free movement or action! Won't you give a thought to it?'

Gora said, 'That's not my responsibility. The society thinks, and thinks on such a colossal scale from such a big premise that I don't even perceive that it thinks. It has thought over millennia and survived—I place my trust here. Just as I do not bother myself with the thought if the earth was revolving round the sun slantingly or vertically, and have lost nothing for my unconcern. That is my approach to my society as well.'

Binoy smiled, 'Gora dear, I too used to prattle just these things just this way—I didn't imagine this will be turned back on me today. I guess I will have to bear the punishment for having spoken parrot-like without conviction in the past. Anyway, it's no use arguing; because I have encountered a truth from very close quarters, which I had not noticed earlier. I have perceived that the course of a human life is like the course of a great river; it can take new unexpected turns in amazingly new directions which were never imagined before—this is the beauty of its onward movement. This unpredictable pace and direction is God's will—it is not a man-made canal, to flow along prescribed route. Since this revelation manifested itself before me I cannot be deluded any more by any flourish of artificial oratory.'

Gora said, 'The moth dancing towards death also argues exactly like you; therefore I won't waste my energy to make you see things.'

Binoy got up from the chair saying, 'That's better. Bye then—but I must see *Mā* once before I leave.'

After Binoy had left Mahim slowly entered the room.

While chewing his betel-leaf, Mahim commented, 'I am afraid you could not cut much ice. Not likely either. Had I not been warning you for a long time, "Take care; symptoms are bad." But you did not care. If we could somehow manage the marriage between him and Shashimukhi at the right time there would have been no problem today. But who warns whom? And who is to listen? Once you got adamant who can make you see things! Now a youth of Binoy's stature deserts your team. Is it a small loss!'

Gora did not reply. Mahim continued, 'So you could not bring him back? Well, let it be. But the proposal regarding Shashimukhi's marriage with Binoy has already received a degree of publicity. Therefore, it is better not to delay it any more. You know very well the kind of society we live in; if they get someone trapped in a vulnerable position they will harass the poor thing to no end. So a suitable boy—oh, no no, you don't worry, you needn't act the matchmaker. That part I have managed myself.'

Gora asked, 'Who is the boy?'

Mahim replied, 'Your Abinash.'

Gora asked, 'Has he agreed?'

Mahim. 'Hasn't he! Is it your Binoy! Indeed, whatever you may say, it appears that this Abinash, among all your followers, is really loyal to you. He jumped at the prospect of tying a knot with someone of your family. He said, "It is my privilege, it is my pride." When I asked him about the financial matters he pressed his palms upon his ears and implored, "Excuse me; please don't mention these matters to me at all." I said, "O.K. Those matters will be settled with your father." I also met his father. The father and son seem to be worlds apart. The father did not shut his ears at all to money-matters; instead he waxed so eloquent on the issue that I had better shut my ear drums. The son too, I found to my consternation, is quite devoted to the father in such matters,—altogether '*pitā he paraman tapa*' syndrome. So it's no use expecting him to mediate on our behalf. This time there seems to be no other way than encashing the Company papers. Anyway, you too tell Abinash one or two things. If he gets encouragement from you—.'

Gora said, 'That won't slash the dowry amount, I'm afraid.'

Mahim said, 'Don't I know that! When filial loyalty becomes materially useful then it gets too tough to resist.'

Gora asked, 'Is it final?'

Mahim. Yes.

Gora. The date and time, etc.?

Mahim. Of course. It is the coming full moon of Magh. There is not much time. The father says, diamond or gems can be sacrificed; but the gold must be solid. Now I have to consult the goldsmith about how to make weighty gold ornaments without burning holes into the purse.

Gora said, 'But what is the great hurry? It is not likely that Abinash will join the Brahmo samaj very soon.'

Mahim said, 'That's true. But perhaps you have not noticed Baba has of late become very weak. He is adding up to his rituals proportionately to the doctors' warning against them.

The monk that has recently lined up with him, has been making him bathe thrice a day, and in addition has started making him practice a form of yoga that is likely to turn his iris, eyebrows, breathing, pulsation, etc. completely topsy-turvy. It is desirable that Shashi is married off before something happens to Baba. If I can have it over before Baba's pension-savings are swindled by his Omkarananda Swamy, then I wont have to worry much. In fact I had broached the matter with Baba yesterday. But I realized it won't be as easy as I presumed. I am contemplating to serve a good dose of *gānjā* for a few days to that scoundrel of a Swamy so that it can be managed through the very same scoundrel. You may rest assured that Baba's savings will come to no avail for the householders who need money most. The crux of my problem is that whereas others' father would screw me for money, my own father—at the very mention of money—starts the yogic exercise of *prāṇāyam*. So I have little choice. Must I tie my daughter of eleven to my neck and drown myself?'

62

Harimohini asked, 'Radharani, why didn't you eat anything last night?'

Sucharita was surprised, 'Didn't I? I think I did.'

Harimohini pointed at the untouched plate, 'Indeed! What is it then?'

Then Sucharita realized that she had forgotten her meal last night.

Harimohini said dryly, 'These are not good symptoms, I must say. I don't think your Pareshbabu,—at least as far as I know him—would approve of such excesses. Seeing him one feels becalmed. Just consider what he might think if he came to know your ways these days.'

Sucharita was left in no doubt about the implication of Harimohini's solicitation. Initially she felt a slight shrinking in her mind. She had never imagined that her relationship with Gora could be perceived as just another average man-woman relationship and be target of such vulgar hints. So her first reaction was a slight diffidence at this taunt from Harimohini. But the very next moment she pushed away the work in her hand and sat up straight to look at Harimohini full in the face. She decided instantly not to fight shy in the least about Gora and said, 'Masi, you know Gaurmohanbabu came yesterday. Our discussion kept me so preoccupied afterwards that I forgot my dinner. If you were present you could have heard about a lot of things.'

The kind of speech that could please Harimohini was not exactly the kind delivered by Gora. She longed to hear about devotion. Devotion did not sound that simple and delightful on the lips of Gora. Gora seemed to be engaged in perpetual fight with some imaginary opponent! He was bent on bringing round the dissenter; but what did he have to deliver to one who had already conformed! Harimohini was indifferent to what excited Gora. She had no genuine grievance at the members of the Brahmo samaj keeping apart from the Hindu society and leading an exclusive life. It was sufficient for her if there was no rupture with her dear ones. Therefore, she did not at all enjoy Gora's talks. Furthermore, when Harimohini came to feel that Gora had won over Sucharita's heart, she found the youth even more distasteful. Sucharita enjoyed complete financial independence, and was a distinct individual in her thoughts, beliefs and ways. So it was beyond Harimohini to establish a total control over the girl. Yet Sucharita was her only prop at this last leg of her life's trudge; therefore any other influence on Sucharita—excepting that of Pareshbabu—made Harimohini feel quite nervy. She began to imagine that Gora was actually a pretender whose real target was to somehow attract Sucharita and grab her property. She decided that Gora was her principal enemy and resolved to herself that she must resist the enemy.

Gora had no appointment with Sucharita today, nor there was any reason for meeting her. But the element of hesitation was next to none in Gora's make-up. When he set himself to some job there was no scope for dribbling; his mind moved along a single track, and went straight to the target like an arrow.

When Gora reached Sucharita's room in the morning Harimohini was at her prayers. Sucharita was neatly arranging the books and papers on the drawing room table when Satish ran in to announce Gaurbabu's arrival. Sucharita was not much surprised; it seemed she had been expecting him to come today.

Taking the chair Gora said, 'At last Binoy has deserted us.'

Sucharita remonstrated, 'Why call it desertion? He hasn't joined the Brahmo samaj.'

Gora said, 'He would have remained closer to us if he really joined the Brahmo samaj. Because he is clinging to the Hindu society it'll be afflicted all the more. It would have been better had he completely abandoned our society.'

Sucharita felt deeply hurt. She said, 'Why do you take the society so intently? You repose such an enormous trust on society; is it spontaneous on your part, or do you force yourself considerably towards this?'

Gora said, 'This forcing itself is a natural act in the present situation. When the ground shakes beneath your feet you have to plant every step with additional force and care. Because of the opposition all around, our speech and action seem to manifest a degree of excess. But that cannot be called unnatural.'

Sucharita said, 'Why do you take this opposition as wholly unjustified or unnecessary? If a society tries to obstruct the process of time, it must receive assaults.'

Gora said, 'The process of time is like tide; it undermines the shore. But I don't think it is the shore's duty to surrender to the breaking process. Please don't assume that I do not notice the difference between good and bad things of the society. Such a judgment is so easy that even a small boy of sixteen can take the seat of the judge. But what is difficult is to perceive reverentially a thing in its totality.'

Sucharita contested, 'But is reverence enough for ensuring truth? Can't we accept untruth as well if led by blind reverence? If I can ask you—can we accept idolatry too with reverence? Would you accept this as truth?'

After a brief silence Gora replied, 'I shall try to tell you my exact feeling. I have accepted these as truth from the very start.

I didn't dismiss them in haste just because they seemed to clash with the European approach, and one could employ some very cheap arguments against them. Personally I have no special religious pursuit. But I cannot unthinkingly smatter such cliché as the identicality of icon worship and idolatry, or that there is no superb manifestation of devotion in icon worship, etc. Since imagination has its scope in art and literature, even in science and historiography, why should I emphatically denounce its place in religion? All the attributes of man find their superb expression in religion. The reconciliation of wisdom, devotion and imagination that has found manifestation in the icon worship of our country has made our religion a more complete truth than it has been in other countries; don't you think so?'

Sucharita said, 'But idol worship was there in Greece and Rome as well.'

Gora said, 'Their idols involved an imagination which was oriented more in aesthetics than in wisdom and devotion. In our country imagination has been deeply embedded in wisdom and devotion. Our Krishna-Radha or Hara-Parvati are not just historical objects of worship; they manifest man's eternal spiritual wisdom. That is why the devotion of Ramprasad or Chaitanyadev had found expression through their attachment to such idols. When did we ever see such profound expression of devotion in the history of Greece or Rome?'

Sucharita asked, 'Won't you accept any change of society corresponding to changing times?'

Gora replied, 'Why not! But change and madness are not the same thing. Man's change should follow the human way. The child eventually changes into an old man. But a man cannot suddenly change into a cat or a dog. India's change must come by the Indian way; a sudden mimicry of the British history may nullify and ruin it all the way. An enormous reserve of accumulated strength and resources lie stored within the country; I have dedicated my life to propagate this message to you all. Do you get me?'

Sucharita said, 'I think so. But I have never heard or thought of such things. When one arrives at an unfamiliar place it takes time to know even an obvious thing. I have that kind of feeling. Perhaps because I am a woman I cannot get the adequate conviction of feeling.'

Gora said, 'Never. I know many men; I have been discussing these ideas with them for a long time. They are sure that they have understood everything whereas I am sure that not a single one among them has attained a fraction of the vision you have glimpsed. The first time I saw you I felt you had this profound perceptivity. That's why I have come to you with all the accumulated thoughts and feelings of my heart, I have spread my whole life out before you without any hesitation.'

Sucharita said, 'When you speak like this I feel a strange turbulence in my mind. What are your expectations from me, how far I can meet them, what is my duty, how should this new emotion surging within me get expressed—I cannot make out anything. Then I feel anxious lest all this trust of yours reposed on me proves illusory to you.'

Gora said in a voice like the rumbling cloud, 'It is no illusion. I shall show you what great strength you carry within yourself. Forget all anxiety—it is my responsibility to bring out that ability within you, depend on me.'

Sucharita did not utter a word; but the silence was sufficiently eloquent to denote her unreserved acquiescence to the dependence. Gora too remained silent. For a long time there was no sound in the room. Outside in the lane the vendor, hawking old crockery, passed by sending his resonant call through the door.

After finishing her worship and rituals Harimohini was set for the kitchen. She did not guess the presence of any one in the silent room. But when suddenly looking into the room she noticed Sucharita and Gora immersed in silence, without even exchanging social niceties, a flame of anger seemed to flash through her like lightning. Controlling herself she came back to the door and called, 'Radharani!'

When Sucharita went up to her she said in low voice, 'It is the eleventh day of the moon, my fasting day. I am not very well too. You please go to the kitchen and light the oven. In the meantime let me have a word or two with Gaurbabu.'

Sucharita left for the kitchen but with some anxiety at seeing Masi's expression. As Harimohini stepped into the room Gora touched her feet. She sat down on the chair without returning the greeting. After maintaining tight-lipped silence for a time she charged, 'I think you are not a Brahmo.'

Gora said, 'No.'

Harimohini asked, 'I hope you respect our Hindu society.'

Gora replied, 'Of course!'

Harimohini came out, 'Then how come that you behave thus!'

Gora could not get the point of her accusation and looked askance at her face.

Harimohini said, 'Radharani has grown up. You are not her relative. Then why should you have to talk to her so much! She is a woman; she should do domestic chores; why should she listen to such talks at all? This can distract her mind. You are supposed to be a knowledgeable person—all the country applauds you—but can you tell me if this kind of thing was ever in vogue in our country or approved by any scripture!'

Gora suddenly received a big jolt. He had never thought that such abuse could be hurled at Sucharita from any quarter. After a brief silence he said, 'She is in the Brahmo samaj; I have all along seen her freely interacting with people; so it did not occur to me.'

Harimohini argued, 'Well, I accept she hails from the Brahmo samaj; but I don't think you at least approve such views. Listening to you so many people are getting restored to their senses! If you, of all persons, behave like this how can people respect you! For instance, you talked with her till night yesterday, and still your discussion was not finished, you appear again this morning! Since morning she neither went to the store, nor to the kitchen; it did not even occur to her that on this eleventh day of the moon she should assist me a little. What kind of training is this, I don't understand! You too have womenfolk in your home; are you giving them this kind of training to neglect all other duties, or would you appreciate another doing so to them?'

Gora on his part had nothing to answer. He only murmured, 'Because she has grown up this way I did not consider it odd in her case.'

Harimohini said, 'She may have grown up in any manner; but so long as she is with me or I am alive I won't allow this sort of thing. I have brought her round to some extent. When she was at Pareshbabu's house there was quite a rumour that she has become a Hindu under my influence. But after shifting to this house, I don't know what went on between your Binoy and her, and again she reverted to the old form. Anyway, he is going to marry into a Brahmo family; I have pushed Binoy out with great difficulty. Then another man, called Haranbabu, used to call. Whenever he came I called Radharani upstairs; he could not make much inroad. Thus after much painful experience she seems to have come back to her senses again. After settling in the new house she had started taking food and drink from all castes. Yesterday I saw she had stopped that practice; I saw her again self-serving her meal and forbidding the bearer too to bring the drinking water. Now son, this is my earnest entreaty to you, please don't spoil her again. I have lost all my near ones in this world excepting her; she too has none else to call exactly her own. Please leave her alone. Aren't there a lot of big girls in their family? There's Labanya, there's Leela; they too are intelligent; they too have been educated. If you want to talk with girls why don't you go to them and talk to your heart's content; nobody will raise a brow there.'

Gora was stunned. After a brief lull Harimohini started again, 'Just consider. She too should settle down in domestic life. Already she is quite old for that. Do you suggest that she should remain a spinster like this for the rest of her life? Don't you think domesticity essential for women?'

Theoretically Gora had no objection to this; indeed he subscribed to identical views about the matter. But he had never applied that angle to Sucharita's case. He could not imagine the prospect of Sucharita being confined within some mundane household, doing the round of daily domestic chores. He seemed to take it for granted that Sucharita would remain perpetually as she is today.

Gora asked, 'Do you have any plans regarding your niece's marriage?'

Harimohini replied, 'I must. Who else is there to worry for her?'

Gora asked again, 'Can she be married into the Hindu society?'

Harimohini said, 'I have to pursue the matter. If she gives no further trouble, and cooperates, I hope I shall pass her off. I have planned everything, but could not dare to proceed in view of her adamant ways. Recently I find her mellowing again, so I feel hopeful.'

Gora thought he should not ask anything more about the matter, but could not restrain from asking nevertheless, 'Have you decided about the prospective bridegroom?'

Harimohini assured, 'Certainly. He is a quite suitable groom,—my brother-in-law, Kailash. His wife expired some time ago. He has been waiting so long because he did not find a suitable big girl of his choice; otherwise such a boy does not have to wait. He will be a fine match for Radharani.'

The more Gora suffered tormenting pricks of a poisoned needle the more he queried about Kailash.

Among all the brothers-in-law of Harimohini Kailash was the only one who had received a little education. How far did he study? Harimohini had no idea. Anyway, he enjoyed the reputation of being the only 'scholar' in the family. When there was an occasion for submitting a petition against the postmaster of the village, it was Kailash who had drafted it in such classy English that some big officer of the department came down in person to inquire into the matter. At this the entire village was impressed by Kailash's amazing skill. Furthermore, in spite of all this education Kailash's faithful adherence to rites and rituals remained intact.

After the life and career of Kailash was narrated, Gora got up, touched Harimohini's feet and left without a word.

As Gora was climbing down the stairs to the courtyard, at the other end of the same yard Sucharita was engaged in cooking. Hearing his steps she came out at the door. But Gora bolted out without lifting his eyes. Sucharita sighed and resumed her cooking.

At the turn of the lane Gora stumbled across Haranbabu. With a mild grin Haranbabu said, 'So early today!'

Gora did not respond. Haranbabu grinned again, 'I think you had been there! Is Sucharita at home?'

Gora just said, 'Yes', and immediately disappeared with long strides.

On entering the house Haranbabu at once spotted Sucharita through the open door of the kitchen. She had no chance to escape; Masi too was not around.

Haranbabu shot his query, 'Just met Gaurmohanbabu. May I assume he was here so long?'

Without replying Sucharita suddenly became busy with her kitchen pots and pans, as if she were too busy to spare a second for him. But Haranbabu was not the man to give up so easily. Taking position in the yard outside the kitchen he started his sermon. Harimohini came down at the staircase, and politely coughed a few times, though without avail. Harimohini could have appeared before Haranbabu; but she had a hunch that once she appeared before him, neither she nor Sucharita will have any chance to escape the irrespressible enthusiasm of this enterprising youth in this house. Therefore, as soon she spotted even the shadow of Haranbabu she used to draw the end of her sari very low over her forehead, indeed so low as might be considered excessive even for the new bride of her times.

Haranbabu sermonized, 'Sucharita, do you know whither are you going? *Quo vadis*? Where will you land at the end? I hope you have heard that Lalita will marry Binoybabu in the Hindu style. Do you know who is responsible for this?'

Getting no reply from her Haranbabu said in low voice with added solemnity, 'It is you.'

Haranbabu had assumed that Sucharita would not be able to bear the brunt of such a terrible allegation. But she continued her work without a word. At seeing this he put in another dose of solemnity into his voice and, while shaking his outstretched forefinger at her, said, 'Sucharita, I say again, you are the culprit. Can you place your right hand on your heart and claim that you should not be accountable for this to the whole Brahma community?'

Sucharita silently poured some oil onto the pan and it crackled on the fire.

Haran went on, 'It was you who had introduced Binoybabu and Gaurmohanbabu into the family, and pampered them so far that today they are closer and more important to you than all the respectable friends in your Brahmo samaj. And don't you see the results? Didn't I warn you from the very beginning again and again? What is the situation today? Who will restrain Lalita? Do you assume the tide is over with Lalita! No, not at all. I have come today to admonish you. It is now your turn. I am sure you are repenting for Lalita's catastrophe; but that day is not far when you too will slide down to the abyss and won't feel the slightest sting of remorse at your own fall. But Sucharita, there is still time to turn back. Just recall once, with what noble hope we had come together, how glaring was our sense of duty, how expansive was our vision of the prospects of Brahmo samaj—what great resolves we had, and how we had accumulated means towards realizing them day by day. Is it all lost? Never. That domain of our hope is still waiting ready for us. Just look back and behold. Come back once more to the fold.'

The sermon was synchronized with the sizzling sound of a good quantity of vegetables being fried in hot oil, to which Sucharita was delivering the appropriate push and shove with a long ladle. When Haranbabu stopped to ascertain the response of his call, Sucharita lifted the pan off the oven, placed it on the floor, and then turning her face said firmly, 'I am Hindu.'

Haranbabu was completely stumped, 'You Hindu!'

Sucharita repeated, 'Yes, I am Hindu.'

Saying this she again put back the pot on the oven and resumed her ladle operation.

Haranbabu took a few seconds to absorb the shock and then cried out in shrill voice, 'Oh, that explains Gaurbabu's visits here day in and day out; I think he has been initiating you regularly, morning and evening.'

Without turning her face Sucharita said, 'Yes. I have been initiated by him. He is my guru.'

There was a time when Haranbabu was certain that he was Sucharita's guru. Perhaps he would not have been hurt so much if Sucharita admitted her love for Gora. But that Gora had appropriated Haran's rights as guru seemed to wound him like a piercing shaft.

He said, 'Your guru may be a big guy—but do you hope the Hindu society will ever accept you?'

Sucharita said, 'I am not bothered about that, not about society, I know only this much that I am Hindu.'

Haranbabu said, 'Do you know that just because you have remained unmarried so long you are an outcaste in their perception?'

Sucharita replied, 'Please don't worry yourself unnecessarily over this. But I tell you again, I am Hindu.'

Haranbabu said, 'So you surrender even the religious training you received from Pareshbabu at the feet of your new guru!'

Sucharita said, 'My God knows about my religion; I don't want to discuss it with any one. But for your information I say again, I am Hindu.'

Haranbabu lost all control and cried out impatiently, 'However ardently you may embrace Hinduism it will bring you no benefit—this is my last warning to you. Don't take your Gaurmohanbabu for another Binoybabu. You may cry yourself hoarse,—I am Hindu, I am Hindu—but don't expect Gaurbabu to accept you socially. It is easy to enjoy the privilege of guru over the disciple, but don't take this as guarantee that he will receive you in his family and happily settle down in conjugal life.'

Sucharita forgot her cooking and instantly turned upon him like the flash of a lighting, 'What did you say!'

Haranbabu said, 'I am saying just this much that Gaurmohanbabu will never marry you.'

Sucharita's eyes flashed anger, 'Marriage! Didn't I tell you he is my guru?'

Haranbabu said, 'Yes, of course you have said so. But we can also guess what you have not spoken in so many words.'

Sucharita said, 'Please get out. Don't insult me. And please remember from this morning onward I shall never come out in your presence.'

Haranbau said, 'Of course. How can you, indeed! You are now a Hindu lady—not to be seen by the sun! So Pareshbabu's cup of sin now touches the brim! Let the old man bear the punishment for his sin—we take our hands off.'

Sucharita closed the kitchen door with a bang, and squatting down on the floor desperately tried to stop the sound of her crying by covering her mouth with the sari end. Haranbabu went out gloomily.

Harimohini had attentively listened to the entire dialogue. What she overheard today was beyond her wildest dream. She puffed up in pride and said to herself, 'Why not! Didn't I worship my God with all attention; should it all go in vain!'

Immediately she ran upstairs to her puja room and throwing herself full length on the floor thanked her God; also promised to increase the quantity of offerings from that day. So long her puja was quiet as it was a consolation in her bereavement. Now, at the prospect of selfish interests, it became at once very pungent, hot, and hungry.

63

Gora had never expressed himself to any one as he unfolded before Sucharita. So long he had drawn out from himself only comments, opinions, instructions for the consumption of his audience. This was the first time that he drew out his own hidden self. The joy of this self-expression pervaded all his ideas and resolves not only with strength but also with a unique jouissance. A beautiful radiance seemed to embrace and encircle his life. The gods, as it were, blessed his pursuit with shower of ambrose.

Carried along on the crest of this joy Gora had been coming to Sucharita everyday recently, but at Harimohini's comments suddenly he recalled how he had scolded and ridiculed Binoy like anything for similar infatuation. Today, discovering himself in the same position without being aware of this before, Gora was startled. As a man, fallen asleep in some wrong place, without proper cover, suddenly jerks himself up at a jolt, Gora tried to whip himself into consciousness. All along Gora preached the message that although many prosperous races in the world have been completely effaced, India alone survived the onslaught of centuries by means of its restraint. Gora wanted no relaxation of that restraint. Gora said, Bharatbarsha was robbed of everything, but hid its life force behind this cuirass of restraint in such a way that no oppressive power could wound it. So long as we are under alien rule we have to firmly obey our strictures. This is not the time to discriminate between the good and bad rules. The person pulled away by a tide grasps whatever he can lay hold on; he does not care if that is beautiful or ugly. This had been his consistent stand. Today when Harimohini criticized his conduct it was like pricking the great elephant with the nailed rod.

When Gora reached home Mahim, sitting barebodied on a roadside bench in front of the door, was smoking tobacco. His office was closed today. Seeing Gora enter he too followed him and called out, 'Gora, come here, I have something to tell you.'

Taking Gora to his own room, Mahim said, 'Brother, please don't take it otherwise. I wanted to ascertain if you too have caught the infection from Binoy. It appears that you are visiting that zone rather too regularly!'

Gora's face reddened. He said, 'Rest assured.'

Mahim said, 'You can never be sure in view of the kind of trend that comes to prevail. Perhaps you assume it is but an eatable thing; you would just gulp it down and return home. But that it has hooks hidden inside you can guess very well from your friend's debacle. Aha, what's the great hurry for leaving! I am yet to come to the point. I come to hear that Binoy's marriage with a Brahmo girl has been finalized. But after that we must not keep any contact with him. I tell you this in advance.'

Gora said, 'Of course, we must not.'

Mahim said, 'But if *Mā* creates trouble that should be very unfortunate. We are ordinary familymen. It is sufficient ordeal to marry off a daughter; in addition to it if you install a second Brahmo samaj inside the house, then I shall be forced to seek another shelter.'

Gora said emphatically, 'That will never happen.'

Mahim said, 'The proposal of Shashi's marriage is about to take a final shape. Our *Behai* will have gold no less in weight than our small girl, because he knows human beings are fragile things while gold lasts better. He is more interested in the diet that is to be taken with medicine than the medicine itself. Calling him *Behai* is but belittling him; he is quite a '*Behāyā*'. I have learnt a lot from the guy—though at some cost to myself—anyway, this will come to good use when my son gets married. I was really tempted to be reborn and get married once again according to the custom, and utilize my potential as a male in this society to the fullest extent through my father. Indeed this is male valour—to maul the bride's father so as to make him eat the dust. Is it easy! Whatever you may say, I can't find the enthusiasm to join your chorus in plauding the Hindu society day and night—my voice is enfeebled,—nay lost altogether. My Tinkode is just fourteen months old—my helpmeet has taken long to correct her initial mistake of delivering a female child. Anyway, Gora, you and your followers please keep the Hindu society alive till

Tinkode's marriage; thereafter let the countrymen go the Muslim way or opt for Christianity as they like, I won't mind.'

As Gora stood up Mahim said, 'Yes, what I had come to say—you must not invite Binoy to Shashi's wedding ceremony. It won't do if you stir up a storm over the issue at the last hour. Please warn *Mā* in time.'

Coming to his mother's room Gora saw Anandamoyee sitting on the floor, with spectacles on, and making some sort of list on a writing pad. Seeing Gora she took off her specs, closed the pad and called, 'Come, sit here.'

After Gora sat down Anandamoyee said, 'I have some discussion with you. I think you know about Binoy's marriage?'

Gora remained silent. Anandamoyee said, 'Binoy's uncle is adamant; none of his family will come. On the other side, it is doubtful if the marriage can be arranged at Pareshbabu's residence either. Binoy has to arrange all by himself. So I have a suggestion. The ground floor of the northern part of our house is let out; the tenant on the first floor too has vacated; so if we can arrange for Binoy's marriage in that portion of the first floor that should be convenient.'

Gora asked, 'How should it be convenient?'

Anandamoyee said, 'If I am not there who will look after the whole thing? The poor boy will be in great trouble. If the marriage is held there I can organize everything from this house, without any problem.'

Gora put his foot down, 'You cannot do that *Mā*!'

Anandamoyee asked, 'Why not? I have got your father's consent.'

Gora repeated, 'No, *Mā*, this marriage cannot be held here—I say this, please listen to me.'

Anandamoyee said, 'But why! Binoy is not marrying according to their custom.'

Gora said, 'That's subtle argument. You cannot cheat the society. Let Binoy do whatever he likes, we cannot accept this marriage. There is no dearth of houses in this city. Doesn't he have his own house?'

That there was no dearth of houses was not unknown to Anandamoyee. But she was pained at the thought that Binoy, completely deserted by friends and relatives, will have to somehow perform the marriage rites at his own apartment. That is why she had decided to hold the ceremony at that portion of the house which was kept separate for tenants. This could give her the satisfaction of organising the auspicious ceremony in her own house, without coming into clash with society.

At the firm objection of Gora she sighed and said, 'O.K. since you are so much against it, I shall have to requisition some other house, though that will be great strain upon me. Anyway, since this cannot be, there is no use lamenting.'

Gora said, '*Mā*, you must not join this ceremony.'

Anandamoyee said, 'What do you say, Gora? How can you? If I do not join our Binoy's marriage ceremony who else will!'

Gora insisted, 'No *Mā*, you must not by any means!'

Anandamoyee said, 'Gora, you may differ from Binoy in matters of opinions; but must that make you behave with him like an enemy?'

Gora got a little excited, '*Mā*, this is unfair. You know how it hurts me that I cannot join the marriage feast of Binoy with gay abandon. You know at least, if none else, how much I love Binoy. But *Mā*, this is not the question of love; neither friendship nor hostility figures here. Binoy has taken the plunge knowing fully well the consequences. We have not deserted him; rather it is he who deserted us. So the separation that is imminent now must not affect him as something beyond his anticipation.'

Anandamoyee said, 'Gora, it is true that Binoy knows you will not be associated with this marriage in any form. But he also knows it for certain that I cannot desert him on this auspicious occasion by any means. If Binoy felt I would not receive his bride with my hearty blessings he would have never taken the step. I am more than sure of this. Don't I know his mind!'

Saying this Anandamoyee quickly wiped off a drop of tear. The deep sadness about Binoy that Gora kept carefully suppressed stirred up at this. Still he said, '*Mā*, you live in the society, and you are indebted to society; please don't forget this.'

Anandamoyee said, 'Gora, I have told you time and again that my ties with the society were snapped a long time ago. Society despises me for that; I too keep apart from society.'

Gora said, '*Mā*, I am most deeply hurt when you speak like this.'

Anandamoyee seemed to touch Gora's whole body with the tearful, soft look of her eyes before she said, 'My son, God knows I do not have the ability to save you from this hurt.'

Gora stood up and said, 'Then let me tell you what I have to do. I am going to Binoy; I shall ask him not to involve you in the matters relating to his marriage and thereby contribute to a further widening of the gulf separating you from the rest of the society; I shall tell him this should be considered very selfish and unfair on his part.'

Anandamoyee smiled, 'Well, do what you can—tell him what you like, and leave the rest to me.'

After Gora's departure Anandamoyee thought for a long time. Then she got up slowly and proceeded towards the suite of her husband.

It was the eleventh day of the moon. So there was no cooking today which he did himself. He had found a new Bengali version of *Gherandasamhitā*. Sitting on a piece of deer-skin he had been reading it.

Seeing Anandamoyee he was surprised and uneasy. Anandamoyee sat at the doorstep keeping quite a good space between them and said, 'Look here, a great wrong is being done.'

Krishnadayal had slipped out of the mundane worldly concerns of right and wrong. So he asked indifferently, 'What wrong?'

Anandamoyee said, 'We should not keep Gora in the dark any more, not for another day. Things are increasingly getting out of control.'

Krishnadayal had a similar feeling the day Gora had mentioned his plan to go in for a *Prāyaśchitta* or cleansing rite; but eventually he had become preoccupied with his own meditation, yoga and various rites and did not have the time to rethink.

Anandamoyee said, 'Negotiations for Shashimukhi's marriage are going on; possibly it will take place in the coming spring. In the past, on every occasion of social rites and feasts in the house I used to, under this or that excuse, leave along with Gora for some other place. No such big event in fact took place in the recent past. But what shall we do with him this time during Shashi's marriage? Wrong has been piling up every day; I have been praying to God, every morning, every evening, for forgiving; for dealing all His punishment to me alone. But I have the fear—perhaps it cannot be resisted any more, perhaps some trouble will stir up about Gora. Please permit me now at last,—I am ready to face the consequence—to disclose everything to him.'

Oh, what was this impediment sent out by Indradev, the lord of gods, in order to ruin Krishnadayal's spiritual pursuit, his absorbed meditation! The pursuit too had become very intense and intricate these days; he was taking training in some very difficult breathing exercise; the intake of food too had been reduced to such a level that it seemed the gap between stomach and back would disappear before long as envisioned. Now what annoying disturbance at this juncture!

Krishnadayal said, 'Are you mad! If this is made public today I may land in great trouble; not only the pension will be stopped; even the police may give trouble. The past is past; now try to steer along as tactfully as you can; even if you cannot it won't matter much.'

Krishnadayal had decided that any catastrophe should be postponed till his death; and in the meantime he would hold himself aloof; and hoped to carry on by ignoring what happened to others in their unawareness.

Failing to decide what she should do, Anandamoyee got up with a desolate expression. Before leaving she waited a moment at the door and said, 'Have you noticed how your health is deteriorating?'

To this foolish remark of Anandamoyee Krishnadayal reacted with a lofty small grunt and said, 'Oh, Health!'

Thus the discussion could not lead to any satisfactory conclusion and Krishnadayal applied his mind again to *Gherandasamhitā*.

At another part of the house, in the drawing room Mahim was then engaged with Krishnadayal's trainer monk in some very high-level spiritual discussion. With great modesty and wistfulness he had raised the question if family men stood any chance of spiritual liberation and then sat down with folded hands to listen, displaying such a mood of devotion and eagerness as if he had staked all his possessions to the last iota in order to achieve the said liberation. The monk was trying to console Mahim by assuring that although family men stood no chance of liberation, still they had the prospect of heaven after this life, but Mahim was inconsolable. He must have liberation; heaven was not on his requirement list. And once he somehow marries off his daughter he will surrender himself at the monk's feet, and engage heart and soul in the pursuit of liberation. No one could stop him at that! But you know marrying off a daughter was no child's play—unless the monk took pity on him.

64

Remembering that he had forgotten himself for a while Gora turned even more austere than he was in the past. He concluded that it was his laxity in maintaining the disciplined life that led to his infatuation and brief oblivion of the social reality.

As Gora entered the room after his morning worship he saw Pareshbabu waiting there. It seemed a lightning flashed through his bosom; even his veins and nerves could not but acknowledge that he was connected with Pareshbabu by the ties of some mysterious kinship. Gora touched Paresh's feet.

Paresh said, 'I think you have heard about Binoy's marriage.'

Gora said, 'Yes.'

Paresh said, 'He does not agree to marry according to the Brahmo custom.'

Gora said, 'Then he should not go through the ceremony of this marriage.'

Paresh smiled a little but did not contradict. Instead he said, 'No member of our community will participate in the ceremony; I come to learn no relative from Binoy's side will join either. On the side of my daughter it is only me alone; on Binoy's side, I guess, there is none else than you. So I have come to consult you in this matter.'

Gora shook his head, 'What use consulting me in this matter? I am not in it.'

In shocked surprise Paresh stared at Gora's face for a few moments, 'Aren't you!'

Gora felt embarrassed for a moment at this surprised reaction of Paresh. But because he felt embarrassed, he repeated with redoubled emphasis, 'How can I be in this!'

Pareshbabu said, 'I know you are his friend. Is it not the time when a friend is needed most?'

Gora said, 'I am his friend. But that is not my only bond in this world, and not even the most important bond either.'

Pareshbabu asked, 'Gaur, do you think Binoy's action is really something wrong or irreligious?'

Gora replied, 'But there are two aspects of religion: one eternal and the other temporal. We cannot disregard religion even where it is manifested in the rules of society; if we do then the society will fall apart.'

Pareshbabu said, 'But there are countless rules. How can we be so sure that all these rules manifest religion?'

Pareshbabu chanced to hit Gora at the very point where a turbulence was going on in his mind for some time and from that churning he had also reached some conclusion. Therefore, the force of his accumulated thoughts enabled him to speak before Pareshbabu at length and without inhibition. The essence of his speech was—unless we completely control the society by means of rules, we obstruct the deepest purpose of society; because that purpose is mysterious and is not palpable to common perception. That's why we should have the stamina to obey society without questioning it.

Pareshbabu listened with calm patience till the end. When Gora stopped at last and felt a bit ashamed at his own garrulity, Paresh said, 'I accept the first part of your argument. It is true that God operates with a special purpose through every society. Neither is it very clear to all. But is it not man's duty to see it clearly? Unconsciously following rules like the plants and trees obeying nature's rules cannot be man's fulfillment.'

Gora said, 'My contention is this: first we have to obey the society completely in all respects; only then can we attain a clarity of perception regarding its purpose. If we clash with it we not only obstruct but also misunderstand it.'

Pareshbabu said, 'There can be no test of truth without opposition or obstruction. The test of truth cannot be final with just a band of wise men having listed it once in some remote past. People of every age have to rediscover truth through obstacles and conflicts. Anyway, I don't want to argue about this. I respect the individual freedom of man. It is by testing against that freedom of the individual that we can come to know which is perennial truth and which is temporal assumption, and the welfare of the society depends upon that knowledge and the aspiration for that knowledge.'

Saying this Paresh got up. Gora too stood up from his seat. Paresh said, 'I thought perhaps I would have to keep a little distance from this marriage at the request of Brahmo samaj, while you, as the friend of Binoy, should look after the whole thing. Here friends are in a slightly better position than relatives, they do not have to bear the brunt of the society's response. But since you too have considered it your duty to desert Binoy then the entire responsibility falls upon me. I have to carry it alone.'

Alone! Gora had no idea how alone Paresh was indeed. Baradasundari had openly defied him; the women of the house were not happy. Apprehending Harimohini's objection he did not involve Sucharita at any stage of his preparation for this marriage. In the meantime the entire Brahmo samaj had turned adamant and hostile against him. And he received a few letters from Binoy's uncle which openly abused him as a scheming, cunning boy-catcher.

As soon as he left Abinash and a few others of Gora's team stepped into the room and were about to burst into hilarious mirth with Paresh as target. Gora sharply squashed, 'If you do not have the sense to respect the respectable, at least get over the meanness of taunting him.'

Gora had to revert back to his accustomed daily chores with his old team. But it was all dull. Oh, how dull it all was! It was empty. It was no work. It had no life. Gora had never before been so struck by the realization that nothing meaningful was being achieved through all this writing, reading, speaking, organizing; rather a lot of meaningless junk was accumulating instead. His life, newly risen at a fresh tide of strength, longed for some genuine direction in order to flow towards its own fulfillment, and nothing else appealed to him.

In the meantime preparations were going on for the ritualistic penance. Gora had been taking a special interest in this preparation. It was not just to cleanse him of the contamination during the prison term; through this ritual he sought to be cleansed in every sense and almost get reincarnated with a fresh life and energy to dedicate himself to his mission once again. The details of the ritual had been decided in consultation with the pundits, the date was fixed, arrangements were made to invite all the eminent scholar-pundits in the Eastern and Western parts of Bengal; the richer members of Gora's team had even raised a fund. All the members of the team were euphoric that something great was about to take place at long last. Abinash has confidentially drawn up a plan with other team-members that on the scheduled day the title '*Hindudharmapradīp*' or 'the lamp of the Hindu religion' will be conferred on Gora through the scholars present on the dais along with the appropriate accessories of rice, green grass, flowers, sandalwood, etc. On the occasion a few lines in Sanskrit verse, signed by all the Brahmin pundits, and printed in gold-tinted letters, should be placed inside a sandalwood box and the box be presented to Gora with appropriate pomp and grandeur. In addition to this a volume of *Rigveda*, published by Max Müller and bound in precious Morocco leather will be presented to Gora through the most senior and respectable scholar as the 'gift of India' to him. The message that Gora was the sole saviour of ancient Vedic religion in these heretical days will be finely underlined by this gift.

Thus Gora's followers were busy drawing up fresh plans and improvisations towards making the programme on the scheduled day as interesting and effective as anything.

65

Harimohini received a letter from Kailash, her husband's brother. He wrote: 'With the blessings of your sanctified feet, things are fine at this place. Please remove our anxious worries by informimg us about your well-being.'

It needs no saying that since Harimohini left their house her in-laws had been burdened with this sort of anxious worries, and yet took no effort to overcome the lack of information regarding her well-being. After finishing his long list of information regarding Khudi, Patal, Bhajahari, *et al.*, Kailash wrote at the conclusion—

'Send me detailed information regarding the girl you have mentioned. You have said she is around twelve or thirteen, but because of her developed physique looks a bit older. I don't think that should matter. Regarding her property which you have mentioned, inquire thoroughly about the terms of ownership, whether it is just life-term, or transferable. After you send full information about the matter I shall broach the proposal with my elders. I hope, they won't object. I feel assured at hearing that the prospective bride has respect for Hindu religion. However, the fact that she has been brought up in a Brahmo family must be kept a tightly guarded secret. Therefore, don't tell anyone about this. The almanac prescribes a dip in Ganga during the lunar eclipse which falls next full moon; if possible I shall go then and have a look at the girl.'

So long Harimohini had somehow spent her days in Calcutta. But now at the slightest hope of returning to her husband's house Harimohini felt she could hardly wait any longer. She longed to instantly tell Sucharita, fix a date and have it over. Still she did not dare to hasten things. The more she was seeing Sucharita from close quarters the more she was realizing that she had not understood her at all.

Harimohini waited for her chance, and became more watchful over Sucharita than before. The hours she used to devote to worship and rituals were reduced; she did not want to lose sight of Sucharita.

Sucharita found Gora suddenly stopped his visits altogether. She guessed Harimohini had told him something. She said to herself, 'Alright. Let him stay away. But it is he who is my guru, my guru.'

The guru in absentia can exert greater influence than the guru visibly present before one's own eyes; because in the former case the mind compensates for the lack of visibility by means of its own resources. Thus, the ideas of Gora on which Sucharita might have argued in Gora's presence are now accepted by her without protest. If she finds them hard to accept she persuades herself to believe that if he were present he would surely convince her.

But the longing to see the bright face of Gora, to hear him speaking in his bass voice! How to overcome it? This unsatiated longing, this intense yearning did not leave her for a single moment and seemed to erode her existence. Every now and then Sucharita remembered with benumbing pain—so many people could see Gora day and night without the least hindrance, yet they knew nothing about the preciousness of this privilege.

During this time one afternoon Lalita came and embraced her, 'Suchididi dear!'

Sucharita responded, 'What is it, my Lalita dear!'

Lalita said, 'All is settled.'

Sucharita asked, 'The date?'

Lalita said, 'Monday.'

Sucharita asked, 'Where?'

Lalita shook her head, 'I don't know, Baba knows.'

Sucharita encircled Lalita's waist by her arm, 'Happy, darling?'

Lalita said, 'Shouldn't I be?'

Sucharita said, 'You got what you wanted. Nothing remains to quarrel over with anybody. That's why I feel apprehensive lest you lose interest.'

Lalita laughed, 'Why? Is there any dearth of quarreling people? The advantage is that now I won't have to go outside to look for them.'

Sucharita patted Lalita's forehead with her forefinger, 'Oh, that's the plan then! I must tell Binoy. There is still time for the poor boy to take precautions.'

Lalita said, 'Your poor boy has no chance to take precautions. He has no respite any more. Whatever was destined in his lot has come true, now it remains only to lament and weep.'

Sucharita became serious, 'How can I tell you dear, how happy I am at this. I only pray that you may be the right partner for a husband like Binoy.'

Lalita said, 'Aha! Indeed! Then does not anybody have to aspire for being the right partner to me! Go and ask him about this. If you get his opinion on the matter you'll be filled with remorse that such a wonderful creature was among us so long and yet we were unaware of her great worth, so blind we were!'

Sucharita said, 'Anyway, at last you've found a discerning jeweller. There cannot be any complain either regarding the price he offers. It is apparent that from now on there will be no need of appreciation from novices like us.'

Lalita said, 'Who told you there will be no need? Of course, there will be great need.'

Saying this she pressed Sucharita's cheeks so hard that she cried out, 'Ooh!' Lalita said, 'I must have your special attention for ever; if you deprive me and smuggle it to confer on another I won't stand it.'

Sucharita put her cheek against Lalita's and said, 'I shall give it to none, to none.'

Lalita asked, 'To none? To no one absolutely?'

Sucharita only shook her head. Lalita then moved a little away and said, 'Suchididi dear, listen to me. You know, don't you, that I could not accept your loving any other person. So long I did not tell you, but today I must say,—when Gaurmohanbabu came for the first time to our house—Oh, no Didi, you must not stop me, please let me say today, I must confess. I have never concealed anything from you, but for that one thing, and I have been all along miserable on its account. Without confessing that I cannot take leave of you. When Gaurmohanbabu used to come to our house I sulked. Why? Did you think I did not understand? I saw that you never even mentioned his name before me; that made me even more resentful. I felt it unbearable that you should love him more than me—oh, no Didi dear, you must allow me to say—I have suffered so much for this. I know that even now you won't say a word about it to me. Well, don't. But my resentment is gone. I shall be so happy, darling, if your—.'

Sucharita agitatedly stopped Lalita by pressing her palm on Lalita's lips, 'Lalita, I entreat you, please don't mention it! I feel ashamed like anything at such suggestions!'

Lalita asked, 'Why dear, is he—.'

Sucharita appealed pathetically, 'No, no, no! Don't talk insane Lalita! Ideas that you cannot entertain in your lonely thoughts should never be uttered in so many words.'

Lalita was vexed at this shyness of Sucharita, 'This is, I must say, a bit too much dear. I have noticed very clearly and I can tell you for certain—'

Sucharita pulled off her hand from Lalita's grasp and rushed out of the room. Lalita ran after her and drew her back saying, 'O.K., O.K., I shall not say any more!'

Sucharita said, 'Never!'

Lalita said, 'I cannot make such a tall promise. If I get my chance one day I shall say, but not otherwise. This much I can promise.'

For the last few days Harimohini had been keeping close watch over Sucharita, and maintaining a tireless vigil. Sucharita gussed this and this suspicious watchfulness of Harimohini weighed down upon her mind like some oppressive burden. She felt restive within, yet could not express it. Today following Lalita's departure Sucharita, mentally exhausted as she was, sat down at the table and laying her head between her two arms wept. The servant came to light the lamp, but Sucharita bade him to leave. It was the hour for Harimohini's evening worship. But she saw from upstairs that Lalita went out and she came down at this unlikely hour, entered Sucharita's room and called, 'Radharani!'

Quickly wiping her eyes Sucharita stood up.

Harimohini said, 'What is this?'

Sucharita did not answer. Harimohini said in a harsh tone, 'What's all this nonsense, I simply cannot understand!'

Sucharita asked, 'Masi, why are you keeping this watch upon me day and night!'

Harimohini said, 'Don't you understand why I keep watch? This neglect of your meals, this weeping, what symptoms are these? I am not a child, that I should not guess the reason.'

Sucharita said, 'Masi, I must tell you, you have understood nothing. Rather you have so grossly misunderstood that every minute becomes unbearable to me.'

Harimohini said, 'Well, if I am wrong then why don't you come out and tell me what is what!'

Sucharita firmly suppressed all her hesitations and shyness and said, 'Well, let me speak then. I have received a message from my guru which is unfamiliar to me, which requires great strength for acceptance; I feel I am lacking in that strength—so I am desperately fighting with myself. But Masi, you perceive our relationship in a distorting way. You have shut him out with insult—what you have told him is all wrong, what you have thought of me is all false. You have done a great wrong! It is beyond you to humiliate such a person as him. But why did you perpetrate such torture on me? What have I done to you?'

Before she could finish Sucharita's voice choked, and she left the room.

Harimohini was bewildered. She said to herself, 'My goodness, never heard of such things in my life, nor in my past seven lives.'

She gave some time to Sucharita to cool down and then called her for dinner. As she sat down at dinner Harimohini resumed, 'Look here Radharani, I am an elderly person. Since my childhood I have been practicing Hinduism and also learnt a lot about it. You don't have this preliminary training in Hinduism; therefore, Gaurmohanbabu is cheating you by throwing the posture of a guru. I have heard scraps of his talks—those are not genuine scripture, but his own imagination and improvisation. These cannot delude us, because we have learnt at our guru's feet. I tell you Radharani, you needn't bother at all. When the time comes my guru—I have my own guru and he is not such a fake one—will give you the right *mantra* or initiation. Have no worry at all. I shall smuggle you inside Hindu society. True you had lived with a Brahma family, but who is to know of it? True you have been a bit overage but there are lots of such physically developed young girls. Who is going to pry into your horoscope? Furthermore, you have the money, and when money is there nothing matters, all will go smooth. I have seen with my own eyes how low caste boys of fishing family are passed off as high-caste Kayastha with the help of money. I shall pass you off into Hindu society through such prestigious Brahmin family that no one will be allowed to raise a finger, because they are at the helm of affairs. For this you have no need to suffer hardship for your guru or waste such flood of tears for his sake.'

As Harimohini went on with her elaborate exposition of the matter, the food went stale for Sucharita, and she could hardly swallow it down. But she forced herself to eat in silence; because she knew her low intake itself could lead to such comments which wouldn't be palatable at all.

When Harimohini failed to elicit any response from Sucharita she said to herself, 'I salute them; indeed, I salute them. She would shed an ocean of tears for Hinduism, and yet pay no heed to the prospect of such a great chance. No need of purification rites, nor any explanation; just loosen your purse and throw some coins judiciously this and that way and you at once get admission to Hindu society; if even such bright prospects fail to enthuse how can she aspire to be a Hindu!' Harimohini was left with no doubt what a great fraud Gora was. Probing the root cause of the trouble she came to the conclusion that the root cause was Sucharita's property and her beauty and youth in addition. The sooner she could rescue the girl, along with her property deeds, and secure her in the confinement of her in-laws' fort, the better. But she would have to wait till the girl softened a bit. With the hope of that ultimate softening she continued to weave narratives about her in-laws' house to Sucharita day in and day out. She described with adequate illustrative examples how extraordinarily powerful they were, how they could achieve the unachievable in society, how any attempt to oppose them landed nice people in terrible ordeals whereas by seeking their patronage how many consumers of Muslim-cooked chickens had passed the difficult trials of Hindusamaj with a smile. She would make her narrative convincing by citing names, places and other details.

Baradasundari made no secret of her wish that Sucharita should not keep contact with her family, because she nursed a sort of pride in her straightforwardness. While behaving with unqualified rudeness to others she frequently used to announce this virtue of hers. Therefore, it was expressed in no uncertain terms to Sucharita that she should expect no welcome at Baradasundari's house. Sucharita also knew that in case she paid a visit Paresh would have to face the consequence, and his peace was to be ruffled. Therefore, she did not go there unless it was absolutely necessary and for the very same reason Paresh came to Sucharita's house everyday once or twice to see her.

For the last few days Paresh could not visit her place because of his various worries and pressure of work. These few days Sucharita has eagerly waited for Paresh, and yet felt a sort of qualm and sadness within her own mind. She knew for sure her relationship with Paresh, the deep benediction in it, could never be snapped, but she could not forget the pain that was caused by some major external pulls against it. On the other hand Harimohini had made daily life unbearable for her. At last Sucharita took the risk of incurring Baradasundari's displeasure and came to see Paresh at his house. It was the last hour of afternoon when the sun had gone down behind the two-storeyed house in the west casting long shadows on the garden. In that shadow Paresh could be seen strolling alone in his garden with bent head.

Sucharita came to join him. She said, 'Baba, how are you?'

Being thus interrupted in his silent thoughts Paresh stopped for a moment, then looking at her said, 'I am fine, Radhe!'

The two strolled on. Paresh said, 'Lalita's marriage is fixed on Monday.'

Sucharita thought she would ask why she was kept out of the planning or execution of this ceremony. But she was hesitant, because she felt she too was answerable in a way. In the past she would not have waited for a call to join.

As Sucharita was turning over this thought in her mind Paresh broached exactly the same issue; he said, 'I could not call you this time, Radhe!'

Sucharita asked, 'Why, Baba?'

Without answering her Paresh watched her face for a time. Sucharita could not bear it any more. Lowering her face a little she asked, 'Did you think some change had come upon me?'

Paresh said, 'Yes. So I thought I won't embarrass you by making any request.'

Sucharita said, 'Baba, I thought I would tell you everything, but I could not see you. That's why I come today. I do not have the articulation to express myself as I would. I am afraid lest I fail to express appropriately.'

Paresh said, 'I know it is not easy to clearly communicate your feelings. You have received something through your emotion, through your feeings, but it is yet to take a definable shape in your thoughts.'

Sucharita felt comforted, 'Yes, it is exactly like that. But my feelings are strong; how can I describe to you? It seems I have come across a new life, a new consciousness. I have never looked at myself from such an angle. So long I was not aware of my connection with my country's past and future. But the realization of the immense magnitude and truth of that connection has thrilled my heart with such an extraordinary wonder that I cannot forget it for a moment. Look here Baba, I am telling you the truth—I could not previously imagine of uttering, I am Hindu. But now I can declare emphatically without hesitation, "I am Hindu." I feel a great joy in being able to do so.'

Pareshbabu said, 'Have you considered all the aspects, all the tentacles, all the implications of this utterance?'

Sucharita said, 'Do I have the ability to think of all the dimensions? But I have studied, discussed. When I did not see from this perspective my attention was focused on the small details—which led to a contempt towards the big whole.'

Pareshbabu was surprised at hearing her. He could clearly understand Sucharita had attained a new perception, she had an unhesitant feeling that she had attained something genuine; it was not that she was being just carried away on the crest of vague emotions like an infatuated person without understanding a thing.

Sucharita said, 'Baba, why should I say I am a small isolated individual cut off from my country, my nation? Why can't I say, "I am Hindu?"'

Paresh smiled, 'That means, *Mā*, you are asking me why I don't call myself a Hindu. Indeed if I think deeply I don't find any incontrovertible argument against it. One of the less important reasons is that the Hindus do not agree to accept us as Hindu; the second reason is my fellow-believers do not call themselves Hindu.'

Sucharita thought silently. Paresh said, 'I have already told you, these are not serious reasons; these are but external causes. One can even ignore them. But there may be another deeper reason. There is no entrance route to Hindu society. At least no main gate, though there may be some backdoor, I am not sure. This society is not a society for all humans; it is only for those who are born into it by chance or a stroke of destiny.'

Sucharita said, 'But does this not apply to all societies?'

Paresh said, 'No. No great society is like that. The great lion-gate of the Muslim society is open for all men; Christianity too invites all. The communities appended to the Christian society also follow the same norm. If I want to be an Englishman that is not an altogether impossible proposition; by living in England and following their custom I may be accommodated in their society, even without converting to Christianity. Abhimanyu knew how to enter an enemy *Byuha*, but not how to come out of the same; it is just the opposite in the case of the Hindu. The entrance to this society is completely sealed, but exit routes are countless.'

Sucharita said, 'But Baba, isn't it true that in spite of this the Hindu society has not been eroded, it is still surviving!'

Paresh said, 'It takes time to realize the erosion of a society. In the past the backdoor of Hindu society was kept open. Through that the non-Aryans entered the mainstream and shared a sense of glory. On the other hand, during the Muslim rule the influence of Hindu kings and landlords was sufficiently strong throughout the country so that it was not easy to strike exit from the society in the teeth of all the obstacles and persecution. Now that the British rule protects everybody under its law, thereby rendering it well-nigh impossible to guard the exit door by artificial means—in recent times we can see a systematic fall in the number of Hindus in proportion to the steady rise of the number of Muslims. If the trend continues the country will be eventually Muslim-dominated; then it would be unfair to call it Hindustan.'

Sucharita exclaimed in painful concern, 'Baba, shouldn't we all try to stop it? Should we too desert the Hindu society and thereby aggravate the erosion? Is it not the time to hold on to it with all our might?'

Pareshbabu affectionately patted her on the back and said, 'Can I make one survive just by clinging to him? There is a natural law of survival. One who abandons that law is eventually abandoned by all others. The Hindu society insults man, rejects man; it is for this reason that its survival is getting daily tougher in modern times; because now it cannot afford to maintain an iron curtain. Doors to the big world have opened; people are gathering from all directions—you can no more resist the contact with others by raising walls of scriptures and strictures. If Hindu society does not tap its power to receive, and allows the eroding trend to aggravate, then this very contact with the outside world will ring its death knell.'

Sucharita was stung with pain, 'I don't understand all this. But if that be true, that it is about to be deserted by all, then how can I desert it at such a time! Shouldn't we stand by its sick bed for the very reason that we are its children of a bad time.'

Pareshbabu said, '*Mā*, I won't raise any objection to the emotion that has stirred within you. You bring your mind to a state of poise by meditation, then consider your ideas by relating them to the truth, the ideal of the desirable that is within you; eventually things will become clear to your perception. Don't belittle one who is greater than all, above any country or person; that won't bring good either to you or to the country. I think like this and seek to submit myself heart and soul to Him. It is only by so doing I feel that I can be true to the country and to every person.'

At this time a person came with a letter for Pareshbabu. Pareshbabu said, 'My glasses are not here, the daylight too has faded—you read the letter for me.'

Sucharita read out the letter. It came from some committee of Brahmo samaj, signed by many a member. The content of the letter was like this—Paresh has given consent to his daughter's marriage according to non-Brahmite custom, and has taken preparation to participate in the ceremony; under such circumstances Brahmo samaj cannot consider him one of its members any more. If he has to say anything in self-defence his letter must reach the committee before next Sunday. The matter will be discussed and decided according to the majority opinion on that day.

Paresh put the letter inside his pocket. Sucharita held his right hand in her own soothing palm and silently strolled with him. Gradually evening receded, darkness thickened, a streetlight appeared on the lane right to the garden. Sucharita said gently, 'Baba, it is time for your prayer; I shall also pray with you today.'

Saying this Sucharita led him by the hand to his quiet chamber for meditation. As usual a mat was spread there and a candle was burning. Paresh silently performed his meditation for a long while, and then ended it with a small prayer.

Coming out from the meditation room he found Binoy and Lalita waiting patiently at the door. Both touched his feet. He placed his hand on their heads and blessed silently. He told Sucharita, '*Mā*, I shall go to you tomorrow. Now I have to finish my duty of today.'

Saying this he left for his room.

Sucharita could not contain her tears anymore. She stood like a motionless idol silently in the darkness of the balcony. Lalita and Binoy too could not say anything for a long while.

When Sucharita was about to leave Binoy came up before her and said softly, 'Didi, won't you bless us!'

Saying this Binoy and Lalita touched her feet. What Sucharita said through her tears was audible to her god alone.

Coming back to his room Pareshbabu wrote his letter to the Brahmo samaj committee. He wrote: 'I have to take the responsibility of the marriage ceremony of Lalita. If you expel me for this it won't be an unjust decision on your part. Now I have only one prayer to God, may He take me out of the shelter of all societies and allow me to take shelter at His feet alone.'

66

Sucharita felt a great longing to share with Gora the ideas that she gathered from Paresh. Gora had widened her vision of Bharatbarsha, had stirred strong love in her mind for this Bharatbarsha, but was he aware that this India was at last being confronted by Time, and was about to erode! So long India had sustaind itself by means of its inner system; it did not require alert effort on the part of Indians. But is there the time now to rest assured like that? Is it sufficient today to cling to the old system and wait indoors?

Sucharita pondered, 'I too have some duty, some mission in this situation. But what is that mission?' Gora should have been here at this time; he should have come forward and guided her, commanded her. Sucharita thought to herself, 'If he could rescue me from all this obstruction and ignorance and make me take my right place then would it not have been much more precious an experience above and beyond all petty slanders, abuses, inhibitions?' Sucharita felt an elation of self-esteem at this thought. She wondered why did not Gora test her, why didn't he command her to do the impossible; was there a single member among Gora's entire team who could dedicate himself so completely like Sucharita without a second thought? Why didn't Gora see the need of such an aspiration for sacrifice, such strength? Is it not a loss for the country to dump such resources unutilized out of the fear of popular inhibition and slander? Sucharita refused to admit the ignominy and pushed it away from her cognition. She said, 'It is impossible that he should desert me like this. He must come back to me. I must search him out. He must get over all inhibition, all hesitation. Howsoever strong he may be, he needs me, he has said this to me in so many words—how come that he abandons me just at the pettiest of petty hints!'

Satish ran in and stood close by Sucharita, 'Didi!'

Sucharita encircled his neck with her arms, 'What is it, Bakhtiyar dear!'

Satish said, 'Lalitadidi's marriage will be held on Monday. From today I shall stay at Binoybabu's house. He has invited me.'

Sucharita asked, 'Did you tell Masi?'

Satish replied, 'Told Masi. She's angry; says, "I don't have anything to say about this, go tell your Didi, let her decide." Didi, please don't say no. My studies will not suffer there at all. I shall study everyday. Binoybabu will help me with my task.'

Sucharita teased, 'I think you will disturb them like anything in their preparations for the festival.'

Satish eagerly protested, 'Oh no Didi, I won't disturb at all.'

Sucharita said, 'Are you taking your doggie there?'

Satish said, 'Of course. I must take it. Binoybabu has specially invited doggie. A separate red printed invitation letter has come in his name—it is written there, doggie must come along with his family and have snacks there.'

Sucharita asked, 'Who is this family?'

Satish was quick in response, 'Why—me, of course, as Binoybabu said! He has also told me to take that toy organ. Didi, please lend it to me. I won't break it.'

Sucharita said, 'Oh, I should be the happiest person if it is broken. So now it is clear—your friend has invited you to play organ during his marriage. It seems he plans to save the money on the Sehnai players.'

Satish was greatly excited and protested as best as he could, 'Oh, no, never, not like that at all. Binoybabu has told me he will make me his *nitbar*. Didi please tell me what the *nitbar* is supposed to do.'

Sucharita said solemnly, 'He has to keep on fast through the whole day.'

Satish completely disbelieved it. Then Sucharita drew Satish close to her lap and said, 'Well, Bakhtiyār bhai, can you tell me what you want to be when you grow up?'

Satish was ready with the answer. His class-teacher represented to him the epitome of unquestionable power and extraordinary scholarship. He had already decided that in future he would be a teacher.

Sucharita told him, 'So much is there to be done, Bhai. We the brother and sister shall work together. What do you say to this, Satish? We must build up our country with the dedication of our heart. Or can we really build it! What is there greater than our country! Rather we have to build up ourselves. Do you know? Do you follow?'

Satish was not one to admit he did not follow. He said a big emphatic 'Yes'.

Sucharita said, 'Do you know how great our country is, how great is our nation. How can I make you understand! It is a wonderful country. God has worked for thousands of years to place it above the rest of the world. So many people have come from so many lands to join this work. So many great men have been born here, so many great wars have been fought, what wonderful messages have been disseminated from here, what extraordinary pursuits have been made here! Religion has been envisioned here in so many ways! So very many solutions to problems of life have been devised here! This is our Bharatbarsha. Remember it as something very great. Never, by any mistake, denounce it. You must come to understand one day what I tell you now. Of course I don't think you understand nothing now. You must ever remember this—that you have been born in a very great country, adore this country with all your heart, and devote your whole life to its work.'

Satish was silent for a little while. Then he asked, 'Didi, what will you do?'

Sucharita said, 'I too shall do this work. Will you help me?'

Satish instantly puffed up his chest and said, 'Yes, I will.'

Sucharita's heart was full to the brim but she could not find any one to communicate. Therefore, at the proximity of this small sibling her emotions surged up. The language she spoke was not fit for a child, but Sucharita did not shrink at that. During this heightened state of her mind she had come to the realization that if you fully outpoured your own genuine feelings everybody—children or elders—can somehow understand it according to their own respective ability. But if you try to dilute or cut it down in order to fit it to others' power of comprehension the truth gets naturally distorted.

Satish's imagination was excited; he said, 'When I grow up and earn a lot, lots of money then—'

Sucharita interrupted, 'No, no, no—please don't mention money; we don't need money, Bakhtiyār—our work will require devotion, dedication.'

At this point Anandamoyee entered the room. There was a sudden splash of blood, as it were, in her bosom. She touched Anandamoyee's feet. Satish was not much of an adept in feet-touching; he shyly had it over somehow.

Anandamoyee drew Satish close to her lap and kissed his head. Then she addressed Sucharita, 'I came to consult you *Mā*—I don't see any one else to consult with. Binoy said, "The marriage will be held at my apartment." I interposed, "That can never be. What great Nawab you think you are that our daughter should go to your place to get married!" That won't do. I have requisitioned a house; it is not far from this house. I am just coming from there. You tell Pareshbabu and take his approval.'

Sucharita said, 'Baba will agree.'

Anandamoyee said, 'Then, you too *Mā* have to join me there. There is not much time. The marriage is scheduled on next Monday. So we have to stay there and immediately start the arrangements. True, I can manage the whole thing myself. But if you are not in it, Binoy will be very unhappy. He cannot request you in so many words; in fact he has not even mentioned your name to me; but that's why I can guess his sadness in this regard. It won't do if you stay away; Lalita too will be deeply hurt.'

Sucharita was a little surprised, '*Mā*, are you joining this ceremony?'

Anandamoyee said, 'What do you say Sucharita! You speak of joining! Am I an outsider who just joins! Is it not Binoy's marriage! Who else can take the lead but me. I have to shoulder the entire responsibility. But I have also told Binoy clearly, "In this marriage I am not in your party, I am the bride's party." He is coming to my house to marry Lalita.'

That Lalita's own mother had abandoned her on this auspicious occasion had filled Anandamoyee's heart with compassion for the girl. That is the reason why she has been trying her best to ensure that there was no trace of lovelessness, or lack of respect about this marriage. She would take the place of Lalita's mother, would dress her up with her own hands, would look after the reception of the bridegroom—in case some rare invitee happened to drop in she would ensure a flawless reception for them, and she would decorate this rented house in such a way that Lalita could get a home feeling. Such was her resolve.

Sucharita asked, '*Mā*, won't you have to face any problem for this?'

Anandamoyee remembered for a moment the furore at home, raised by Mahim on the issue, and said, 'May be. But why bother! Problems come; but if you wait with patience, eventually they disappear as well.'

Sucharita knew Gora was not joining this marriage ceremony. She was curious to know if Gora had tried to stop Anandamoyee in this matter. But she could not ask it in so many words, and Anandamoyee did not even mention Gora's name.

Harimohini had got the news. But she took some time before entering the room, 'Didi, how are you? You seem to have made yourself scarce: no visit, no connection!'

Without addressing the allegation Anandamoyee said, 'I have come to take your niece.'

Saying this she explained her purpose of coming. Harimohini did not hide her displeasure. A sullen silence was followed by her declaration, 'I cannot get involved in this.'

Anandamoyee said, 'No sister, I did not ask you to join. And don't worry about Sucharita—I shall be with her.'

Harimohini said, 'Let me speak then. Radharani has been going public with her claim that she is Hindu. These days she has taken to the Hindu ways. So, if she chooses to opt for the Hindu society, she has to be careful. Even as such there will be lot of problems; those I can counter somehow. But she has to be cautious for some time from now on. The first thing people will ask about her—why still a spinster at such age? That can be suppressed somehow, and even a good bridegroom too can be secured at some effort. But if at this stage the lady reverts to her earlier ways, you tell me, how can I manage? You too are a born Hindu, why don't you understand? If you had a daughter of your own could you have sent her to attend this marriage? Wouldn't you have to think—how to marry off your daughter?'

Anandamoyee looked at Sucharita in surprise. Her face flushed crimson. Anandamoyee said, 'I don't want to force. If Sucharita has any objection I....'

Harimohini did not allow her to finish, 'I don't understand your behaviour. It is your son who has converted her to Hinduism, and you pretend you are as innocent as the new-born babe!'

Where was the Harimohini who stayed in Pareshbabu's house like a timid guilty intruder, and eagerly clung to any person at the slightest sign of sympathy? Today she had assumed the posture of the tigress to retain her new possessions. The suspicion that antagonistic forces were active on all sides to seduce her Sucharita away from her clutch kept her ever on the alert. She could not clearly identify who were the friendly party and who belonged to the enemy camp, and this allowed her no peace of mind. In the past when the world became empty for her she eagerly sought the succour of her god; now the worship of that god too failed to give her peace. Once she was deeply involved in mundane domesticities. When terrible bereavements led to a spirit of withdrawal she could not imagine that she would ever develop the slightest attachment again to money, property and relatives. But as soon as she started recovering from her emotional wound the lure of that old life came back with all its attraction; all the starved hopes and aspirations had stirred up again with their insatiated hunger. The desire to go back to what she had supposedly left behind for ever grew so aggressive and overpowering as to make her more restive than when she had a regular family life. Anandamoyee was stunned at this radical change in Harimohini's expression, look, posture, manner and speech within such a short time, and her affectionate soft heart went out to Sucharita in a spirit of deep intuitive compassion. She found it quite a problem how to protect Sucharita from hurt.

When Harimohini alluded to Gora in her ramblings Sucharita lowered her face and silently left the room.

Anandamoyee said, 'Don't worry sister! I did not know this earlier. Anyway, I won't insist. You too don't say her anything. She has grown up in one way; now if you put too much pressure all of a sudden that won't work.'

Harimohini said, 'Don't I know that, being such an elderly person! Let her speak before you, if I ever gave her any cause for complaint; she has her own ways in everything, I never utter a syllable; I say, may God keep her alive, that's enough. In view of the kind of luck that I am born with, I am always on tenterhooks at what may happen and when.'

As Anandamoyee was leaving Sucharita came out of her room and touched her feet. Anandamoyee touched her with compassionate affection and said, 'I shall come, *Mā*, I shall come and tell you everything—there will be no problem; with God's blessing the auspicious ceremony will be held without a hitch.'

Sucharita did not say a word.

The following morning as Anandamoyee, with the assistance of Lachmya, had practically unleashed a flood to wash out the accumulated dust of the rented house, Sucharita arrived. Anandamoyee threw away her broom and hastened to hug her and hold her in a close embrace.

Then the festival of cleaning, scrubbing, arranging and decorating was launched with great zest. Pareshbabu had given Sucharita the necessary money for meeting the expenses. With this fund in hand they got busy drawing up so many lists and so many corrections and improvisations of the same.

Before long Paresh himself arrived with Lalita. For Lalita her home had become unbearable. No one dared to challenge her, but their silence wounded her at every step. Finally when Baradasundari's friends lined up at the door to offer their condolences, Paresh decided it was better to move Lalita from this house. On the eve of leaving Lalita went to touch Baradasundari's feet; she turned away and shed tears. Labanya and Leela were privately quite curious and eager to attend Lalita's marriage, and if they somehow got the chance they would not take a minute to make for the ceremony hall. But when Lalita took leave they put on very grave look as was befitting in view of the stern duties of a Brahmo family. While coming out she ran across Sudhir for the flash of a moment. But as Sudhir was flanked by a few elders of their samaj, there could not be any exchange. On boarding the carriage Lalita saw a small packet at a corner of the seat. Opening the packet she found a flower vase of German silver, carrying an inscription in English,—'May God bless the happy couple', and a card containing only one letter, 'S', the first letter of Sudhir's name. Lalita had toughened herself to the resolve that on this day she won't shed a drop of tear. But while holding this only gift, a gift from a childhood friend, in hand at this last moment of bidding farewell to her father's house, tears rolled down her cheeks inconsolably. Paresh sat upright and still with his eyes closed.

'Come in, come in, *Mā*, come in', saying this Anandamoyee warmly received Lalita, clasped both of her hands and took her inside, as if she had been specially waiting for her arrival right now.

Pareshbabu sent for Sucharita and told her, 'Lalita has left my house this day for good.'

His voice choked.

Holding Paresh's hand Sucharita said, 'Baba, here she will not miss any affection or care.'

As Paresh was about to leave Anandamoyee, covering her head, appeared before him and greeted him with folded hands. Paresh hastened to return the greeting, folding his hands. Anandamoyee told him, 'Have no worry for Lalita. The one to whom you have handed her over will give her no cause for sorrow; and God has now granted my one need—I did not have a daughter, today I have been bestowed with one. For a long time I had been waiting for Binoy's bride so that she could take the place of my daughter. True, God has taken a long time to grant my prayer but he has given me such a wonderful daughter and in such a wonderful way that I could never imagine I would be so fortunate.'

Since the beginning of the upheaval regarding Lalita's marriage this was the first time that the heart of Pareshbabu spotted a shoreline in the turbulent ocean and was genuinely soothed.

67

Since his release from the prison everyday Gora had so many visitors, and they pestered him so much with flattery, eulogies, suffocating talks, endless discussions that the situation became unbearable for him.

Gora, therefore, resumed his tour of villages as he did in the past.

In the morning, after having some food he would set out and return home after nightfall. He boarded a train from Calcutta and getting down at some station nearby would walk into the heart of some village. There he sought hospitality at those areas of the village which were inhabited by low-caste working people like the oil-maker, the potter, the fishermen, etc. Why this very fair, heavily built Brahmin was visiting them from door to door, was inquiring about their well-being was an enigma to them. They were even suspicious of him. But completely disregarding their hesitation and suspicion Gora continued to move among them. Sometimes he had to hear unpleasant things, but still he was not deterred.

The more he came to know them the more a thought haunted his mind. He saw that in these areas social ties were much stronger than among the educated genteel society. The eating, drinking, sleeping, leisure, work of every house were perpetually under the unblinking eye of a watchful society. Every person had a natural unquestioning faith in social custom. Yet the social tie or the respectful adherence to custom did not impart to them any strength in the practical field of work. It was doubtful if another such society existed in this world, so diffident, helpless, incapable of judging for their own benefit as they were. They can only follow custom, and won't recognize any other benefit, nor accept the idea even if it is explained to them. The only thing they understand is taboo or stricture, which is imposed through punishment and petty cliquing. The series of "Don'ts" enmeshed their nature through imposition at every step. But this enmeshing net was the net of debt, with knots tied by the creditor, not the king. It involved no great unity which could bring all to stand together in adversity or prosperity. Gora could not but notice how by using the weapon of custom man was sucking the blood of man, was mercilessly pauperizing man. He saw many instances when, on the issue of social rituals one did not show another the least kindness or consideration. One's father had been ailing for a long time, and the poor man was pauperized meeting the expenses of the treatment of his father. No one helped him then. But in the meantime the villagers decided that he must perform a purification ceremony as his father has been perpetually sick, and that again must have been the consequence of some unknown sin. The poor man's poverty, his incapability was not unknown to any one. Still there was no relenting. This was the rule in all sorts of rituals. As an act of dacoity is a lesser evil for a village than the police-inquiry that follows the dacoity, similarly the funeral ceremony for the death of one's parents becomes a greater misfortune than the bereavement itself. Nobody will consider the excuse of limited income or limited ability. You must somehow meet the heartless demands of social custom cent per cent. On the occasion of a marriage the bridegroom's party will do their best to make the burden as heavy as possible for the bride's father; no trace of compassion for the poor man is to be found. Gora saw this society did not help a member during his need, did not give support during a crisis; it only makes him feel insecure by clamping its strictures and forcing him to surrender to the same.

So long as Gora moved among the elite society he was oblivious of this reality, because in that society the trend of organized activity towards common benefit was operative, at least under the impact of the world outside. Various unifying efforts were emerging. There his chief concern was to stem the possibility of these collective efforts getting misdirected towards futile mimicry.

But deep within the backwater villages, where the conflicting trends of the big world did not reach it was total passivity; in this passivity Gora saw the entrenched vulnerability of the country in its naked form. The religion that was supposed to strengthen people in the form of service, love, compassion, self-sacrifice,—to sustain, to bring benediction, was nowhere visible. The custom that only drew lines of division, that only constrained, that paid no heed to intelligence, that kept love at a distance, served only to put up obstacles at every step. The damaging impact of this stupid compulsion was so apparent to Gora as he saw how it assaulted people's health, knowledge, activity and religious sensibility from every possible angle, that it was impossible for him to take cover of his earlier romantic illusion any more.

At the very start he noticed, owing to the low count of women among the low class people of the village or for some other reason, brides were available only on paying heavy dowry. Many men had to remain unmarried all their lives, whereas many others had to wait till an advanced age for marriage. On the other hand there was strict taboo against widow-marriage. As a result of this society was getting polluted, and its disadvantage and damage were felt by everybody. But they were compelled to carry on with this evil, they had no scope for seeking remedy. Gora, who never allowed any laxity of custom among the elites, mounted an assault on custom here. He was able to win over the priests to his side, but could not prevail upon the common people. They were angry with Gora, and announced, 'Very well. Let the Brahmins first marry their widows, then we shall follow suit.'

The main reason of their resentment was the assumption that Gora was despising them as low caste, and had come here specifically with the purpose to preach the message that people like them should desirably follow despicable ways.

While moving about in the villages Gora had also noticed that among the Muslims there was an element which enabled them to stand unified. Gora had noted in case of crisis or need in the village the Muslims offered such a show of solidarity as the Hindus never did. Gora thought again and again, why this world of difference between the two neighbours who lived close to each other? He felt too reluctant to get reconciled to the answer that rose in his mind. His heart ached to admit that the Musalmans were united by their religion, and not by custom alone. On the one hand the bondage to custom had not rendered them inactive, on the other hand the bond of religion among them was strong and genuine. They had together embraced something which was not just negation,—'Don't'—, but which was positive, —'Do'. For the sake of this ideal all of them could stand in a body and lay down their lives without a second thought.

When Gora used to write, debate, deliver speech, convince others, persuade others to his opinion in the educated society, he had automatically added splashes of charming colours to them by applying his imagination; he had covered up even the crude things with subtle oratory; he had projected even the junk of relics as magic pictures by filtering them through the charming moonlight of romantic imagination. As a group of countrymen turned away from the country, looked down on everything of the country as despicable, Gora—out of sheer love for his country—tried to protect his country from the insult of this loveless glance by means of covering up everything with the shimmering veil of romanticism day and night. He had become accustomed to this. When Gora claimed that everything of the country was fine, that even what you called blemish was virtue in another sense, not that he fought for his case like a lawyer; he had come to believe this with his whole heart. Even in altogether impossible situations he had defiantly held this faith high in firm grip like some victory flag, alone in the face of hostile jeering opposition. He had only one commitment,—he must restore the reverence of countrymen to the country before he could turn to anything else.

But these days when he enters a village there is no rapt or hostile audience to listen to him, there is no one before whom he has to prove anything, there is no need to mobilize your power of aggression in order to defeat the attitude of contempt and hostility. So here he is not required to envision truth through any veil. It is the very intensity of his patriotism that lends an extraordinary sharpness to his vision of truth.

68

In a Chinese coat of raw silk, with a *cādar* around the waist, a canvas bag in hand, Kailash himself arrived in person to touch Harimohini's feet. He was around thirty-five, a short stout body; a few days' unshaven face looked like some thorny stiff grassland.

Seeing a relative from her marital house after a long time Harimohini was delighted, 'Oh, it is *Thakurpo*! Come, come, sit down.'

Saying this she hastened to spread a mat, and asked, 'Would you like to wash?'

Kailash dismissed her proposal, 'No need. Anyway, you appear in fine health.'

Harimohini considered it an abuse to keep in good health and remonstrated, 'Oh, not at all!'

She furnished a long list of ailments which she clinched with the exclamation, 'It is a pity this rotten body refuses to die altogether!'

Kailash expressed objection to such avowals of indifference to life, and indicated the family's great benefit in the survival of Harimohini, although his elder brother had taken the route to heaven. As evidence of this benefit he cited, 'For example, because you are here, I could come to Calcutta and get a shelter in this city.'

After imparting all the information about all the relatives and neighbours in the village, Kailash suddenly cast a glance around and asked, 'Is it her house?'

Harimohini said, 'Yes.'

Kailash said, 'It appears to be solid structure.'

Harimohini, in order to fan up his interest, assured, 'Solid of course; everything is solid.'

Kailash carefully noted that the beams under the ceiling were of good Sal wood, whereas the doors and windows were not of cheap mango wood. Whether the walls were of double bricks' width or just one and a half also did not escape his attentive consideration. He also inquired about the total number of rooms on the upper and lower floors. On the whole the thing pleased him. It was difficult for him to guess how much it had cost to build the house; because he had no idea of the prices of such building materials. He thought hard, placed one of his legs upon another and while stirring both thought to himself, 'It must be not less than ten to fifteen thousands.' He slashed it while speaking, 'What do you say, *Bauthān*, I think it may be around seven to eight thousands?'

Harimohini expressed surprise at Kailash's rustic ignorance, 'What are you saying *Thakurpo*? Seven to eight thousands indeed! It will be not one paisa less than twenty thousand.'

Kailash silently surveyed the furniture around with meticulous attention. The thought that just by nodding his assent he can be the sole owner of this concrete building including its Salwood beams, and Segunwood doors and windows gave him great satisfaction. He asked, 'So all this is seen. But what about the girl?'

Harimohini quickly replied, 'She has to go to her paternal aunt on a sudden invitation; it may take a few days before she returns.'

Kailash was fidgety, 'Then what about interviewing the girl? I have a court case, I must leave by tomorrow.'

Harimohini said, 'Hang your case for the time being. Before you finish your work here you won't be allowed to leave.'

Kailash pondered for a while and finally decided, 'The case may be lost in the absence of defence counsel. Anyway, let it be.' To assess the prospect of compensation he could get here, he cast his glance around once again. Suddenly he noticed a small puddle of water at one corner of Harimohini's puja room. As there was no drainage system attached to this room, and yet Harimohini was all the time cleaning and scrubbing this room with adequate water, a small quantity of water always accumulated at one corner. Kailash got concerned at once, '*Bauthan,* that's not good.'

Harimohini asked, 'Why? What's not good?'

Kailash said, 'Look there, the water soaking at the corner, that won't do.'

Harimohini expressed her helplessness, 'What can I do *Thakurpo*?'

Kailash asserted, 'No, no, that won't do. The floor will be damaged. I tell you *Bauthakrun*, you must stop using water in this room.'

Harimohini had to stop short. Kailash then expressed curiosity about the girl's appearance.

Harimohini assured, 'You'll see for yourself. I can only say this much that your family did never have such a bride.'

Kailash said, 'What do you say! Have you forgotten our second daughter-in-law—.'

Harimohini protested, 'Comparing what with what? Your second daughter-in-law stands no chance by her!'

Harimohini was not quite pleased at this projection of the second lady as the epitome of beauty in the family, 'Whatever nonsense you people may say, I think the fifth daughter-in-law is a much better beauty than the second one.'

Kailash felt no interest in the comparative study of the beauty of the second and fifth. Instead he was trying to insert the thinnest nose and largest eyes to some peerless form in addition to thick hair rolling right down to the ankles, and was quite lost in this creature of his confused imagination.

Harimohini guessed that situation on this side was perfectly satisfactory. She even felt the serious social handicaps on the bride's side might not be considered insurmountable obstacles after all.

69

Binoy knew that these days Gora went out in the morning; so he arrived at his house at the dark hour of dawn on Monday. He headed straight for the bedroom. But failing to find him there asked the servant who said that Gora was in the worship room. He was a little surprised at this. Coming to the door of the worship room he saw Gora sitting inside as if at worship. He was wearing a silk dhoti and *cādar*, which left large parts of his huge white body uncovered. Binoy was more surprised at seeing Gora at worship.

Hearing the rustle of his shoes Gora turned back and anxiously admonished, 'Don't enter this room.'

Binoy said, 'Have no fear. I am not entering. I have come to see you.'

Gora came out then, changed dress, and took Binoy to his second floor room.

Binoy said, 'Bhai Gora, it is Monday.'

Gora said, 'Of course it is Monday. Even if the almanac mistakes you won't miss this day. At least you are right that it is not Tuesday.'

Binoy said, 'Perhaps you are not coming, I know—but today, without seeing you once, I could not proceed. So after getting up at dawn I have first come to you.'

Without uttering a word Gora sat still.

Binoy said, 'So is it decided that you won't join my marriage ceremony?'

Gora said, 'No Binoy, I can't.'

Binoy remained silent. Concealing his heartache Gora smiled and said, 'Even if I don't go, does it really matter? It is you who have won. Haven't you won over *Mā* to your side? I tried so hard, but failed to detain her by any means. So finally I have to lose to you even on the issue of my own mother! Binoy, does it signal that eventually "*sab śeş ho jāyegā*", it will be total enemy occupation! Shall I remain the single occupant of my territory at the end!'

Binoy said, 'Anyway, don't put the blame upon me, brother. I had told her very emphatically, "*Mā*, you must not come to my marriage." *Mā* said, "Look here Binu, those who will not go to your wedding will not come even if you invite, and those who will join will do so in spite of your forbidding. Therefore, I advise you,—neither you invite anyone, nor forbid anybody; you just keep quiet!" Gora, you have been defeated, but is it by me? You have been defeated by your mother, yes, a thousand times over. Where to find another such *Mā*!'

Although Gora had tried his best to hold Anandamoyee back, she refused to be cowed down by any obstruction, and without showing any consideration for his anger or pain, left for Binoy's marriage; but he did not feel any real resentment at this, and instead had a sense of relief. Binoy had received a share of his mother's unlimited affection. The assurance that even if Gora and Binoy separated from each other, Binoy won't be deprived of his share of that deep affection, instilled a peace and contentment in Gora's mind. Binoy might drift from him in all respects, but thanks to this common bond of the unshakable affection of *Mā* the two perpetual friends would remain closest to each other in a most intimate way.

Binoy said, 'Bhai, I leave now. If you cannot go by any means, don't; but don't keep any resentment in your mind. If you can feel what great fulfillment this union lends to my life you can never withdraw your love and good wishes from this marriage. About this I am certain.'

Saying this Binoy got up from his seat.

Gora said, 'Binoy, sit down. I think your auspicious moment is not before nightfall, what is the great hurry now!'

At this unexpected gesture of affection from Gora Binoy melted at once and sat down again.

Then, after many days at this hour of dawn the two again started their leisurely talk as they used to do in the past. Gora stroked the particular string of the lyre of Binoy's heart which had been tuned at the top pitch for some time. Binoy spoke endlessly. So many small events, which, put in so many words, could appear even ridiculous; Binoy's narration of those little things seemed to attain fresh charm like the everrepeated and yet everrenewed melody of music surging up again and again. The wonderful tide that had been curling up at the shore of Binoy's heart these days, became manifest as Binoy went on describing it in all its exquisite and variegated charm by means of his excellent language and a very subtle and deeply emotive manner. How superb this experience was! Binoy had received this indescribable experience filling his heart to the brim; is this granted to everybody! Do they have the strength to receive it! The union of men and women that usually takes place in this world does not strike this note. Binoy appealed to Gora repeatedly not to compare him with other common people. Binoy had the feeling that perhaps such an experience had never happened to any one before. If this was a common phenomenon then the entire society would have burst into the tumultuous overflow of blossoming life, just as one zephyr from the spring makes the entire forest burst into delighted clusters of fresh flowers and soft twigs. In that case people could not go on like this with their eating, sleeping, smooth-going slithery ways. Then all the potential for beauty and strength in everybody would have flowered up in variegated colours and got manifested everywhere. Wasn't it that magic stick of gold? Who could afford to ignore its magic touch and remain unresponsive! Couldn't it turn a commoner into an extraordinary entity! If one got the taste of this tumultuous extraordinary at least once in life he would stand face to face with the true vision of life!

Binoy said, 'Gora, I can tell you for certain, the means to wake up the entire human nature in an instant is this love. Whatever be the reason the advent of this love is weakened in our life. That's why each of us is deprived from the realization of its full impact. We do not know what we possess; we cannot express what is hidden within us. It is impossible for us to spend what we have stored—that's why it is so joyless all around us, so joyless. That's why the embedded nobility within us is realized by only a few like you; to the common man's perception it does not exist.'

Binoy's spontaneous overflow stopped when Mahim left his bed with a loud yawn and noisily went to wash his face in the basin. He took leave of Gora and left.

Standing on the roof top Gora looked at the vermilion sky on the east and sighed. He strolled long on the roof top. He didn't feel like going to the village today.

Recently Gora had been feeling a void within his heart, a longing, a lack of contentment which he could in no way get over. Not only it was he alone, all his works also seemed to aspire, to reach out, to clamour for 'some light,—some bright, beautiful light.' As if all the other accessories were ready, as if diamond, jewel, gold, silver were not really costly; as if all the armour and equipments were attainable, but where was that beautiful light, cool and glowing like dawn, luminous with hope and consolation! There was no need to make any effort to augment what was already there. But what was needed was the inspiration to make it radiant, and charming.

When Binoy said at some rare moment of divine bliss an inexpressible uniqueness manifested itself through the love of man and woman, Gora could not laugh it away as on earlier occasions. Gora admitted to himself it was no mundane union, it was fulfillment, whose very touch lent value to everything. It gave a shape to imagination, and lent the body the beauty of soul. It not only enhanced liveliness of life, and cerebration of the brain, it showered a new joy over all.

On this day when he was cut off from Binoy on the social plane, Binoy's heart transmitted its music to Gora's heart in an unbroken symphony. Binoy went away. The day advanced. But the music did not stop. As it happens when two sea-going streams converge, the love of Binoy met Gora's love to overlap each other; as a result endless ripples came dancing up on the crest of endless ripples and flooded everything under the murmuring surge. So long Gora had tried to resist something, by avoiding it, enfeebling, it, looking away from it; today that came up to inundate both the banks and irresistibly assert itself in unmistakable terms. Gora did not have the strength today to condemn it as wrong, to ignore it as trivial.

The day passed like this. At last when afternoon was fading into evening Gora picked up a *cādar* and went out into the street. Gora said to himself, 'I must take her who is mine. Otherwise I am incomplete in this world; without her I shall be nullified.'

Gora did not have the least doubt that in this wide world Sucharita was alone waiting patiently for his call. Today, this very evening, he will fulfill that expectation.

Gora walked fast through the crowded Calcutta streets. Nothing, no one, seemed to receive his cognition. His mind ran before the body towards the goal.

Arriving at the house Gora suddenly came to a halt. He had come here so many times, but never did he see the main entrance closed. He gave a push and found it was shut from within. Standing at the door he thought a little. Then he knocked a few times on the door.

The bearer came out. Seeing Gora there standing in the evening twilight he told without waiting for him to ask, 'Didi is not at home.'

Where is she?

Since the last few days she has been busy elsewhere in connection with Lalitadidi's marriage.

For the fraction of a second Gora thought he would proceed towards the ceremony hall when an unknown man came out from inside and said, 'Yes, sir, what do you want?'

Surveying him from head to foot Gora replied, 'No, nothing.'

Kailash waxed cordial, 'Why don't you step in and have a smoke!'

Kailash was dying in want of a companion. He would coax anybody to drop in so that he could start a gossip and thus have some respite. During daytime he stands by the roadside, hookah in hand, and watches the passers-by, but after evening he feels exasperated inside the room. Whatever he had to discuss with Harimohini had been exhausted. Harimohini's ability at conversation was very limited too. Therefore, Kailash sat on a cot in the small room near the main entrance, hookah in hand, and from time to time called the servant to gossip with him and thus pass the time.

Gora refused, 'Sorry, I cannot sit with you now.'

Before Kailash could properly repeat his request Gora had crossed the turn of the lane.

Gora had an idea firmly rooted in his mind that most events of his life were not chance sequences, nor did they take place just because of his own volition. He was born to serve some special purpose of the deity or destiny that ruled his country.

Therefore, he tried to read special meanings even into the small events of his own life. Today when he rushed towards Sucharita's door under the impulse of such a strong desire and then heard she was not there, he took this as a sign of that divine purpose. The power who had been directing Gora's life signaled his inclination this way. In this life Sucharita's door should remain closed to him, Sucharita was not destined for him. A man like Gora must not be carried away by his personal desires, longings; for him there must not be any scope for personal happiness or personal misery. He was the Brahmin of Bharatbarsha, and he was destined to worship God on behalf of Bharatbarsha; his mission was to dedicate his life in the service of Bharatbarsha. Attachment, or fondness was not for him. Gora said to himself, 'God clearly revealed to me what attachment was like; he showed to me it was not white, not calm; it was crimson like wine and pungent like wine; it does not allow the intellect any rest, it confuses your vision; I am an ascetic; this has no place in my pursuit.'

70

After a prolonged torment for days Sucharita found such comfort and solace with Anandamoyee as she had never received before. Anandamoyee drew her so close and with such perfect ease that Sucharita forgot there was a time when she was not known or close to her. Somehow she had seen through her mind, and without uttering a word could convey a deep solace to the girl. Sucharita had never before mentioned the word '*Mā*' this way with the whole of her heart. Even without any need for calling, but just for the pleasure of voicing the address, she would find pretexts to call Anandamoyee as '*Mā*'. When Lalita's marriage was over, and Sucharita went to bed, exhausted with the day's work, she could not sleep; the thought that tormented her was how would she leave Anandamoyee and go away. She murmured to herself, '*Mā*, *Mā*, *Mā*!' As she chanted the call her heart swelled and tears rolled down. At such a time she saw Anandamoyee suddenly lifting the mosquito net, and entering her bed. She touched her fondly and asked, 'Were you calling me?'

Then Sucharita became conscious that she was calling, '*Mā*, *Mā*.' Sucharita could not answer and instead pressing her face in Anandamoyee's lap wept inconsolably. Without saying a word Anandamoyee consoled her by the affectionate touch of her hand. That night she slept in the same bed.

Anandamoyee could not take leave immediately after Binoy's marriage was over. She said, 'Both of them are novice—how can I leave without getting them started a little in their new life?'

Sucharita said, '*Mā*, in that case I shall also stay with you.'

Lalita also eagerly enjoined, 'Yes, *Mā*, let Suchididi too stay on with us these few days.'

On getting scent of the discussion Satish too ran in and hanging from the neck of Sucharita kicked his feet and announced, 'Fine, Didi, I am also staying on.'

Sucharita said, 'Don't you have to study Bakhtiyār?'

Satish said, 'Binoybabu will help me with the study.'

Sucharita said, 'Binoybabu cannot coach you now.'

Binoy shouted from the adjacent room, 'Of course I can. I don't think I have become so inept within these few days, and the little I learnt by burning midnight oil over the years is forgotten in one night.'

Anandamoyee asked Sucharita, 'Will your Masi agree?'

Sucharita said, 'I am writing a letter to her.'

Anandamoyee said, 'You needn't write. Leave it to me.'

Anandamoyee knew Harimohini might resent if Sucharita wished to stay on. But if the request was made by her she should be the target of Harimohini's resentment, and that did not matter.

Anandamoyee wrote, she will have to stay at Binoy's house for a while in order to get Lalita started on her new domestic responsibilities; in this situation if Sucharita too stays on with her that should be of great help.

Harimohini was not only angry at this letter but also a serious suspicion stirred in her mind. She thought since she had debarred the son to her house, now the mother enters the scene and throws her net in order to trap Sucharita. She clearly envisioned the conspiracy of mother and son. She also recalled that during their very first encounter she did not like Anandamoyee's ways. She must not make any delay and secure Sucharita inside the haveli of the famous Roy clan as early as possible. Furthermore, how long could she keep Kailash waiting thus? The poor fellow had already blackened the walls of the house with his tobacco soot.

The very next morning after receiving the letter Harimohini herself came to Binoy's house in a palanquin along with a servant. Sucharita, Lalita and Anandamoyee were then downstairs, already engaged at preparation for the day's cooking. On the upper floor Satish was noisily preparing his lesson, memorizing English words, along with their spellings and Bengali synonyms at the top of his voice. At home such sonority of his voice was not audible—but here he was under the compulsion to prove that he was not neglecting his studies, and he had to add unnecessarily a lot of zeal and pitch to his voice.

Anandamoyee received Harimohini with special honour. But without paying any heed to social manners she came straight to her point, 'I have come to take Radharani back with me.'

Anandamoyee said, 'Very well. Take her. But please drop in for a while.'

Harimohini refused, 'No, my worship, etc. are yet to be done. I have not yet recited my daily chant. I cannot wait here at this hour.'

Without saying a word Sucharita continued chopping gourd. Harimohini addressed her directly, 'Do you hear? It is getting late.'

Lalita and Anandamoyee sat silently. Sucharita left her work and said, 'Come, Masi.'

Harimohini was about to proceed towards the palanquin when Sucharita held her hand and said, 'No, come inside to this room once.'

Taking her inside the room Sucharita said firmly, 'As you have come to take me I won't send you back before others. I am coming with you, but this very noon I shall come back here.'

Harimohini was vexed, 'What an idea indeed! Why don't say instead you'll stay here forever!'

Sucharita said, 'I am not that lucky. That's why I wont leave her these few days when I am fortunate enough to live in her proximity.'

Harimohini was annoyed to the core at this reply but considered it wiser not to express her feelings right now.

Sucharita came to Anandamoyee and said smilingly, '*Mā*, I am going home just for a short break and shall come back quickly.'

Anandamoyee asked no questions and said, 'Very well, *Mā*!'

Sucharita whispered into Lalita's ears, 'I shall come back for lunch.'

Standing before the palanquin, Sucharita asked, 'What about Satish?'

Harimohini said, 'Leave Satish alone.'

Lest Satish's presence proves an obstacle to her scheme she preferred Satish's absence from the scene.

After the two boarded the palanquin Harimohini tried to broach the matter. She said, 'So Lalita got married. Well, it is fine. Pareshbabu's worries—for at least one daughter—are now over.'

This was followed by a discourse on the guardian's unbearable, worrying responsibility regarding an unmarried daughter, 'How can I tell you, I have no other preoccupation. Even when I chant god's names the same thought disturbs me. To tell you the truth, I cannot apply my mind to worship as I could earlier. I ask my god, 'Oh Gopiballabh, you had relieved me of every distraction, then why have you entrapped me again in this new mesh!'

Harimohini gave the impression that this was not just mundane domestic anxiety for Harimohini, but it was also obtruding her way to spiritual emancipation; but even the prospect of such a grave crisis failed to elicit any response from Sucharita; Harimohini could not make out the exact reaction in her mind. She recalled the proverbial cliché—silence meant assent—and sought solace by citing it in her favour. She presumed Sucharita had softened a little.

Harimohini gave the hint that she had nearly achieved the impossible job of securing the entry of a girl like Sucharita into Hindu society. Such a chance was quite imminent when she could join the feast at the same row with high families in the Hindu hierarchy and yet none would dare to raise a finger.

When the introductory remarks came upto this point the palanquin reached the house. The two got down at the door. While making for the upper floor Sucharita saw an unknown man in the room by the gate; a bearer was giving him an oil massage with a lot of noise and slaps. He did not show any embarrassment, but watched her with remarkable curiosity instead.

Reaching upstairs Harimohini informed about the arrival of her brother-in-law. Sucharita rightly guessed the implication of this event by relating it to Harimohini's introductory lecture. Harimohini tried to convince her,—since there was guest in the house it won't be good manners to leave him unattended and go back in the noon.

Sucharita shook her head emphatically, 'No, Masi, I must go.'

Harimohini said, 'Well. Do go. But why don't you stay today and go tomorrow?'

Sucharita said, 'I shall take my bath now, and immediately after that I start for Baba's house for my lunch there; from there I shall go to Lalita's house.'

Then Harimohini said unambiguously, 'But he has come specifically to see you.'

Sucharita went red in the face. She said, 'What's the point of seeing me?'

Harimohini said, 'Hear her! Is it possible these days to do away with this part of "seeing"? That could do in the olden days. Your uncle had never seen me before the marriage ceremony.'

Saying this she instantly hastened to add a number of distractors; how before her own marriage the famous Roy family had sent to her father's house an old employee of the clan, Anathbandhu by name, along with an old maid-servant, named Thakurdasi, who were flanked by two turban-wearing stick-wielding gatekeepers; how her guardians were anxious and eager to please those attendants of the Roy clan by food and other pleasantries. Finishing the description of that memorable event she let out a sigh and observed that times had changed since.

Harimohini said, 'There's no occasion for any fuss; he will just see you for five minutes before leaving.'

Sucharita said, 'No.'

That 'No' was so emphatic, so clear that Harimohini had to beat retreat. She said, 'Well, have your way. In fact this seeing is not necessary at all. However, Kailash is a modern youth, and like you does not obey old customs; he says, "I shall see the bride with my own eyes." So, I thought,—as you meet all sorts of people—"Well, what is there in it—I shall introduce her to you any day." Anyway, since you feel shy seeing can be dispensed with.'

Saying this she proceeded with her narration regarding the extraordinary education of Kailash, how he had endangered the village postmaster by one scratch of his pen; moreover, she explicated with energy how indispensable Kailash was whenever anybody of the neighbouring villages had the occasion to file a court case or write an application. And regarding the moral character—to say anything is superfluous. After his wife's death he was not at all agreeable to the proposal of a second marriage; it was only after the immense insistence of relatives that he had agreed, and that too only in order to obey the order of his elders. Harimohini herself too had to exert a lot before he could agree to the present proposal. Did he agree to listen! And why should he! Aren't they a great family! What great prestige do they command in society!

Sucharita did not agree to lower this prestige by any means. No she won't. She did not consider her own glory or interest. She even appeared not to care for the bleak prospect of never getting a chance to enter Hindu society. To make Kailash agree to marry by means of great persuasion was no small cause of honour for Sucharita. But she was too much of a fool to grasp the point. Not only that, she even took this as insult. Harimohini was thoroughly puzzled by this absurd approach of modern times.

Then in her fury she started throwing abusive suggestions about Gora. 'However much Gora may boast of his Hinduism what is his position in the Hindu society! Who cares for him! If out of greed he marries some propertied girl from a Brahmo family, how will he escape the verdict and condemnation of his society! Then won't the entire money go by the gutter towards stopping the foul mouthed public.' She rambled on this way.

Sucharita said, 'Masi, why do you say such things! You know very well how baseless all this is.'

Harimohini then said that she had reached an age when it was not possible for anyone to deceive her. She kept her eyes and ears open. She sees all and understands all, and this has left her in stunned silence. She expressed her conviction that Gora, in complicity with his mother, was trying to marry Sucharita, and the secret purpose of that marriage was not noble at all, and if she could not save Sucharita with the assistance of the Roy clan, sooner or later that will be Sucharita's fate.

It became unbearable for Sucharita in spite of her habitual patience. She said, 'I admire and respect the persons whom you are abusing. Since you'll never understand my relationship with them, I have no choice—I leave at once; I shall return only after you calm down and I feel I can live with you alone in the house.'

Harimohini said, 'If you are not in love with Gaurmohanbabu, if there has been any such decision that you two won't marry each other, then what's wrong with this suitor? You are not going to remain a spinster!'

Sucharita said, 'Why not? I won't marry.'

Harimohini's eyes widened in amazement, 'Going like this till old age—.'

Sucharita said, 'Yes, till death.'

71

This jolt ushered a change in Gora's mind. He probed the cause—why and how Sucharita came to take possession of his mind. He saw that he had mixed with them on a regular basis, and in course of this had got involved without being aware of it. He had defiantly transgressed the traditionally forbidden frontier. This was not the way of our country. If one did not respect one's limits he knowingly and unknowingly causes harm to himself, while also losing the pure energy to ensure good to others. Proximity stirred up various emotions which adversely affected knowledge, dedication, strength.

He had stumbled upon this realization not only through his connection with girls of a Brahmo family. Gora went out to meet common people, and there too he was about to lose himself by being caught in a sort of cesspool; because at every step he was mortified by kindness, a kindness that conditioned his condemnation—this was bad, this was wrong, this must go, etc. But didn't this very instinct of compassion curb our impersonal judgment of right and wrong? As our instinct for kindness grows strong, proportionately our ability to have a detached view of truth declines; the soot arising from the smoke of compassion accumulates on everything and even a light coloured object looks deep through it.

Gora reasoned with himself,—this is the reason why the people in whom the responsibility of collective good was reposed were expected to maintain detachment according to the traditional custom of our country. That an intimate connection of the king with his subjects was the way to good administration was a completely baseless idea. The kind of knowledge the king should command about his subjects did but get polluted by his direct contact with the people. This was the reason why the subjects willingly kept the king apart, encircled by his distance. The moment the king became one of them his relevance too was lost.

Similarly, the Brahmin too should maintain his distance, his detachment. Since the Brahmin was committed to bring good to the society, he had to necessarily deprive himself of the proximity of many.

Gora told himself, 'I am that Brahmin of traditional Bharatbarsha.' There were Brahmins these days who had become involved with all, who had become engrossed in trade, who had—out of materialistic greed—willingly put on the noose of slavery around the neck; Gora did not count them among living items of his country, and rather looked down upon them as worse than the Sudra; because the Sudra survived in his own right as Sudra, whereas these renegade Brahmins were dead in the absence of real Brahminism in them, and thereby impure. Bharatbarsha today was undergoing the humbling *Aśauc*, the period of impurity.

Gora whipped up his mind to the resolve that he would invoke that spirit of that ideal Brahminism and pursue the ideal of reviving the same through his own life. He told himself, 'I must be extremely pure. I am not standing at par with others. Friendship is not essential for me; I am not of that category for whom female company is the one great pleasure; and any intimate involvement with the lowly people should be completely forbidden for me. As the earth wistfully watches the sky for signs of rain, they have been waiting for the Brahmin—if I get too close with them who will save them?'

Prior to this Gora had paid no attention to the actual ritual of icon worship. Since the time his heart had risen, he found it difficult to restrain himself, work had turned stale and devoid of meaning, his existence had been split up—with one half of it languishing in pain,—Gora was seeking to absorb himself in the act of worshipping. Sitting motionless before the image of God, Gora tried to concentrate on the image. But he did not feel the stirring of the right emotion within. He can interpret God in rational terms, he must turn it into a symbol for his acceptance. But you could not offer the love of your heart to a symbol. You could not worship an abstract spiritual idea. Rather he got a better feel of joy and devotion when, instead of trying to concentrate on worship inside the puja room, he let himself to be carried away by his thoughts and words in arguing with himself or with somebody else in his own study.

Still Gora did not give up. Everyday he sat down at his worship, he took this as a discipline. He persuaded himself to believe that when one failed to connect with others through emotion then one could relate through discipline at least. Whenever Gora entered a village, he would enter the local temple and deeply meditate, 'Here is my special place; on the one side there is God, on the other the devotee; the Brahmin is to serve as the bridge between the two.' Eventually Gora arrived at the conclusion that the Brahmin had no need for devotion. Devotion was for the common man. The bridge between the devotee and his object of devotion was a bridge of knowledge. As the bridge connects the two, simultaneously it also helps to maintain the frontier between the two. If pure knowledge does not stand as a space between the devotee and God, then things become distorted. Therefore, the ecstasy of devotion is not for the Brahmin to indulge in. A Brahmin should be engaged in the pursuit of maintaining the purity of this devotion for the use of the common man while himself sitting on the peak of this knowledge. Just as in the material world the Brahmin is denied the comfort of hedonistic pleasure, so he should deny himself the pleasure of devotion in his worship. This precisely was the glory of the Brahmin; in material world he is to be guided by rules and restraint, whereas in religious pursuit knowledge is his domain.

His heart had subjugated him; for that offence Gora passed the verdict of banishment on his heart. But who was to lead it to exile! Where was the army to execute the order!

72

Preparation was going on for the purification ceremony which was to be held at a garden by the Ganga.

Abinash was unhappy that the ceremony was going to be held outside Calcutta and thereby it wouldn't attract adequate public attention. Abinash knew Gora needed no purification for himself, but the country needed it. The moral effect could be of good use. And that was the reason why it should have been held right in the midst of the crowd.

But Gora did not agree. The kind of huge fire-rite he envisioned, in accompaniment of Vedic mantra, would not seem befitting in the heart of the city. That required a *tapovan*. He envisioned the rite, on the lonely Ganga bank—made resonant with Vedamantra and radiant with the lustre from the altar fires, as his invocation to the ancient India which was the guide to the world; he would take his dip in the river, and thus purified he would receive his initiation into a new life at the hand of this guide. Gora was not concerned about the moral effect.

Being left with no other choice Abinash finally sought the help of newspapers. Without informing Gora he advertised the ceremony in all the big papers. Not only that, he also arranged for lengthy articles on the Editorial page. These essays claimed that a pure valiant Brahmin like Gora could not be touched by any contamination; still taking on his own shoulders all the sins of Bharatbarsha which had fallen in the present times Gora was opting for this purification ceremony. Abinash wrote, 'Just as our country was suffering for its own evil deeds in the prison of foreign ruler, Gora too in his own life embraced this misery of imprisonment. Thus, he has borne the country's misery on his back, and in the same way he also gets ready to undergo purification for all the aberrations of the country. Therefore, my dear Brethren of Bengal, my dear two hundred fifty million unhappy children of India, you—' etc., etc.

Gora was vexed like anything at reading these papers. But Abinash was incorrigible. Even when Gora scolded him he did not mind; rather he was happy at being scolded, 'My guru mentally lives on a divine plane, and does not know a thing about the ways of this earthy world. Like Narad, a dweller of heaven, he plays his lyre to make Bishnu melt to create Ganga, but channelising the Ganga downward to the earth and thereby restore the ashes of King Sagar's children was the job of Bhagirath and not of a heaven-dweller. The two things were completely different.' Therefore, when Gora flared up at Abinash's interferences, Abinash only laughed to himself and his devotion to Gora only increased proportionately. He says to himself, 'Our Guru looks like Shiva, and his nature too is like that deity; he understands nothing, has no practical sense; gets angry at no cause, and again takes not long to cool down.'

Thanks to Abinash's enterprise Gora's plan for purification sent ripples all around. The crowd swelled by each passing day to see Gora in his house, to know him. Everyday brought so many letters that he stopped opening letters. Gora felt as if the austere purity of the ceremony as envisioned by him got eroded by this publicity; it became a matter of ostentation. Perhaps that was the rule of the times.

Krishnadayal did not even touch a newspaper these days. But the rumour eventually reached the interior of his *Sādhanāśram*. Krishnadayal's flatterers informed him with appropriate pride that his worthy son Gora was set for a grand purification, and expressed the hope that by following the sanctimonious footsteps of his father he too would eventually emerge as another divinely blessed monk like him.

It was so long ago since Krishnadayal had last stepped into Gora's room. He changed from his silken puja costume into common cotton cloth and went up straight into Gora's room. He could not see Gora there.

He asked the servant. The servant informed him Gora was in the worship room.

He was visibly jolted. What was he doing in the worship room?

He worships.

In a great haste Krishnadayal made for the puja room and reaching there found that Gora was really seated at puja.

Krishnadayal called from outside, 'Gora!'

Surprised at his father's sudden appearance here Gora stood up. Krishnadayal had installed his own deity in his *Sādhanāśram*; although theirs was a Vaishnavite family he personally had opted for the Shakta cult, and had no direct connection with the family deity since a long time.

He shouted out to Gora, 'Come, come, come out this instant.'

Gora came out. Krishnadayal was petulant, 'What is this! What is your business here!'

Gora did not reply. Krishnadayal peevishly said, 'There is the family priest employed for doing this. He is daily performing the rituals, that is enough for all the members. Why have you been interfering in this!'

Gora said, 'There is nothing wrong in this.'

Krishnadayal said, 'Nothing wrong! What do you say! Everything's wrong. Why must one take up a work for which one is not entitled? It involves offence. It involves wrong not only on your part but also on the part of the whole family.'

Gora said, 'If you consider the question of genuine devotion then very few are indeed entitled to sit before God. But do you mean to say that Ramhari priest has the right to do puja here whereas I don't have even that right?'

Suddenly Krishnadayal was at a loss for words. After a little silence he said, 'Look here, worship is Ramhari's family trade. The offence incurred in course of trade does not count before God. But you have no such excuse. So why must you enter this room?'

It was indeed surprising that there could be such an objection even against such an orthodox Brahmin as Gora regarding his entering the puja room; but since the objection came from none other than a man like Krishnadayal it did not sound too odd. Gora, therefore, patiently listened and did not say anything.

Then Krishnadayal said, 'I have been hearing another thing Gora! Is it true that you have invited pundits for performing a purification ceremony?'

Gora said, 'Yes.'

Krishnadayal burst into a great excitement, 'I won't allow this so long as I am alive. No, not by any means.'

Gora was about to explode in defiance; 'But why?', he asked.

Krishnadayal was exasperated, 'What why! Didn't I tell you earlier, no purification can be held.'

Gora said, 'Yes, you said. But you did not explain the reasons.'

Krishnadayal said, 'I don't see any point in explaining. We are your seniors, you should obey us. There is no custom of doing these scriptural rites without our permission. Do you know you have to perform *śrādhba* rites for your ancestors during such a ceremony?'

Gora asked in surprise, 'But what is the obstacle to such rites?'

Krishnadayal got angry and said, 'There is every obstacle. I cannot allow it.'

Gora was hurt to the core; he said, 'Look here, this is my own plan. I am doing this in order to be restored to my purity. Why do you take the trouble of arguing in vain on the matter!'

Krishnadayal said, 'I tell you Gora, don't jump into arguments at every chance. These are not matters of argument at all. There are many such things which are beyond your understanding as yet. I am telling you once again,—this your assumption that you have been able to enter the Hindu society is a complete mistake. You do not have that ability. Every drop of your blood, your existence from head to foot, goes against it. One cannot be a Hindu all of a sudden, even if one longs to be! It needs the accumulated good deeds of many births.'

Gora's face turned crimson. He said, 'I do not know of rebirths. But can't I claim the right that runs through the blood of your line?'

Krishnadayal rebuked, 'Arguing again! Don't you hesitate to defy me in the face! Yet you call yourself a Hindu! Indeed how to do away with the Western pungency! Do what I say. Stop this all.'

Gora stood silently with lowered head. After a time he said, 'If I don't undergo purification I may not sit in the same row with others at the marriage feast of Shashimukhi.'

Krishnadayal looked enthused and said, 'Well, let it be. It does not really matter. They can arrange a separate seat for you.'

Gora said, 'That means in any case I shall have to remain ostracised in the society.'

Krishnadayal said, 'That is not bad either.'

Noticing Gora's amazement at his remark Krishnadayal explained, 'Look at me for instance. I do not participate in community feast nor join any invitation. What connection do I have with society? Since you want to adhere to the pure ascetic life I think this should be your way too. I envision only your good in this.'

At midday Krishnadayal sent for Abinash, and asked, 'I think it is you people who have enthused Gora into this madness.'

Abinash said, 'What do you say! It is your Gora who enthuses us, whereas he himself remains calm in comparison.'

Krishnadayal said, 'But my son, I tell you, I won't have those programmes of yours—that purification—cleansing, etc. I do not give my consent to this. You must stop it immediately.'

Abinash thought, what a wrongheaded oldie! Of course there were many historical examples of incorrigible fathers who could not appreciate the nobility of their eminent sons; Krishnadayal obviously belonged to this class of fathers. Indeed Krishnadayal would have done better if he sought to learn from his own son instead of keeping the company of some worthless monks day and night.

Abinash was a clever man; he was not one to waste energy where it was no use arguing or trying to secure moral effect. He said, 'Alright Sir, if you don't want it won't come off. Anyway, since all the preparations are complete, invitations too have been sent out, and the time too is short; let us do one thing—let Gora stay away, we shall perform the purification rites—you know there is no dearth of sins among countrymen.'

At this assurance from Abinash Krishnadayal felt relieved.

Indeed Gora had never much respect for Krishnadayal's opinions. Today too he did not mentally accept his admonition. In the context of a life which was higher than domestic life, Gora did not consider it obligatory to abide by the commands of parents. But still through the whole day he felt a certain heaviness of heart. He had a vague hunch that some truth was hiding behind the apparent absurdity of Krishnadayal's admonitions. A shapeless nightmare was, as it were, haunting him, which he could not get over by any means. He had a curious feeling that someone was trying to push him back from all sides. The magnitude of his loneliness suddenly became apparent to him. The field of work stretching before him was immense in its expanse, the work envisioned was gigantic, yet there was no one by his side on this day.

73

Purification ceremony will be held tomorrow, and according to the plan Gora will stay in the garden from tonight. When he was about to start Harimohini appeared. Gora did not feel too happy at seeing her. Gora said, 'You have come—but I must start right now—*Mā* too is not at home for the last few days. If you want to meet her then—.'

Harimohini said, 'No son, it is you I have come to meet. You must sit for a while and listen to me. I shall not take long.'

Gora sat down. Harimohini started with reference to Sucharita. She said, the girl has improved a lot under the good guidance of Gora. Indeed, she did not even drink water from each and everyone as she used to earlier and thus was showing signs of all-round improvement in this regard. 'My son, did I have a small worry for her! I cannot tell you in so many words how you have helped me by bringing her round to the right path. May God make you a lord of lords. Marry a nice obedient girl from a good family, worthy of your family status, may your house be illuminated, may you acquire wealth, happiness and sons.'

After this she broached the real issue—Sucharita was already grown up, she should not delay a day in getting married, if she grew up in a Hindu family by now she would have been showered with children. Gora would surely agree with her that this delay in marriage was a serious departure from the custom. After suffering unbearable anxiety over a prolonged period regarding the problem of Sucharita's marriage, Harimohini has at last, by means of a lot of pleading and coaxing, persuaded her brother-in-law Kailash to come over to Calcutta and tie the knot. All was settled, the bridegroom's party won't even take any dowry, and raise no objection about her past history; Harimohini had squashed all such potential problems with her wonderful strategy; but now at this turn—people will be surprised to know that Sucharita has turned defiant. Harimohini has no idea what is in her mind; God alone knows if she has been misled by somebody, or if she has fallen in love with someone—.

'But son, let me tell you frankly, she is not the right bride for you. If she is passed off as bride in some remote village nobody will know of her antecedents there; somehow that will be managed. But you live in the city; if you marry her you will not be able to face the public.'

Gora angrily cried, 'What nonsense are you talking about! Who told you that I visited her to negotiate marriage with her!'

Harimohini said, 'How do I know dear! I hear it has come out in the papers and since then I am nearly dying of shame.'

Gora guessed Haranbabu or some of his friends had gone to the media over the matter. Gora clenched his fist and shouted, 'Damn'd lie!'

Harimohini started at the thunderous voice and said, 'That's my belief too. Now I have a request to you, please don't say no. Please come to see Radharani for once.'

Gora asked, 'Why?'

Harimohini said, 'You just once try to make her see reason.'

Gora's mind prompted him to rush at once for Sucharita on this excuse. His heart told him, 'Come, have a last look at her today. Tomorrow is your purification—thereafter you will be an ascetic. This night is the only time in between, and you are to get just a brief slot even of this little time to see her. It will not be sin. And even if it be, the sin will be burnt to ashes tomorrow.'

After a little silence Gora asked, 'Tell me what am I to convince her.'

Nothing much but this—according to Hindu custom a girl of Sucharita's age should marry without delay and that it was amazing good luck for a girl in Sucharita's position to get a good bridegroom like Kailash in Hindu society.

It seemed to pierce his heart from end to end like some missile. Gora was tormented like anything to recall the man he had seen at the door of Sucharita's house. That man will have Sucharita! Even the imagination was unbearable to Gora. His mind cried out in rebellion, 'No, no, it cannot be, no, never.'

It was impossible that Sucharita should be united with another; her silent deep heart, brimming with intelligence and profound emotions, was never disclosed to any second person in this world apart from Gora, and will never be. How wonderful it was! How exquisite! What an indescribable soul dwelling within the core of that mysterious mansion had been revealed to him! How many times one could be seen like that, and how many could be seen that way! The person who had seen Sucharita by the blessing of some benevolent destiny in this intense truth, had felt her essence with all his being, was the one who really got her. Who else could have her ever!'

Harimohini said, 'Shall she remain a spinster till death! Is it right!'

That too was true. Will not Gora have his purification tomorrow? After that he will turn an immaculately pure Brahmin. What will happen to Sucharita then? Will she remain unmarried for ever! Who has the right to impose such a lifelong burden on her? What could be heavier for a woman to bear!

Harimohini rambled on. It did not reach Gora's ears. Gora thought on, 'Baba has been so intently forbidding me against undergoing purification; does his command have no value? The life I have been planning for me may be just my imagination, it is not natural for me perhaps. I may stumble, being crippled under the weight of that unnatural burden. Under that endless burden I will not be able to do anything at ease. I can see for myself what a longing pervades and wrings my heart. How shall I remove this rock! Baba has somehow seen through me, and known that deep within my heart I am not the Brahmin, the ascetic; that's why he forbade me so emphatically.'

Gora said to himself, 'Let me go to him. This very evening I shall ask with all the strength of my appeal what has he perceived in me. Why did he say even the path of purification was closed to me? If he can make me understand I shall be free. Free!'

Gora told Harimohini, 'You wait just a bit. I shall come back soon.'

Gora hurried towards his father's suite. He had a hunch that Krishnadayal knew something which could free him at once.

The door of *Sādhanāśram* was closed. He banged on it twice; it did not open, neither did anybody respond. Fine aroma of incense sticks and powder floated out from the closed room. Tonight Krishnadayal closed all the doors to his suite and was practicing some very intricate and very difficult yogic procedure along with his monk coach. Tonight no one was to have access there.

74

Gora said to himself, 'No, the purification is not to wait for tomorrow. It has started this very day. A much bigger fire than the one to be lit tomorrow has flared up. It is because I have to make a great sacrifice on the eve of my new life that God has stirred such a great longing in my mind. Otherwise, why should such a strange thing happen? I had been in another world.

There was no chance of my meeting them on social plane. Nor do people of such opposed ideas normally come close in this world. Again, nobody could have imagined that this meeting could wake up such an uncontrollable longing in an indifferent person like me. Yes, this was necessary. Exactly such a desire was needed today. So far whatever I gave to my country was given easily without costing me any pain. I could not understand why should people hesitate to sacrifice anything for the country. But a great mission is not performed with such easy gifts. It demands suffering. It is by cutting off the umbilical chord that I should get reborn. Tomorrow morning I shall undergo the ritualistic part of my purification before the public. Just the night before it my ruling destiny has knocked on my door. If I do not have my real purification at the innermost core of my heart how shall I receive the external purification to be bestowed on me tomorrow! It is only after offering to my God the one gift which involves most acute pain for me that I can be really shorn of every possession, be really pure; it is only then that I will be a Brahmin.'

As soon as Gora came back Harimohini pleaded, 'Son, please come with me for once. If you come, if you say one sentence all problems will be over.'

Gora said, 'Why should I go? What is my connection with her? Nothing!'

Harimohini said, 'Don't you know how she adores you like a God, looks up to you as her guru.'

A red-hot shaft of lightning seemed to rend his heart from end to end.

Gora said, 'I see no need of going. There is no chance of my ever meeting her again.'

Harimohini was highly pleased, 'Of course, of course. It is not decent either to meet such an old spinster. But Baba, I won't leave you before you do this little service to me. After this I shall never disturb you again.'

Gora shook his head repeatedly. No more, by no means. It is over. He has already made his offer to his God. He won't allow anything to stain his purity any more. He won't go to see her.

When Harimohini realized it was not possible to persuade Gora she said, 'If you cannot go by any means then please do one little favour my son! Please write a note to her.'

Gora shook his head. That cannot be. No communication any more.

Harimohini suggested, 'Well, you can address me in your note. Just write two lines. You know all the scriptures, suppose I have come to you for some instruction.'

Gora asked, 'What instruction?'

Harimohini said, 'That the highest mission of a grown up Hindu girl is to get married and perform the domestic duties.'

Gora fell silent for a time and then said, 'Look here. You don't try to drag me into this matter. I am not the authority to issue instructions.'

Harimohini then said a bit sharply, 'Why don't you clearly admit the secret wish of your mind? You trapped her first, and then refuse to loosen it, saying, "don't drag me". What's the meaning of this? The crux is, you don't want her to shake you off from her mind.'

If it were another time Gora would have flared up in anger. He could not have accepted even such a genuine allegation. But today his purification had started; so he did not get angry. He probed deep within himself and saw Harimohini was right. He was about to slash ruthlessly the strong bond he had with Sucharita—yet longed to leave some subtle chord untouched, pretending he did not notice it. He had not yet been able to completely forego his longing for Sucharita.

But this miserliness won't do,—this offering through one hand and retaining the same by the other hand.

He immediately pulled out a sheet of paper and wrote in big bold letters,—'Marriage is the religion for women, domesticity is her principal pursuit. This marriage is not for fulfillment of desire, but for the welfare of all. Whether the family life is happy or unhappy, the mission of the woman's life is to embrace that life, and by being chaste pure loyal she will keep religion manifest within the four walls of her homestead. That is their mission.'

Harimohini said, 'Could you please add a few words about our Kailash in this note, my son?'

Gora said, 'No, I don't know him. I cannot write about him.'

Harimohini carefully folded the piece of paper, tied it neatly in a knot at the end of her sari, and returned home. Sucharita was still with Anandamoyee at Lalita's place. Apprehending that Lalita's house would not be convenient for her discussion, and moreover hearing the adverse opinions of Lalita and Anandamoyee about the marriage proposal Sucharita might waver, Harimohini sent message to Sucharita to come to her once during the day; she had some urgent matter to discuss; after this she could go back to Lalita in the afternoon.

The following day Sucharita had braced herself up to a stern stance before she came. She knew her aunt would again pester her with the same proposal. She had decided to stop her finally today by some very assertive reply.

After lunch Harimohini said, 'Last evening I went up to your guru.'

Sucharita shrank at the idea. Did Masi again insult him under some excuse!

Harimohini said, 'Don't worry, Radharani, I did not go to pick up a quarrel with him. I was alone, so I thought why don't I go to him to hear some good talk. In course of conversation your name was mentioned. I found that he too shared my opinion in this matter. He didn't seem to be favourably inclined to the idea that a girl should remain unmarried too long. He holds it to be against religion. It may be common among the Europeans, but won't do in Hindu society. I have also told him frankly about our Kailash. Yes, he is a wise man indeed.'

Sucharita was dying in shame and agony.

Harimohini said, 'I think you look up to him as guru. Shouldn't you obey his command?'

Sucharita remained silent. Harimohini said, 'I told him, "Son, come and convince her yourself; she does not obey us." He said, "No, I should not meet her any more. That is against the custom of our Hindu society." I asked, "Then what's the way?" Then he wrote this in his own hand. Just look at this.'

Saying this Harimohini slowly untied the knot of her sari and unfolding the paper held it before Sucharita's eyes.

Sucharita read. She felt she could not breathe. She sat stiff like a wooden doll.

There was nothing in the note that was new or unreasonable. Sucharita did not even disagree with the words as such. But the implication of sending the note through Harimohini tormented her to the core. Why this command from Gora today? Of course, a time will come when she may have to marry; but what was the compunction on Gora's part in thus hastening the matter? Was all the work of Gora with her over altogether? Had she posed any obstacle or affected Gora's duties in any way? Did she have nothing more to offer to Gora, nor anything to expect from him? But she had never thought this way; she was still waiting for him. Sucharita tried desperately to struggle with this unbearable pain but found no consolation.

Harimohini gave her a long time to think over. In the meantime she even stole a nap as was her daily habit. On waking up she came to Sucharita's room and found her still in the same posture.

She said, 'Radhu, why are you brooding so much? What is there to think about at all? Has Gaurmohanbabu written anything wrong?'

Sucharita said quietly, 'No, he has written the right thing.'

Harimohini was immensely relieved and said, 'Then what's the point in delaying any more?'

Sucharita said, 'No, there is no point. I shall go to Baba for once.'

Harimohini said, 'Look here Radhu, your father will never like the idea of your marrying into Hindu society. But if he who is your guru—.'

Sucharita lost her patience and sharply turned back, 'Masi, why do you pester me with the same nagging theme? I am not going to Baba to discuss marriage. I am going just to see him.'

The very company of Paresh was a source of solace for Sucharita. Reaching Paresh's house Sucharita found him busy packing clothes in a wooden trunk.

Sucharita asked, 'Baba, what is this!'

Paresh smiled a little and said, '*Mā*, I am going for a trip to the Simla hills. I shall start tomorrow morning.'

Sucharita came to learn the story of the great turmoil that lay hidden behind this smile. His wife and daughters at home, and his friends and acquaintances outside did not allow Paresh a moment's respite. If he did not go away for a time a turmoil will continue to seethe around him. He had decided to leave the following day, and yet he had no near one today to help him with the packing; he had to do it himself. Seeing this Sucharita felt deeply mortified. She stopped Pareshbabu and first completely emptied the trunk. Then she neatly folded the clothes with great care and arranged them again in the trunk and placed his favourite books so that they would not be damaged in movement. Thus while doing the packing Sucharita asked in a soft voice, 'Baba, will you go alone?'

Paresh sensed a sadness in this query and said, 'But you know Radhe, that is no problem for me.'

Sucharita said, 'No Baba, I shall go with you.'

Paresh watched her face. Sucharita said again, 'Baba, I won't give you any trouble.'

Paresh said, 'Why do you say so? Did you ever cause me any trouble, my daughter?'

Sucharita said, 'It will be no good to me if I stay away from you. I cannot understand many things. If you do not instruct me I shall lose my way. Baba, you tell me to depend on my own intelligence, but I don't have that intelligence, nor do I get that strength within. Baba, you please take me along with you!'

Saying this she turned her back to Paresh and bent her head very low on the clothes inside the trunk. Drops of tears rolled down from her eyes.

75

When Gora handed over the note to Harimohini he felt he had signed off Sucharita in a no-claim deed. But the work was not over instantly just by signing the deed. His heart completely disowned the deed. True, Gora's willforce had signed the deed, but it was only a signature of pen; the deed did not carry the signature of the heart. The heart, therefore, refused to obey. So great was the disobedience that he was about to rush towards Sucharita's house that very night! But at the very moment the church clock struck ten and Gora became conscious that this was not the time for paying social visit. After that Gora had heard all the following gongs of the church clock from hour to hour; because his plan of going to the garden at Bali that night did not materialize. He sent message that he would reach there the following morning.

He reached the garden early in the morning. But where was that clear and strong mind with which he had envisioned to receive purification!

Many scholar-pundits had arrived. Many more were on the way. Gora greeted all, spoke to all. They applauded Gora again and again, praising his consistent devotion to ancient religion.

The garden became increasingly crowded and noisy. Gora was supervising all around. But in spite of all the noise and pressure of work a voice was ringing deep within him—it told him without pause, 'You have done a wrong! Done a wrong!' He had no time to think clearly what the wrong was, but he could by no means stop this voice protesting deep within himself. Amidst the grand preparation for the ceremony some indwelling enemy was continuously reminding him, 'The wrong remains.' This wrong was not the neglect of rules, not the mistake in chanting mantras, not the violation of the scriptures. This wrong was perpetrated against nature itself; and therefore Gora's entire heart remained aloof, turned away from all the grandeur of the ceremony.

The time for the ceremony drew closer. The hall was made with bamboo frame and canvas walls and covering. After taking the holy dip in the Ganga Gora was changing dress when a restlessness became visible among the crowd. Some anxiety seemed to spread quickly through the entire gathering.

At last Abinash came to report despondently, 'Message has come from your home. Krishnadayalbabu has vomited blood. He has sent messenger with carriage to take you to him immediately.'

Gora hurried back. Abinash was about to board with him. Gora stopped him, 'No, you stay back at reception. You must not leave.'

On entering Krishnadayal's room Gora saw him lying in bed and Anandamoyee sitting at his feet while her hands slowly ran over his feet. Gora anxiously looked at both. Krishnadayal signed him to sit on the chair by his bed. Gora sat down.

Gora asked his mother, 'How is he now?'

Anandamoyee said, 'Slightly better now. A British doctor has been sent for.'

Inside the room there were Shashimukhi and a servant. Krishnadayal waved towards them to go outside.

When he saw all were gone he silently looked at Anandamoyee's face and then addressed Gora in low voice, 'I don't have much time now. Something was kept secret to you till this day, but in case I pass away without telling you about it, I cannot be free.'

Gora turned pale. He sat still. For a long time no one uttered a word.

Krishnadayal broke the silence, 'Gora, those were the days when I did not care about anything; that's why I could make such a blunder. But afterwards there was no way to rectify it.'

Saying this he again lapsed into silence. Gora too sat motionless without making any question.

Krishnadayal resumed, 'I thought perhaps there won't be any need to tell you; things would go on as they did all these years. But now I find that cannot be. How can you perform the funeral rites after my death?'

Krishnadayal seemed to shudder at the very prospect of such a blunder. Gora was growing impatient to know what the secret was. He directly addressed Anandamoyee, '*Mā*, you tell me, what is the mystery. Don't I have the right to perform the funeral rites?'

So long Anandamoyee had been sitting speechless with her face bent down. At Gora's question she raised her head, looked straight at his face, and said, 'No, dear, you have not.'

Gora shrieked, 'Am I not his son?'

Anandamoyee said, 'No.'

Like the erupting volcano the cry shot out—'*Mā*, are you not my *Mā* then?'

Anandamoyee felt her heart was going to burst. She said in the voice of tearless weeping, 'Baba Gora, you are my son, the son of this childless mother. So much more a son you are, Baba, than the son borne in one's own womb.'

Then Gora turned to Krishnadayal and asked, 'Where did you get me then?'

Krishnadayal said, 'It was the time of mutiny. We were at Etawa then. Your mother had run away in fear of the soldiers and took shelter in our house during the night. Your father had died the previous day in an encounter. His name was—'

Gora thundered, 'Don't. Please don't mention names. I don't want to know.'

Surprised at this outburst of Gora Krishnadayal stopped. Then he said, 'He was an Irishman. That very night your mother died after giving birth to you. Since then you have been with us.'

Within a moment Gora found his entire life turned into a strange dream. The foundations on which his life evolved for so many years since childhood collapsed altogether. He could not make out who he was, or where did he stand. As if behind him there was no such thing as a past, and before him the definite image of future, envisioned by him all these years with intent dreams, was suddenly erased to the last dot. Between these he was just trembling like dew-drop on the lotus leaf in a fleeting moment. He had no mother, no father, no country, no race, no name, no clan, no deity. His entire identity was made of one big 'no'. What will he clutch on, what will he do, where will he start at again, what new target will he set himself again, from where and how will he again accumulate the equipments of living day after day step by step! Amidst this strange void without a signpost in any direction he sat dumb like one with a broken compass amidst a vast sea. Looking at his face no one dared to speak another word.

At this time the British doctor arrived along with the Bengali house physician. As the doctor looked at the patient he could not but notice Gora; he wondered, 'Who is this fellow?' Gora's forehead still bore the tilak mark drawn with the sediment from the Gangabank; the silk cloth he had put on after his bath was still on him. He wore no shirt; his huge body was visible through the sparse covering of the silk *cādar*.

Till the other day the very sight of an English doctor would automatically generate a hostility in Gora's mind. Today as the doctor was examining the patient Gora watched him with particular curiosity. He asked himself repeatedly, 'Is this fellow my nearest kin among all the people present here?'

After examining and making some queries the doctor said, 'I don't find the condition that serious. Pulse is not bad, the organs of the body too are functioning alright. If proper care is taken I don't think the symptom will recur.'

After the doctor's departure Gora was about to get up from the chair and leave without a word.

At the doctor's arrival Anandamoyee had withdrawn into the adjacent room. She rushed in and held Gora tightly by the hand; she said, 'Gora, my son, don't be angry with me, please. If you are angry I will not survive!'

Gora said, 'Why didn't you tell me so long! There could have been no harm.'

Anandamoyee took all the blame upon herself; she said, 'My son, it was the fear of losing you that led me to such grave error. If at last that very fear materializes, if you go away from me today, I cannot blame anybody, Gora, but that will be the verdict of death for me, son.'

Gora in answer said only '*Mā*!'

Hearing that address on Gora's lips, the repressed tears of Anandamoyee gushed out at last.

Gora said, '*Mā*, I shall now go to Pareshbabu's house for once.'

Anandamoyee felt the weight lifting from her bosom. She said, 'Yes, my son.'

Krishnadayal became very apprehensive at realising that he was not going to die soon, and yet the secret was already disclosed to Gora! He said, 'Look here Gora, I don't think it is at all necessary to disclose this to anybody. Just you intelligently keep along a middle path. Things will go on as it was going on all along, no one will get a hunch.'

Without answering him Gora went out. He felt comforted at remembering that he had no blood ties with Krishnadayal.

Mahim had no scope to cut office without notice. After making all the necessary arrangements about doctors, treatment, etc., he had just run up to the office to meet his English boss and take leave officially. As Gora was about to leave Mahim returned to run into him. He stopped Gora, 'Gora, where are you going?'

Gora said, 'It is good news. The doctor came. He says the danger is over.'

Mahim was visibly relieved. He said, 'Thank you. The day after tomorrow happens to be an auspicious one. I shall marry off Shashimukhi that very day. But Gora, you'll have to exert yourself a little. And another thing, please warn Binoy, lest he chances to appear here on that day. Abinash is an orthodox Hindu; he has expressed his wish in so many words against the presence of this kind of people at his marriage. I have also another request to you, my brother: I shall invite my British bosses that day; you please don't rush to give them a good thrashing. It is not much; just incline your neck a little and say, "Good evening, Sir." I don't think your Hindu scriptures will get nullified by that little; later on you can consult the pundits about remedial measures. Do you understand, brother? They are the ruling race; curbing your pride just a little before them won't amount to humiliation.'

Without saying anything in response to Mahim's expostulation Gora went out.

76

As Sucharita was bending low over the trunk to hide her tears and pretending to be busy with her packing news reached that Gaurmohanbabu had come.

Sucharita hastened to wipe her tears and was about to leave the room when Gora entered.

Gora still bore the tilak on his forehead, he did not simply remember it. He still had the silk dress on. Normally people did not pay social visit in such a dress. Sucharita recalled the first day she met Gora. Sucharita knew that day Gora had dressed up to signal war. Did it carry the same message today!

Gora entered and the next moment he greeted Paresh by first touching the floor with his forehead and then touching his feet. Paresh hastened to pick him up in embrace saying, 'Come, come in my son, come in and sit down.'

Gora said, 'Pareshbabu, I am released today from all ties.'

Pareshbabu was surprised, 'What ties?'

Gora said, 'I am not a Hindu.'

Pareshbabu said, 'Not a Hindu!'

Gora said, 'No. I am not Hindu. I came to know today I was picked up as an infant during the mutiny; my father was Irish. Today I am shut out from the doors of all the temples in India—from the extreme north to the extreme south. Today I have no place in any row at any community feast in India.'

Paresh and Sucharita sat astounded. Paresh could not think out what to say to Gora.

Gora said, 'Pareshbabu, I am free today! I have no more any fear of being ostracized, of falling to the level of the outcaste. Today I do not have to bother about shielding my purity at every step.'

Sucharita stared at his radiant face in amazement.

Gora said, 'Pareshbabu, so long I have devoted my heart and soul to get at the heart of Bharatbarsha. But all the time there was one or another hitch. I had tried to reconcile my reverence with those hitches. I had tried day and night for all these years. I had been obsessed with this effort of establishing my reverence on some solid foundation. That was my only pursuit which kept me away from other concerns of life. That's why I have again and again gone out to serve India with my eyes open to her reality, and again and again I had to beat retreat in fear. I had tried to make an impersonal emotional fine construct of India in order to protect my reverence safely inside that seamless fort; what fight did I launch with everybody and everything around me for this! Today that illusory citadel has been blown away in one moment like some dream. Today I have been suddenly released into a great truth! The good and evil, happiness and sorrow, knowledge and ignorance of the entire Bharatbarsha have been splashing at my bosom. Today I have at last earned the true right of service; the field of true work now expands before me—it is not the field created by my imagination—it is the real field of work for the good of the twenty-five crores of real people outside that imaginary construct.'

The strong tide of Gora's emotions that surged in the wake of his freshly acquired experience sent ripples to Paresh's heart as well; swayed by its thrust, he could not remain sitting, but got up from his chair.

Gora said, 'Do you get me? I have become today what I had wanted to become day and night for all these years and could not. Today I am an Indian. Today I am not in conflict with any community, Hindu, Muslim or Christian. Today all the castes of India are my caste, the food of all is my food. I tell you, I have wandered through many districts of Bengal, I have sought hospitality in localities inhabited by most lowly people—don't think I have just delivered speeches before urbane gatherings—but I could not take my seat alongside all people by any means. I have always carried along with me an invisible distance which I could never cross. For that I had a sense of great void in my mind. I have tried to disown this void by various means; I have tried to garnish this void with beautiful decorative touches; because I could not accept any accusation against that part of the image where I could glimpse the Bharatbarsha which I love more than my life. Today I am happy Pareshbabu that at last I have been freed of that compulsion of futile effort to cover up my void with artificial decoration.'

Pareshbabu said, 'When we realize truth it comforts our soul in spite of its bareness—we do not simply feel like decorating it up with redundant accessories.'

Gora said, 'See Pareshbabu, last night I had prayed to God, that I might wake up into a new life this morning, that I might completely burn out the shell of falsehood, of impurity that covered me since childhood and get reborn into a new life. God paid no heed to the particular form in which I envisioned the object of my prayer. But he startled me by dropping the gift of his own truth directly on my palm. I never dreamt that he would thus remove my impurity in one single stroke. Today I have emerged so pure that I run no risk of contamination even at the home of a *Chandal*. Pareshbabu, this morning I am born into the lap of Bharatbarsha with my bared soul. At long last today I have come to the fullest realization of what is called mother's lap.'

Paresh said, 'Gaur, you have been restored to your rightful place in your mother's lap; you also draw us into the fold of these rights.'

Gora said, 'Do you know why I have rushed to you and you alone immediately on attaining freedom?'

Paresh said, 'Why?'

Gora said, 'You alone know the mantra of this freedom. That is why you have no place today in any society. You make me your disciple. You teach me the mantra of that God, who is the god of all—be they Hindu, Musalman, Christian, Brahmo, and whatever else—, whose temple doors do not shut out any race, any caste, any individual, who is not just the God of the Hindus, but the God of Bharatbarsha!'

A profound beauty of devotion cast its soothing shade on Paresh's features; he stood silently with lowered eyes.

Now at last Gora turned to Sucharita. Sucharita had been sitting motionless on her chair.

Gora smiled and said, 'Sucharita, I am not your guru any more. I pray to you now—please hold my hand and lead me to your guru.'

Saying this Gora stretched out his right hand and went up to her. Sucharita got up, and placed her own hand in his. Then Gora and Sucharita together touched the feet of Pareshbabu.

THE END

When Gora returned home it was already evening. He saw Anandamoyee silently sitting in the balcony in front of her room. Gora at once sought her feet and placed his head there. Anandamoyee lifted his head with both hands and kissed it.

Gora said, '*Mā,* it is you and you alone who is my mother! You are the *Mā* I had been looking for outside while all the time she was waiting here in my own house. You have no consideration of race, no discrimination, no hatred—you are the image of benediction! It is you who are my Bharatbarsha. ...

'*Mā,* now you call your Lachmya. Tell her to bring me a glass of water.'

Then Anandamoyee brought her mouth near his ear, and softly said in a voice quivering with tears, 'Gora, now let me send for Binoy.'

Glossary

Ācārya—preceptor.

Agrahajaṇ—the eighth month of the Hindu calendar from the middle of November to the middle of December.

Annapurṇā—mythical concept of the giver of food; wife of Lord Shiva who can give alms even to Shiva.

Aśauch—the 'impure' phase following the death of some close kin, when traditionally a Hindu is supposed to observe certain restrictions.

Baba—Father; also an endearing form of address to one's son or some young person.

Bakhtiyār—An endearing name—after Bakhtiyār Khilji, a Sultan of Delhi—for a chatterbox. The pun is lost in translation. In Bengali to '*bakā*' means being talkative.

Bāmun—a Bramhin cook.

Baradidi—eldest sister.

Bāul—a sect of Indian devotees who worship God through their dance and song. 'Bauls' can belong to either of the Hindu and Muslim communities.

Baudi—wife of one's elder brother.

Bauthān; Bauthākruṇ—Same as *Baudi.*

Bhrgu—Mythical figure.

Behāi—the fathers of the bride and bridegroom are 'behai' to each other.

Behāyā—shameless.

Binoybodh—a book containing exposition of Binoy's thoughts.

Brāhmo—a religious sect and also one who belongs to that religious sect.

Brāhmo-Sabhā—meetings of the Brahmos.

Brāhmo samāj—the society of the Brahmos.

Cādar—a light scarf which was part of the formal costume of the Bengali babu in those days.

Champā—A beautiful fragrant flower of light golden colour.

Chārupāth—School textbook of grammar and composition for the primary level.

Commisseriat—semi-government job.

Dādā—elder brother.

Dādāthākur—a combination of '*Dādā*' (elder brother) and '*Thākur*' (deity), it refers to a respectable person.

Damaru—a kind of small tabour shaped like an hour glass and played by moving it in one hand.

Dhāpā—a garbage zone of Calcutta at the time of the story.

Dhārāpāt—a book of arithmetical enumeration.

Dharma—religion.

Dhoti/Dhuti—a long piece of unstitched cloth, usually white,—conventional costume of Bengali menfolk.

Didi—elder sister.

Doshād—An 'untouchable' caste.

Ghāt—Steps on the river bank leading down into the water.

Goālā—a person who is a milkman either by profession or by caste.

Gorā—a person of very fair complexion; another name of Sri Chaitanya, a Vaishnavite saint of Bengal, who was very fair.

Gurguri—a hookah or a hubble-bubble, or a pipe to smoke tobacco.

Hinduānī—Rituals and practices of Hinduism.

Jagatdhātrī—an image of Durga, representing benediction, prosperity, protection, etc.

Jām—a huge sprawling tree of dark green leaves and small sweet fruits, once common in Bengal and various places of India.

Jāmāiśashthī—The sixth lunar day in the month of June which is the special day marked out for offering gifts and entertainment to the son-in-law.

Kābāb—roasted meat.

Kamandalu—an accessory of Indian monks,—a pot that is shaped like a combination of a bowl and a kettle.

Kāminī Kāncan—women and gold, which were supposed to be held in equal contempt by conventional ascetics in India.

Kārtik—the beautiful warrior son of goddess Durga.

Kāshi-Bhātpārā—Benaras and a small region on the banks of the Hooghly river which were known as seats of Hindu Brahmin scholarship as well as citadels of orthodoxy.

Katkī—produced in Katak, the then capital of Orissa.

Kāzī—Judges during the Mughal period in Bengal.

Khāndā—the large falchion, a kind of sword wielded by goddess Durga, and Kali.

Khude—An endearing term for something very small.

Kīrtan—devotional songs sung by the Vaishnavite cult, once very popular folksong in Bengal.

Kuber—the god of wealth.

Lakshmī—daughter of Durga and goddess of wealth.

Mā—Mother; a young girl may also be affectionately addressed as 'mā.'

Mādur—light mattress made of fine grass.

Mem—A British lady; acting as private tutor to the girls in the present context.

Mleccha—heathen; belonging to an alien religion and culture.

Mukti—liberation.

Nāmābalī—a piece of cloth carrying the printed names of deities.

Namaskār—Greeting one with folded hands; a common Indian custom.

Nitbar—a small boy dressed up as a small bridegroom who accompanies the original bridegroom during the wedding ceremony.

Pāgrī—a long piece of cloth rolled into a headpiece, and used to cover the head.

Pankh—fine masonry work of old times related to polishing and painting the inside walls and ceilings of a room.

Pānpatra—the formal engagement according to traditional Hindu custom of marriage.

'*pita he paraman tapa*'—One's father is the deity to deserve one's best worship.

Prāṇāyam—Yogic breathing exercise.

Prasād—fruits and sweets first offered to the idol and then taken by the worshipper as sanctified left-over of the deity's meal.

Pujā—worship.

Pundit—a Sanskrit scholar well-versed in the Hindu scriptures.

Sadhanāśram—a private recluse where one retires in pursuit of God.

Sāri—a long piece of unstitched cloth worn round the body by Indian women.

Sindhkāti—the iron stick and handle used by the burglars in the olden days to make holes into mud walls.

śrādhha—funeral rites.

'*Swādhīnatāhīnatāy ke bācite cāy re...*' (Who wants to live without freedom)—Alludes to a very popular patriotic song of the times composed by the poet Rangalal Bandyopadhyay.

Tāndava—the wild dance of Lord Shiva.

Tāntrik—one who worships in accordance with the *Sāstras*.

Tapasyā—penance.

Tapovan—hermitage.

Tattwa—ceremonial gifts on prescribed days in the calendar to be sent to the in-laws of the bride by her parental house or to the bride's house by the bridegroom's family.

Tiki—a small tuft of hair at the centre of a cleanly shaven scalp, a custom of orthodox Hindu Brahmins in the earlier ages.

Thākurpo—the traditional address of a married woman to the younger brother of her husband.

Tilak—a vertical mark made by sandal paste on one's forehead.

Tol—private residential schools run buy eminent Sanskrit scholars in the past.

Tumi—an informal way of addressing second person in singular number.

Yagna—ceremonial religious sacrifice.

Yama—God of death.